The St. Martin's
WORKBOOK

Lex Runciman

Through letters there is no road too distant to travel, no idea too confusing to be ordered.

from the Wen Fu *of Lu Chi (4th century)*
translated from the Chinese by Sam Hamill

The St. Martin's WORKBOOK

Lex Runciman
OREGON STATE UNIVERSITY

ST. MARTIN'S PRESS
NEW YORK

Senior Editor: Mark Gallaher
Developmental Editor: Julie Nord
Project Editor: Joyce Hinnefeld
Manuscript Editor: Bruce Emmer
Editorial Assistant: Robyn Feller
Text Design: Helen Granger/Levavi & Levavi, Inc.
Cover Design: Darby Downey

For information, write: St. Martin's Press, Inc., 175 Fifth Avenue,
New York, NY 10010

ISBN: 0-312-00836-8

Acknowledgments
    Epigraph (page ii): from *The Art of Writing* (Breitenbush Books, 1987). Re-
printed by permission of the publisher.
    Page 81: from *In the Shadow of Man* by Jane van Lawick-Goodall.
Copyright © 1971 by Hugo and Jane van Lawick-Goodall. Reprinted by permission of Houghton Mifflin Company and William Collins Sons and Company Ltd.
    Page 391: from Dylan Thomas: *Poems of Dylan Thomas*. Copyright © 1945
by the Trustees for the Copyrights of Dylan Thomas. Reprinted by permission of New Directions Publishing Corporation. In Canada, published by
Dent. Reprinted by permission of David Higham Associates Ltd.
    Page 406: from *Machine Dreams* by Jayne Anne Phillips. Copyright ©
1984 by Jayne Anne Phillips. Reprinted by permission of the publisher, E.P.
Dutton/Seymour Lawrence, a division of NAL/Penguin, Inc.
    Pages 471–472: from *The Sea around Us*, Revised edition, by Rachel L.
Carson. Copyright © 1950, 1951, 1961 by Rachel L. Carson, renewed 1979 by
Roger Christie.
    Pages 479–480: from *Waiting for Nothing* by Tom Kromer. First Amer-
ican Century Series edition March 1968 by Hill & Wang. Copyright © by
Emogene Kromer. Reprinted with permission of Emogene Kromer.

Preface

The St. Martin's Workbook is designed as a multifaceted resource for both teachers and student writers. Everything in this book proceeds from two basic assumptions: first, that every college student can become a skilled and successful writer; and second, that successful writing proceeds from both a knowledge of how English works and a knowledge of what writers do.

In fact, writing is a complicated and challenging and satisfying activity. In order to write well, writers engage in some combination of brainstorming, freewriting, outlining, drafting, revising, and proofreading. They often consider their readers' knowledge and expectations, struggle with their own intentions, and revise on the basis of preliminary responses to their rough drafts. In its chapters on the essay, argumentation, and the research process, *The St. Martin's Workbook* provides structured opportunities for students to understand and practice these various writing activities. A working knowledge of writing strategies cannot help but contribute to one's confidence.

The vast middle portion of this book is devoted to discussion and exercises dealing with the formal complexities and conventions of written English as it is typically used in college writing. Again, a working knowledge of these conventions encourages writers to believe that English is indeed their language and can be used to serve their own purposes—in a college essay, a research paper or technical report, a job application, a short story, or a poem.

The St. Martin's Workbook shares its organization with *The St. Martin's Handbook*: the books' chapter and part numbers and titles parallel each other, and the numbers that follow major text heads in the *Workbook* (*1a, 1b*) correspond to numbered *Handbook* sections in which the same material is covered. The two texts can easily be used together, with the *Workbook* providing many additional exercises. Like the *Handbook*, the *Workbook* highlights the twenty errors most commonly found in college essays, providing explanations and exercises to enable student writers to identify such errors and to correct them. The *Workbook* may also be used alone, as either a primary or a supplemental text. Teachers are directed to the Instructor's Manual for a discussion of how courses may be structured.

Teachers who wish to may use exercises in this book as the basis for classroom discussion and as the basis for work in small groups; the Instructor's Manual identifies exercises which particularly lend themselves to this approach. In fact, this is one of the first workbooks designed to encourage students to talk with each other about writing and to use one another as preliminary readers. Such collaboration is widespread in business and professional writing and is encouraged in many rhetoric texts; it is time for such strategies to find their way into workbooks.

But perhaps most important, this book attempts to give student writers a realistic image of the good writer. We tend to think that good writers write effortlessly, quickly, and perfectly. That is simply not so. All writers struggle with questions of content, purpose, and audience. All writers must sometimes look up fine points of grammar and punctuation. And when at last we see that our words communicate almost precisely what we wish them to, when we have worked through and conquered the confusions, looked up misspellings and nailed down every comma, the elation we feel is real and well earned. *The St. Martin's Workbook* aims to make such success more practically and more frequently attainable.

This large project could not have been completed without the devoted efforts of many people. Thanks to Nancy Perry and to the *Handbook* authors Andrea Lunsford and Bob Connors; without the three of you, there would be no *St. Martin's Workbook*. Julie Nord and her assistant, Robyn Feller, worked tirelessly on behalf of this book and its Instructor's Manual. Even under deadline pressures, their intelligence and good cheer never flagged; thank you both. Kay Fleming gave us valuable help, as did Peter Herman. Thanks also to Marilyn Moller, to copy editor Bruce Emmer, and to project editor Joyce Hinnefeld; your keen attentions have made this book better.

Grateful thanks also to the several reviewers who read this book in draft form and whose responses were both useful and encouraging: Karen L. Greenberg, Hunter College, CUNY; Barbara R. Sloan, Santa Fe Community College; Douglas Krienke, Sam Houston State University; Bonnie Lee, University of Oregon; and Arthur A. Wagner, Macomb Community College.

A different but no less emphatic thanks to my Oregon State University colleagues, and particularly to Lisa Ede and Barbara Hogg, who have provided crucial (sometimes daily) encouragement and support; your generosities and kindnesses are deeply appreciated. Thanks to the O.S.U. Writing Lab student staff; your openness, your varied interests, and your consistent enthusiasm for good writing make it easier to come to work each day. And finally, personal, heartfelt thanks to my family, to Debbie and to Beth and to Jane, who made room for this project and who are the sources of so much joy.

Lex Runciman

Contents

The St. Martin's
WORKBOOK

Lex Runciman

PART

1

The Writing Process

These questions are designed to help you, the student, decide what you need to study. Read the following statements and indicate whether they are true or false. (Answers to preview questions are found at the back of the book.)

1. Skillful writers do not need to revise. _____

2. Those who do not demonstrate marked writing skill before college are not destined to become successful writers. _____

3. Freewriting allows a writer to think on paper, without worrying about the correctness of the ideas or of the writing itself. _____

4. Writers should never consider the nature of their readers when writing. _____

5. Comparison and contrast and cause and effect are the only two logical relationships that can form the basis of an essay's organization. _____

6. The drafting process demands time, concentration, and the flexibility to follow where our thought processes lead us. _____

7. Revision helps writers understand what they want to say, and how readers are likely to interpret their words. _____

8. Experienced writers never discuss their work with others. _____

9. An outline is useful because it allows writers to see an entire paper's organization, so that they can spot inconsistencies. _____

10. An arguable statement presents assertions for which no certain answers or solutions exist. _____

11. Tone is an important element in an essay's persuasiveness. _____

12. Successful arguments rely solely on emotional appeals to convince readers.

_____

13. Deductive reasoning moves from a general principle to a specific instance.

_____

14. A *non sequitur* ties together two logically related ideas. _____

15. A paragraph is a group of sentences focusing on one main point. _____

16. Transitional words and phrases help both the writer and the reader to make connections and to achieve clarity in a paragraph. _____

1

Understanding the Writing Process

Writing as an Activity |1a|

Consider all that we read. We read billboards, newsmagazines, daily comics, and the front covers of whatever is stacked near the grocery checkout counter. We read weather forecasts, advice columns, building directories, transit schedules, box scores, editorials, advertisements on the insides or the outsides of buses. We read neon signs, cereal boxes, product directions, romance novels, thrillers, biology textbooks, *Mad* magazine, recipes, *Huckleberry Finn* and other novels, poems such as Robert Frost's "Stopping by Woods on a Snowy Evening."

All of these are finished pieces of writing. Very little of what we read is not a final product. It is not surprising, therefore, that when we think of the writing *process*, we forget just how much of it consists of *getting to* those final products. Many of us even think that practiced, skillful writers produce polished prose immediately, in a single draft. From time to time, a very experienced writer will manage this. But much more often, such writers spend hours and hours making notes, jotting down ideas, scribbling aimlessly just to get some thoughts on paper, rewording, reorganizing, starting all over, going back and looking for more information. . . . This sort of work makes up the real writing process.

As you work through the first chapters of this book, you may find that you have already done many of these activities or ones like them. Perhaps the only difference between your current writing process and a more successful one (the one you may imagine that more experienced writers go through) is just how often you have done these things, what you have learned from doing them, and how you have adapted to make them work for you, to make them into your tools.

Beginning with Exercise 1.1, this book will give you many opportunities to experience every stage of the writing process—those just listed and others as well. You will be able to reflect on each stage and to hone your own unique writing process to suit you and to help you improve as a writer.

EXERCISE 1.1 FREEWRITING

When you think of the word *writing*, what do you think of? On your own paper, copy this sentence: "When I think of the word *writing*, I think of . . ." Finish that sentence and keep right on writing. Do not worry about correctness; do not worry about where your train of thought takes you. Just follow that train of thought. If you run out of something to say, set the exercise aside and come back to it later. Whether you write this exercise in one sitting or in several, fill at least half a page. (This kind of writing is called "freewriting." Chapter 2 will discuss this technique further.)

This book will add to your knowledge about writing and language; it will also help you to understand and refine your own writing habits. It begins, however, with two basic assumptions. They are mentioned in what you have just read, but they are important enough to be worth stating again:

1. Writing is a process, a set of many actions that *eventually* lead to a finished product. Whether you are conscious of it or not, you already have experience with many of these actions. That experience amounts to your writing habits, which in turn constitute the writing process that you know.
2. You are a writer. You use written language to produce grocery lists, notes to yourself, letters. You have written school assignments, you will write more of them, and your job will probably require you to write such things as business letters, memos, evaluations, perhaps even proposals or reports. Above all, it is within your power to learn how to write all these things more easily and with better results.

Your first step is to examine your own current writing habits.

EXERCISE 1.2 REVIEWING YOUR WRITING PROCESS

Assume that you have been asked to write a short essay that discusses your own history as a writer and tells readers what you normally do to complete a writing task. Assume that you have been given several days to complete this assignment. *Do not write that essay.* Instead, use your own paper to answer the questions below. Use several sentences to answer each question, making your answers as specific and as candid as they can be. It is important, as you begin this book, that you know your own writing habits and attitudes.

1. Would you be eager to begin this assignment? Would you begin working on this writing assignment right away, or would you put it off? Explain why.

2. Describe the step-by-step process you would be most likely to use to complete the assignment. Include any procrastination that you might be prone to. Be as detailed as you can be: what would you do first? second? after that? Include all significant steps. This answer will be the longest of the four you write for this exercise.

3. Are you entirely happy with the process you just described? Would that process enable you to produce your absolutely best work? Would your final reader give your writing the response that you would want? Explain.

4. Would you consider the writing process you described typical of the way you normally work as a writer? Explain why or why not.

Planning, Drafting, Revising |1a, 1b|

In this book, when we speak of writers, we are speaking of ordinary people who use written language to teach themselves and to communicate with others. How do these ordinary folks write? They think; they struggle; they use pen, pencil, keyboard, paper. And you can be sure of this: few writers sit down and effortlessly compose a perfect sentence, followed by another, followed by another. To do so would be roughly equivalent to sitting down at a piano for the very first time and playing, effortlessly and expertly, a Mozart sonata or a blues improvisation.

Put in the simplest terms, writers plan, draft, and revise (each of these major activities will be discussed in a following chapter). This sounds like it should be a straight-line process: plan first, then draft, then revise. Actually, though, the process is rarely that simple. More often, it looks like this: a writer *plans* (thinks, researches, takes notes, brainstorms), *drafts* (writes quickly, letting the thoughts take their own shape), *rereads,* then perhaps *plans* some more (conducts more research, for example), *keeps drafting,* or *revises* what has been drafted before and then *drafts* some more. Any one of these activities might occupy a writer for hours or days; a writer could just as easily be involved with all these activities in the space of only a few minutes.

This movement from drafting to revising to planning to more drafting is called *recursion*; hence, writing is often called a *recursive activity.*

Experienced writers may involve others in these activities. They brainstorm with others, talking out part of a draft as a way of provoking additional thought; often they seek responses from unbiased readers in order to focus the revising process and make it more efficient. But whether alone or in concert with others, writers typically engage in the three main processes or activities of planning, drafting, and revising. Let us look at each briefly.

Planning

How should I begin to write? What do I know about this topic? What else do I need to know? What will be easy about this particular writing task?

What will cause me trouble? Should I try brainstorming or freewriting? These are all planning questions. Planning includes asking such questions. It also includes everything you do as you prepare to write words readers might actually read. Many writers use writing as a way to plan. That is, they write notes or outline or freewrite. No one else reads this material. Many writers plan with others, sharing information as they go and using the responses to help shape the planning process.

The planning stage for an in-class essay exam might last only a few minutes and be done entirely solo. The planning stage for a lengthy research paper might extend over several weeks. As writers plan, they work toward an understanding of both what they want to say and how they will organize those thoughts. Chapter 2 will address the planning part of the writing process in considerable detail.

Drafting

When writers draft, they consciously shape their content into consecutive sentences and paragraphs. Many of these sentences and paragraphs will be changed later, but that does not matter at this stage. As writers draft, they tell themselves what they think, believe, or know to be true. Thus, drafting often becomes the most creative and surprising stage of writing. In effect, drafting is thinking. Sometimes the pen (or fingers at a typewriter or computer keyboard) simply will not move fast enough. Writers learn to do whatever will encourage this sustained thinking. They often draft as quickly as they can, and they pay almost no attention to matters of correctness. Is a word misspelled? Leave it, keep going, you can come back and correct later: stay with the thought and the momentum it has built. Chapter 2 will provide you with additional drafting techniques.

Revising

When writers read over what they have written, they will read either to continue drafting (to rebuild momentum) or to check, scrutinize, tinker, rephrase, add, cut—in short, to revise. Writers revise to satisfy themselves as readers and to satisfy their actual intended readers. Writers trying to satisfy themselves examine their sentences and paragraphs to see whether or not the marks on the page actually reflect their own thoughts and intentions. Thus, writers reading their own work are asking themselves, is this what I want to say? Writers revising with their actual readers in mind ask themselves a different set of questions: Will my readers understand this? Are these sentences sufficiently detailed? Is this organizational structure going to be clear to strangers? The responses of others can be tremendously useful to writers at the revising stage. A simple report of what a reader understands or does not understand (a kind of "mirroring" of content) can give writers some degree of objectivity. And if a reader is having trouble understanding some main point or transition, a writer can often revise on the spot, testing each revision until the words in fact say what the writer wishes.

EXERCISE 1.3 ANALYZING YOUR OWN WRITING PROCESS

Use Exercise 1.2 to help you analyze your own writing process further. Use your own paper for this exercise.

1. Review your answer to the second question from Exercise 1.2. Which parts of your step-by-step process would you classify as planning?
2. Which parts of your process would you consider drafting?
3. Which parts of your process would you consider revising?
4. Of these three stages of the writing process, which is your strongest and which is your weakest? Use several sentences to explain your answers.

Understanding Your Own Writing History

This discussion of writing and experienced writers' approaches to it would be incomplete unless it also focused on you, what you have done in the past, and your attitudes toward writing. In this chapter, you have explored your own writing process. You are also aware of your feelings and attitudes about writing, about whether you like it or not, whether you are successful at it or not, and so on. These attitudes are holdovers from your writing past; every writing task you have been judged or graded on has contributed to them. If your writing past has been successful, reviewing your writing history will make you even more aware of that success and should make the next writing task easier. If you have not been entirely successful as a writer, reviewing your writing history may be the first step toward putting that history in perspective and going beyond it. The following exercise asks you to perform just such a review.

EXERCISE 1.4 REVIEWING YOUR WRITING HISTORY

Answer the following questions with full sentences. There are no right or wrong answers here, only incomplete ones. Use your own paper for this exercise.

1. What kinds of writing have you been most frequently asked to do? Have you most frequently written history papers? papers analyzing literary works? memos for a job? personal experience papers? essay exams? Use at least two examples to illustrate your answer.

2. How have your final readers (teachers, employers) usually judged your writing in the past? Do you agree with their judgments? Why or why not?

3. All writers have their strengths and weaknesses. What are your strengths as a writer? Use examples to illustrate your answer.

4. What are your weaknesses as a writer? Use examples to illustrate your answer.

2

Planning and Drafting

Deciding to Write |2a|

As you know if you have worked through Chapter 1, writing is more than something others read—it is also something writers *do*. Effective, experienced writers know what kinds of activities and writing strategies work for them. How do such writers get started?

The first step is usually just deciding to write. The alternative is procrastination, the I-can-do-it-tomorrow syndrome. Unfortunately, procrastination today makes procrastination tomorrow easier. And all too often, an inexperienced writer ends up face to face with a deadline that will not go away. The writer panics, decides that anything is better than nothing, writes hastily, and hopes for the best. This writing "process" is a recipe for failure at worst, mediocrity at best. It does not give the writer a chance to do good work. Practiced consistently, it will eventually convince a writer that he or she will never write well. Furthermore, this approach teaches people to hate writing. After all, nobody enjoys panic; nobody enjoys handing in work knowing that it could and should be better.

Experienced writers have learned the importance of beginning early. They begin thinking about writing as soon as the task is assigned. Further, they know what kinds of thinking will help them get started (more about these kinds of thinking in the next section of this chapter).

EXERCISE 2.1 LOOKING AT PROCRASTINATION

Answer the following questions with full sentences. Use your own paper for this exercise.

1. Think about all the required writing you have done—book reports, essays, history papers, argumentative papers, research papers, and so on. What kinds of writing assignments have you had trouble starting? Identify two such assignments, explain each, and discuss why you did not start right away.

2. Look at each of the writing tasks you just identified. How successful were your final products? Did they elicit positive judgments from teachers? Do you feel that you handed in the best work that you were capable of writing?

3. Consider now your overall history as a writer and your feelings about writing at this moment. Explain why procrastination is or is not a problem for you.

Understanding Writing Assignments |2b|

Suppose that you must write an application letter for a job. You know that the letter should be relatively short, that it must contain specific information about your qualifications, and that its goal is to get you a job interview. This kind of writing task is quite specific: you already know what the content, length, and format of the writing should be. (For more about job application letters, see Chapter 44.)

Some college assignments are directive, too. In a lab report or a case study, for instance, the topic is clear, your role is clear, and your readership is clear, and all of these combine to dictate a particular kind of organization for your writing.

But college writing assignments often seem to lack this clarity. You know who your reader is: your college instructor. But you may not feel you know what that instructor is "looking for." This is made even more difficult if the instructor leaves the topic selection up to you, as in "Discuss a person who has changed your life" or "Examine one aspect of the Industrial Revolution."

Whether your assignment seems directive or nondirective, first look at it systematically to determine exactly what you are expected to do. Here is a list of questions to help you begin.

1. What does this assignment ask you to do? Look at the imperative verbs (words like *define, analyze, discuss, argue*). Do these verbs give you clear directions? If not, ask for clarification. [If you were beginning the Industrial Revolution assignment, for example, you might ask your instructor questions like these: Can you explain more what you mean by the word *examine*? Are we being asked to argue something? Should this paper address a cause? an effect? a cause and effect? Should it just list facts?]

2. What do you need to know in order to complete this writing task? [Questions for the instructor: Do you expect that we will need to read beyond our already required reading? Do you want us to quote other historians, or are we to stay only with our own readings and opinions?]

3. Does the assignment allow you to limit or broaden the assignment's focus? [Question for the instructor: Can you give us some examples of what you mean by "one aspect of the Industrial Revolution"?]
4. Does the assignment specify a length or a particular organization? What is your deadline? [Questions for the instructor: Do you have a length in mind? What is our deadline? Can you suggest a particular organization, or are we to determine that based on our topic selection?]
5. What is your purpose as a writer in this particular writing situation? [Question for the instructor: Should we assume a particular purpose for this writing beyond demonstrating our understanding of the topic?]
6. What kind of reader constitutes the audience for what you will be writing? How will this reader affect what you include or omit? [Question for the instructor: How much should we assume our readers already know about the topic?]

Will your instructor always answer the questions you ask? Perhaps not. Perhaps your instructor has left the assignment open-ended precisely to see how *you* answer them. Either way, your first step is to begin analyzing the writing task.

EXERCISE 2.2 ANALYZING ASSIGNMENTS

Use the six questions presented in this section to analyze each of the following writing assignments. Use your own paper for this exercise. As you analyze each assignment, copy the question down before you answer it. When you have finished the analysis for each assignment, answer the final question.

A. What are the qualities of "home" for you? Describe one place that possesses those qualities, and make sure your readers understand why you value them.

B. Assume that a friend or relative is to begin college. Identify three problems this person may face, and give advice for overcoming each of them. Explain both problems and solutions clearly. Order your paper so that the most significant problem is discussed last.

Final question: Suppose you were given a choice to do either of these two writing assignments. Which would you prefer? Briefly explain why.

Exploring a Topic |2*e*|

Analyzing an assignment is just the first step toward a rough draft. Even after such an analysis, you may not be sure what to do next. Should you go directly to a rough draft? Should you go directly to the library to look up every single bit of information on your topic? Faced with such questions, experienced writers frequently use some sort of strategy to explore this new, perhaps strange topic systematically. Four such modes of exploration will be discussed here: brainstorming, freewriting, looping, and questioning. Each of these methods will help you explore a topic; they will also help you determine your interests and your level of knowledge about each topic.

Brainstorming

To brainstorm, simply make a list of words or phrases that seem connected to your topic. The idea here is to push yourself to focus on the topic without judging your results. Work fast, and do not censor yourself. At the top of a notebook page, jot down your topic; then note under it anything that comes to mind. Figure 1 shows what a brief brainstorming session might produce after some reading or class discussion of the Industrial Revolution.

Brainstorming works best when writers already have some knowledge of their topic. It is even more effective in a group. Even two people brainstorming together will normally produce much more material than an individual.

Freewriting and Looping

Like brainstorming, freewriting asks writers to suspend judgment, banish hesitation, and simply think on paper. Instead of making notes, freewriting involves writing sentences, or something approximating sentences. What do you write? You write whatever comes into your head after you have thought for a minute. The key to freewriting is to keep right on going, even if all you are writing is, "I don't know what to say now." If you have written "I don't know what to say now" two or three times and you really seem

Industrial Revolution

new machines to speed up production
all kinds of products → like what? textiles — weaving
    mass production — clothes, household goods
"sweatshops" working conditions — long hours
safety — child labor

rev. in America — Henry Ford. England?
Shift from country to city
less reliance on agriculture / weather / forces of nature / God
more dependence on mill owners, market forces
— lives out of control?
standardized products, not unique hand-made ones

pollution   rich get richer / poor get poorer
    less self-sufficiency
transportation vastly improved

Figure 1   Brainstorming

stuck, go back to the last substantive sentence and recopy it. But keep writing. How long should you keep going? Plan on seven minutes. Set a timer if you like. Write nonstop for seven minutes, and if there is more to say, keep right on saying it.

Here is a freewrite on "one aspect of the Industrial Revolution."

> I'm supposed to write on one aspect of the Industrial Revolution. That's a big one. There's what happened to technology—all those machines doing things that people used to do. Tremendous efficiency in comparison with the old ways. I need some examples here. But what's the price? the consequences of all this? Were people better off? happier? Some probably were, some not. So which ones were happier and which ones were not? Fine, all I'm coming up with are questions. And now I'm running out of things to say about the Industrial Revolution. Except that word revolution revolution revolution revolution—something ———→ connected to other revolutions. These are big changes we're talking about here—generation gaps. Makes me think this revolution isn't over. If anything, speeded up. The big, boxy radios we had as kids now small enough to fit *inside* a set of headphones. TVs with 2 inch screens, and my grandparents didn't know tv at all as kids. Not to mention space travel, people on the moon, nuclear energy, nuclear bombs . . .

Freewriting can be effective as you begin a writing task, and it can be equally effective later on as you explore a subtopic. Since freewriting is easy, you can try it on several possible topics as a way of helping to settle on one.

Writers can also use freewriting repeatedly in a method that the writer and educator Peter Elbow calls "looping." Say you have written a freewrite that looks something like the one just shown. Choose a sentence in it that for some reason appeals to you—for instance, "Makes me think this revolution isn't over." These words now become the starting point for your second freewrite, with your goal being to explore the ideas contained in that sentence further.

Questioning

One of the oldest ways to explore a topic is systematically to ask questions about it. You can pose and answer questions entirely on your own, or you can use any of the sets of questions in this section as a basis for group discussion.

The ancient Greek philosopher Aristotle first proposed these four questions as a way to generate information:

1. What is it? (definition or description)
2. What caused it? (cause and effect)
3. What is it like or unlike? (comparison/contrast)
4. What do others say about it? (testimony)

[13]

The journalistic questions *who, what, when, where, why,* and *how* are also widely used and are particularly helpful if your overall purpose is to explain.

Finally, the modern philosopher Stephen Toulmin designed a way to help writers analyze their thinking when their aim is to persuade. Toulmin's analytic model is shown here in modified form as a series of brief questions:

1. What is the *claim* I am making?
2. What are the *grounds* or *good reasons* that support my claim?
3. What *underlying assumptions* support the grounds of my claim?
4. What *backup evidence* do I have or can I find to add further support?
5. What *refutations* can be made against my claim?
6. In what ways is or should my claim be *qualified*?

Note that these question sets may require that you perform research in order to answer them adequately. Such research may be useful and necessary, but there is no point in conducting research until you have some idea of how you will use the information you gather. At an early stage in the writing process, you may not need to answer any of these questions completely. Their value lies in their ability to focus your thinking so that you can begin to determine what you know and what you need to find out.

EXERCISE 2.3 EXPLORING A TOPIC

Respond to the following questions using your own paper.

1. Have you ever used any of the strategies discussed in this section? If so, which strategies have you used, and what were you writing when you did so?
2. Do you use other strategies to explore a topic? If so, describe them briefly.
3. Of freewriting, looping, and brainstorming, choose the strategy *least* familiar to you and use it to analyze this topic: "college life."
4. Now use one of the question sets—either Aristotle's, the journalists', or Toulmin's—to analyze this same topic, "college life." Copy each question first; then fill in your answer. If you are unable to answer a particular question, indicate that and also indicate very specifically what you could do to obtain an answer.

ESSAY EXERCISE 1 EXPLORING YOUR TOPIC

Use either brainstorming or freewriting to begin exploration of one of the topics listed here (or one of your or your instructor's choosing). Then use one of the question

sets to help you determine what you already know about your topic and what you need to find out. Use your own paper for this exercise.

A. Almost all of us recall at least one of our grade school teachers. Select one such teacher. Tell readers why this teacher was memorable and what this teacher taught you about education and about yourself.

B. When we were youngsters, we had somewhat strange notions about what it meant to be an adult. Now that we are no longer youngsters, we probably have very different notions of what it means to be an adult. Compare and contrast your childhood vision of being an adult with the reality you experience now.

Understanding Purpose   l2cl

Your purpose in writing anything can be determined on two levels: **your purpose as writer** and **the purpose of the writing for your readers**.

Let us return to the assignment "Examine one aspect of the Industrial Revolution." This kind of assignment gives writers the opportunity to think and learn more about a specific topic. It invites them to teach themselves something significant about it. Once they understand this, writing can become an intellectual adventure, something akin to solving a mystery or traveling to a new place. If you approach your writing with this sense of active inquiry, you have developed a writing purpose.

Satisfying this personal interest will rarely be your only reason to write; more often, part of your purpose will be determined for you. For example, an assignment may read, "Some historians argue that the Industrial Revolution hurt people more than it helped; agree or disagree." Here part of your purpose is clearly persuasion. Other common purposes include explanation, comparison and contrast, and description of process.

What about your audience, your readers for this assignment? What purpose does this writing serve for them? In many cases, your reader is likely to be your college instructor—someone who knows far more about the assigned topic than you do. However, teachers devise assignments to encourage the kind of deeper thinking on a topic that only writing can provide. A writing assignment forces every class member to become intellectually involved.

And though a college instructor is likely to know more about an assigned topic than students in the class, he or she does not know what particular individuals understand. Most college instructors care deeply about what their students think. They are eager to know whether or not their students have grasped the complexities of a topic and eager to see how different students will interpret or weigh the same basic information. These variables change with each student; only you can tell your instructor what you have taught yourself. Your final purpose here is perhaps the most obvious.

College students write in order to demonstrate their best, clearest thinking; many course grades depend on students' abilities to demonstrate that thinking. As we discuss the relation between student writers and teacher readers, we come very close to addressing the question of audience. But we shall save that discussion for the next section of this chapter.

EXERCISE 2.4 DETERMINING PURPOSE

Assume that you have been given this assignment: "Write about some aspect of television and you." You have been asked to produce an essay of about five pages, due in seven days. Use these questions to help you discover your purpose for writing this essay. Write your answers on your own paper.

1. "When I think of television, the first thing that comes to mind is . . ." Complete this sentence.
2. Freewrite to expand on the sentence you just wrote. Why did you think of that? Continue with this train of thought, using full sentences. Write quickly and do not worry about spelling, grammar, or punctuation. Instead, concentrate on where your thought is leading you. Write at least half a page.
3. Identify the worst television show (or series) you ever saw. Why was it so bad?
4. Identify the best television show (or series) you ever saw. Why was it so good?
5. What controversial questions surround television use? What do commentators argue about? Do any of these issues touch you or your friends or family?
6. What else intrigues you or interests you about television programs, television production, or television stars?
7. Based on your answers to questions 1–6, identify two possible topics for your essay on television. Be as specific as you can.
8. Now consider what your purpose might be with each of the two possible topics. What would your purpose be for yourself? What would your purpose be with regard to your readers?
9. If you were forced to choose today, which of these two topics would you choose to write about? Why?

ESSAY EXERCISE 2 DETERMINING YOUR OWN PURPOSE AS A WRITER

You have received an assignment and done some exploration of your topic. Now it is time to make some preliminary decisions about your topic and your purpose. To do so, answer the following questions; write out your answers on your own paper.

1. Based on your explorations (Essay Exercise 1), identify two possible topics for your essay. In each case, be as specific as you can.

2. Look again at the two options you have identified.

   a) What would interest *you* about the first possibility? What would you be teaching yourself or discovering for yourself?

   b) What would interest *you* about the second possibility? What would you be teaching yourself or discovering for yourself?

3. Based on your answer to question 2, which possible focus would you choose right now? Why?

_____

Considering Audience |2d|

Most college and job-related writing is read and used by other people. Instructors read and grade what you write. Employers read your application letters. Published research results are read by other experts. None of this is surprising, yet writers often do not evaluate their writing from the point of view of those who will read and use it. Once writers do begin to consider their readers, they often find that the writing task becomes clearer. Remembering your readers' point of view will also help you determine an appropriate tone and even in some cases an effective organization for what you write.

We touched briefly on this question of audience when we identified it as one of several ways to begin analyzing a writing task, in this case the assignment "Examine one aspect of the Industrial Revolution." The question and an answer to it are given below:

6. What kind of reader constitutes the audience for what you will be writing? How will this reader affect what you include or omit?

> Since I'm presumably writing to demonstrate my knowledge, that probably means that I ought to assume a reader who doesn't know very much about the Industrial Revolution. If I assume that sort of reader as my audience, I will be forced to explain my reasoning and my conclusions, thus demonstrating my knowledge. In a sense, I'm not writing for the instructor (who presumably has done more thinking about all this than I have); rather, I'm writing for someone like myself before I took this class. In effect, I'm trying to teach someone what I've learned.

As this reasoning shows, though your course instructor remains your primary audience, it is often helpful to identify and speak to a different kind of audience altogether. If part of your purpose in writing is to demonstrate your knowledge, it is reasonable to target an audience that does not possess that knowledge—in this case, someone like yourself before you took the class.

Thinking about audience also helps writers determine appropriate language and style. Chapter 26 identifies three general levels of language and style: familiar, informal, and formal. We need not discuss these levels here, except to note that our audience is often crucial to both what we say and how we say it. A twenty-year-old might describe a rowdy weekend in one way when talking to a friend and in quite another way when telephoning home. The vocabulary of the two descriptions would be quite different; so would the level of detail. The telephone discussion might be briefer and more general than the discussion with a friend.

Considering audience in this way is particularly important when your writing task calls for you to argue a point. When writing to convince others, what they believe and what they know become as important as what you as writer believe and know.

To learn more about how important awareness of your audience is in any writing task, complete the following exercise.

EXERCISE 2.5 CONSIDERING AUDIENCE

Use your own paper to respond to the following questions.

1. Assume that a history professor has asked you to write a five-page paper that identifies and discusses the economic causes of the Civil War. How can thinking about audience help you as you approach this assignment?
2. Assume that you are writing a short note—half a page or less—to a student friend who has asked you whether she should take a class from Professor **X**, whose class you took last term. Also assume that the dean has asked everyone from last term's class to write a letter about Professor **X**'s teaching. In what ways will the note to your friend differ from the letter to the dean? Be as specific as you can.

ESSAY EXERCISE 3 UNDERSTANDING AUDIENCE

Use these questions to help you understand the audience for your essay. Be specific, and use full sentences. Respond on your own paper.

1. Who are the readers for your essay?
2. Why have your readers requested this writing? How will they use it?
3. What do your readers already know about your topic?
4. What do your readers already know about what *you* are going to say?
5. What is it that only you can tell your readers?

Establishing a Working Thesis   12f1

As writers explore a topic, their major goal is to develop a working thesis to guide them as they begin to draft. A thesis is a one-sentence statement that presents an essay's main point and suggests the writer's purpose for that essay. A *working* thesis is tentative and subject to change or refinement. Your working thesis evolves as you explore your topic and ultimately becomes your final thesis. Though a working thesis is likely to change, establishing one early makes the drafting process smoother.

A good working thesis has two parts: a topic portion and a comment portion. The topic portion states the subject, while the comment portion makes an important point about that subject:

topic

The theory of a "nuclear winter," though supported by several computer

comment

studies, remains highly controversial.

comment   *topic*

Three major factors account for the U.S. farm crisis of the mid-1980s.

These examples could, in fact, be final theses rather than working ones. What makes them working theses is the simple fact that the writer is still at work on them. He or she might later revise the second working thesis by reducing the number of factors from three to two. The writer of the first example might decide after further research that the phrasing of the current working thesis puts too much emphasis on controversy. A working thesis is simply one that the writer might still change.

How do you know if you have a strong working thesis? A strong one provokes audience interest, is phrased as specifically as possible, and limits and focuses the subject to make it manageable for the writer. Here is an example of a working thesis evaluated for interest, specificity and clarity, and manageability.

FIRST VERSION

topic   *comment*

My friend Deena is an important friend I have known for years.

INTEREST   *Is this interesting to the writer? Will this be interesting to readers?* Certainly this must be interesting to the writer, someone who has known Deena for a long time and presumably shared many experiences with her.

Readers might not yet find this interesting. Readers (strangers, after all) do not know Deena and may not know the writer. So this working thesis seems to leave readers out of the picture.

SPECIFICITY AND CLARITY The topic focus on Deena is clear. The comment section, however, is very vague. Why is Deena important? Is it just that the writer has known her for years? The writer needs to answer this question and then rephrase the working thesis to make it more specific.

MANAGEABILITY Right now it is difficult to judge the manageability of this working thesis. If the writer plans to discuss the entire friendship with Deena, the topic is probably too large.

CONCLUSIONS This working thesis needs revising, particularly so that the comment part is more specific. That specificity should help make the working thesis more interesting to readers and should also limit the topic so that it can be reasonably handled by the writer.

REVISED WORKING THESIS

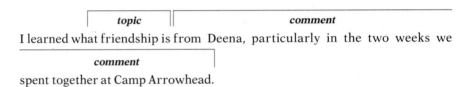

Notice that the topic has shifted to "what friendship is." The comment part is also now much clearer, and the writer has committed to discussing only a limited amount of experience. This revised version is, in addition, far more interesting to readers. Now the proposed essay clearly deals with an important topic and with experience that has the potential to be both humorous and serious.

EXERCISE 2.6 DEVELOPING AND TESTING A WORKING THESIS

In Exercise 2.3, you used one exploratory strategy to generate information on the topic "college life." Use the results of that exercise to formulate *two* possible working theses pertaining to this topic. On your own paper, analyze each working thesis according to interest, specificity and clarity, and manageability. If your analyses suggest that you should revise your original versions, do so. Use the text immediately preceding this exercise as an example.

ESSAY EXERCISE 4 DEVELOPING AND ANALYZING YOUR WORKING THESIS

Use your own paper to respond to the following questions.

1. Based on all you have done thus far on your essay, determine a preliminary working thesis. If in light of your own purposes and those of your readers, you need to do additional brainstorming (or the like), do so and turn it in with your working thesis.
2. Identify the topic portion of your working thesis by circling it. Identify the comment portion by underlining it.
3. Now analyze your working thesis for interest, specificity and clarity, and manageability. Your analysis should include discussion of each of these three criteria.
4. Finally, revise your working thesis as your analysis suggests.

Gathering Information |2g|

You have analyzed a writing assignment, begun to explore the topic, and arrived at a working thesis. The next step depends on your own habits of thinking and writing. Some writers will go directly to writing a draft. They do so knowing that what they will produce may be disorganized and full of holes. But they also know that for them, drafting constitutes one way to evolve an organization and to identify gaps that additional research must fill.

However, several factors may make it impossible to go directly to drafting. In some cases, the writer simply does not know enough to begin. In other cases, what the writer does know is confusing and makes drafting difficult. When drafting seems impossible, there are many ways of gathering further information before beginning to write.

One is to consult written sources. Often the textbooks you already have will provide all the information you need in order to begin drafting. If you need additional information, consult your school or community library (see Chapter 38 for more on library research). If you use written sources, remember that you must document your research by citing your sources (see Chapter 41 for more on documentation).

Information can also be obtained through interviews, field observation, and surveys. Each of these techniques can provide much knowledge and often new insights into your subject. But each must be carefully planned to bring good results. You will be most successful if you decide in advance what questions you want to answer; whom or what you are going to interview, observe, or survey; and how you will manage to keep from gathering too much unrelated material.

ESSAY EXERCISE 5   ANALYZING AND GATHERING INFORMATION

Thinking of all you have done so far on your essay, answer the following questions. Use full sentences, *be specific,* and write your answers on your own paper.

1. Do you need to gather additional information before you can begin drafting? If not, why not? If so, what information gathering techniques will help you obtain the information you need?

2. In general, do you prefer to gather a wealth of information before beginning to write a rough draft, or would you rather use the drafting process itself to help you identify what you do not know? Explain and give examples.

Organizing Information |2*h*|

Once writers have gathered enough information, some immediately begin work on a first draft. They trust that by immersing themselves in their material, they will discover how to organize it. For writers inclined to work this way, organizing the essay becomes part of the revision stage.

Other writers begin by considering which organizational form seems best suited to the material. For many writers, choosing an appropriate, though tentative form for an essay helps determine how it should begin and makes drafting easier. (Note that many of the organizational strategies for essays can be applied to individual paragraphs or clusters of paragraphs within an essay. For more on organizing paragraphs, see Chapter 5.)

Using Spatial Relationships Descriptive material that deals with particular locations is often presented **spatially**. If your aim is to describe a particular view, room, or building, for example, you might well organize your presentation by telling readers what is visible on the left, then in the middle, then on the right.

Using Chronological Relationships Any material organized according to time (what happened first, what happened second, what happened third, and so on) is organized according to **chronological relationships**. When you describe an auto accident to your insurance agent, you probably use time as your principle of organization. Almost all instructional writing ("How to Knit the Cable Cardigan," "How to Change a Tire") employs this form of organization. And many narrative essays (essays that tell a story to help make their point) also rely on time as one major way of organizing.

Using Logical Relationships In many writing situations, your material does not lend itself to an exclusively chronological organization. Your decision to enter one particular college, for example, probably rested on your analysis of that school's advantages and disadvantages—factors that are related logically rather than temporally.

Several common essay forms are based on logical relationships. The **cause-effect** pattern can work in either of two ways, by trying to explain why something happened (thus working from effect back to cause) or by trying to forecast something that is likely to happen (thus working from current causes to possible effects). A newspaper article that tries to explain a politician's defeat may begin by acknowledging an effect (the defeat), then discuss its probable causes. A business report analyzing a proposed price change would discuss the price change (the cause) and its probable effect on sales.

The **problem-solution** pattern identifies and describes a problem, explores possible solutions, and typically ends by recommending one solution as preferable. Such a pattern would be appropriate with, for example, a paper urging commuters to solve their parking problems by taking the bus.

An essay employing **illustration** provides concrete examples to support the essay's main idea. If your essay's purpose is to describe the promising future awaiting liberal arts graduates, you might well begin by proposing that thesis and then using examples to illustrate it.

Closely related to the illustration essay is the **definition** essay, which describes what something is and, often, what it is not. For example, an essay that sets out to define the character of people raised in the Midwest would essentially be a definition essay. This same topic could also be organized as a **comparison and contrast** essay. By its nature, a comparison and contrast essay focuses on two main topics or subjects, examining their similarities and their differences. Thus a writer might contrast Midwestern cultural values with Southern cultural values.

Writers can organize comparison and contrast essays in two ways. Using block comparison, an essay would speak about one topic (one block), then discuss the second topic in light of the first (the second block). Here is an organizational sketch for a paper comparing and contrasting American working conditions in 1890 with those in 1990:

A. Introduction
B. Block 1: Working conditions in 1990 (hours, pay, safety)
C. Transition
D. Block 2: Working conditions in 1890 (hours, pay, safety)
E. Conclusion

The other possibility is to organize according to major points, comparing each point separately and then moving on to the next. This is called alternating comparison:

A. Introduction
B. Working hours in 1990 vs. working hours in 1890

[**23**]

C. Brief transition
D. Pay scales in 1990 vs. pay scales in 1890
E. Brief transition
F. Workers' safety in 1990 vs. workers' safety in 1890
G. Conclusion

Two other logical relationships can also form the basis for essay organization: **division** and **classification**. An essay based on division begins by examining an idea in its entirety, then proceeds to identify and discuss parts of it. Suppose you are asked to write an essay that describes "the good teacher." You might identify and discuss the components that you believe go into a good teacher—knowledge of subject, enthusiasm, respect for students, and so on. You might then follow this discussion with your explanation of how these various traits are related to one another.

To classify means to group according to categories. You might choose to describe your particular college courses this term by classifying them as science/math or liberal arts.

Writers often use some combination of several of these organizational strategies. Considering this question of organization before beginning a rough draft should give you a sense of direction, control, and confidence as you begin drafting.

EXERCISE 2.7 CONSIDERING ORGANIZATIONAL STRATEGIES FOR ESSAYS

Assume that you have been asked by your college newspaper to write an essay for a column that carries the general title "A Day in the Life." Since it is midterm time, your editors have asked you to focus your essay on some aspect of test taking. They have told you that your essay may be serious or humorous. Using your own paper, respond to the following questions.

1. Begin this exercise by either freewriting or brainstorming on your topic. If you need to review these techniques, see the earlier sections of this chapter.

2. Based on your explorations for question 1, select a working thesis for your essay. Circle the topic portion and underline the comment portion. Review the section on working theses if necessary.

3. Now consider your working thesis. Which of the organizational strategies presented in this section would work well for this paper? Would you organize your essay primarily by using spatial relationships, chronological relationships, or logical relationships? Explain, being as specific as you can.

4. If you were going to begin drafting this paper, how would the thinking you did for questions 1–3 help you as you drafted? Explain.

ESSAY EXERCISE 6 ANALYZING AND CHOOSING AN ORGANIZATIONAL STRATEGY

Think about all you have done on your essay so far as you consider and respond to the questions below. Write your answers on your own paper.

1. If you have already begun to draft your essay, which of the organizational schemes presented in this chapter does your draft most resemble? Explain this in detail. How does it help you to analyze your draft in terms of organizational strategies? (If you have not yet begun drafting, go to the next question.)

2. If you have not yet begun drafting, which two organizational schemes might work as you think about drafting? Describe the two schemes, as you would use them for your essay, and explain what advantages there would be to using each one.

3. If you had to choose right now, which organizational plan would you select? Why?

Writing a Plan for Drafting |2*i*|

Once you have reviewed the organizational forms, it is useful to take that mental work one step further and write yourself a plan for your draft. The plan can be as formal as an outline or as informal as a set of sketchy notes. The key here is to *write it down.* Your drafting process may take several sittings, and by its nature drafting requires you to focus on the details of content as well as the mechanics of sentence and paragraph construction. As you consider these things, it becomes very easy to lose track of your overall direction and organization. A written plan will help keep you on track.

Earlier, we presented two possible organizations for a comparison and contrast essay discussing working conditions in 1990 vs. working conditions in 1890. In one sense, these are already plans. The nature of the block organization as a plan becomes even clearer with some slight rewording:

```
Organizational Plan: First Draft

      Introduction
          **establish the essay's purpose, namely to compare working con-
             ditions a century apart


                      discuss working conditions in 1990

                      --hours
      BLOCK #1
                      --pay

                      --safety
```

[*25*]

```
                        Transition

           **should draw tentative conclusions based on this first half


                         discuss working conditions in 1890

                         --hours
          BLOCK #2  {
                         --pay

                         --safety


                Conclusion: bring together the topics here
```

As you can see, an organizational plan for drafting is really a set of notes written by the writer for his or her own use. No one else is likely to read such notes, and the plan they present may well be altered before the revising process is complete. If this plan helps the writer begin drafting and provides a clear overview of the writer's content, it is doing its job.

EXERCISE 2.8 WRITING A PLAN FOR DRAFTING

To complete this exercise, you will need to have already completed Exercise 2.7. If you have already completed that exercise, refer to it now. Otherwise, complete Exercise 2.7 before reading further.

Using Exercise 2.7, determine a plan for drafting an essay dealing with some aspect of test taking. Your plan could be an outline, or it could be a set of notes similar to those presented in this section. Whatever its form, your plan should clearly show how you would organize this essay. Write this plan on your own paper.

ESSAY EXERCISE 7 PLANNING YOUR DRAFT

If you have not yet begun drafting, turn your organizational scheme (identified in Essay Exercise 6) into a plan for drafting. Indicate the plan on your own paper. If you already have a substantial start on your draft, go on to Essay Exercise 9 in Chapter 3. (If you are having trouble coming up with a plan for drafting, go back to some of the activities discussed earlier in this chapter.)

Producing a Draft *12j1*

At some point, your thinking, information gathering, and planning must lead you to writing sentences and paragraphs that will eventually add up to a rough draft of your essay. Where should you begin? You could begin with the introduction if you know what it should say. But if beginning with the introduction seems difficult (as is often the case), start drafting some middle part of the paper—some part you know well. But do begin. (For more on writing introductions, see Chapter 3.)

What, in general, can be said about the drafting process?

- *Drafting demands flexibility.* As you write, you are thinking, concentrating with more intensity and interest than earlier. As a result, you will probably find it necessary to revise your plans as you go along. This should not surprise you or dismay you; in fact, you should expect that as you draft, you will probably not follow your own plans to the letter.
- *Drafting demands paying attention to your content and to your process.* What should you do if you realize as you draft that you lack certain information or that you are not making use of information that you spent hours gathering? All writers encounter such situations at one time or another. They are normal and must be accepted. Sometimes that means continuing to draft but writing a note to yourself that you have skipped over a key point and will have to come back to it later; or it might mean that you will simply omit some information to provide a tighter, more manageable focus for your paper. Such adjustments should not be cause for panic or frustration.
- *Drafting demands time.* No matter how much planning you have done or how much information you have gathered, chances are that your drafting will proceed fitfully and will require more than one sitting. If your drafting goes forward without a hitch, consider yourself lucky. The advice here is to anticipate that your drafting will take longer than you want it to; so avoid last-minute, hurried drafting if you wish to rise above mediocrity. Also realize that juggling other concerns and responsibilities is part of the writer's lot. Even full-time writers cannot escape entirely the sometimes chaotic reality of their daily lives.

Many writers also find it useful to think about the conditions that make them comfortable and productive. Some writers prefer particular places to write; they may prefer certain pens or pencils, even a particular kind of paper. Such concerns are not trivial if they contribute to writing success.

Perhaps the most important advice about drafting is this: generate a train of thought and stay with it. Do not stop to look up words in the dictionary (circle them and come back to them later). Do not stop to ponder paragraph breaks or the rules regarding quotation marks. Write in bursts of at least ten minutes, longer if the words are coming easily. If you have access to a computer, consider drafting at the keyboard (for more on computers and the writing process, see Chapter 45).

If you cannot finish a draft in one sitting, stop at a point where you know what you will say next. Suggest that information with a couple of phrases jotted on the page. You will be grateful for those notes to yourself when you next look at the draft.

What if you get absolutely stumped and can see no way to proceed? Do not panic. Reread what you have written, looking for wrong turns or imprecise expressions in the last page or so of your writing. If you are still stumped, set the draft aside and do something entirely different, something that will allow you to forget the writing task altogether. Jog. Do laundry. If your deadline allows you to stay away from the writing overnight, do so. A brief time away will often give you a new perspective and enable you to resume drafting. One more possibility is to skip the section that is giving you trouble. This may be possible if you know what you want to say further on. By the time you have written the rest of the paper, you will probably have figured out how to address the problem portion of the draft.

All of these tactics you can try by yourself, but perhaps the best remedies involve other people. Talk to someone about your writing. If your campus has a writing lab, talk to one of the writing assistants. Talk to your instructor. Talking about a draft helps you see that draft more objectively, and that new outlook may be all you need to continue drafting.

EXERCISE 2.9 UNDERSTANDING HOW YOU DRAFT

Answer the following questions, using your own paper.

1. What particular conditions must you have to work comfortably as you draft an essay? Discuss where you like to work, the time of day you prefer, as well as any particulars that help you feel comfortable as a writer.
2. In the past, have you done conscious planning before you draft, or have you gone directly to writing a draft? Has this practice helped you produce your best possible writing?
3. What planning and drafting methods discussed in this chapter were new to you?
4. Right now, what do you consider the hardest aspect of writing a first draft?
5. What strategies could you adopt to reduce the difficulty you identified in your answer to question 4?

ESSAY EXERCISE 8 DRAFTING YOUR ESSAY

Based on all your thinking, note taking, exploring, and planning, begin drafting your essay. Begin at the beginning or in the middle, whichever seems appropriate. As you draft, pay attention to both your content and your process.

3

Revising and Editing

Revision Strategies |3b|

Even the best writers often turn out first drafts that are sketchy, wandering, and incomplete. This is just a stage in their writing process. The next stage involves revision strategies. Revision strategies typically have two main goals: helping writers understand what they want to say and helping them read as their final readers will. Such strategies enable writers to turn even the most confused first drafts into well-organized, complete, and successful final drafts.

Strategy 1: When unsure of what to say next or after completing a full first draft, give yourself time.

How much time should you give yourself? Of course, you must remember your deadline. You do not want simply to put off writing and thus put more pressure on yourself later, but you do want to stay away long enough to forget your literal sentences. Even an hour away from your writing might be useful. As Chapter 2 suggested, do something unconnected with words. Dust. Go bowling. When you come back to your writing, do so with strategies 2, 3, and 4 in mind.

Strategy 2: Read critically for content only.

Whether you have what you believe to be a full draft or only a partial one, repeatedly rereading what you have written is crucial. Before you reread, determine what you wish your rereading to accomplish. You might reread looking for a possible wrong turn, a place where the draft veered off in an unexpected and unproductive direction. Try focusing on topic sentences—

the big picture. Or you might be checking for completeness, making sure that each step in your thinking has in fact been represented on the page. If you have not yet written an entire first draft, you may be rereading to remind yourself of what the next main idea ought to be.

Notice that with this revision strategy, you do not pay specific attention to spelling or punctuation rules. You should focus instead on content, on whether your sentences and paragraphs indeed say what you want them to say. This strategy should lead to more writing, rewriting, or a search for additional information. If such rereading leads only to stalemate, turn to another strategy.

EXERCISE 3.1 UNDERSTANDING REVISION STRATEGIES 1 AND 2

Respond to the following questions on your own paper. Be specific and use examples.

1. Revision strategy 1 involves giving yourself a time-out period as part of your drafting and revising process. Have you ever used this strategy successfully? If not, what has prevented you from doing so? If you have used this strategy successfully, describe one instance and discuss your results.

2. Almost every writer has used rereading as a revision strategy. Describe exactly how and when you have used it. Has this strategy proved successful for you? If so, why? If not, what will you change to make this strategy successful for you?

ESSAY EXERCISE 9 A ROUGH DRAFT PROGRESS REPORT

Respond to the following questions on your own paper.

1. List the activities you have already completed as you have worked on this essay.

2. How much of the rough draft have you written so far?

3. Are you now having problems drafting? If so, explain what has happened to cause these problems.

4. Do you foresee problems ahead? If so, explain.

5. When you resume work on this writing assignment, will you be continuing drafting, or will you need to double back to do some reevaluating or information gathering? Explain.

6. How soon do you plan on having a complete rough draft? (Indicate a date here.)

7. What do you want to remember about this drafting process in order to make your next writing task easier? (If the drafting has gone well so far, what did you do to make it go well? If the drafting has not gone well so far, what could you have done to make the process smoother?)

_____

Seeking the Responses of Others |3c|

Sometimes rereading seems tremendously productive. Changes get made, and you feel both surprised and proud. Sometimes no amount of rereading pays off. Either way, you also need to seek the responses of others. Hearing another person discuss your content may be all it takes for you to see it more objectively.

Strategy 3: Ask objective readers to mirror, question, and discuss your content.

To understand the usefulness of this strategy, consider the intensity of any writer's thinking process. Writing well requires uncommon concentration over a relatively long time. Because writing involves so much intellectual (and often emotional) activity, you may not get all of it on the page. Why not? As writers, we know our subjects too well. Our writing may appear absolutely clear to us, but our final readers, less familiar with the subject, may understand only with difficulty or not at all. One solution is to seek outside readers beforehand; they can often tell us what is clear, what is unclear, and what may be missing.

One source of readers is your campus writing center. (If you are not sure whether your campus has such a center, consult a campus directory or call the English Department.) Writers often turn to friends for responses, but be wary. Some people find it difficult to be objective when appraising the work of friends.

Identifying Questions to Pose to Readers

Asking a reader a vague question like "Will you read this and tell me what you think?" is likely to produce an equally vague, hence not very useful, response. Much better would be the question "What is this paragraph saying?" or "Is this example clear to you?"

If you have even a partial rough draft, reread it to identify parts that strike you as unclear. Ask your reader to focus on those areas. If your drafting process has gone well this far, you will still find it useful to ask readers to tell you about what you have written. Ask them to explain the paper's purpose as they understand it so far. Ask them to identify your paper's major points. Ask them to explain how the paper supports or explains its major points. Ask them what they can sense has been left out, if anything. Their answers will help you see your own draft and hear it in someone else's words.

EXERCISE 3.2 ACTING AS A READER

Reproduced below you will find the opening paragraphs of a rough draft. The writer assures you that this draft is very rough and preliminary. Your aim here is to provide this writer with useful response to this work. The writer's assignment is "Analyze and discuss your first week of college. Assume that you are writing for students who have yet to begin college study, though they soon will. Use your experience to let them know what they might expect."

DRAFT

    My first week of college was anything but what I expected. Registration, I had been told, would be a horrible experience. But it wasn't. My brother and sister both warned me about the possibility that I would not like my roommate. I worried about this all of Sunday afternoon as I unpacked my things. Next door, other new roommates were getting acquainted, but mine didn't show up. It's turned out alright though. My roommate was unpacking when I came back from dinner. It turns out we have a lot in common.

    In fact, I think that many of the fears new students have are unnecessary. Registration worked out well for me. I talked with my advisor and everything. My roommate and I went out to see a movie together the second night we were here. Classes have been hard though. I didn't quite expect that they would ask us to read so much. And some of them have over a hundred students. Plus there are so many responsibilities . . . I have to worry about things like the laundry, and when I'll study, and whether or not to get involved with outside activities. It's been rough sometimes, but interesting too.

    Last weekend, for instance, . . .

The writer has asked you these questions. Using your own paper, respond to each.

1. What is the main purpose of this draft as it stands now? If you have trouble identifying the main purpose, tell why that seems difficult. Be specific.
2. What would you expect this draft to go on and talk about? If you cannot anticipate that, indicate why not. Either way, be specific.
3. What is the strongest, most interesting part of this draft so far? What makes it so?
4. What *three* questions do you want to ask to understand more fully?

ESSAY EXERCISE 10 SEEKING RESPONSES TO AID IN FOCUSING CONTENT AND PURPOSE

Read Exercise 3.2 and note the questions it uses to obtain useful information from readers. Review the rough draft you have been working on. Based on the questions in

Exercise 3.2 and on your own sense of your rough draft, compose questions that you can use with readers of your rough draft. Use your own paper for this exercise.

1. What questions would you want to put to readers to determine their understanding of what you have written in this essay? List at least three questions that are specific to your rough draft.

2. What three questions would you want to ask to help you gain some direction for revising? Again, make your questions as specific to your draft as you can.

3. Now select a reader (perhaps another class member), and ask that reader to use your questions to respond to your rough draft. Have your reader give you brief written answers to your questions.

4. Read over the responses you receive. Do you wish you had asked other questions? If so, what other questions should you have asked? Explain.

ESSAY EXERCISE 11 USING RESPONSES

You obtained written responses to your rough draft in Essay Exercise 10. Guided by these written responses and your own understanding of your rough draft, answer the following questions. Write your answers on your own paper.

1. What are the strengths of your rough draft as it now stands? Be brief but specific.

2. What two or three problem areas did your readers identify as in need of significant revision?

3. Do you agree with your readers about the problem areas? Explain why or why not.

4. Based on your responses and on your own sense of things, would it be useful for you to gather further information before continuing to draft or revise? If so, what information do you need, and where will you obtain it? If not, explain why not.

5. When you next sit down to work on your draft of this essay, what will be your plan for that working session? Be specific.

Analyzing the Organization of Your Draft |3d|

Strategy 4: Chart the organization of your draft.

Some writers routinely outline as a way to forecast their content and help them stay on track as they draft. Outlining or otherwise charting your content can also be a tremendously helpful revision strategy. Your outline need not rigidly follow any particular format. Your aim is simply to picture your entire paper's organization in one glance so that you can spot inconsistencies. If you cannot outline your first draft, that should tell you the draft needs considerable attention.

Reread the rough draft you responded to in Exercise 3.2. Here is an outline of the first paragraph of that draft:

```
                          OUTLINE

        First week of college not what expected
              --registration not horrible
              --roommate OK
```

Based on that brief outline, we can see that this opening does have a thesis, but it lacks specifics. Why was registration "not horrible?" Why is the roommate "OK?" These omissions will need to be remedied through revision.

EXERCISE 3.3 OUTLINING TO CHART ORGANIZATION

Read the following paragraph carefully, paying attention to both the content and its organization. Use your own paper for this exercise.

The first thing I did was ask Shelly, a senior who lives down the hall, which course instructor to specify on the registration form. I really did not want to take my required math class from a bad teacher. Then I looked in the catalog to figure out what other required classes I could take this term. After developing a long list of possibilities, I was jotting down the courses I was interested in when the phone rang. It was my brother, Jack. He graduated last June and has a good job in L.A. But he couldn't help me much with courses in my major, since he majored in international business and my major is anthropology. I also think that students ought to make a real effort to see their advisors. After all my worrying about which classes to take next term, I found almost all my questions were answered after talking with Prof. Rollings.

1. Outline the paragraph.
2. Based on what you learned from question 1, suggest revisions.

ESSAY EXERCISE 12 CHARTING THE ORGANIZATION OF YOUR DRAFT

Using your own paper, answer either question 1 or question 2.

1. Read through your draft, numbering each paragraph as you go. Write a brief sentence or phrase that summarizes each numbered paragraph. Eventually you should have a numbered list of sentences or phrases, each representing one paragraph in your draft. Look only at your summary sentences or phrases. Now that your paper is set before you in this way, analyze the progression of ideas by using the following questions.

a) Do you see any material that is unnecessary? If so, which numbered paragraphs can you cut or consolidate?

b) Do you see any holes in the flow of the content? If so, what needs to be added, and where will this material fit?

c) Do any of the main ideas seem to be in the wrong place? Is the movement from point to point logical? If not, how can you reorganize?

d) Finally, can you see any sudden shifts in content? If so, does the draft now provide effective transitions so as not to lose readers? Will you need to add or revise any transitions?

2. If you have what you believe to be a complete rough draft, read through it, outlining as you go. Circle any parts of the outline that you feel need revising, and make marginal notes to yourself to help with that revising. As you go along, keep these questions in mind:

a) What parts seem out of place? Where should they be placed?

b) Is any of this material repetitive or off the point? Can it be cut?

c) Are there any holes? What needs to be added to this draft?

d) Does the draft employ effective transitions, particularly when it shifts from one major section to the next?

Considering Titles, Introductions, and Conclusions   3f

Strategy 5: Reconsider your essay's title and introduction.

The title and opening paragraph should introduce the essay's topic and should convey the writer's reasons for writing. What makes a good title?

- A good title is specific; it would be appropriate only with the paper that follows it.
- A good title is interesting, intriguing; it asks questions or raises expectations that readers will want to satisfy.

It is useful to ask yourself to come up with one or two alternative titles. By forcing yourself to come up with alternatives, you give yourself choices; revision involves making such choices.

An introduction can take any of these forms:

- A general-to-specific paragraph that states a generality and then modifies and limits it, thus indicating the essay's limited topic (for more on the general-to-specific paragraph, see Chapter 5)

- A quotation that the essay will either agree with or contradict
- A brief story that dramatizes the essay's topic
- A question or series of questions that the essay will address
- A strong assertion of opinion

To draft an effective introduction, you need to review your purpose and your topic. Then consider which form best suits the purpose and topic. Ask yourself questions like these: Should I begin with a thesis statement or with an example? What if I tried it the other way? Stories make statistics come alive; if I am beginning now with statistics, could I begin instead with a story, even a fictional story identified as such? If I'm beginning now with a story, would beginning with the statistics be the better way to start?

Strategy 6: Review Your Conclusion

How should your essay end? That can be an intimidating question, better thought of in these terms: What has all of your planning, drafting, and revising taught you about your topic? What has it led you to that you did not understand before? What do you want your readers to understand as a result of reading your essay? Do you want them to act, and if so, how? These are the kinds of questions writers use to help draft and revise conclusions. Here are some general criteria for good conclusions:

- Good conclusions proceed from all that comes before them. They are consistent with earlier content, do not contradict that content unless accompanied by reasonable explanations, and do not normally introduce entirely new topics.
- Good conclusions reveal the writer in control of the essay's materials. The essay does not simply stop abruptly. Good conclusions complete the paper's thought process.

Many conclusions use the specific-to-general paragraph pattern (discussed in Chapter 5). Such a conclusion presents the last bits of specific evidence and then moves to generalizing about this evidence and ultimately about all that has gone before it. An essay can also effectively end with a quotation, as does Martin Luther King's "I Have a Dream" speech:

> When we let freedom ring, when we let it ring from every village and every hamlet, from every state and every city, we will be able to speed up that day when all God's children, black men and white men, Jews and Gentiles, Protestants and Catholics, will be able to join hands and sing in the words of the old Negro spiritual, "Free at last! Free at last! Thank God almighty, we are free at last!"
>
> —MARTIN LUTHER KING, JR.
> "I Have a Dream,"
> August 28, 1963

Essays can also end with warnings or calls to action. If your essay has been devoted to giving advice on how to shop for a used car, it could easily end with a list of warnings. If your essay has been devoted to urging citizens to support a particular candidate for political office, it could end with an exhortation to action—to vote for your candidate.

EXERCISE 3.4 CONSIDERING TITLES, INTRODUCTIONS, AND CONCLUSIONS

TITLES

Five pairs of titles are given. For each pair, indicate the title that would be more likely to move you to read whatever would follow it. Then explain briefly the reason for your choice. Use your own paper for this exercise.

EXAMPLE

Looking at College Life after Two Years Away   *or*   Returning to College: Back in the Saddle Again

The second version, "Returning to College: Back in the Saddle Again," would be my choice. Besides giving a fairly clear indication of the essay's topic, this version suggests a somewhat humorous tone, which suits the topic. The first version does a good job of identifying the topic but does not have the human interest of the second version.

1. Recovery from Pollution   *or*   The Columbia River: A Comeback Story
2. Federal Taxes and You   *or*   Do New Tax Laws Mean You'll Pay More?
3. What High Schools Don't Want Students to Read   *or*   Censorship
4. Caffeine and Pregnancy   *or*   Jury Undecided?
5. Occupational Death   *or*   English Working Conditions in Textile Mills during the Industrial Revolution

INTRODUCTIONS

You want to write a persuasive paper aimed at convincing students that they ought to learn how to administer cardiopulmonary resuscitation (CPR). The class lasts only two hours. You have statistics on the numbers of lives saved by people who administered CPR. You have talked with a heart patient who was revived using CPR. You have interviewed several reluctant students, so you know why they are reluctant. You have interviewed the CPR instructor, who has stressed the importance of CPR.

1. Specifically identify two ways that this persuasive paper could be introduced.
2. Explain how you would begin this paper. What factors will influence your decision?

CONCLUSIONS

Having identified a possible introduction, decide how you might end this paper. Would you follow the specific-to-general format? Would you end with a quotation? a warning? a call to action? Explain your decision.

Examining Paragraphs, Sentences, Word Choices, and Tone   13g1

> *Strategy 7: Reconsider your paragraphing, sentence structure, word choices, and tone.*

Once you feel reasonably happy about an essay's content and organization and your draft has assumed the overall shape it will probably keep, reread with an eye toward technical choices. As you reread, consider these questions:

Paragraphs

- Do these paragraphs group sentences effectively?
- Are they consistently too long? Do I pack too much information into one paragraph?
- Are they consistently too short? Do they lack examples and explanations?
- Are the transitions from one paragraph to the next smooth and clear?

If you charted the organization of your draft as suggested earlier in this chapter, you have an easy way to check your transitions between paragraphs. Your chart will tell you where your major shifts in thought occur. Chapter 5 discusses the use of transitions *within* paragraphs, and those same devices can be used between paragraphs. Sometimes, especially in long papers, writers find it helpful to compose transitional paragraphs. Here is an example:

> So far in Chapter 3, we have looked at several revision strategies aimed at helping writers determine their content, structure it carefully, and anticipate the responses it will provoke from readers. The rest of this chapter will focus on smaller-scale concerns: sentence structures, word choices, tone, and correctness in spelling and punctuation.

A paragraph like that one tells readers exactly what comes next. (For more on paragraphs, see Chapter 5.)

Sentences

- Are all of these sentences the same length?
- Do they all employ the same structure?

A paragraph composed of nothing but short sentences begins to sound like a grade school reader: "I went to the store. Jack went with me. At the store, bread filled at least four shelves. I could not decide which kind to buy. Finally, I recognized our usual brand. . . ." A series of unnecessarily long sentences, on the other hand, often exasperates the reader and makes meaning harder to grasp. Varying sentence length keeps the reader's attention better.

This use of variation also holds true for sentence structure. The most common (and most direct) English sentence structure is the simple, one-clause, declarative sentence: subject ⟶ verb ⟶ object. This structure is excellent. But if it is the only structure you use, you will have a hard time showing relationships between ideas. If every sentence sounds and looks the same, the ideas in those sentences will seem the same, too. Varying sentence structure will help you accentuate some ideas and downplay others. Thus, variation allows you to be more expressive as a writer.

It is* and *There are   The first effort at drafting demands that writers find a way to express new and perhaps bewildering content. *It is* and *There are* may be the two easiest ways to start a sentence. Anything can follow them. But these two phrases rarely add any meaning to a sentence. Writers can almost always revise to eliminate such vague openings and make stronger, more precise sentences. Here are two examples.

> There are three techniques that experienced writers use to tighten their writing.
> Experienced writers use three techniques to tighten their writing.

> It is worth noting that all three share common elements.
> Note that all three share common elements.

(For more on sentences, see Chapter 6 and Chapters 17–21.)

Word Choices

- Does the essay use specific words rather than general ones—*spaghetti* rather than *dinner, sneakers* rather than *shoes, sprinted* rather than *ran*?
- Does the essay use active verbs whenever reasonable, and does it stay away from excessive use of the verb *be* (*is, was, were*)?

Words like *fun, large, messy, great,* and *slow* are all defined by context, as are generic nouns like *food, movie, building.* If the writing does not provide a detailed context, these words often leave readers in the dark. After all, how big is *large*? How messy is *messy*? Which *movie* did you see? What kind of *building* was it? When you revise to use more specific words, you give your readers far more information. (For more on word choices, see Chapter 25.)

[*39*]

Remember too that essay writing improves when writers use the active voice. In addition to simply conveying more action, the active voice demands subjects as the agents of the verbs' actions. (For more on active and passive voice, see Chapter 21.)

Jeff Bridges was kissed in the movie *The Morning After*. [*Who kissed him?*]

Jane Fonda kissed Jeff Bridges in the movie *The Morning After*. [*Now we can picture it, and we have more information.*]

Writers often employ the passive voice in a variety of useful ways, but if you find that you lapse repeatedly and unconsciously into the passive, try rewriting in the active.

Tone

- Do the word choices create a tone appropriate to the topic and intended audience?
- Is the language formal enough, too formal, too informal?
- Does the essay employ words your readers will find out of place or offensive?

If you and your audience possess similar values and backgrounds, your instinctive word choices will probably not offend your readers. However, if your readers possess values or attitudes quite different from your own, you will probably need to pay close attention to your use of language. Contrast the vocabulary you would use in writing to a friend with the vocabulary you would use in writing to a prospective employer. (For more on tone, see Chapter 26.)

EXERCISE 3.5 REVISING PARAGRAPHING, SENTENCE STRUCTURE, AND WORD CHOICES

Read this passage and answer the questions that follow it. Use your own paper for this exercise. (Note that the sentences have been numbered for easy reference.)

The first television was in our house one day when I was about five years old.[1] Since I don't recall its arrival, someone must have brought it home while I was doing something else.[2] The set was maybe fifteen inches wide and encased in a dark wood cabinet with polished doors.[3] When the doors were closed, it looked like any other piece of furniture.[4] The set was added to the room, but nothing else was changed.[5] The chairs were grouped around the fireplace and arranged for conversation; not one of them faced the television itself.[6] Weird, don't you think?[7] The nearest chair was large, overstuffed, with a closely woven green cover.[8] Since it was facing mostly away from the TV screen, we took turns sitting sideways on one of the arms.[9] It wasn't particularly comfortable.[10] Eventually, we wore the covering completely away, revealing a smooth length of hardwood frame.[11] I remember *Howdy Doody; Kookla, Fran, and Ollie;* Red Skelton; Lucy, Fred and Ethel; Milton Berle; *Zorro; Sky King;* Tonto and the Lone Ranger; Lassie and Timmy.[12] I remember the Burma Shave ad jingle, the original *College Bowl.*[13] Eventually, the television got relocated to a back room, the chair was re-covered with a beige fabric it still wears, and that old set was history, *kaput.*[14] Later still, our family also bought a portable.[15] The Vietnam War was watched while eating dinner just like the Olympics and *You Asked for It* and the Channel 8 weather forecast.[16] By then, the tube was a habit for us.[17] Until 1968 the news must have been watched by us every night with dinner.[18] Robert Kennedy was killed that year, as was Martin Luther King.[19] Both deaths brought back too many memories from 1963.[20] These were unpleasant memories.[21] Then the television stayed off.[22] We began to learn to talk to each other.[23]

1. Does this really need to be just one paragraph, as it is now? Would you recommend reparagraphing? If so, how? If not, why not? Explain your reasoning.
2. Would you recommend any changes in sentence length or sentence structure? Identify your changes, if any. Explain your reasoning.
3. Would you recommend any changes in word choice? If so, what words would you change?
4. What else would you say to help this writer improve the passage? Discuss both strengths and weaknesses.

ESSAY EXERCISE 13   USING STRATEGIES 5, 6, AND 7

Now that your draft has been revised so that its overall content and organization reflect your intentions and purpose, it is time to look closely at your introduction and conclusion as well as your preliminary decisions regarding paragraphing, sentence length and structure, word choice, and tone. Respond to these questions on your own paper.
   Reread only your introduction, keeping these questions in mind:

- Does it accurately reflect the paper that follows it?
- Is this the best way for this paper to begin?
- Why will readers want to continue reading after seeing this introduction?

1. Based on these questions, what changes, if any, should you make in your introduction?

Continue rereading your revised draft, keeping these questions in mind:

- Do these paragraphs group information in ways helpful to readers?
- Are there too many long paragraphs or too many short ones?

- Are the transitions from one paragraph to the next clear?
- Are these sentences consistently too long or too short?
- Are long and short sentences used effectively?
- Are the word choices specific?
- Will any of the vocabulary here be unfamiliar to readers?
- Are the word choices appropriately informal or formal?

2. Based on these questions, what changes, if any, should you make in your decision regarding paragraphing and the use of transitions?
3. What types of sentence changes should you make?
4. What types of wording changes should you make?

Editing Your Final Draft |3*h*|

In most cases, experienced writers edit (that is, check for correctness) only after they have completed their large-scale revisions; after all, there is little point in correcting sentences that will be changed or possibly cut later. Since it often comes nearly last in the writing process, editing is one step inexperienced writers sometimes skip. The result may be a clearly organized piece of writing that contains numerous errors.

What do writers look for as they edit their own work? They look for errors, expecially errors that have given them trouble before. Reading in this way involves training yourself to pay *little* attention to your content and *close* attention to individual sentences and words. Reading aloud often helps writers focus in this way. Many writers also read backward, sentence by sentence. Such backward reading makes the content difficult to follow and frees the mind to concentrate on spelling and punctuation. Whatever your method of rereading, simply mark each error (or possible error) and keep reading. Then return to reexamine and remedy the errors.

Successful editing depends on your ability to spot errors. If you write infrequently, you will probably find it harder to recall the rules and harder to edit your own work. In some cases, a sentence may "sound wrong" or "look wrong" even though you cannot say why. If you suspect an error, note the sentence, finish your reading, and then ask someone to help you with those problem sentences—your course instructor, a knowledgeable student, or a writing assistant in your writing center. Do not let any of these resource people simply correct your work. Besides being unethical, such correcting by others robs you of the opportunity to learn. Ask instead for an explanation of the error. Once you understand, you can make the correction.

If none of these resource people is available, you will need to do what many experienced writers do: consult a source book. This is one such book. The table of contents and the index should help you locate answers to specific questions of punctuation and grammar. If you need to review the meanings of various grammatical terms, Chapter 6 should prove useful.

In addition, maintain your own personal editing checklist, a record of the sorts of errors caught during editing. Include the errors you catch and those your instructor notes. Most of us make the same errors over and over. By identifying these repetitions, we should be able to spot and correct them next time. Reviewing your checklist before editing a new paper should help you catch the kinds of errors made on the previous ones.

Error	*Context*	*Look for*
wrong preposition	*to* for *on*	use of *to*
spelling	*seperate* for *separate*	*seperate*
sentence fragment	starts with *-ing* word	use of *-ing* words at start of sentence
apostrophe	*it's* for *its*	use of *it's*
comparison of unlike things	"a winter as cold as Buffalo" should be "a winter as cold as Buffalo's"	as . . . as

If you find that many or most of your checklist entries refer to spelling errors, consider keeping a separate spelling checklist (see Chapter 22).

➤ *Checking your writing for the top twenty errors found in student writing*

The authors of *The St. Martin's Handbook* have conducted extensive research into the error patterns of college writers. This research has resulted in a list of the twenty errors most often made by college students in their writing. Throughout this book you will find coverage of the rules and guidelines you need to correct each of these problems. Each of the specific errors requires more explanation than can be provided here, but the list that follows identifies each error and the chapter that will help you with it. (Note that the most common error made by student writers was misspelling. If you have trouble in this area, study the spelling tips provided in Chapter 22.)

The Top Twenty Errors in Student Writing

1. No comma after introductory expression (see Chapter 27)
2. Vague pronoun reference (see Chapter 11)
3. Missing comma in compound sentence (see Chapter 27)
4. Wrong word (see Chapters 23–26)
5. No comma with nonrestrictive modifer (see Chapter 27)
6. Wrong verb ending (see Chapters 8 and 9)

7. Wrong or missing preposition (see Chapter 6)
8. Comma splice (see Chapter 13)
9. Missing possessive apostrophe (see Chapter 30)
10. Shift in tense (see Chapter 12)
11. Shift in pronoun or point of view (see Chapter 12)
12. Sentence fragment (see Chapter 14)
13. Wrong tense (see Chapter 8)
14. Lack of subject-verb agreement (see Chapter 9)
15. Missing series comma (see Chapter 27)
16. Lack of pronoun agreement (see Chapter 9)
17. Unnecessary comma with restrictive modifier (see Chapter 27)
18. Fused sentence (see Chapter 13)
19. Dangling or misplaced modifier (see Chapter 15)
20. *Its/it's* confusion (see Chapter 30)

Since so many students fall into these twenty error patterns, chances are that several of them may end up on your personal editing checklist. You could *begin* your checklist by looking through your writing for some of the twenty errors just listed. After all, one of the hardest things about correcting your own writing is knowing what mistakes to look for. This list can give you some ideas, but bear in mind that learning what mistakes you routinely make will take time. You will probably keep adding items to your checklist long after you finish using this book. As you do, you will be actively making yourself a stronger, more accomplished writer.

Proofreading Your Final Copy |3*i*|

As a writer, you need to make your final draft absolutely correct. That means one final rereading even after you think you have caught every single error. Read slowly aloud. Check for punctuation marks, letters left out or transposed, and any other typographical errors. If you have been doing your drafting and revising on a computer, you should be able to produce an absolutely clean and error-free copy. (If you use a word processor, you should have little trouble adapting this chapter's revision strategies to computer use. See also Chapter 45, which is devoted entirely to computers and the writing process.)

ESSAY EXERCISE 14   EDITING YOUR ESSAY

It is time for a careful reading of your revised draft to identify and correct any errors. Read backward, sentence by sentence. Pay attention to each sentence's grammar, its use of punctuation marks, and the spelling of each word. Use the rest of this book to help you correct any errors. Finally, on your own paper, construct an editing checklist with headings as shown on page 43 (you need not list any error more than once).

ASSIGNMENT 3A CONSTRUCTING AN EDITING CHECKLIST

Assume that you have been employed for some time as a retail salesperson at a small store in your local mall. Since you must regularly close the shop at the end of your shift, you know the procedures well. The manager has asked you to write down those procedures for new employees to be hired over the holiday season.

You have written a draft that you feel is complete and worded as you want it. Your next step is to edit. Read the following passage, first to acquaint yourself with its content, then a second time to edit. Underline any errors you find. Then enter those errors in the editing checklist begun below. (In the example, the first error has been underlined and a checklist entry made.)

Instuctions for Locking the Store

1. At ten minutes before closeing, turn off half of the store lights. Marked in red on the electirical panel, which you'll find on the north wall in the overstock room.
2. After turning out half the lights. Ring up any last minute purcheses, and then let any remaning customers know that the store will be closing at 7 pm. Be freindly!
3. At 7, walk from the back of the store to the front, keeping any remaning customers in front of you. Usher them out the door (tell them "thanks for shopping at Smith's"), and lock the door behind them. Put the closed sine in the window.
4. Check and clean the fitting rooms. Look for any stray pins have been removed from the carpets!
5. Check and turn out bathroom.
6. Close cash register, tally receipts (see the separate list instructions for this task).
7. Connect the off-hours answering machine.
8. Check the front door once more turn out remaning lights. Exit out the employee's door, locking it behind you.

Error	Context	Look for
spelling	*instuction* for *instruction*	letter left out

This exercise is intended to help you practice writing process skills in composing a single paragraph. You will be asked to make revisions and corrections in differently colored inks or pencils. Two colors are all you need; simply alternate between them. If you need to write drafts or notes that you cannot fit into the spaces provided, by all means do so. Hand in all of your notes along with what you have written on the following pages.

1. Begin by brainstorming, freewriting, or just thinking about the following question (or any other question that you and your instructor have agreed upon): Why did I decide to go to college, and what will my college education bring me? Then create an informal plan (an outline or a list, for instance) for a one-paragraph answer to that question. Write your plan below.

2. Now use the space below to write a first draft of your paragraph.

3. Use revision strategy 2 (page 29) to identify things you might revise in your rough draft. Then use revision strategy 3 (page 31) to identify other revision ideas you may have overlooked. List below all the ideas for revision that these two strategies have helped you gather.

4. Now use the plans you have listed above to revise your draft. You may want to work directly on your rough draft; if so, use a different color of ink or pencil so that it is clear which of your writing is your draft and which is your revision. Copy your revised paragraph below. (It is fine to make further changes as you recopy.)

5. Use revision strategy 7 (pages 38–40) to further revise and improve your paragraph. Working in a different color again, add your revisions of sentences, word choices, and tone directly on the draft you wrote for question 4. Copy this third draft below (again, feel free to make further revisions in recopying).

6. Following the guidelines given on pages 42–44, edit your third draft for spelling, punctuation, grammar, and mechanics. Read the draft once to see what you can spot on your own. Then check it carefully for each of the student writing errors listed on pages 43–44. Correct all the errors that you find (in a different color on the copy you have written above), looking up any rules you are unsure of in the other chapters of this book. If there is anything you still feel uncertain about, circle it and jot down your question about it in the margin. Copy your best edited version below.

7. Set this assignment aside for at least an hour or two—or a day if you can manage the time—and do something completely unrelated to it. Then come back and proofread your final edited paragraph very carefully. Use a different color to correct any mistakes that you find.

4

Understanding and Using Argument

Recognizing Argument 14a

During the course of a day, we hear a variety of straightforward, factual statements:

> "My biology class starts at one-thirty." [*A quick look at the schedule of classes verifies this.*]

> "I hadn't planned on this rain, so I left my umbrella in the car." [*The speaker's wet face verifies this.*]

Such statements are unarguable; they present simple truth. Other statements may not be so simple:

> "Cindy ought to add a P.E. class; she'd love bowling." [*Would Cindy really love bowling? Does her schedule have room for another course? If so, would she be better off adding something else?*]

> "The Democratic candidate is dead wrong on that issue." [*The Democratic candidate will certainly disagree here.*]

> "The new Italian restaurant is the best place in town." [*Not everyone likes Italian food.*]

Such statements are opinions. As such, they are open to argument.

College writers are asked to present all sorts of arguments. A business ethics class asks you to decide whether or not public employees should be permitted to strike. Scholarship committee members wonder why they should award you a scholarship. Your first task in these writing situations is to identify which questions involve verifiable fact and which involve personal opinion.

In general, an arguable statement will possess at least one of these three characteristics:

1. It will attempt to convince readers to change their minds or to do something.
2. It will address a question for which no ready answers or solutions exist.
3. It will present information or assertions with which readers could reasonably disagree.

The statement "Public employees such as police officers and firefighters should not be legally allowed to strike" possesses all three characteristics; it is an arguable statement.

EXERCISE 4.1 RECOGNIZING ARGUABLE STATEMENTS

Look at the following numbered sentences. Indicate which are argumentative (questions of opinion) and which are factual (questions of objective fact). Be ready to explain your answers.

EXAMPLE We recently purchased a computer system. ___factual___

1. Being a golf caddy is not really what it's cracked up to be. _____

2. The California Bears finished the season with a record of 11–7. _____

3. Everyone ought to give skydiving a try. _____

4. No governmental funds should be spent on experimental medical procedures.

_____

5. Last night, the power went out for forty-five minutes. _____

Formulating an Argumentative Thesis |4b|

Chapter 2 discusses formulating a working thesis as one of the early steps in the writing process. Such a thesis contains two parts: a topic part and a comment part. An argumentative paper also requires a two-part working thesis: a claim about what *is* (the topic part) and a claim about what *should be* (the comment part). Here is an example:

| *claim about what is (topic)* | *claim about* |
Since air bags can significantly reduce automobile injuries, air bags ought to

what should be (comment)
be required equipment on all new cars.

Formulating such a working thesis is an important part of the planning process; with such a thesis in place, a writer can begin to anticipate the task ahead. Clearly, the writer of the argumentative working thesis in the example will need to be able to show that air bags do significantly reduce automobile injuries.

EXERCISE 4.2 FORMULATING AN ARGUMENTATIVE WORKING THESIS

Compose three argumentative statements, and identify their two parts: circle the claim about what is, and underline the claim about what should be. Use your own paper for this exercise.

EXAMPLE

Since the law allows public employees to join labor unions and since many of their typical grievances—pay, working conditions, benefits—are similar to those of other employees, public employees ought to be able to strike.

Establishing Credibility   14d1

As current events indicate, the point of a gun may temporarily persuade those at whom it is aimed; however, that persuasion typically does not last long. Real persuasion occurs only through the careful presentation of reasons, on the one hand, and careful listening, on the other. Without both, no lasting agreements can be reached. Centuries ago, the Greek philosopher Aristotle identified three kinds of good reasons that can make for real persuasion: reasons that establish credibility, those that appeal to logic, and those that appeal to emotion. Let us begin with the first sort, reasons that establish credibility.

Whenever you write, you present an image of yourself. If the image is acceptable to your readers, chances are that they will continue to read; present an unacceptable image, however, and your readers will probably dismiss what you say and simply stop reading. How do readers judge a writer's image as acceptable or unacceptable? The first criterion is credibility, which can be demonstrated in any of three ways:

1. By showing ample knowledge about your subject
2. By indicating respect for your readers' points of view
3. By demonstrating fairness and evenhandedness

Showing Knowledge ⏐4d1⏐

How much knowledge is enough knowledge? The answer is particularly important when it comes to persuasive writing. Use the following questions to help you determine whether or not you have enough knowledge on a given topic:

- Can you support your claim with information from several outside sources (library materials or testimony by qualified experts, for instance)?
- Will your sources be considered reliable by your readers?
- Do any sources contradict one another? If so, can you resolve the contradictions?
- If you have personal experience relating to your claim, will your readers agree that it is applicable?

Establishing Common Ground ⏐4d2⏐

One of the best ways to convince readers to listen carefully to your argument is to discover and point out any values you may hold in common. For example, it is likely that writers on both sides of the gun control issue value freedom and human life. Both sides may also agree that safety in cities is a problem. If an argument establishes these common points of agreement, even hostile readers will be more willing to listen to the entire argument. And readers who read it all are probably the only readers you have a chance to convince.

EXERCISE 4.3 ESTABLISHING COMMON GROUND

Consider these controversial topics. On a separate sheet of paper, list three values or relevant statements that are likely to be shared by both sides of the argument.

EXAMPLE

Banning smoking in public places infringes on the rights of smoker.

Common value 1: Public freedoms are an important part of American life.
Common value 2: Actions by some citizens should not endanger the health of other citizens.
Common value 3: Any legal limitation on public freedoms should be based on solid evidence, careful consideration, and considerable public input.

A. Capital punishment is cruel and unusual punishment.
B. Public schools ought to allow prayer in the classrooms.
C. People should live together before marriage.
D. The draft is a legitimate way to provide for the nation's defense needs.
E. Employers should not be able to require drug tests of prospective employees.

Demonstrating Fairness |4d3|

Establishing a Neutral Tone In a persuasive essay, fairness has to do with both content and tone. Tone is a matter of word choice. Writers who wish to persuade must be very careful when it comes to word choices. If, for example, you call a group of people "terrorists," you have automatically condemned them. If you are trying to convince these "terrorists" to change their tactics, you might begin by giving them a more neutral label. "Activists" might be less offensive, for instance.

Avoiding Ethical Fallacies |4d4|

Fairness has also to do with the argumentative tactics writers use. A writer who blasts the mayor's new anticrime program because the mayor is "a lazy, no-good, self-serving politician" is not really commenting on the anticrime program. Such personal attacks (usually on an individual's character or intelligence) are often called *ad hominem* attacks. They are a convenient way to side-step issues. Writers who use such tactics usually do so because they can think of no better methods.

Guilt by association is another version of the personal attack. In the middle of this century, the playwright Arthur Miller (author of *Death of a Salesman*) was unfairly accused of being a Communist simply because he had attended various open meetings. The illogic of this is not difficult to see. By the same logic, everyone attending a Catholic wedding must necessarily be Catholic.

EXERCISE 4.4 RECOGNIZING INFLAMMATORY WORD CHOICES AND ETHICAL FALLACIES

The following paragraph is an attempt at argumentative writing. Read the paragraph. Then, on a separate sheet of paper, answer the questions that follow it.

As a taxpaying member of this community, I'm sick to death of our smug politicians who think they can hoodwink us into paying for another boondoggle program. These are the same people who brought us a tax increase on gasoline to pay for road repair. Now they're talking about a new mall for downtown. This proposal has been cooked up by the same party that brought you Watergate. They're just eager to get and spend public money, and they're in league with the fat-cat businessmen downtown who see our wages as a way to finance their profits. The plan stinks. Vote no next Tuesday on Measure 99.

1. Make a list of any problematic word choices in the paragraph.
2. Make a list of any ad hominem attacks in the paragraph.
3. Make a list of any examples of guilt by association in the paragraph.
4. Explain, in a few sentences, whether the argument in the paragraph seems effective. Why or why not?

Appealing to Logic |4e|

Providing Examples and Precedents |4e1|

Successful arguments do more than simply establish their credibility. Logic and emotion also play their parts. We shall now begin to discuss how writers present the logic of their arguments.

Well-conceived examples go a long way toward the logic of making arguments effective. Suppose that you want to change majors, but your parents are against it. Suppose further that one of your best friends changed majors last year. And also assume that this friend has done wonderfully—has, in fact, gone from being a mediocre student to a mainstay on the dean's list. If you use your friend as an example as you present your case to your parents, then they may well be more willing to agree to your change of major.

That friend's experience may also act as a precedent. The word *precedent* means literally "what came before." If you decide to use your friend's experience as a precedent, you are arguing that your friend's circumstances are just like yours and that the end of both stories will also be the same.

Not all examples are precedents. By themselves, examples may not argue a point. But examples are almost always crucial to readers' understanding, and readers must understand what you say before they can assent to it. Precedents, by contrast, are by their nature argumentative. A writer who says, "Look what happened last time," is arguing a point and using precedent to do so.

EXERCISE 4.5   UNDERSTANDING EXAMPLES AND PRECEDENTS

For each of the following general topics, list two examples and one precedent. Use your own paper for this exercise.

EXAMPLE   Justice

1. *Precedent: Roe* v. *Wade* (a Supreme Court decision). By their nature, almost all Supreme Court decisions become precedents.
2. *Example:* A fairly played sporting contest—the best team wins.
3. *Example:* Any prime-time detective show—the villains are always caught.

EXAMPLE   Taxes

1. *Precedent:* Any earlier tax law could potentially be used as a precedent for a later similar law. Prohibition is seen by some as a precedent indicating the futility of legislating morality.
2. *Example:* A sales tax.
3. *Example:* Social Security withholding.

A. College regulations
B. Responsible driving
C. Civil rights discrimination

_____

Using Testimony and Authority 14e2

In addition to examples and precedents, argumentative writers often call on **authorities** to help back their claims. A writer arguing for reasonable treatment of AIDS patients might cite information provided by the Centers for Disease Control. Most researchers and most of us in the general populace would agree that this authority is reliable. Some states have begun to use advertisements featuring the victims of drunk drivers. The experiences of these individuals give their arguments against drunk driving considerable persuasive power.

Citing authority is a time-honored argumentative technique, but it must still be done carefully and intelligently. These guidelines should help you use authority effectively:

- *The authority should be timely.* (It would be foolish, for instance, to argue that the world is flat simply because many medieval authorities said so.)
- *The authoritiy should be qualified to judge the topic at hand.* When the American Medical Society urges a health position (say, the encouragement of AIDS education), it is arguing from authority. If the AMA advocated cars made by one company over cars made by another, we might reasonably wonder if the AMA is qualified to act as an authority on automobiles.
- *The authority should be known and respected by readers.* Many investors will listen to advice from large investment firms like Merrill, Lynch. Not many investors will listen to an unknown stock analyst publishing a newsletter out of a garage.

Many writers also employ **testimony** from authoritative individuals. Suppose the victim of a drunk driver says, "Thanks to him, I'll never walk. I'll never run on a beach. I'll never teach my own children to ride a bicycle. Don't do this to anyone else; don't do it to yourself." That is testimony presented by an authority. Such testimony can be an effective and persuasive tool for writers. However, like any information from an authority, testimony should be used carefully. Irrelevant testimony abounds in advertising. What makes a sports hero an effective advertising personality is name recognition, not necessarily any real expertise. It is not logical to assume that a person renowned for hitting golf balls a long way has any special knowledge about what you should eat for breakfast.

Linking Causes and Effects 14e3

Linking causes with effects sounds like it should be easy, and sometimes it is. An egg dropped on the floor (a cause) creates a mess (effect). When causes and effects are obvious, there is little likelihood for argument. When the link is more difficult to see, there may well be considerable disagreement.

Identify an effect that you know to be unfortunate—for example, the number of accidental injuries from handguns. What causes these injuries? Some writers might argue that these injuries are the result of negligence on the part of handgun owners. Their solution might be to require that all handgun owners take a firearm safety class. Other writers might argue that so long as the law allows the private ownership of handguns, accidents will occur. These writers might argue for laws banning the private ownership of handguns.

Will these arguments convince readers? They will do so only to the extent that they can link the effect (accidental injuries) with the cause they identify. Such definite linkage is often difficult to prove. However, whenever you can confidently trace cause and effect, you have a potent weapon for argument.

Now turn to Assignment 4A at the end of this chapter for practice in analyzing cause and effect arguments.

Using Inductive Reasoning |4e4|

When you work from a number of specific instances to some general statement, you are thinking inductively. Inductive reasoning is one way to establish a cause-and-effect relationship. Suppose that your family goes out to dinner. Later that evening, one family member becomes ill; no one else is affected. Reasoning inductively, you can eliminate several possible causes: Since you all drank the water, that can be eliminated. Since two of you had the same vegetable, that can be ruled out. Since three of you had fish, that can be eliminated. In fact, all that is left is the oysters, which were eaten only by the person who became ill. Inductive reasoning has led you to a probable cause.

In the example just given, inductive reasoning is used to work backward to a cause. Inductive reasoning can also be used to work forward to a choice. Suppose you need to write a paper that takes a position on the question of whether or not abortions should be legal. As you begin, you realize only that the issue is complicated and controversial. Deciding to use inductive reasoning, you start by trying to identify the most frequent instances when people turn to abortion. Eventually, you compose a list of such typical situations. By understanding these specific instances, you work closer and closer to your own generalization regarding the question of legal abortions.

Accomplished writers of arguments know that inductive reasoning can be a powerful persuasive tool. If you can lead readers to understand a succession of specific facts, chances are that you can also lead them to agree with the conclusion (the inductive generalization) you arrive at through those facts.

Now turn to Assignment 4B at the end of this chapter for practice in using inductive reasoning.

Using Deductive Reasoning |4e4|

At a large party, you are introduced to someone your age named Judy. The host introduces you by saying something to the effect that you are a college student at O.S.U. Immediately Judy's face brightens, and she talks to you like a long-lost friend. What has happened here? Perhaps Judy has deduced that since she found so many great friends at O.S.U., chances are you will also be a friend. She has worked from a general principle (O.S.U. students make great friends) to a specific instance (you are going to be a great friend). That is deduction.

A short time ago, we used the example of inductive reasoning to determine that oysters were the probable cause of a family member's illness. We can take that inductive generalization, that conclusion, and make it the major premise in a deductive line of reasoning: since oysters made Dan ill before, they will make him ill again. Hence, he ought to avoid oysters. However, deductive reasoning is trustworthy only to the extent that the major premise is accurate. Was it the oysters or the sauce that made Dan ill? In the example in this section, you and Judy might well have become good friends. But the major premise that all O.S.U. students would necessarily be good friends is suspect. Friendship is more complicated than that.

Sometimes you will hear deductive statements based on major premises that are implied but unspoken. "Don't bother to ask for Jack's help with this physics problem—he's a jock." The implied premise here is that jocks are stupid, so they cannot possibly be of any help with physics. Being able to spot implied premises will help you analyze the truth (or lack thereof) in deductive reasoning.

EXERCISE 4.6 USING DEDUCTIVE REASONING

This exercise asks you to do three things. First, write a major premise that you believe applies to each group named. Then work from that major premise to a specific instance you believe to be accurate. Finally, combine the major premise and the specific instance in one sentence. (Use your own paper for this exercise.)

EXAMPLE

Group: College students
Major premise: College students are busy people.

Specific instance: We shouldn't expect many student volunteers.
Combination: Since college students are busy people, we shouldn't expect that many of them will volunteer.

1. *Group:* Soap opera watchers
2. *Group:* Parents
3. *Group:* Tourists

Each of the following sentences asserts an argument based on one or more implied major premises. In each case, identify and write down at least one implied major premise. (Again, use your own paper.)

EXAMPLE   Animals cannot talk; therefore, they cannot feel pain as humans do. [*Implied premise:* Pain does not exist unless it is expressed in words.]

1. Since a majority of Americans still do not use their seat belts regularly, we ought to require seat belt use by law.
2. Nothing can be done about the alcoholic who denies the problem.
3. The United States ought to overthrow that government because it is Marxist.

Recognizing and Avoiding Logical Fallacies |4e5|

Logical fallacies are errors in reasoning. We have already discussed the difficulties writers often face in linking causes and effects, as well as the potential pitfalls of inductive and deductive reasoning. Several other argumentative techniques are illogical and will only anger careful readers.

Begging the Question Suppose a politician roars out in a speech, "We must defeat those ultraliberal Democrats in November!" This statement is "begging the question" because *it treats several unproven, debatable points as if they were settled facts.* It assumes that all Democrats are "ultraliberal," that we all share the same definition of "ultraliberal," and that we all agree that being "ultraliberal" and being a Democrat constitute sufficient grounds for defeat.

The Post Hoc Fallacy The post hoc fallacy is *the assumption that because event B happened after event A, B must have been* caused *by A.* Suppose you are driving your car down the highway and run over some broken glass. Ten minutes later you have a flat tire. You might automatically assume that the broken glass caused your flat tire. You may in fact be right, but until you actually prove this is so, you are guilty of the post hoc fallacy.

The Non Sequitur *Non sequitur* means literally "it does not follow." This fallacy is the attempt to tie together two or more logically unrelated ideas: "Since it was raining outside, I felt the book was simply not well written."

The Either/Or Fallacy A child walks up to her parent and says, "Either you give me a candy bar, or I'll be entitled to a cookie." That child has used the either/or fallacy. This type of argument is illogical because it pretends that only two options exist when in fact there are many more. In this case, the child's parents could offer her an apple or could say, "Not until after dinner."

The Hasty Generalization A hasty generalization bases one or more conclusions on too little evidence or on evidence not carefully analyzed; for example: "I couldn't understand the lecture today, so I'm sure this course will be impossible."

Oversimplification Oversimplification is too simple a relationship between causes and effects. "If all high school students were required to learn touch typing, they would be able to write superior papers once they got to college." That sentence grossly oversimplifies the skills required to write well. While typing is a useful skill for writers to have, not all writers must be good typists (think, for example, of Shakespeare, who had no access to typewriters).

Assignment 4C at the end of this chapter provides practice in recognizing logical fallacies.

Appealing to Emotion |4f|

Consider a poster that reads "DRINKING + DRIVING = (skull and crossbones). The poster's message is clear and logical; it argues that two causes produce an effect.

Now let me tell you a story. In this story, I am a college teacher, and you are a student in my writing class. It is a small class (seventeen or eighteen students), and after several weeks we all recognize each other. In the past three weeks, several students have distributed copies of their papers in rough draft form so that the rest of us could respond—praise, ask questions, suggest changes.

Jill's rough draft was discussed last week. In her paper, Jill wrote of her response to the great American play *Death of a Salesman*. She wrote that she had begun to understand how Willy Loman, the main character, felt worthless because he had lost his job. She had lost a summer job once, through no fault of her own, and that had been bad enough. As a result of that rough draft, we had a spirited discussion; we all realized something about how Americans tend to confuse salary with self-worth.

A week and a half later, I come into class and tell you that Jill was killed early that morning; her car was hit head-on by a drunk driver. Without even thinking, you look over and see her empty chair.

Which is more persuasive, the poster with its message in block letters or the story? The poster does not really appeal to your emotions; it probably does not induce much *feeling*. The story, however, may well give you pause; it might make you feel some of the pain that can result from drunk driving. It might make you think twice. If so, it is a successful piece of persuasion.

Stories constitute one example of emotional appeals. Photographs often evoke emotions. Direct quotes from individuals may often be quite emotional (hence, useful as emotional appeals). And we should not forget humor. The stupid commercial that provokes laughter (on purpose) may not logically make any promise for its product. But we remember the laughter and perhaps purchase the product as a result. Remember that the more specific the details of your appeals (either logical or emotional), the greater the impact of your writing.

Ideally, serious persuasion is a matter of addressing readers as whole people, as people who can think and feel. The most successful persuasive writing often interweaves both kinds of appeals.

EXERCISE 4.7 USING EMOTIONAL APPEALS

One possible logical appeal has been provided for each of the following persuasive topics. Supply a possible emotional appeal. See the example below.

Drug abuse means trouble; say no.

Logical appeal: Doctor's discussion of the clinical effects of long-term drug addiction.
Emotional appeal: Interview with a divorced father whose parental rights have been denied due to his violent behavior while under the influence of drugs. As a result of what the father says, we see his remorse and his pain.

1. Couples ought to live together before deciding to marry.

Logical Appeal: Divorce statistics over the past ten years indicate that more marriages fail than succeed. Perhaps this failure can be attributed to the fact that couples do not really know how to handle the inevitable day-to-day tensions of living under one roof. Such tensions include decisions about budgeting, the division of household chores, even seemingly insignificant things like meal preferences. Included here would be testimony from marriage counselors.

Emotional Appeal: _____

_____

2. Over the next decade, nuclear power ought to be phased out entirely.

Logical Appeal: The costs to maintain aging nuclear power facilities continue to rise (this would be documented). New technologies—especially in solar power, thermal power, and wind power—promise increasing amounts of power at decreasing cost. And nuclear waste continues to be a problem mostly lacking acceptable scientific answers.

Emotional Appeal: _____

_____

_____

Using Analogies   14f31

An analogy is a comparison: *x* is like *y*. Here's a brief example:

> My life is like the top of my desk: it's a mess. My desk has papers strewn all over it. My days are just as disorganized and scattered. . . .

Analogies can be quite effective when introducing a point or stressing one. For example, if you are trying to write a business paper that argues against the hostile takeover of corporations, you could compare such a takeover to a forced marriage between unwilling partners. Some readers may not understand the intricacies of stock takeovers, but most readers will understand the notion of a forced marriage.

EXERCISE 4.8 USING ANALOGIES

Using your own paper, respond to the following questions.

1. Look back at the sample analogy. In this example, words like *mess* and *disorganized* imply criticism. Rewrite the example so that its point is positive. That will mean changing how the analogy is interpreted. Make sure this new version runs at least five sentences.

2. Freewrite for several minutes to extend each of these two analogies. See how many things you can think of that would *support* each analogy. Consider, also, any limitations each might have: ways in which the comparison is untrue or weak. Include these limitations in your freewriting.

> **A.** Becoming a good writer is like becoming a good tennis player.
> **B.** Filling out income tax forms is like being tortured.

3. Now write just a few sentences answering these questions: Which analogy would you be able to extend more successfully? Why? When you are done, turn in both freewrites, as well as your answers to these questions and to question 1.

Recognizing Emotional Fallacies |4f5|

Emotional appeals constitute a valid, often necessary, and useful part of argumentative strategy. However, some emotional appeals seek to preclude the use of any logical or factual investigation or decision making. Such emotional appeals are flawed and unfair, and they should be avoided. Knowledgeable readers will see right through them.

The Bandwagon Appeal   The candidate who argues that because the polls show ever-increasing support, undecided voters should "get on the bandwagon" makes an argument by appealing to the human fear of being left out or left behind. This appeal tries to eliminate any use of fact or logic, and it has no real bearing on politics.

Flattery   Typically, a writer using flattery praises readers for possessing certain qualities, then indicates that because readers possess these qualities, they must certainly agree with the writer's position: "As civic-minded and caring individuals, I am sure that you will want to support the sheriff's posse benefit dinner by purchasing two tickets." Such an appeal asserts that anyone who does not purchase two tickets is automatically the opposite of civic-minded and caring. The argument is thus deflected away from any logical or factual line of discussion. Is the sheriff's posse benefit dinner really a worthy cause? Why?

Veiled Threats   This fallacy also ignores the real issues in a question; it tries to intimidate an audience instead: "If People's Utility does not get an immediate fourteen percent rate hike, it may be forced to discontinue service to its customers." The thought of losing electricity may well inspire considerable fear on the part of customers, and that is exactly the writer's intent.

EXERCISE 4.9 RECOGNIZING EMOTIONAL FALLACIES

Analyze this letter to the editor. Does it employ emotional fallacies? (Note that the sentences have been numbered so that you may refer to them easily.) List any emotional fallacies you can find, and say whether they increase or decrease the effectiveness of the writer's argument.

When I think of the residents of our town, I think of Gordon Johnson, who has devoted so much of his time to the development of community theater.[1] We have all benefited enormously from his dedication and hard work; last month's production of *Cat on a Hot Tin Roof* is only the latest example.[2] When I think of the residents of our town, I think of Anne Sherry, whose promotional efforts on behalf of the Downtown Association resulted this year in a wonderful and much appreciated holiday parade designed to kick off the holiday season and showcase downtown merchants.[3] We all have a right to take pride in such upstanding citizens.[4] And when I think of the residents of our town, I think of you good people.[5] I know that next Tuesday, you will be willing to vote yes for Tax Measure A.[6] I know you care about this town, I know you work hard on its behalf, and I know that with your support we will continue to go forward.[7]

ANALYSIS _____

_____

_____

_____

_____

Organizing an Argument |4g|

The Classical Five-Part Argument This chapter has presented only very brief arguments as examples; however, chances are that your own arguments will be lengthier and more difficult to organize. There is no sure-fire formula for organizing an argument successfully, but many writers use the classical five-part argument format. This organizational scheme begins with an introduction, then presents any necessary background information, moves on to the actual lines of argument, refutes any objections, and concludes with a call to action (if appropriate) or a call for agreement. If you find it difficult to organize your argumentative writing, try following this format.

EXERCISE 4.10 ORGANIZING AN ARGUMENT

Take the following notes and, on a separate sheet of paper, reorganize them into the classical five-part argument under these headings: "Introduction," "Background," "Lines of Argument," "Refutation of Opposing Opinions," and "Conclusion." The issue is this: should University X switch from the quarter system to the semester system? The writer of these notes has taken the position that the switch to semesters is a good idea. (You will see that since these are notes, the writer has not proofread.)

NOTES

four similar schools have switched to semesters in last three years

Those opposed say that semester system does not provide enough flexibility. Counterargument: Whatever is lost in terms of flexibility is gained by the greater length of time students have with their subjects.

```
        Those opposed say that switch to semester system will force faculty to
dramatically alter their course syllabi.  Counter:  Agreed, and these
alterations can only be accomplished after a careful review of course
goals, teaching methods, tests, etc.  All this reevaluation is a good
thing.

        reasons for switch:
        --easier transfer to other institutions (majority of similar schools
are on semester system
        --reduced registration costs (2 times per year instead of 3)
        --careful review of courses campuswide
        --students spend more time with each subject:  more depth, greater
understanding of complexities, more practice
        --allows greater student-faculty interaction:  students get to know
faculty better

        this switch has been a topic of campus debate on and off for the past
decade

        all of us want quality education

        those who agree should express that agreement by signing the petition
at the information desk in the Student Union building.
```

Now that you have arranged those notes into an organizational format, evaluate what you have arranged. What parts of this five-part organization still seem seriously incomplete to you? Why?

EXERCISE 4.11 ANALYZING AN ARGUMENT

Carefully read the following argument. (The sentences have been numbered for easy reference.) Using your own paper, analyze the argument for its use, misuse, or failure to use logical, ethical, and emotional appeals.

Everyone knows that the American way is a cooperative, democratic way.[1] And none of us likes to feel pushed around or dictated to.[2] That's why some Americans are bothered by proposals that ban smoking in public places.[3] Think about the term "public places."[4] "Public" means "for everyone."[5] And in this country, "everyone" includes a large number of smokers.[6] If we start giving in to a vocal minority that wants to ban smoking in public, we risk losing what our forefathers fought and died for.[7] We risk losing our freedom.[8]

ASSIGNMENT 4A ANALYZING CAUSE AND EFFECT ARGUMENTS

Examine the following cause-effect analyses. In the space given, indicate briefly whether or not you believe the analysis is valid.

EXAMPLE

Effects: In Teacher B's physics class, more students get grades of A and B than get grades of C, D, or F. In Teacher C's physics class, most students receive grades of C or below.

Cause: Teacher B must be a superior teacher.

Discussion: Teacher B may well be a superior teacher. But it is also possible that Teacher B asks so little of students that only the most lackadaisical have trouble meeting the criteria. The cause-effect assertion is not well established here.

1. *Effect:* Your five-year-old car fails to start the day after you bought gas at a new gas station.

Cause: The station sold you tainted gas.

Discussion: _____

_____

_____

_____

2. *Effect:* Your neighborhood is plagued by repeated break-ins and thefts.

Cause: Most of your neighbors haven't bought handguns.

Discussion: _____

_____

_____

_____

3. *Effect:* A popular class suddenly registers a dramatic decline in enrollment.

Cause: Though the class is taught by the same instructor and covers the same material it always has, it used to be a night class; now it is offered only at 10 A.M.

Discussion: _____

_____

_____

_____

In each of the following questions, you are provided with examples of specific information. Draw a reasonable conclusion supported by those examples.

EXAMPLE

The first time you saw Dave, he was wearing a shirt and tie.
The second time you saw him, you noticed he was wearing polished shoes.
The third time you saw him, he was wearing a deerstalker hat.
The fourth time you saw him, he had a pipe in his mouth.
The fifth time you saw him, he asked you if you'd seen Watson.
The sixth time you saw him, he said something like "Elementary, my dear," in an affected British accent.

Inductive Generalization: Dave has been reading Sherlock Holmes stories and is enjoying them immensely.

1. Jack S. is a business major and lives in a fraternity house.
   Pete Y. is an art history major and lives in a dorm.
   Julie K. is a business major and lives in a sorority house.
   George L. is a business major and lives with his family in married student housing.
   Kelly F. is a political science major and lives in a dorm.
   Fred J. is a business major and lives in a fraternity house.

Inductive Generalization: _____

_____

_____

2. On February 5, the rainfall measurement was 0.34 inch.
   On February 6, the rainfall measurement was 0.16 inch.
   On February 7, there was no measurable rain.
   On February 8, the rainfall measurement was 0.89 inch.
   On February 9, the rainfall measurement was 0.22 inch.

Inductive Generalization: _____

_____

_____

3. Small business owner Anne K. notes the following things during the course of a month:

Orders for the company's goods are at an all-time high level.

The two workers in the shipping department have fallen ever further behind; what was once a three-day lag between the receipt of an order and its shipment has stretched to sixteen days.

Both individuals in the shipping department have become irritable; one has been ill twice in the past two weeks.

The company accountant reports that the company's financial position is the best it has ever been.

A few customers have noticed that their orders take more time to process.

Inductive Generalization: _____

_____

_____

ASSIGNMENT 4C RECOGNIZING LOGICAL FALLACIES

Each of the following sentences illustrates one of the logical fallacies identified in the text. Identify the fallacy, and briefly explain why the sentence is illogical.

EXAMPLE

If we prohibit the sale of alcohol, we will get rid of the problem of drunkenness.
Fallacy: Oversimplification
Analysis: The sentence argues that the only reason for drunkenness is that alcohol is for sale. There are, in fact, a whole host of personal and societal problems which may cause people to abuse alcohol.

1. If I wash my car on Saturday, we are certain to have rain on Sunday.

Fallacy: _____

Analysis: _____

_____

2. We must approve mandatory bicycle registration because there are so many bicycles on campus.

Fallacy: _____

Analysis: _____

_____

3. I shouldn't consider a medical career; one high school chemistry class was enough to teach me that.

Fallacy: _____

Analysis: _____

_____

4. Passing this civil rights legislation will eliminate prejudice.

Fallacy: _____

Analysis: _____

_____

5. Either we provide our children with sex education in school, or they will get their sex education on the streets.

Fallacy: _____

Analysis: _____

_____

6. We must support Senator Smith's worthy proposal against the efforts of those who would weaken it by amendments.

Fallacy: _____

Analysis: _____

_____

5

Constructing Paragraphs

Understanding Paragraphs |5a|

A paragraph is a group of sentences that focus on one main point, with each sentence clearly related to the others and each providing specific details to support or explain the main point.

Some writers working at the drafting stage ignore paragraphs altogether; their drafts look like one big paragraph. Other writers actually draft their essays using paragraph breaks right from the beginning. But whatever their habits at the drafting stage, virtually all writers recognize that paying conscious attention to paragraphing is a vital part of the revising process.

EXERCISE 5.1 MAKING NOTES FOR PARAGRAPHS

On your own paper, jot down the things you do on a typical Monday morning, beginning when you first wake up. *Do not write sentences.* At the top of your page, write "Typical Monday Morning." Underneath, write notes and phrases. Fill at least half a page with your notes.

A few hours later, return to the notes you made. Is anything major left out? If so, add it. Now number each item chronologically. Save these notes; you will use them later in this chapter. Your notes might begin with entries like these:

1. wake up too early
2. coffee, must have coffee
3. take shower

Developing Paragraphs by Providing Details |5d|

Often the difference between a well-written paragraph and a poorly written one is the inclusion of details. Without them, a writer's message is a mystery. With them, the message is clear and unmistakable.

Consider this short paragraph:

> Even though the weather was bad, we had a good Sunday. We drove out into the country and looked at the country. Sometimes it seemed like we were miles away from town. After two hours, we were home again. The drive had been a welcome way to enjoy the weekend.

This is not very good writing. Though the sentences are grammatically correct, they are also so general that they tell us very little. What exactly does "good" mean, for instance? Since the sentences paint no pictures and convey no real emotion, they tend to exclude readers; only the writer knows what was good about this particular Sunday.

EXERCISE 5.2 USING SPECIFIC DETAILS

Return to the notes you made for Exercise 5.1 now and expand them to include specific details. For example, under "eat breakfast," indicate exactly what you frequently eat. Do you eat cold pizza? cereal with milk and sliced bananas? Under each general point in your notes, list one or more specifically detailed statements. Again, use your own paper for this exercise. Save this exercise; you will need it for Exercise 5.3.

EXAMPLE

1. wake up too early
   alarm set for 6:06
   first voices those of Morning Edition hosts (National Public Radio)
   groan
2. coffee, must have coffee
   in kitchen, Mr. Coffee machine, black, hot
3. take shower
   finally begin to actually wake up
   bathroom steamy

Building Coherence into Paragraphs |5c|

Using Chronological Order |5c1|

All good paragraphs present details. They may be sensory details—how something looks, tastes, smells, feels, or sounds. They may be intellectual details—the specific nuances of ideas. They may be emotional details—how something made someone feel. But how do you present these details? How do you decide what order they should follow?

One common answer to this question is simply to tell the story as it happened. If you are writing a paragraph that tells a story, you are writing a narrative paragraph. Such paragraphs are organized chronologically: what came first is said first, what came second is said second, and so on.

EXERCISE 5.3 WRITING CHRONOLOGICALLY ORDERED PARAGRAPHS

Using your own paper and drawing on your notes from Exercise 5.2, write a chronologically ordered paragraph that tells the story of your typical Monday morning.

EXAMPLE

> My typical Monday morning starts sometime after 6:06 when the clock radio comes on to "Morning Edition." Maybe I hear Burton Bolag talking about politics or Bob Edwards reading the national news. After twenty or so minutes of groaning at how hard it is to get out of bed (sometimes my wife and I do this as a duet), I get up and stumble into the kitchen and Mr. Coffee. The cups are in the cupboard over the stove; I like the large white ones with the blue sailing ships. I don't really begin to wake up until the shower water hits my face. Some mornings I don't even remember turning on the water; I just realize, at some point, that the room is warm and steamy—I have probably forgotten to turn on the fan. Breakfast normally consists of another cup of coffee, vitamins (I eat the same chewables that my kids eat), and a bowl of Raisin Bran or Special K. And so the day begins.

Using Spatial Order |5c|

Both chronologically ordered and spatially ordered paragraphs have something in common: the order is already provided for you. Time provides the order in a chronological paragraph. In a spatially ordered paragraph, the actual arrangement of objects provides the order. In these paragraphs, readers are urged to picture some view or setting. Reading spatially ordered paragraphs is like looking through a camera as it moves from one part of the scene to another.

Two things are important to the clarity and success of spatially ordered paragraphs. First, the relation of things (what is next to what, above it, or behind it) must be clear. The description should not jump around; it should move naturally: left to right, near to far, bottom to top. Second, the description should be specific, not generic: not "a big painting" but "a painting six feet tall and ten feet wide." The idea is for readers to be able to visualize the description, and everything we see is detail.

Note that many spatial paragraphs function quite well without topic sentences. The description itself provides all the focus readers need. If a topic sentence is used, it may be found at the beginning of the paragraph; it may also often be found at the end, where it serves to summarize and name what has been described.

EXERCISE 5.4 WRITING SPATIALLY ORDERED PARAGRAPHS

On your own paper, describe a room where you live. Make sure your eyes move consistently in one direction, and make sure you tell readers what direction that is. Pay particular care to specific characteristics (instead of generic ones). You might want to make notes before you begin. If you can write this paragraph while you are actually in the room, that may help you be more specific. Make your last sentence the topic sentence, and underline it.

Using Repetition, Pronouns, and Parallelism |5c2, 5c3, 5c4|

In a coherent paragraph, the sentences are related to each other not just by their content (unity is a function of content) but also by their sentence structures and word choices. As a writer, you should be aware of three important techniques for creating coherence: repetition, pronoun usage, and parallelism.

Repetition is the multiple use of key phrases or words. The following paragraph uses repetition to achieve coherence:

> Why do some college students succeed, while others struggle? Some succeed because their educational backgrounds have prepared them for college-level work. Others succeed because they are effective time managers: they have set aside time for study and time for play. Others succeed because they are motivated. If a class seems too difficult, they recognize the difficulty and seek help. Successful students are also determined students. And finally, successful students do not ask themselves to be superhuman; they are aware of their strengths and not discouraged by their weaknesses.

As you can see, several words and phrases are repeated from sentence to sentence, including the word *succeed* and the phrase *successful students*. This paragraph uses just about the maximum amount of repetition that any paragraph can stand without sounding affected, forced, or insincere.

In this sample paragraph, one important noun phrase is *college students*. Three pronouns—*some, others,* and *they*—consistently refer to the college students named in the topic sentence. This linking reminds readers that the paragraph is still addressing the subject it began with. It is another way writers can increase the coherence of their paragraphs.

The next paragraph uses the third technique, parallel sentence structures, to add coherence. In this paragraph, every sentence shoves its subject right up against its verb, without allowing any clauses or phrases to fall in between them. Where this has been done, the subject-verb combination has been underlined. (Note that the topic sentence for this paragraph has been placed last.)

> Strolling through the fairgrounds, curious <u>visitors notice</u> cowpokes in tall straw hats and paunchy ranchers wearing turquoise jewelry and bolo ties. The fancier <u>natives sport</u> fancy Tony Lama boots. <u>Women flounce</u> by wearing square-dance dresses. Inside a roped-off arena, a mechanical <u>bull throws</u> all who attempt to ride it. Outside, novice tractor <u>drivers try</u> not to disturb the orange cones as <u>they maneuver</u> their large machines down a narrow, winding course. <u>Sheep bleat.</u> Two <u>holsteins stand</u> placidly chewing their cud. It's all part of Mayville's Agriculture Daze festival.

EXERCISE 5.5 UNDERSTANDING COHERENCE

This paragraph employs the three techniques for promoting coherence. Read the paragraph carefully. Then, using your own paper, discuss how the paragraph uses repetition, pronouns, and parallel sentence structures to achieve coherence. Use one paragraph to make your point that the sample is indeed coherent. The sentences have been numbered for easy reference.

> Some folks vacation by lakes; others adore the mountains.[1] Our family prefers the ocean.[2] We prefer to fall asleep each night with the sound of surf a constant and constantly varying noise—never thunderous, always there.[3] We prefer the ever-changing spectacle of the beach itself.[4] One day, the beach is a repository of seaweed whips, wave-buffed clam shells, mussel shells dark blue and movable like wings.[5] The next day, an entire small tree washes ashore, its trunk mostly stripped of branches, its roots like tangled hair.[6] We like to note how the sand advances or retreats with the seasons.[7] In summer, mounded dunes invite picnics.[8] In winter, the scoured shore reveals rocks and agate beds.[9] Winter or summer, the ocean seems to us like a living thing.[10] Its consecutive waves washing up and ebbing seem to us like breathing.[11] The alternation of tides seems almost the equivalent of sleeping and waking.[12] Yes, we like lakes, and we admire mountains.[13] We prefer the ocean.[14]

Using Transitions to Achieve Clarity |5c5|

Transition words and phrases such as the ones listed here are writers' tools for making connections.

nevertheless	often	but when	as a result
of course	when	other	in short

If you have not consciously used transitional words and phrases in the past, doing so in the future will probably make a big difference in the way readers react to your writing. In addition, consciously using transitional words forces writers to make sure that their paragraphs are indeed care-fully organized. If you have difficulty making a transition, then either a sentence (or more) has been left out of the paragraph, or the paragraph has jumped to a new topic. Paying careful attention to transitions is an impor-tant part of the revision process.

EXERCISE 5.6 USING TRANSITIONS

Read the paragraph below. You'll see that transition words and phrases have been left out. Select the most appropriate transition word or phrase for each blank from the list of possible words and phrases below the paragraph. Pencil the number of the blank next to the appropriate word or phrase. (You will not use every transition word or phrase in the list.)

My grandfather hated flying. _____(1)_____ , I remember train stations. _____(2)_____ , it's not just the stations themselves I remember, though they were beautiful and cavernous and full of echoes. I remember the luggage carts, especially the squeaky sounds their wheels made. _____(3)_____ I'd even get to ride on one as it bounced over track after track. _____(4)_____ we'd arrive at track 9 or track 6 or whatever track it was. _____(5)_____ I'd seen it all _____(6)_____ , I'd be thrilled by that bright white eye getting larger and nearer. _____(7)_____ , the engine would rumble by, the long procession slowing to a crawl and then to a full stop. _____(8)_____ Grandpa and Grandma would bend down to say goodbye, their lips moving but their words lost in the hissing of steam brakes. My grandparents never did fly anywhere together. That's one of the things I remember them for. _____(9)_____ , I have a fondness for train stations.

then	here	at last
of course	and	even though
eventually	all in all	sometimes
before	because	until
thus	immediately	even now

Focusing Paragraphs |5b|

Using Topic Sentences |5b1|

Chronological paragraphs such as the one you wrote for Exercise 5.3 are frequently the easiest to write: their order is based on time, and they often do not need a topic sentence (more about topic sentences in a moment). Chronological paragraphs do have limitations. Basically, writing only chronological paragraphs makes you a slave to actual events. Chronological paragraphs tell what happened, but they do not allow for much emphasis or variety. They do not handle critical or intellectual material very well.

If time does not organize a paragraph and determine what goes in it, something else must. Often a single statement of the paragraph's main idea—the topic sentence—is the organizer of a paragraph. In addition to stating the paragraph's main idea, a topic sentence acts to exclude any information that does not contribute to this main idea. Consider your narrative paragraph on your typical Monday morning. Since time ordered that paragraph, you simply told about what normally happens on Monday morning, starting at the beginning. Your point was simply to tell the story.

But suppose you wanted to tell the story to make a point. Your point might be that your Monday mornings are hectic, sluggish, or particularly unwelcome. As a writer, once you have a point to make, you have a reason to include some details and omit others. Which details will support or prove your point? Those are the details you include. Which details do not contribute to your point? Those details you leave out.

What about the topic sentence—should it come early in the paragraph? Can it come late in the paragraph? Those are good writing questions, ones that a writer must answer on the basis of both material and purpose for writing. As you continue reading this chapter, you will encounter topic sentences in both positions. Here is a revision of the sample narrative paragraph from the preceding section. Some new details appear now to illustrate the underlined topic sentence. Note that the paragraph still uses chronology to provide one element of order.

> My Monday mornings are often difficult. Part of the problem lies with my own internal body clock. It's set to keep me awake and alert until late in the evening, sometimes past midnight. When the clock radio comes on at 6:06, my internal clock says it's way too early to climb out of bed. Since I'm groggy and not exactly eager to wake up, I tend to be grouchy. Even after I've had my shower and begun to feel conscious, I can get irrationally angry when there isn't a full bowl's worth of Grape Nuts left; never mind that there's an unopened box of Raisin Bran in the pantry. If it's raining when I go out to get the paper, I'll probably curse the weather and the paper. About 7:30 or so, I realize that I've been less than charitable to my family (I've probably blamed them for the stray sock in the hall and for the page one headlines). Realizing that, I feel guilty, sheepish. If I'm lucky, I can tease them out of being mad at me. But some Monday mornings, it's tough going.

As you can see, the topic sentence is positioned as the very first sentence in the paragraph. Every sentence that follows it adds some new example or detail to support the statement made in the topic sentence.

EXERCISE 5.7 DEVELOPING PARAGRAPHS AROUND TOPIC SENTENCES

By now you have written a narrative paragraph that details your typical Monday morning. For this exercise, take the same subject and write a paragraph which uses a topic sentence to make a point about your typical Monday morning. Use your own paper for this exercise. Position your topic sentence at the beginning of your paragraph, and underline it. Then make sure that your following sentences support and detail the topic sentence. Add new details or omit some, as necessary.

Revising to Achieve Unity |5b2|

In a unified paragraph, all the information contributes to the paragraph's main point; nothing irrelevant is included. In chronologically ordered or spatially ordered paragraphs, unity is not hard to achieve. So long as each sentence contributes to the chronology or the description, the paragraph will have a basic unity. Sentences that have no bearing on the chronology or the description are generally easy to spot. But in paragraphs that deal with ideas, unity sometimes presents problems. Consider this paragraph:

> Sometimes Oregon winters are cold, but most of the time they are just rainy. People walk around with coats like second skins. Sometimes you do see crazy people walking around in shorts like it's really August. They're just like those people who wear swimsuits to the Denver Broncos' home games. Those people are really strange. You can see them on television every time a Denver home game is broadcast. They're wearing nothing but earmuffs and a swimsuit, even when the temperature is 22 degrees.

What is this paragraph about? It begins with a discussion of Oregon winters, and you could reasonably expect that the rest of the paragraph would discuss those winters. Instead, the paragraph wanders off to a discussion of Denver Broncos football fans. This kind of wandering is often what our minds do, and this is the kind of paragraph that sometimes turns up in freewriting. The only cure for such a disunified paragraph is revision. The writer needs to make some decisions about the paragraph's main point. Is this to be a paragraph on Oregon winters? Is it to be a paragraph about the odd behavior of some Oregonians and Coloradians? The paragraph cannot be sucessfully revised until these questions have been answered.

To analyze a paragraph for unity, first determine its topic sentence. Then ask yourself whether each of the other sentences illustrates, explains, or adds to your knowledge of the main point identified in the topic sentence. If you cannot determine the paragraph's topic sentence, the paragraph probably needs substantial revision.

EXERCISE 5.8 REVISING TO ACHIEVE PARAGRAPH UNITY

Look back at the paragraph that begins "Sometimes Oregon winters are . . . ." On your own paper, write a new, more unified version of that paragraph. You might begin by underlining the topic sentence in the original paragraph and then circling everything that does not relate to the idea the topic sentence presents. Omit the unrelated details from your new version, and add details that do support the main idea. (If you do not know anything about Oregon winters, just use your imagination.)

Patterns of Paragraph Development and Organization |5d|

If you are having difficulty drafting a paragraph, there are a number of patterns you can follow to help you decide what to include. These same patterns are useful during revision. When you have a paragraph but feel that it is disorganized or meandering, you can try rewriting it to follow any one of these patterns to make your point more plainly.

Using Illustration and Examples Suppose that neither chronological nor spatial order is really appropriate to your topic. You might then consider developing your paragraph by illustration. Notice how the following paragraph illustrates a main idea by means of several examples:

> The 1960s was a turbulent time in American history. Civil rights marches, sit-ins, and boycotts challenged many people's assumptions about race and racial equality. The deaths of three public heroes—John Kennedy, Robert Kennedy, and Martin Luther King—forever changed the lives of those who witnessed these events on television. Overseas, American troops took on an ever more active role in the Vietnam War. This involvement frequently provoked protests and antiwar demonstrations. For the first time, many Americans felt separate from their country and its policies. The decade began with President Kennedy saying, "Ask not what your country can do for you; ask what you can do for your country." It ended with rioting in the streets. It ended with a small memorial flame burning at Kennedy's grave.

You can also use illustration by presenting a single extended, detailed example.

EXERCISE 5.9 USING ILLUSTRATION AND NARRATION

Consider this topic sentence: "American eating habits are based on convenience rather than on nutrition." Using your own paper, write two different paragraphs supporting this topic sentence. Label each paragraph as using illustration or using narration, and underline the topic sentence of each paragraph.

In the first, use illustration as your pattern of development (that is, support the topic sentence with factual examples). *Hint:* Make a list of American eating habits that strike you as based on convenience rather than on nutrition. Then refer to your list to illustrate that main point.

For your second paragraph, use narration as your pattern of development. Begin with the topic sentence; support it with a story from your own experience. *Hint:* What from your recent experience will support this topic sentence?

The General-to-Specific Format How do you handle material that does not lend itself to narration or spatial ordering? You may be able to use the general-to-specific pattern of organization. This kind of paragraph begins with the paragraph's most general sentence, the topic sentence, which introduces the main idea. The second sentence limits and focuses the writer's message, and the rest of the paragraph illustrates or supports this narrower focus.

Pets have been a part of human society at least since the days of the Pharaohs. Recently, however, doctors and other health care workers have begun to use pets as an integral part of their recommended treatments, particularly with children and the elderly. In some children's hospitals, cancer wards use dogs and cats, even gerbils, as ways to provide patients with unrestricted acceptance. Kids whose hair has fallen out or who find themselves in casts or bandages sometimes wish to withdraw from contact with their family or friends because they do not wish to be seen "that way." But pets don't care. Their love is unconditional. The elderly respond in much the same way. To these people, often in pain and sometimes without nearby family or friends, pets provide instant companionship and instant distraction. As a result, some older folks take a greater interest in their own well-being and in the life around them.

The Specific-to-General Format As you have no doubt guessed, the specific-to-general paragraph is organized so that the sentences providing explanations or examples come first. Positioned at the end of the paragraph, the topic sentence serves to unite the explanations and examples. This organizational format creates a quite different reading experience. A successful specific-to-general paragraph draws readers in with its specifics, then unites those specifics with a topic sentence that provides a neat summary.

Visitors cannot help but notice cowpokes in tall straw hats and paunchy ranchers wearing turquoise jewelry and bolo ties. Some sport fancy Tony Lama boots. Women flounce by wearing square-dance dresses. A mechanical bull systematically throws all who attempt to ride it. Novice tractor drivers try not to disturb the orange cones as they maneuver their large machines down a narrow course. Sheep bleat. Two holsteins stand placidly chewing their cud. It's all part of Mayville's Agriculture Daze festival.

EXERCISE 5.10 USING THE GENERAL-TO-SPECIFIC AND SPECIFIC-TO-GENERAL FORMATS

1. Choose one of the following four topic sentences, and write a paragraph that uses the general-to-specific method of organization. Begin with the topic sentence of your choice, then write a sentence that restricts and focuses your topic. The sentences that follow should all illustrate your narrower focus. Use your own paper for this exercise.

A. Television is well worth watching.
B. For some people, fast food is a way of life.
C. Photographs rarely tell the whole truth.
D. The American dream is not the same for everyone.

2. Choose another of the topic sentences. Write a paragraph organized in the specific-to-general manner. Make sure that the paragraph presents several examples. Then use a final sentence that unites them all. Make sure that your examples are specific and detailed. Again, use your own paper for this exercise.

The Problem-Solution and Question-Answer Formats A problem-solution paragraph states a problem first, then provides one or more solutions. Similarly, a question-answer paragraph opens by raising a question, then providing one or more answers.

Process Analysis Paragraphs A process analysis paragraph is chronologically organized. It specifies a particular action or set of actions, then proceeds to tell readers how they regularly occur. Here, for example, is a nontechnical process analysis describing how a car is started:

> The process of starting a car begins when the driver inserts the car key into the ignition. Turning the key (typically to the right) completes a circuit and sends electricity from the car's battery to the starter motor and to the spark plugs. The starter motor sets the pistons in action. The spark plugs begin to fire, and the pistons begin to rise and fall on their own. At this point, the driver disengages the starter motor and depresses the gas pedal slightly to give the cold engine the fuel it needs.

Cause-Effect Paragraphs A cause-effect paragraph examines why something happened (emphasis on causes), tries to predict what will happen (emphasis on effects), or does both (cause and effect given equal billing). The typical television weather forecast is often a cause-effect analysis with an emphasis on effects.

Comparison and Contrast Paragraphs Another quite useful organizational pattern is comparison and contrast (you *compare* similar things; you *contrast* dissimilar things). This pattern is discussed in Chapter 2 as an essay organizational format. The paragraph you examined in Exercise 5.5 (it begins, "Some folks vacation by lakes; others adore the mountains") could easily be rewritten as a comparison and contrast paragraph. You would simply follow up on that first sentence with supporting details for both of its halves. You would list what people like so much about lakes and then what others like so much about mountains. (See Chapter 2 for further details on the comparison and contrast format.)

Special-Purpose Paragraphs   15e, 5f

Occasionally essays, especially narrative essays, will use quoted dialogue to present the actual words of several speakers. The conventions of paragraphing dialogue are simple: every time you present a new speaker, use a new paragraph. Recognizing that convention, you know how to write and how to read this exchange:

> "Want to jump rope?"
> "Nah. I'm tired."
> "Want to play gin rummy?"
> "Nah."
> "Want to watch TV?"
> "We've already watched an hour's worth, and you know what Mom said."
> "Well, then—"
> "What about if we kick the soccer ball in the backyard?"
> "I thought the ball was flat."
> "It was until Mom pumped it up again."
> "OK, let's go."

Short stories and novels follow the same convention for paragraphing dialogue: every time there is a new speaker, there is a new paragraph.

The introduction and conclusion of an essay, as discussed in Chapter 3, require special types of paragraphs that relate to the entire essay. Transitions from paragraph to paragraph also need special attention; consult the part of Chapter 3 that deals with the use of transitions.

ASSIGNMENT 5A FINDING PARAGRAPH BREAKS

PART ONE

The passage below is from Jane van Lawick–Goodall's 1971 book *In the Shadow of Man*. Here she writes of some of her observations in East Africa's Gombe Stream Game Reserve. Read the passage and determine where you believe the paragraph breaks should come. Mark each paragraph break with a slash (/). For each paragraph you identify, underline the topic sentence.

During that month I really came to know the country well, for I often went on expeditions from the Peak, sometimes to examine nests, more frequently to collect specimens of the chimpanzees' food plants, which Bernard Verdcourt had kindly offered to identify for me.[1] Soon I could find my way around the sheer ravines and up and down the steep slopes of three valleys—the home valley, the Pocket, and Mlinda Valley—as well as a taxi driver finds his way about the main streets and byways of London.[2] It is a period I remember vividly, not only because I was beginning to accomplish something at last, but also because of the delight I felt in being completely by myself.[3] For those who love to be alone with nature I need add nothing further; for those who do not, no words of mine could ever convey, even in part, the almost mystical awareness of beauty and eternity that accompanies certain treasured moments.[4] And, though the beauty was always there, those moments came upon me unaware: when I was watching the pale flush preceding dawn; or looking up through the rustling leaves of some giant forest tree into the greens and browns and black shadows that occasionally ensnared a bright fleck of the blue sky; or when I stood, as darkness fell, with one hand on the still-warm trunk of a tree and looked at the sparkling of an early moon on the never still, sighing water of the lake.[5] One day, when I was sitting by the trickle of water in Buffalo Wood, pausing for a moment in the coolness before returning from a scramble in Mlinda Valley, I saw a female bushbuck moving slowly along the nearly dry streambed.[6] Occasionally she paused to pick off some plant and crunch it.[7] I kept absolutely still, and she was not aware of my presence until she was little more than ten yards away.[8] Suddenly she tensed and stood staring at me, one small forefoot raised.[9] Because I did not move, she did not know what I was—only that my outline was somehow strange.[10] I saw her velvet nostrils dilate as she sniffed the air, but I was downwind and her nose gave her no answer.[11] Slowly she came closer, and closer—one step at a time, her neck craned forward—always poised for instant flight.[12] I can scarcely believe that her nose actually touched my knee; yet if I close my eyes I can feel again, in imagination, the warmth of her breath and the silken impact of her skin.[13] Unexpectedly I blinked and she was gone in a flash, bounding away with loud barks of alarm until the vegetation hid her completely from my view.[14] It was rather different when, as I was sitting on the Peak, I saw a leopard coming toward me, his tail held up straight.[15] He was at a slightly lower level than I, and obviously had no idea I was there.[16] Ever since arrival in Africa I had an ingrained, illogical fear of leopards.[17] Already, while working at the Gombe, I had several times nearly turned back when, crawling through some thick undergrowth, I had suddenly smelled the rank smell of cat.[18] I had forced myself on, telling myself that my fear was foolish, that only wounded leopards charged humans with savage ferocity.[19] On this occasion, though, the leopard went out of sight as it started to climb up the hill—the hill on the peak of which I sat.[20] I quickly hastened to climb a tree, but halfway up there I realized that leopards can climb trees.[21] So I uttered a sort of halfhearted squawk.[22] The leopard, my logical mind told me, would be just as frightened of me if he knew I was there.[23] Sure enough, there was a thudding of startled feet and then silence.[24] I returned to the Peak, but the feeling of unseen eyes watching me was too much.[25] I decided to watch for the chimps in Mlinda Valley.[26] And, when I returned to the Peak several hours later, there, on the very rock which had been my seat, was a neat pile of leopard dung.[27] He must have watched me go and then, very carefully, examined the place where such a frightening creature had been and tried to exterminate my alien scent with his own.[28]

PART TWO

Turn back to page 3 of this text. The first three paragraphs of Chapter 1 were originally written as one paragraph. In the space below, explain briefly why you think new paragraphs were begun at *All of these* and *As you*, whether you think this paragraphing improves the passage, and why or why not.

PART

2

Sentences: Making Grammatical Choices

These questions are designed to help you, the student, decide what you need to study. Read each sentence and underline the word or words specified in parentheses or underline the correct word of the two provided within the sentence. (Answers to preview questions are found at the back of the book.)

1. Meryl drove her car to the supermarket. (nouns)
2. The Washingtons brought their pet to the doctor. (nouns)
3. Makiko will get a new dress after she finishes her exams. (verbs)
4. Juan might speak to his father about going to the ball game. (verbs)
5. Anybody could buy Prince's record, but only those who went downtown could buy his new single. (pronouns)
6. Which restaurant do you want to go to? (pronouns)
7. Until nine o'clock she waited under the bridge, but then she gave up and walked away. (prepositions)
8. Celia and (I, me) are very close friends.
9. The audience did not know (who, whom) to applaud.
10. (Who, Whom) did you call this morning?
11. Both (he, him) and (her, she) were chosen for the play.
12. They invited both John and (I, me) to the party.
13. I (be, am) a marvelous cook.
14. That woman (don't, doesn't) want anyone to help her.
15. Sarah (give, gave) John a piece of candy yesterday.
16. John (lay, lied) on the bed until he felt better.
17. If I had done better (will, would) you be satisfied?
18. Neither I nor anyone else (want, wants) trouble.
19. The class assembled at (its, their) usual time.
20. Each student should bring (his, a) notebook to class.
21. My family (travel, travels) to India tonight.
22. The members of my family (has, have) much in common.
23. The news (is, are) always on at six o'clock.
24. She began to feel (good, well) after a few days.
25. Dave was the (more, most) handsome of the three.
26. He wrote a (real, really) hard exam.
27. Marianne is (more nice, nicer) than her brother, but her father is the (nicest, nicer) of all of them.

On a separate sheet of paper, list at least one of each of the following, taken from any of the sentences above: a complete subject, a complete predicate, a direct object, an indirect object, a possessive pronoun, a linking verb, a past tense verb, a future tense verb, and a compound subject. Check your answers against the material presented in the next five chapters; if you need help, ask your instructor.

Constructing Grammatical Sentences

Recognizing the Parts of Speech |6b|

The parts of speech are the basic building blocks of language. There are eight different parts of speech: nouns, adjectives, verbs, adverbs, pronouns, prepositions, conjunctions, and interjections. This chapter will begin by introducing each.

Recognizing Nouns

Nouns name things (or places or people or ideas or concepts). The following words are all nouns: *cup, wood, paper, St. Louis, lake, Einstein, Jordan, love, gravity, justice.* Proper nouns like *St. Louis* name specific people or specific places; their first letters are capitalized (for more on capitalization, see Chapter 33).

Plural Nouns Most nonproper nouns can be made plural by adding *-s (lake, lakes; paper, papers)* or *-es (church, churches; lunch, lunches).* However, mass nouns cannot be made plural because they name things that cannot be easily counted. Examples here include *dust, peace,* and *tranquillity.*

Possessive Nouns Nouns use a possessive form to show ownership; you can form the possessive by adding *'s* (for more on using apostrophes, see Chapter 30). Thus, if you wished to talk about a thought that was unique to Einstein, you would refer to it as *Einstein's,* because it belonged to him.

Articles Any discussion of nouns would be incomplete without mentioning articles (sometimes called noun markers): *a, an,* and *the.* Nouns always follow these words, as in *the bank, an apple, a dime.*

REVIEW

- Nouns name things, places, people, ideas, or concepts.
- Proper nouns name specific people or specific places.
- Possessive nouns indicate ownership by using *'s*.
- Articles are always followed by nouns.

EXERCISE 6.1 IDENTIFYING NOUNS

Underline all the nouns in these sentences.

EXAMPLE The soprano strode onto the stage.

1. For an hour, Leonard chopped wood.
2. Marcia wore dark glasses.
3. Angie and Hank drove for three hours on the freeway.
4. The quiche served at The Valley tastes delicious.
5. A dog grows extra hair to prepare for winter.
6. *Sports Illustrated* featured an article on Mike Tyson.
7. My mother's chocolate chip cookies always tasted great.

Recognizing Adjectives

Adjectives describe or limit nouns. In the following pairs of words, the underlined word is an adjective, while the second word is a noun:

red ball   crowded store
sleepy man   empty bucket
beautiful sunset styrofoam cup

As you can see, adjectives often precede the nouns they modify. (For more on using adjectives, see Chapter 10.)

EXERCISE 6.2 IDENTIFYING ADJECTIVES

On a separate sheet of paper, compose six adjective-noun pairs. Underline each adjective you use.

Recognizing Verbs

Verbs show action *(run, sleep, scratch)* or occurrence *(become, happen)* or a state of being *(be, live)*. The verb is underlined in each of these examples:

The cat <u>scratches</u> with its paw.

A tadpole slowly <u>becomes</u> a frog.

Mrs. Byron <u>is</u> Sadek's teacher.

Verbs are often combined with other words called auxiliary verbs to indicate time or obligation. The most common auxiliaries are forms of *be, can, do, have, may, must, shall,* and *will.* A verb combined with an auxiliary is called a verb phrase. In the following examples, the verb phrase is underlined.

Josh <u>will go</u> to the store for bread.

Yukiko <u>has finished</u> her letter.

Tonight I <u>must get</u> some sleep!

Chapter 8 provides a complete discussion of the forms and functions of verbs. Chapter 9 provides a discussion of subject-verb agreement.

EXERCISE 6.3 IDENTIFYING VERBS

Underline the verbs or phrases in the following sentences.

1. The clock on the wall reads 2:15.
2. The cleaners will be finished with your coat on Friday.
3. Alice, you must tell me before tomorrow.
4. That mug on his desk has not been washed in three weeks!
5. Grosbeaks make a distinctive sound.
6. I will always choose broccoli over asparagus.
7. Music lifts my spirits.

Recognizing Adverbs

Adverbs describe or limit verbs, adjectives, other adverbs, or (rarely) entire sentences. Adverbs frequently end in *-ly,* though some common adverbs, such as *always, soon, rather, very, not, never,* and *well,* do not. The adverbs are underlined in the following examples:

Virginia and Kim <u>recently</u> visited Santa Fe. [*adverb modifies verb*]

They had an <u>absolutely</u> marvelous time. [*adverb modifies adjective*]

Kim had <u>not really</u> expected to like New Mexico. [*adverb* not *modifies adverb* really, *which in turn modifies verb phrase* had expected]

<u>Clearly</u>, we should consider visiting Santa Fe. [*adverb modifies whole sentence*]

[*87*]

Unlike other parts of speech, adverbs can often be shifted to different positions within a sentence without significantly changing sentence meaning. Examine these variations:

Virginia and Kim *recently* visited Santa Fe.

Virginia and Kim visited Santa Fe *recently.*

Recently, Virginia and Kim visited Santa Fe.

(For more on using adverbs, see Chapter 10.)

EXERCISE 6.4 IDENTIFYING ADVERBS

Choosing from the following list, add adverbs to sentences 2–7 in Exercise 6.3. Write your new sentences out on a separate sheet of paper. The adverbs to choose from are *early, promptly, really, almost, thoroughly, willingly, usually, always,* and *gladly.* Feel free to use others if you prefer. Sentence 1 from Exercise 6.3 has been done for you as an example:

The clock on the wall *clearly* reads 2:15.

Recognizing Pronouns

Pronouns are used in place of nouns, making repetition unnecessary. In practice, we use pronouns frequently. Consider this sentence: *Marion lost the watch, but she found ten dollars.* In that sentence, the word *she* refers to *Marion.* Without a pronoun, the sentence would read this way: *Marion lost the watch, but Marion found ten dollars.* In most cases, pronouns refer to specific earlier nouns, called antecedents. The antecedent of *she* in the example is *Marion.*

Pronoun Types There are many types of pronouns. *She* is a **personal pronoun** because it refers to a person. Personal pronouns take different forms depending on how they are used in sentences. For now, you should simply be able to recognize the personal pronouns:

I, my, mine, our, ours, we, us

you, your, yours

she, her, hers, he, him, his, one, it, its, they, them, theirs

There are quite a few other kinds of pronouns. **Reflexive pronouns** refer to the subject:

> Jack likes *himself.*

> Sue prepared *herself* for the interview.

Myself, ourselves, yourself, yourselves, himself, herself, itself, and *themselves* are reflexive pronouns.

    Indefinite pronouns do not indicate gender:

> *Everyone* saw the winning play.

> *Nobody* likes going to the dentist.

All, another, any, anybody, anything, anyone, both, each, either, everybody, everyone, everything, few, very, most, much, neither, nobody, none, no one, one, someone, and *something* are indefinite pronouns.

    Demonstrative pronouns single out or point to some particular thing:

> *That* song is by Bon Jovi.

> *These* socks are disgusting!

This, that, these and *those* are demonstrative pronouns.

    Interrogative pronouns are used to ask questions:

> *What* pizza do you like best?

> In *which* direction is the wind blowing?

Who, which, what, when, why, how, and *whose* are interrogative pronouns.

    Relative pronouns introduce noun or adjective clauses (more about clauses later in this chapter):

> The day *that* it rained I caught a cold.

Who, whom, whose, which, that, and *what* are relative pronouns.

    Note that several pronouns *(who, whose, which, that, what)* appear in more than one list. How these pronouns are used determines their particular classification. (Further information and advice on correct pronoun use is provided in Chapters 7, 9, and 11.)

EXERCISE 6.5 IDENTIFYING PRONOUNS

Underline all the pronouns in the following sentences. The first sentence has been done for you.

1. That cup, which you found on the coffee table, is mine.
2. Our assignment is due Wednesday.
3. Jeb noticed that his lawn was full of dandelions.
4. Most of us enjoy a good movie occasionally.
5. Her superiors praised her work for the EPA.
6. Everyone who is fascinated by cities should see New York.
7. The eagle that we sighted yesterday has its nest on Sauvie Island.

Recognizing Prepositions

Prepositions are combined with nouns (and their adjectives) to form phrases. *Under the stairs, with the boxes,* and *of old clothes* are prepositional phrases. In each case, the preposition begins the phrase. Here is a list of commonly used prepositions:

about	as	beyond	inside	onto	to
above	at	by	into	out	toward
across	before	down	like	over	under
after	behind	during	near	past	until
against	below	except	of	regarding	up
along	beneath	for	off	since	with
among	beside	from	on	through	without
around	between	in			

Sometimes prepositions are combined into compound forms:

according to	except for	in place of	next to
because of	in addition to	in spite of	out of
due to	in front of	instead of	with regard to

A prepositional phrase always has at least one noun as the object of the preposition. In each of the following examples, the entire prepositional phrase is underlined:

According to yesterday's phone call, the orders never arrived. [*The compound preposition is* according to; call *is the noun object of the preposition;* yesterday's *and* phone *are adjectives modifying the noun.*]

Carry this painting through that door, down the hall, and into Gallery A. [*This example contains three prepositional phrases in a row.*]

For Janice and Jake, twenty dollars is a large sum of money.

➤ *Student Writing Error 7: Wrong or Missing Prepositions*

Prepositions are small words, and when working quickly, we may not pay much attention to them. This is probably why the seventh most common student writing error is a wrong or missing preposition.

MISSING PREPOSITION Mo went the store.

WRONG PREPOSITION I took that part out in the story.
I took that part out from the story.

Checking for incorrect preposition use is a simple matter of rereading your draft very slowly to be sure that each preposition you have used is the most appropriate ("I went *to* Texas" rather than "I went *at* Texas"; "I took that part *out of* the story" rather than "*out in* the story"). Checking for missing prepositions is perhaps best done by reading your draft aloud. Reading silently, our minds often fill in words that are not actually on the page, just because we are used to seeing them there. But reading "Mo went the store" aloud makes it obvious that something has been omitted.

EXERCISE 6.6 IDENTIFYING PREPOSITIONAL PHRASES

Underline the prepositional phrases in the following sentences. The first sentence has been done for you.

1. We finally purchased the light bulbs <u>for that lamp</u>.
2. I'll meet you in the hotel lobby after work.
3. After a meal of turkey, potatoes, and creamed onions, I had no room for dessert.
4. With the exception of my chemistry class, I'm having a good term.
5. With so many blouses in stock, we should probably have a sale.
6. The computer ribbons for your Panasonic printer arrived in the latest shipment.
7. Contestants for the poetry prize should mail their <u>entries before April 1</u>.

Recognizing Conjunctions

Conjunctions introduce or join words or groups of words. In so doing, conjunctions indicate logical relationships. For example, the conjunction *but* indicates a reversal or a contradiction, whereas *and* indicates an addition. There are four kinds of conjunctions; each kind will be explained briefly. (Conjunctions sometimes join clauses; do not worry about that now. It will be discussed later in this chapter.)

Coordinating conjunctions join grammatically equivalent words, phrases, or clauses. The most common coordinating conjunctions are *and, but, for, nor, or, so,* and *yet.*

In sixth grade, I ate tuna *and* pickles sandwiches for lunch. [*The conjunction* and *joins two adjectives—*tuna *and* pickles*—which both modify the noun* sandwiches.]

Work *and* play are two sides of the same coin. [*The conjunction* and *here joins two nouns.*]

Cindy enjoys softball, *but* basketball is her favorite sport. [*The conjunction* but *works with a comma to join two sentences.*]

Correlative conjunctions come in pairs and serve to join equivalent words or word groups. The most common correlative conjunctions are *both . . . and, either . . . or, neither . . . nor, not only . . . but also,* and *whether . . . or.*

Both Monica *and* Suki will graduate this term. [*The correlative conjunctions join two nouns.*]

Either I mow the lawn now, *or* I take a nap. [*The correlative conjunctions join two independent clauses.*]

Subordinating conjunctions introduce dependent clauses. The most common subordinating conjunctions are these:

after	even though	since	unless
although	if	so that	until
as	in order that	than	when
because	once	that	where

I understood the material *once* I reread it carefully. [*The subordinating conjunction* once *introduces a dependent clause.*]

Although I enjoy writing, I also find it hard work. [*The subordinating conjunction* although *introduces a dependent clause.*]

Some conjunctions—*before*, *since*, and *until*, for example—can also be used as prepositions. When they are followed by whole clauses, they are considered subordinating conjunctions. When they are followed only by nouns plus any adjectives, they are considered prepositions. Compare these examples:

After the lecture, I understand the material more clearly. [After *acts as a preposition here;* lecture *is the object of the preposition;* After the lecture *is the complete prepositional phrase.*]

After I heard the lecture, I understood the material more clearly. [After *acts as a subordinating conjunction; the complete dependent clause is* After I heard the lecture.]

Recognizing Interjections

Interjections express emotions or exclamations. They often stand alone, as fragments (rather than full sentences). Even when they are included in sentences, interjections are not grammatically related to the rest of the sentence. The most common interjections are *Oh! No! Hey!* and *Yeah!* Interjections are most frequently used in informal writing and dialogue:

"*Hey!* Wait for me!"

EXERCISE 6.7 IDENTIFYING CONJUNCTIONS AND INTERJECTIONS

Read the following sentences. Underline conjunctions once and interjections twice. The first sentence has been completed for you.

1. Hey! Even though I'm little, I still want to go with you.
2. Before you order dessert, make sure you have enough money to cover it.
3. After breakfast, either I'll rake the leaves or I'll go for a walk.
4. Ouch! That score wasn't what I'd anticipated.
5. Jake and Sandy, Elly and Hank, and Sally Jo and Michael all plan to travel together and attend the conference.
6. Dee is arranging her schedule so that she can chair next week's meeting.
7. Our parts shipment did not arrive yesterday, so I cannot fill your order.

Turn now to Assignment 6A at the end of this chapter for more practice with parts of speech.

Recognizing the Parts of a Sentence: Subjects and Predicates |6c|

As you have seen, every word in a sentence can be talked about as a part of speech. The words of a sentence can also be talked about according to how they function in that sentence. But before we go further, we need a definition of the word *sentence*.

What is a sentence? Answered most simply, a **sentence** is a grammatically complete group of words that expresses a thought. To be grammatically complete, a sentence must contain at least these two structural parts: a **subject**, which identifies what the sentence is about, and a **predicate**, which asserts or asks something about the subject. The simplest sentences are composed of a one-word subject and a one-word predicate—for example, *Marcellus sneezed.* Here the subject is *Marcellus* and the predicate is *sneezed.* By now you should recognize that *Marcellus* is a noun and *sneezed* is a verb. In this sentence, then, *Marcellus* is a *simple subject*—a noun acting as the sentence subject—and *sneezed* is a *simple predicate*—a verb acting as the sentence predicate.

Of course, most sentences contain more than two words. Consider a sentence like this one: *The drawing shows her latest design.* The nouns in that sentence are *drawing* and *design. Shows* is the verb. You should also be able to identify *The drawing* as the subject of the sentence and *shows her latest design* as the predicate.

subject	predicate

The drawing shows her latest design.

Note: We said that a sentence must contain at least two parts: a subject and a predicate. A subject and a predicate that combine to express a complete thought can also be called an independent clause.

EXERCISE 6.8 IDENTIFYING SUBJECTS AND PREDICATES

In each sentence, underline the subject once and the predicate twice.

EXAMPLE   Life is just a bowl of cherries.

1. His coffee tasted too strong.
2. The phonograph needle skips every time.
3. That telephone has rung constantly all morning.
4. April rains have refilled the reservoirs.
5. The fishing season opens soon.
6. The typewriter ribbon was fixed last night.
7. Her letter answers every question.

When a predicate contains more than a verb, as in *shows her latest design,* we call it a *complete predicate.* A *complete subject* also contains more than a simple, one-word subject. It might be *The drawing on the north wall by the door* instead of just *The drawing.*

A complete predicate may include a number of sentence elements that provide information that makes the thought, idea, or action of the sentence complete. As we mentioned before, the simple subject–simple predicate pattern of *Marcellus sneezed* presents a complete thought or action. But this is not always the case. *The train was* and *Abby caught* follow the same pattern as *Marcellus sneezed,* but clearly we need more information in these sentences if they are to tell us anything.

The four grammatical elements that can be added to the predicate to complete the meaning of a sentence are subject complements, direct objects, indirect objects, and object complements.

A **subject complement** is a noun, noun phrase, adjective, or adjective phrase that is used with a linking verb to describe the subject of the sentence (more about linking verbs in the next section). In the compound sentence *The train was an express, but it was late,* both the noun *express* and the adjective *late* act as subject complements.

A **direct object** receives the action of the verb. In *Abby caught the ball, ball* is the direct object; it is the thing that is *caught.*

An **indirect object** literally receives the action of the verb indirectly. It is used along with a direct object—never without one—when subject, verb, and direct object still do not tell the whole story. In the sentence *Rafael made Lisa breakfast, Lisa* is the indirect object of *made,* and *breakfast* is the direct object. Without *Lisa,* this sentence tells a very different story.

An **object complement** relates to the object in a sentence the way a subject complement relates to the subject: it describes the object, particularly with respect to the state of being that the verb establishes. Consider the sentence *Rafael's thoughtfulness made Lisa very happy. Very happy* is the object complement of *Lisa;* it describes the effect resulting from the action of the verb.

Common Sentence Patterns

The sentences you have just read follow patterns that are used over and over in English. Not all sentences you write must or even should follow these patterns. However, it may help you to refer to them during revision of your own writing, if you have trouble deciding whether a sentence is complete or whether you have arranged its elements in the correct order. The patterns are as follows:

subject + verb + subject complement

subject + verb + direct object

subject + verb + indirect object + direct object

subject + verb + direct object + object complement

Note that indirect objects and object complements are always used with direct objects, never by themselves. *Rafael's thoughtfulness made Lisa* and *Rafael made very happy* are not complete sentences.)

These patterns, and the patterns of most complete English sentences, boil down to subject + verb + [more information to complete and specify the action of the verb]. Thus, in our earlier example, *late* and *an express* both answer the question *the train was what?* and *the ball* answers the question *Abby caught what?* Also, the *type* of verb used in a sentence often determines, at least in part, which of the four predicate elements must follow it.

Verb Type and Sentence Structure

A verb can be classified as one of three types: linking, transitive, and intransitive. Linking verbs generally require subject complements, transitive verbs generally require direct objects, and intransitive verbs generally require neither (intransitive verbs are the ones used in the sentence pattern subject+verb; *sneezed* in *Marcellus sneezed* is an intransitive verb). Let us look at these three types of verbs and how they help to determine sentence structure.

Sentence Structures Using Linking Verbs Linking verbs act exactly as their name implies: they link a subject with a subject complement.

> The actress *was* Lana Turner.
>
> Coffee *is* a beverage.

In each case, the subject complement (*Lana Turner, beverage*) is a noun that renames the subject (*actress, coffee*). Nouns used in this way are called *predicate nouns.*

When the subject complement describes rather than renames the sentence subject, we call it a predicate adjective:

> The actress was *beautiful.*
>
> Coffee is *hot.*

These examples used *is* or *was*—forms of the verb *be*. Other verbs such as *feel, look, taste, seem, appear,* and *become* can also function as linking verbs. Note that these verbs can almost always be interchanged with a *be* verb without substantially affecting sentence meaning. For example, *The actress looked beautiful* can become *The actress was beautiful.*

Turn now to Assignment 6B at the end of this chapter for more practice with linking verbs and subject complements.

Sentence Structures Using Transitive and Intransitive Verbs Consider this sentence: *The door opened slowly.* You should be able to identify *The door* as the subject of the first sentence and *opened* as the verb. You should also be able to identify *slowly* as an adverb modifying the verb *opened*.

Now consider this sentence: *Reynaldo opened the door.* Here, *Reynaldo* is the subject and *opened* is the verb. But what is *door*? It is the direct object of the verb *opened*. In this second sentence, *opened* is a transitive verb; the action implied in the word *opened* is transferred to something, in this case, *the door.* Transitive verbs transfer their action to a noun other than the sentence subject. That other noun is called the direct object of the verb. All of the following sentences have transitive verbs, which are underlined once; the direct objects are underlined twice. Direct objects typically answer the question *what?* or *whom?*

Stevie <u>replaced</u> the typewriter <u><u>ribbon</u></u>. [*replaced what? the* ribbon]

The elms <u>dropped</u> their <u><u>leaves</u></u>. [*dropped what? their* leaves]

Don <u>finished</u> his <u><u>laundry</u></u>. [*finished what? his* laundry]

How does *opened* function in the sentence *The door opened slowly?* There, *opened* is an intransitive verb. It does not take an object. It cannot transfer its action to the noun *door* because that noun is already the sentence subject.

Now consider this sentence: *The lioness gave her cubs food.* You should be able to identify *lioness* as the noun subject and *gave* as the verb, in this case, a transitive verb. What did the lioness give? She gave *food,* which makes *food* the direct object. And who received the food? *Her cubs.* In this example, *cubs* is the indirect object of the verb *gave.* Note that if a sentence contains both a direct object and an indirect object, these elements follow a typical order: subject, verb, indirect object, direct object. Here is another example:

subject	verb	indirect object	direct object
John	sent	Kate	a birthday card.

Here, *a* and *birthday* are adjectives modifying the direct object, *card.*

Indirect objects in such sentences can easily be converted to prepositional phrases. For example, *Jack sent Kate a birthday card* becomes *Jack sent a birthday card to Kate.* In the second sentence, *Kate* is the object of the preposition *to.* The process can also be reversed.

Since pronouns frequently replace nouns, pronouns can also act as direct objects and indirect objects:

subject	verb	indirect object	direct object
You	should give	me	that.

Direct objects and indirect objects are never parts of a prepositional phrase:

subject	verb	prepositional phrase	prepositional phrase
They	sailed	to Africa	for a vacation.

EXERCISE 6.9   IDENTIFYING AND USING DIRECT AND INDIRECT OBJECTS

Read the following sentences. Underline each direct object once and each indirect object twice. If a sentence has no direct or no indirect object, leave the sentence as is. The first sentence has been done for you.

1. Jerry poured his <u>coffee</u> into a flamingo pink cup.
2. After dinner, we went to the store for oranges and a loaf of bread.
3. The candidate delivered an impassioned speech.
4. Digital technology gives listeners almost flawless sound.
5. The flicker landed in the tree and sang to us.
6. You should give Mrs. Zanefeld a copy of your poem.
7. Mr. Boggs called the principal over the intercom.

Using the following verbs, construct pairs of sentences, one using an indirect object and one converting that indirect object to the object of a preposition.

EXAMPLE   Verb: sent

     a. *indir. obj.* The president sent his secretary a memo.
     b. *obj. of prep.* The president sent a memo to his secretary.

8. Verb: gave

a. *indir. obj.* _____

_____

b. *obj. of prep.* _____

_____

9. Verb: threw

a. *indir. obj.* _____

_____

b. *obj. of prep.* _____

_____

10. Verb: handed

a. *indir. obj.* _____

_____

b. *obj. of prep.* _____

_____

Turn now to Assignment 6C at the end of this chapter for more practice with verbs.

Recognizing and Using Phrases

A phrase is simply a group of words that are associated in some grammatical way but do not contain both a subject and predicate. There are six types of phrases: noun phrases, verb phrases, prepositional phrases, infinitive phrases, gerund phrases, and participial phrases. We shall look at each in turn.

Noun phrases are composed of a noun and all its modifiers. *The blue sweater, an exciting day,* and *a moderately priced air conditioner* are noun phrases. (For more on noun modifiers, see the section on adjectives.)

Verb phrases are composed of a verb and its auxiliaries (for more on auxiliaries, see the earlier section on verbs). *Are composed, must arrive,* and *should have been explained* are all verb phrases.

Prepositional phrases are composed of a preposition plus one or more nouns and their adjectives. (For more on prepositions and prepositional phrases, see the earlier section on prepositions.) In these examples, the preposition comes first; the nouns plus any modifiers complete the phrase: *to Grady's store, for the next assignment, after supper.* Prepositional phrases act as either adjectives or adverbs, depending on what they modify. Consider this example: *In the morning, she will call.* Here, the prepositional phrase *In the morning* modifies the verb *will call* by specifying when this action will take place. Since it modifies a verb, this prepositional phrase acts as an adverb. Now, consider this example: *Your directions to the store were clear.* Here the prepositional phrase *to the store* modifies the noun *directions* by specifying which directions. Since it modifies a noun, this prepositional phrase acts as an adjective.

EXERCISE 6.10 USING PREPOSITIONAL PHRASES

Add a prepositional phrase to each of the following sentences. Circle the phrase you add, use an arrow to indicate the word your phrase modifies, and indicate whether the phrase functions as an adjective or an adverb.

EXAMPLE   Carrie slept.

(After dinner,) Carrie slept.   Phrase functions as an adverb.

1. Hamid felt ill. _____

    _____

2. Her speech convinced me. _____

    _____

3. The barn is a local landmark. _____

    _____

4. The plumbers will repair that leak. _____

    _____

5. LuAnne announced that she was leaving. _____

    _____

                    _____

   The three remaining types are all *verbal phrases.* They are made from
verbs but function as nouns, adjectives, or adverbs. The verbal phrases are
infinitives, gerunds, and participles.

   Infinitive phrases are made by adding *to* before the verb. Thus, *to run, to
sleep,* and *to enjoy the ball game* are all infinitive phrases. Here are examples:

> *To sleep late on Saturdays* is a habit at our house. [*This infinitive phrase in-
> cludes a prepositional phrase; the entire infinitive is a noun and acts as the
> subject of this sentence.*]

> *To draw plans* is a good way *to begin.* [*This example contains two infinitive
> phrases. The first is a noun and acts as the subject of the sentence. The second
> modifies the noun* way *and so acts as an adjective.*]

> She coughed a little *to clear her throat.* [*Here, the infinitive phrase modifies
> the verb* coughed *and so acts as an adverb.*]

   Be careful to distinguish infinitives from prepositional phrases. The
word *to* is used to introduce them both. In a prepositional phrase, *to* is
followed by a noun; in an infinitive, *to* is followed by a verb.

Though busy, Harry found time *to run*. [*infinitive as adjective modifying time*]

LuAnne ran *to the store*. [*prepositional phrase*]

Gerunds are formed by adding *-ing* to a verb for use as a noun. (When an *-ing* form of a verb acts as an adjective, it is called a participial phrase; more on participles in a moment.) **Gerund phrases** are composed of gerunds and all modifying words. Since they always act as nouns, gerunds and gerund phrases may occur in any sentence position that nouns would occupy. Here are examples:

Running every other day is good exercise. [*The gerund phrase acts as the subject of the sentence.*]

Alicia enjoys *running every other day*. [*Now the gerund phrase is functioning as the direct object of the verb* enjoys. *Enjoys what? Enjoys* running every other day.]

Participial phrases may be either in the present tense or in the past. Present participles are formed by adding *-ing*; past participles are usually formed by adding *-ed* or *-en*. Some past participles (*gone*, for example) have irregular forms. All participles function as adjectives. Note that the present participial form and the gerund form are identical: both are made by adding *-ing* to the verb. What differentiates gerunds and participles is their function. Gerunds always act as nouns; participles always act as adjectives. Here are examples of both present and past participles:

Tired by a long hike, the dog slept before the fire. [*The participial phrase acts as an adjective modifying* dog.]

The stereo *blaring next door* made sleep difficult. [*The participial phrase acts as an adjective modifying* stereo.]

Note that participial phrases may either precede or follow the nouns they modify.

EXERCISE 6.11 USING INFINITIVES, GERUNDS, AND PARTICIPLES

Add the specified phrase to the given sentence.

EXAMPLE

I discovered the book _____. (Add the past participle of *hide* to modify *book*.)

I discovered the book hidden under the couch.

1. Joan enjoyed _____. (Add the gerund form of *run* to complete the sentence.)

2. _____, I arrived just as class began. (Add a present participial phrase modifying the subject *I*.)

3. Alan tried _____. (Add an infinitive phrase to complete the sentence.)

4. _____, you should count calories and exercise regularly. (Add an infinitive phrase.)

5. _____, it is a good idea _____. (Add two infinitive phrases.)

6. Our family has always enjoyed _____. (Add a gerund phrase.)

7. _____, the house needed a lot of work. (Add a past participial phrase.)

————————————————————

Two other types of phrases remain to be discussed: absolute phrases and appositive phrases.

An **absolute phrase** is formed by combining a noun or pronoun and a participial phrase. Absolutes modify an entire sentence and are always set off from the rest of the sentence by commas. Here are two examples:

The big cat waited, *its nostrils flaring slightly.*

Feet aching, I finally crossed the finish line.

Absolute phrases can often be moved in the sentence without destroying the meaning: *Its nostrils flaring slightly,* the big cat waited.

An **appositive phrase** is a noun phrase that renames the noun that immediately precedes it. An appositive phrase is always set off by commas. Here are two examples:

Victor Atiyeh, *a former governor,* lives in Portland. [*This appositive phrase is composed of a noun,* governor, *and its modifying adjective,* former.]

The police officer fed Scarlet, *the stationhouse mascot.*

Turn now to Assignment 6D at the end of this chapter for more practice with phrases.

Recognizing and Using Clauses

There are two types of clauses: **independent clauses**, which can stand alone as sentences, and **dependent clauses**, which cannot stand alone. Clauses always have subjects and predicates. For example, *The weather* *forecast calls for snow* and *I'll start the fire* are both independent clauses; they are also sentences.

Dependent clauses are always coupled with independent clauses in order to make a complete sentence. By themselves, dependent clauses are sentence fragments that do not express a complete thought. Some dependent clauses are introduced by subordinating conjunctions:

> *After the snow stops*, Alice and I will shovel the driveway. [*dependent clause introduced by the subordinating conjunction* after]

> *Whenever we go outside*, the neighbor's dog barks at us. [*dependent clause introduced by the subordinating conjunction* whenever]

(For more on subordinating conjunctions, see the section on conjunctions in this chapter.)

In other cases, dependent clauses are introduced by relative pronouns such as *who, which,* and *that* (for more on relative pronouns, see the section on pronouns in this chapter).

> The dog *that I chose at the pound* has become a member of the family. [*dependent clause introduced by* that *and acting as adjective modifying subject* dog]

In addition to functioning as adjectives, dependent clauses may also act as nouns or as adverbs. Here are some examples:

> We have agreed *that we should arrive early.* [*dependent clause introduced by* that *and acting as a noun, in this case, the direct object of the verb* agreed]

> Typists *who memorize the keyboard* will not have to look at their fingers. [*dependent clause introduced by* who *and acting as an adjective modifying the noun* typists]

> *When I am confident*, tests do not bother me. [*dependent clause introduced by the subordinating conjunction* when *and modifying the main verb* do not bother]

> *When I am confident that I will pass*, tests do not bother me. [*Here are two dependent clauses, one embedded inside another.* When I am confident that I will pass *is an adverbial clause modifying the main verb* do not bother. *Within that adverbial clause is another adverbial clause*, that I will pass, *which modifies the predicate adjective* confident.]

REVIEW

- Dependent clauses are always introduced by a subordinating word.
- Dependent clauses always contain a subject and predicate.
- Dependent clauses must be combined with an independent clause in order to form a full sentence.

EXERCISE 6.12 IDENTIFYING DEPENDENT CLAUSES

Read the following passage and underline the dependent clauses. The first dependent clause has been underlined for you.

Dick and I remember that afternoon well. The sun glinted off the ocean <u>as we pulled into the state park.</u> Dick said that the surf looked a little high. Even so, we weren't worried. After we were seated in the kayak and headed into the waves, we began getting worried. Each wave washing over us put us lower in the water. Before we had time to think, we found ourselves underwater. It was quiet and pale blue under there. When we struggled to shore half an hour later, a man who had been watching strolled over to us. I'll never forget what he said. "Well, you made it, though for a while there I wasn't sure that you would."

Classifying Sentences according to Function and Form   l6dl

Sentences can be classified according to both form and function. There are four basic sentence functions: *declarative sentences* state facts or opinions, *interrogative sentences* ask questions, *imperative sentences* give commands, and *exclamatory sentences* express strong feeling.

Most of the sentences in this book are declarative sentences. [*declarative sentence*]

Why is English such a curious language? [*interrogative sentence*]

You must think of language as a set of tools. [*imperative sentence*]

At last I am beginning to understand this language! [*exclamatory sentence*]

Sentence forms are determined by the type and number of clauses in them. (For more on clauses, see the preceding section in this chapter.) A sentence made of a single independent clause *(Jack sneezed)* is called a **simple sentence**.

A **compound sentence** is composed of two or more simple sentences, that is, two or more independent clauses: *Jack sneezed, and the dog jumped.* The independent clauses that make up a compound sentence are joined by commas and coordinating conjunctions (see also Chapter 27) or by a semicolon (see also Chapter 28).

A **complex sentence** is composed of one independent clause and at least one dependent clause. When the dependent clause opens the sentence (as it does this one), a comma is used to separate it from the independent clause. No comma is necessary when the dependent clause follows the independent one (as in this sentence).

A **compound-complex sentence** contains at least two independent clauses with at least one dependent clause attached to one of them.

REVIEW EXAMPLES

The independent clauses have been underlined.

- Simple sentence (one independent clause):

  A flicker sometimes sings in our yard.

- Compound sentence (two or more independent clauses):

  A flicker sometimes sings in our yard, and the neighbor's cat watches it.

- Complex sentence (one independent clause + at least one dependent clause):

  Some afternoons a flicker sings in our yard while the neighbor's cat watches.

- Compound-complex sentence (more than one independent clause + at least one dependent clause):

  When the sun comes out, I open the windows, and fresh air fills the rooms.

Questions To understand the form of a question more easily, revise the question into a statement. Once you have done so, the clauses will be easier to identify.

EXAMPLE   Will Ann pick me up after her racquetball lesson is over?

REVISED AS A STATEMENT   Ann will pick me up after her racquetball lesson is over.

INDEPENDENT CLAUSE   Ann will pick me up

DEPENDENT CLAUSE   after her racquetball lesson is over

The original question is therefore a complex sentence.

EXERCISE 6.13   UNDERSTANDING FUNCTION AND FORM

Underline each independent clause in the sentences that follow. Then identify each sentence according to function and form.

EXAMPLE

Will you take me to the store when I get home from school?
Function: interrogative
Form: complex

1. Either you take me to the store, or I'll run away!

Function: _____

Form: _____

2. Although we received considerable precipitation during April, the drought is not over.

Function: _____

Form: _____

3. Is it true that Lake Park Roller Rink has been closed?

Function: _____

Form: _____

4. While we were sleeping, Alec went to the store for us, and he has even fixed us dinner!

Function: _____

Form: _____

5. I can still taste the delicious Cajun chicken that you prepared for us last night.

Function: _____

Form: _____

Turn now to Assignment 6E at the end of this chapter for more practice with clauses.

ASSIGNMENT 6A IDENTIFYING THE PARTS OF SPEECH

Identify the part of speech of each underlined word as it functions in the sentence.

EXAMPLE

> The car door slammed into the utility pole.
> car: adjective   door: noun   into: preposition

1. The car sped down Main Street and barely missed two pedestrians.

_____

_____

2. You should have read two chapters before tomorrow's class.

_____

_____

3. As the Mississippi winds south toward the delta, it grows and widens and becomes something awesome, magical, even terrifying.

_____

_____

4. Yes, Rochester, New York, did receive over ten inches of snow on April 27.

_____

_____

5. That particular essay question gave everyone trouble.

_____

_____

ASSIGNMENT 6B USING LINKING VERBS AND SUBJECT COMPLEMENTS

With the subjects provided, construct sentences using linking verbs followed by predicate adjectives.

EXAMPLE

> cup
> The cup was broken.

1. lights _____

_____

2. sweater _____

_____

3. ocean _____

_____

4. perfume _____

_____

5. painting _____

_____

Using the subjects provided, construct sentences using linking verbs followed by predicate nouns. The predicate nouns may be modified by adjectives.

EXAMPLE

sand wedge
A sand wedge is a golf club.

6. this car _____

_____

7. that track star _____

_____

8. a piano _____

_____

9. those buildings _____

_____

10. two celebrities _____

_____

ASSIGNMENT 6C UNDERSTANDING LINKING, TRANSITIVE, AND INTRANSITIVE VERBS

The following sentences give a subject and a verb. Complete each sentence by adding an indirect object and a direct object. Underline the direct object once and the indirect object twice.

EXAMPLE

> The school sent Mary her grades.

1. Beth handed _____.

2. The dog brought _____.

3. Charlie passed _____.

4. Sally threw _____.

5. Music gave _____.

Identify the underlined verb in each sentence as either transitive, intransitive, or linking.

EXAMPLE

> The race started with a pistol shot. intransitive
> This fettucine tastes divine. linking
> You should wear a coat today. transitive

6. These fossilized clams are twenty-five million years old. _____

7. Mingo Construction erected that chain-link fence. _____

8. My supervisor has requested a copy of your report. _____

9. Out on the lake, the loon called for a long time. _____

10. The Taylors' cat seems sick today. _____

Combine or add to the following sentences as specified.

> EXAMPLE   Harold phoned Monica. (Add infinitive phrase)
> Harold phoned Monica to ask her for a date.

1. Monica called Harold. (Add only a prepositional phrase.)

2. Harold called to cancel their date. (Add a present participial phrase.)

3. Havre, Malta, and Glasgow were named by the railroad. All these towns can be found in Montana. (Combine using a past participial phrase.)

4. William Carlos Williams established himself as an important 20th-century American writer. He was also a medical doctor. (Combine using an appositive phrase.)

5. Lisa likes to swim every other morning. It keeps her fit. (Combine using a gerund phrase as the subject.)

6. You should watch your diet and exercise regularly. (Add an infinitive phrase.)

7. Test the water. (Add a prepositional phrase with a gerund functioning as the object of the preposition.)

8. The warehouse burned fiercely. (Add a present participial phrase.)

9. Robert Cray is a blues singer. He is gaining a national reputation. He will appear in concert next week. (Combine using an appositive phrase that contains a present participial phrase.)

_____

_____

10. My ears were ringing and my hands were aching. I left the concert and headed for my car. (Combine using an absolute phrase.)

_____

_____

ASSIGNMENT 6E **USING CLAUSES**

Determine whether each clause is independent or dependent. Then add a clause of your own.

EXAMPLES

when lightning hit the roof   (Make into a complex sentence.)
(dependent clause)   Every bulb in the place blew out when lightning hit the roof.

the alarm sounded   (Make into a compound sentence.)
(independent clause)   The burglar shattered the window, and the alarm sounded.

1. before you decide   (Make into a complex sentence.)

_____

2. Bruce caught the ball on the run   (Make into a compound sentence.)

_____

3. the candy had disappeared   (Make into a complex sentence.)

_____

4. the class that you suggested   (Make into a complex sentence.)

_____

5. when Horowitz appeared   (Make into a compound-complex sentence.)

_____

6. a gentle wind stirred the yard   (Make into a compound sentence.)

_____

7. the abandoned car was covered with rust (Make into a complex sentence.)

_____

8. after we'd finished dinner (Make into a compound-complex sentence.)

_____

9. the paper was nowhere to be found (Make into a compound sentence using any coordinating conjunction except _and._)

_____

10. she closed the file drawer (Make into a complex sentence.)

_____

Select six of the ten sentences you have just written (all declarative sentences). Convert two of them to interrogative sentences, two to imperative sentences, and two to exclamatory sentences. You may shorten your original sentences to single dependent clauses.

EXAMPLE

> The burglar shattered the window, and the alarm sounded. (declarative sentence)
> Tell me what time the burglar shattered the window. (imperative sentence)

11. interrogative sentence:

_____

12. interrogative sentence:

_____

13. imperative sentence:

_____

14. imperative sentence:

_____

15. exclamatory sentence:

_____

16. exclamatory sentence:

_____

7

Understanding Pronoun Case

Native English speakers generally know that some sentences require *I* instead of *me* or *they* instead of *them*. When we distinguish between these pronoun forms, we are distinguishing between *cases*. Intuition, unfortunately, does not always help us choose the correct pronoun to use. For example, many writers have trouble recalling the distinctions between *who* and *whom*. Fortunately, if you know enough grammar to identify subjects, predicate nouns, and objects, you can use that knowledge to determine correct pronoun usage. (For an introduction to pronouns and to basic sentence grammar, see Chapter 6.)

In general, pronouns may take different forms to indicate singular and plural and also when functioning as subjects, objects, or possessives. We shall discuss each of these cases. The one pronoun not much discussed in this chapter is the pronoun *you*. This pronoun is easy to use because it stays the same whether it is singular or plural, in both subjective and objective cases.

Using the Subjective Case |7*a*|

When pronouns function as subjects, they take the subjective case. Here are the forms for personal pronouns used in the subjective case:

Subjective Case Personal Pronouns

Singular	*Plural*
I	we
he, she, it	they

Subjective case pronouns can appear in a variety of grammatical constructions; examples follow.

Pronouns as Subjects of Sentences and Clauses

Excited and eager, *we* drove to the hospital. [*In this simple sentence with one independent clause,* we *acts as the subject of the verb* drove.]

Although *they* were tired, the chorus sang well. [*In this complex sentence with one dependent and one independent clause,* they *acts as the subject of the verb* were.]

Pronouns as Subjects of Subordinate Clauses

The store closed before *she* arrived. [*subject of noun clause*]

When *he* arrived, the store had already closed. [*subject of adverb clause*]

Irwin returned the book *he* had borrowed. [*subject of adjective clause*]

Using Personal Pronouns as Predicate Nouns

- Predicate nouns follow linking verbs and rename the subject. Because they rename the subject, they take the subjective case.

The only students who didn't get the flu were Barbara and I. [Barbara *and* I *are predicate nouns renaming the subject,* students.]

EXERCISE 7.1 USING SUBJECTIVE CASE PRONOUNS

Read each of the following sentences, replacing the underlined noun or nouns with the appropriate subjective case pronoun. Then copy each sentence, including the pronoun you have selected, on a separate sheet of paper. As you write each sentence, ask yourself whether the pronoun sounds right to you. If it does not sound right, reread the preceding section of the text and consider whether you have chosen the correct pronoun.

EXAMPLE Jack and *George* visited the zoo.

REWRITE Jack and I visited the zoo.

1. Whenever Jeri, David, and Sean visited the beach, the weather was bad.
2. As the cattle crossed the road, the cattle stopped all traffic.
3. Chris was a better tennis player than Al.
4. The rhododendrons are most beautiful in May when the rhododendrons bloom.
5. Jody, Susan, Scott, and I were the only people still in the building.
6. Tom wondered if Tom was smarter than James.
7. Allison was curious to see whether or not Allison would be asked to work late.
8. Symphonies are popular, but not all cities have symphonies.

9. The cars slowed to a stop whenever <u>the cars</u> approached an on ramp.
10. Dick, Brad, and I have a great time whenever <u>Dick, Brad, and I</u> get together.

Using the Objective Case I7b I

      When pronouns function as objects of a verb, a verbal (an infinitive, gerund, or participial word or phrase), or a preposition, they take the objective case. The objective case forms for personal pronouns are as follows:

Objective Case Personal Pronouns

Singular	*Plural*
me	us
him, her, it	them

      Following are examples of pronouns used as objects.

Pronouns as Direct Objects of Verbs

      Al caught the ball and threw *it* to Robert. [It *acts as the object of the verb* threw.]

      Gordon asked Debbie and *me* to go to the party. [Me *acts as one of the objects of the verb* asked.]

Pronouns as Indirect Objects of Verbs

      Thursday's unexpected blizzard gave *us* an unscheduled holiday. [Us *acts as the indirect object: the blizzard gave what?* holiday *(direct object); gave holiday to whom?* us *(indirect object)*]

Pronouns as Objects of Verbals

      It has taken me years to know *him* well. [Him *acts as the direct object of the infinitive* to know.]

      Wishing *us* luck, Professor Decker said we could begin the final exam. [Us *acts as the indirect object of the participle* wishing.]

      In helping *us* this way, Professor Ede showed real concern for students. [Us *acts as the direct object of the gerund* helping.]

Pronouns as Objects of Prepositions

      Bjorn handed the graphite racquet to *her.* [Her *acts as the object of the preposition* to.]

      With *him and Jack,* no two hunting trips were ever the same. [Him *acts as one of two objects of the preposition* with.]

Turn now to Assignment 7A at the end of this chapter for more practice with objective case pronouns.

Using the Possessive, Intensive, and Reflexive Cases |7c|

Possessive case pronouns are used to indicate ownership or possession. Such pronouns take one form when they are used alone to replace nouns and a separate form when they are used as adjectives to modify nouns. These pronouns are as follows:

Possessive Case Personal Pronouns

Singular		Plural	
Noun Form	*Adjective Form*	*Noun Form*	*Adjective Form*
mine	my	ours	our
yours	your	yours	your
his, her, its	his, her, it	theirs	their

(Note: The possessive pronoun *its* is often confused with the contraction *it's*. If you share this confusion, try reminding yourself that *it's* is a shortened form of *it is*.)

Possessive Forms as Adjectives

The adjectival forms are used only before a noun or a gerund, as in these examples:

> *Her* running keeps her fit. [Her *precedes the gerund* running.]

> *Your* shoes are worn, especially at the heels. [Your *precedes the noun* shoes.]

> *Their* sleeping late caused them to miss the train. [Their *precedes the gerund* sleeping.]

Be careful to distinguish between gerunds and participles. Gerunds always act as nouns, so when pronouns precede gerunds, they always take the possessive case. But the same word may function as a gerund in one sentence and as a participle in another. Consider this example: *I remember his singing well.* Here, *singing* is a gerund; it functions as a noun and is the direct object of the verb *remember.* Thus, the possessive pronoun *his* is accurate. The singing is *his.* The original sentence could be rearranged in this way without changing its meaning: *I well remember his singing.* After all, *well* is an adverb, and adverbs cannot modify nouns.

Now consider this example: *I remember him singing well.* Only one word has changed, but the pronoun *him* creates a sentence with a very different meaning. Now the adverb *well* must modify the participle *singing.* Here we know the quality of his song: he sang well.

EXERCISE 7.2 USING PRONOUNS TO DISTINGUISH BETWEEN GERUNDS AND PARTICIPLES

Identify the underlined word as either a gerund or a participle. Be able to explain the different meanings and constructions for each pair of sentences.

1. a. We saw their <u>signaling</u> clearly.
   b. We saw them <u>signaling</u> clearly.
2. a. We heard them <u>singing</u> without regard for our comfort.
   b. We heard their <u>singing</u> without regard for our comfort.
3. a. We watched his tightrope <u>walking</u> cautiously.
   b. We watched him tightrope <u>walking</u> cautiously.

Possessive Nouns

Functioning like the nouns they replace, possessive pronouns may also be used by themselves, often appearing in sentences using some form of the verb *be.* Here are two examples:

> *Theirs* was the toughest schedule in the league. [*possessive noun as subject*]

> The one coat left must be *hers.* [*possessive noun as predicate noun*]

Intensive and Reflexive Forms

Intensive and reflexive pronouns are formed by the addition of the suffix *-self* (for singular forms) or *-selves* (for plural forms). An intensive pronoun is one that immediately follows its noun, emphasizing it (*The instructor* himself *couldn't be sure of the answer*). A reflexive pronoun acts separately from its antecedent, as if they were two different things (*The instructor asked* himself *how this could be true*). The singular intensive and reflexive pronouns are *myself, yourself, herself, himself,* and *itself.* The plural ones are *ourselves, yourselves,* and *themselves.*

Caution: Do not substitute *myself* for *me* or *I.* The sentence *Myself called the police* is not grammatically correct; the correct version would be *I called the police.* To say *My husband and myself called the police* is also incorrect; the correct version would be *My husband and I called the police.*

Turn now to Assignment 7B at the end of this chapter for more practice with pronouns.

Using *Who, Whom, Whoever,* and *Whomever*   17d1

Using Who *and* Whom *to Begin Questions*

Although everyday speech often does not preserve the distinction between *who* and *whom,* much formal and academic writing still does. Thus, *who* and *whom* often give writers trouble. The rule is simple enough: use *who* as a subject, and use *whom* as an object. However, that rule is sometimes difficult to apply when the sentence is a question. Should you write *Whom did the consultant interview?* or *Who did the consultant interview?*

You can determine which pronoun to use by constructing a possible answer for the question and using a personal pronoun in that answer. The case of that personal pronoun will tell you the case of the interrogative pronoun. Though this sounds confusing, it is really not very difficult. The following examples should help:

> Who/Whom is a good teacher? [*Answer:* He *is a good teacher.* He *is the subject; therefore, the pronoun must be the subjective form:* who.]

> Who/Whom did the consultant interview? [*Answer: The consultant interviewed* her. Her *is the object; therefore, the pronoun must be the objective form:* whom.]

> Who/Whom should I send this report to? [*Answer: I should send this report to* her. Her *is the object of the preposition* to. *Therefore, the pronoun must be the objective form:* whom. *In a formal writing situation, this sentence would probably be reordered to read* To whom should I send this report?]

EXERCISE 7.3   USING *WHO* AND *WHOM* TO BEGIN QUESTIONS

Underline the correct pronoun in each of the following sentences.

1. Who/Whom did you consult before purchasing the car?
2. Who/Whom took that wonderful photograph?
3. Who/Whom should receive first prize?
4. Who/Whom was the Baby Ruth candy bar named after?
5. Who/Whom was the first to run a mile in less than four minutes?

Using Who, Whom, Whoever, *and* Whomever *to Begin Dependent Clauses*

The pronouns *who, whom, whoever,* and *whomever* are called relative pronouns; often they begin independent clauses. How the pronoun functions *inside that clause* determines which form should be chosen. If the pronoun is the subject of the dependent clause, use the subjective form *who* or *whoever:*

I'll award a prize to <u>whoever</u> can recall the name of the first Russian cosmonaut.

How can you tell that *whoever* is the subject in that subordinate clause? One simple way is to write out only the subordinate clause. Doing that, you get *whoever can recall the name of the first Russian cosmonaut*. The verb in this clause is *can recall*; the subject of that verb must be the subjective case pronoun *whoever*.

A second test is again to isolate only the subordinate clause and then substitute a personal pronoun in place of the relative pronoun:

She identified the clerk _____ had given her the wrong change.

The relative pronoun is the subject of the verb *had given*. By itself, the subordinate clause reads _____ *had given her the wrong change*. Substituting the objective pronoun *him* makes the clause read *him had given her the wrong change*. Clearly, the objective case *him* is incorrect in this clause. The correct choice here is the subjective form: *who*.

The objective forms of these relative pronouns are *whom* and *whomever*. The same methods and criteria apply for identifying the correct use of these pronouns; the function of the pronoun within the dependent clause determines the choice. If the relative pronoun functions as an object, the correct choice is either *whom* or *whomever*.

At the party, Alice talked to _____ she found interesting.

By itself, the subordinate clause reads _____ *she found interesting*. This is a somewhat awkward word order; a more normal word order would yield *she found* _____ *interesting*. The accurate personal pronoun here would be *them*, which is the objective form. Thus, the correct relative pronoun here is the objective *whomever*.

EXERCISE 7.4 USING *WHO, WHOM, WHOEVER,* AND *WHOMEVER* TO BEGIN DEPENDENT CLAUSES

Work through the following four sentences to determine whether to use a subjective or an objective relative pronoun. For examples, see the discussion preceding this exercise.

1. Jack said he would be glad to speak to _____ showed up to listen.

The subordinate clause by itself is _____

_____ .

Inserting a personal pronoun (he/she/him/her/they/them) yields

_____ .

Does this personal pronoun act as the subject or as an object? _____

Thus, the correct relative pronoun in this sentence is _____ .

2. She shared the secret with those _____ she trusted.

The subordinate clause by itself is _____

_____ .

Inserting a personal pronoun (he/she/him/her/they/them) yields

_____ .

Does this personal pronoun act as the subject or as an object? _____

Thus, the correct relative pronoun in this sentence is _____ .

3. _____ he instructed to write this brief certainly did not do a thorough job.

The subordinate clause by itself is _____

_____ .

Inserting a personal pronoun (he/she/him/her/they/them) yields

_____ .

Does this personal pronoun act as the subject or as an object? _____

Thus, the correct relative pronoun in this sentence is _____ .

4. Today's weather forecast should please anyone _____ enjoys skiing on fresh powder.

The subordinate clause by itself is _____

_____ .

Inserting a personal pronoun (he/she/him/her/they/them) yields

_____ .

Does this personal pronoun act as the subject or as an object? _____

Thus, the correct relative pronoun in this sentence is _____ .

Turn now to Assignment 7C at the end of this chapter for more practice with *who, whom, whoever,* and *whomever.*

Using the Correct Case with Compound Objects or Subjects |7e|

You will often encounter personal pronouns used as compound subjects or compound objects. If you simply drop the other half of the compound, you should have no trouble determining the correct pronoun case. For example, take the sentence *Margaret and her went to the movie.* Keep the pronoun, drop the other half of the compound subject, and you have this sentence: *Her went to the movie.* That sounds wrong, and it is wrong. You now know that the correct case is the subjective: *Margaret and she went to the movie.*

Using the Correct Case with Elliptical Constructions |7f|

Elliptical constructions are sentence patterns in which one or several words are omitted because the writer assumes that readers will understand without them. Such constructions are used often; if we never left any words out, our writing would be very repetitive indeed. But leaving out words can make it easier to make mistakes, especially with pronoun usage. Consider this sentence: *Bruce is younger than me.* Is the pronoun *me* used correctly? To find out, you must determine which words have been left out of the sentence and put them back in: *Bruce is younger than me am.* Clearly, that sounds incorrect. *Me* is an objective case pronoun; we never hear it used as the subject for a verb, so it sounds unnatural to us. The correct pronoun to use in this sentence is the subjective case one, *I: Bruce is younger than I (am),* because this pronoun is the subject of the dependent clause *than I am.*

Using the correct pronoun case in elliptical constructions is often crucial to your readers' understanding of your sentence meaning. Consider these two sentences:

I like Fred better than he. [*If fully written out, this sentence would read* I like Fred better than he likes Fred.]

I like Fred better than him. [*If fully written out, this sentence would read* I like Fred better than I like him.]

As you can see, changing the pronoun from *he* to *him* alters the meaning considerably.

[*121*]

Using the Correct Case with Appositives   I7gI

Sometimes an appositive (a noun that renames) will follow a pronoun. In such sentences, dropping the appositive should make the case of the pronoun clear.

> Those of we/us baseball players who attended the reunion were glad we did. [*The appositive phrase here is* baseball players. *Dropping it produces this sentence:* Those of we/us who attended the reunion were glad we did. *Here the pronoun is the object of the preposition* of; *hence, the correct pronoun with this appositive is the objective form* us.]

> After lunch, we/us sun worshipers sunbathe on the south lawn. [*The appositive phrase is* sun worshipers. *Dropping the appositive produces this sentence:* After lunch, we/us sunbathe on the south lawn. *The pronoun here acts as the subject of the verb* sunbathe; *hence, the subjective pronoun* we *is the proper choice.*]

In other sentences, you may find a pronoun as part of an appositive. When this happens, the pronoun takes the case of the noun it renames. Here are two examples:

> Two great fishermen, my father and me/I, were skunked again today. [*The appositive phrase is* my father and me/I. *This phrase renames the noun* fishermen. *Since* fishermen *is the subject of this sentence, the pronoun in the appositive must also be the subjective form.* I *is the proper choice.*]

> That one coastal cedar defeated two great tree climbers, Beth and I/me. [*The appositive phrase is* Beth and I/me. *This phrase renames the noun* climbers. *Since* climbers *is the direct object of the verb* defeated, *the pronoun in the appositive must also be the objective form.* Me *is the proper choice.*]

Turn now to Assignment 7D at the end of this chapter for more practice with pronoun case in appositives.

ASSIGNMENT 7A USING OBJECTIVE CASE PRONOUNS

Several of the following ten sentences use objective case pronouns incorrectly. Identify the incorrect sentences, and rewrite them in correct form. If the sentence is already correct, place a *C* on the line below the sentence.

EXAMPLE Whenever we order a drink, the bartender asks we for a drink.

REWRITE Whenever we order a drink, the bartender asks us for a drink.

1. With a long week behind we, a brisk Saturday walk gives Tom and I some much needed exercise.

_____

_____

2. When Pam finished dinner, Julie reminded she to study physics.

_____

3. Charlie asked her to give he a call later.

_____

4. Eventually the headwaiter told Kim, Sidney, and I that we could be seated.

_____

5. After three days of steady rain, gale force winds toppled several trees and left they looking like huge, spilled matchsticks.

_____

_____

6. For Bill, Ubijo, and I, running 15 miles a day was our training for the marathon.

_____

7. Before we could say anything more, Amy loaned Oscar and I thirty dollars.

_____

8. Though even the idea of hang gliding made her nervous, she gave it a try.

_____

9. Harry called she before him left the house.

_____

Substitute pronouns for the nouns shown in parentheses after each blank. See the example below.

They (Jerry and David) drove their (Jerry and David's) own car to the convention so that they (Jerry and David) would not have to rent one.

1. _____ (Ron's) sleeping late made _____ (Diane and me) late for our first class.

2. _____ (The ducks') arriving so early will mean some of _____ (the ducks) may starve.

3. While Linda carries the baby, would you mind carrying _____ (Linda's) suitcase?

4. _____ (Arnie) asked _____ (Arnie) if _____ (Arnie) had made the right decision.

5. Whether _____ (Carrie) goes or whether _____ (Carrie) stays, _____ (Jackson's) love for _____ (Carrie) doesn't change, nor does _____ (Carrie's) love for _____ (Jackson).

Now rewrite each of the following sentences on the lines provided, adding the pronouns specified in parentheses.

I prefer a table by the door, but Carlos insisted that we take one in the back. (Add an intensive pronoun modifying *I*.)
I *myself* prefer a table by the door, but Carlos insisted that we take one in the back.

6. The crowd was standing, and their screams made it impossible for the players to hear. (Add an intensive pronoun modifying *players*.) _____

_____

7. Jake asked how his own garden could have become so productive. (Add a reflexive pronoun modifying *Jake*.) _____

_____

8. The cat washed and licked until its fur gleamed. (Add a reflexive pronoun modifying *the cat*.) _____

_____

9. The students prepare everything served in their cafeteria. (Add an intensive pronoun modifying *the students*.) _____

_____

ASSIGNMENT 7C **USING *WHO, WHOM, WHOEVER*, AND *WHOMEVER***

Underline the correct pronoun choice in each of the following sentences and briefly explain the reason for your choice. See the example below.

> The woman who/<u>whom</u> I met is, I discovered today, the sales manager.
> *Whom* functions as the object of the verb *met*.

1. The government officials to who/whom we were referred have refused to see us.

_____

2. Whoever/Whomever informed you of the test location made a mistake.

_____

3. Who/Whom should we notify in case of illness?

_____

4. I was contacted by the officials who/whom you describe.

_____

5. The salesperson who/whom Dad called is here to speak with whoever/whomever is interested in buying the new vacuum cleaner.

_____

6. Who/Whom called this salesperson?

_____

7. The client who/whom phoned you earlier is on the line again now.

_____

8. People who/whom do not vote have no cause to complain.

_____

In each of the following sentences, determine which pronoun form should be used. Write the entire correct sentence on the lines provided.

1. City life is what we/us New Yorkers thrive on.

2. For we/us Virginians, history is everywhere.

3. For two Missourians, she/her and Bernie, the ruggedness of California came as quite a shock. _____

4. As newcomers Dale and I/me found out, Butte has a long history of mining. _____

5. Lute Johannson always claimed he was the best of us/we chili cookers. _____

6. There is only one whiskey to we/us real Scots.

7. Two Irish writers, she/her and William Butler Yeats, must share the title of best writer. _____

8. The committee gave the two finest storytellers, Ed and I/me, citations of merit.

9. That country house looked good to we/us longtime apartment dwellers.

10. Even to Les and he/him, the computer eventually proved to be a powerful tool.

8

Using Verbs

➤ Student Writing Error 6: Wrong Verb Ending

Verbs identify action, occurrence, or state of being. They are crucial to our understanding of experience, and using them correctly and well is central to mastering English grammar. We use verbs to tell what we do: *sleep, wake, yawn, eat, talk.* We use them to tell what is or was or will be: *The sunshine* is *warm. The rain showers* felt *refreshing. The weekend* will be *partly cloudy.* As these examples begin to indicate, we change a verb's form to make it agree grammatically with its subjects and to indicate tense, voice, and mood. Understanding how verbs work will allow you to select the form that communicates your meaning precisely.

Verb mistakes in student writing are very common. These mistakes take many forms and represent any number of confusions about verb use that trouble the student writers who make them. Pay careful attention to the material that follows: some of it may be new to you, some of it may be things you once knew but have forgotten, and some of it will help you to become more sure of yourself as a verb user.

Except for *be* (more about this irregular verb later), all English verbs can take five forms. Examples of regular verbs follow. (Irregular verbs deviate from this pattern; they will be discussed later in this chapter.)

Base Form	-s Form	Present Participle Form	Past Tense Form	Past Participle Form
cheer	cheers	cheering	cheered	cheered
type	types	typing	typed	typed
discuss	discusses	discussing	discussed	discussed

The *base form*, sometimes called the present form, is the form found in the dictionary. Writers use this form to indicate action that is happening now—in the present. The base form (without *-s* or *-es*) is used whenever the subject is a plural noun or the pronoun *I, we, you,* or *they.* Here are two examples:

> Dogs *howl.* [*plural noun subject,* Dogs]
>
> I *howl.* [*pronoun subject,* I]

The *-s form* is simply the present form with the addition of *-s* or *-es.* The *-s* form is used whenever the subject preceding it is a singular third person noun, as in *The dog howls.* (For spelling rules indicating whether to add *-s* or *-es,* see Chapter 22.) The *-s* form is also used with many indefinite pronouns (*everyone* and *someone,* for example). The *-s* forms are underlined in the following chart.

	Singular	*Plural*
FIRST PERSON	I wish	we wish
SECOND PERSON	you wish	you wish
THIRD PERSON	he/she/it *wishes*	they wish
	the child *wishes*	children wish
	everyone *wishes*	

Note: Some speakers use the base form instead of the *-s* form with a third person singular subject. However, in all but the most informal writing situations, readers will expect the *-s* form with third person singular subjects; when it is not present, they will assume the writer has made a mistake.

> **INCORRECT** She *live* in a high-rise apartment.
>
> **CORRECT** She *lives* in a high-rise apartment.

The *present participle form* is made by adding *-ing* to the base form. By itself, a present participle forms a verbal, which acts to modify something (see the discussion of verbals in Chapter 6). So, in fact, many times a participle is not a verb. But a participle can also be combined with an auxiliary verb (often some form of *be* or *have*) in order to indicate continuing or prolonged action. Here are two examples:

> *Barking* all night, the dogs disturbed the neighbors. [*The participle* barking *acts as a verbal; it modifies* the dogs.]

> Those dogs *were barking* all night. [*Present participle* barking + *auxiliary verb* were *form the predicate, the main verb of the sentence.*]

The *past tense form* indicates action that happened in the past, as in *Dogs barked.* As you can see, the past tense form is made in regular verbs by adding *-ed* (again, more on regular and irregular verbs later in this chapter).

The *past participle form* of regular verbs is identical to the past tense form; irregular verbs have different past participle forms. Like present participles, the past participle form may function as a verbal when used alone (see Chapter 6). Consider this example:

> *Encouraged* by her own success, Erin *encouraged* Mary Lou and Jeanette to study harder.

The first *encouraged* is a past participle and functions as a verbal; it modifies (tells us about) Erin. The second *encouraged* is the past tense form and functions as the main verb of the sentence; it tells us what Erin did. Now consider this example:

> Erin's parents *were encouraged* by her success.

Here the past participle form, *encouraged,* has been combined with an auxiliary verb (a form of *be* or *have,* in this case, *were*) to form the predicate (main verb) of the sentence. (More on auxiliary verbs later in this chapter.)

Turn now to Assignment 8A at the end of this chapter for practice with verb forms.

Using the Verbs Be and Have

Since these verbs are commonly used as auxiliaries and since they possess several forms, the verbs *be* and *have* require special attention. We begin with *be.*

Base Form	-s Form	Present Participle Form	Past Tense Form	Past Participle Form
be	is	being	was	been
	am		were	
	are			

As you see, *be* takes eight different forms. In addition, *be* is the one verb that takes present tense forms that are different from the base form. The base form and the present form of *cheer* are the same: *I cheer for the Cubs.* But the present tense form for *be* may be any of three forms: *am, are,* or *is.*

Present Tense Forms of the Verb *Be*

	Singular	*Plural*
FIRST PERSON	I *am* a Cubs fan.	We *are* Cubs fans.
SECOND PERSON	You *are* a Cubs fan.	You *are* Cubs fans.
THIRD PERSON	She *is* a Cubs fan.	They *are* Cubs fans.

Some speakers retain the base form rather than using the appropriate present tense form, saying, "I *be* a Cubs fan." This is unacceptable in academic or formal writing, so such speakers must be especially careful to use the correct present tense form.

Be also takes two different forms in the past tense, *was* and *were*:

Past Tense Forms of the Verb *Be*

	Singular	*Plural*
FIRST PERSON	I *was* a Cubs fan.	We *were* Cubs fans.
SECOND PERSON	You *were* a Cubs fan.	You *were* Cubs fans.
THIRD PERSON	She *was* a Cubs fan.	They *were* Cubs fans.
	Joe *was* a Cubs fan.	

Again, some speakers substitute the past participle form *been* for the appropriate past tense forms, saying, "I *been* a Cubs fan when I lived in Chicago." In formal or academic writing, such speakers must be extra careful to use the correct past tense form.

The verb *have* presents fewer complications than *be*. With the exception of the third person singular, the present tense is regular:

	Singular	*Plural*
FIRST PERSON	I *have* an idea.	We *have* an idea.
SECOND PERSON	You *have* an idea.	You *have* an idea.
THIRD PERSON	She *has* an idea.	They *have* an idea.

The forms of *have* are as follows:

Base Form	*-s Form*	*Present Participle Form*	*Past Tense Form*	*Past Participle Form*
have	has	having	had	had

EXERCISE 8.1 USING APPROPRIATE FORMS OF *BE* AND *HAVE*

Circle the appropriate form of *be* or *have* for each of the following sentences.

1. Grandma Berry am/be/is the oldest living member of the family.
2. She was/were raised in Colorado before World War I.
3. I is/be/am related to her by marriage.
4. Her maiden name is/be/am Boone.
5. Daniel Boone been/was/were her great-great-grandfather.
6. She have/has lived quite a life.

Using Auxiliary Verbs |8a|

We use auxiliary verbs (some teachers and textbooks call them *helping verbs*) in combination with other verb forms to create a variety of specific verb tenses and meanings. The most commonly used auxiliaries are forms of *be, has,* and *do,* as well as *shall* and *will.*

I *am working* hard. [*present progressive tense*]

Candice *has been working* hard. [*present perfect progressive tense*]

Carol *will approve* of that concept. [*simple future tense*]

Aaron *does* not *enjoy* wearing a tie. [*simple present tense to form a negative*]

You *will have seen* your present by this time on Friday. [*future perfect tense*]

One commissioner *did* not *agree*. [*simple past tense to form a negative*]

Although some speakers use the base form *be* as an auxiliary, this is generally not appropriate for academic or formal writing. In addition, sometimes speakers leave out the auxiliary when academic or formal writing would require it:

DIALECT   I *be working* hard today.
         I *working* hard today.

ACADEMIC WRITING   I *am working* hard today.

In academic or formal writing situations, you should also be careful to distinguish between the contractions *doesn't* and *don't*. Use *doesn't* only with singular subjects; use *don't* only with plural subjects.

DIALECT   The character *don't understand* her situation.

ACADEMIC WRITING   The character *doesn't understand* her situation.
         The characters *don't understand* their situation.

[*131*]

Several other auxiliaries, called modal auxiliaries, are used to indicate necessity, obligation, or possibility. The most commonly used modal auxiliaries are *can, could, may, might, must, ought, should,* and *would.*

I *could* not *work* harder.

Ernie *can substitute* for me.

The government *must address* issues of poverty.

The Mets *ought* to *win* tonight. [*The preposition* to *almost always accompanies* ought.]

The Mets *should have won* last night.

EXERCISE 8.2 USING AUXILIARY VERBS

Underline the auxiliary and main verb in each sentence below. If an incorrect auxiliary has been used, pencil in the correct auxiliary above it. If a needed auxiliary has been left out, pencil it in. If the sentence is correct, write *C* next to the number of the sentence.

is

EXAMPLE Grandma be feeling better this morning.

1. I is running for the position of class president.
2. After careful study, we inclined to accept the consultant's report.
3. Whenever Veronica misses school, you can bet she has developed another ear infection.
4. Since Jared has been reading Robert Louis Stevenson, he don't watch much television.
5. When the alarm bell rings, we must leave the building immediately.

Using Regular and Irregular Verbs |8b|

Most English verbs form their principal parts in the same way: the past tense and past participle forms are made by adding *-d* or *-ed.* The verbs specified in Assignment 8A are all regular verbs. There are several hundred English verbs that do not follow this regular pattern. Called irregular verbs, these special cases must simply be memorized or their forms looked up in a dictionary.

As you look over the following list of commonly used irregular verbs, you will notice several patterns. Some irregular verbs change forms by altering an interior vowel (as in *begin, began, begun*). Other verbs do not change at all (as in *hurt, hurt, hurt*). Still others make quite radical changes (as in *go, went, gone*). For convenience, only the base, past tense, and past participle forms are listed.

Commonly Used Irregular Verbs

Base Form	Past Tense	Past Participle
arise	arose	arisen
awake	awoke/awaked	awoke/awoken/awaked
beat	beat	beaten
become	became	become
begin	began	begun
bite	bit	bitten
blow	blew	blown
break	broke	broken
bring	brought	brought
build	built	built
burn	burned/burnt	burned/burnt
buy	bought	bought
choose	chose	chosen
come	came	come
cost	cost	cost
dive	dived/dove	dived
do	did	done
draw	drew	drawn
drink	drank	drunk
drive	drove	driven
eat	ate	eaten
feel	felt	felt
fly	flew	flown
forget	forgot	forgotten/forgot
freeze	froze	frozen
get	got	gotten
give	gave	given
go	went	gone
grow	grew	grown
hear	heard	heard
hide	hid	hidden
hurt	hurt	hurt
keep	kept	kept
know	knew	known
lead	led	led
let	let	let

lose	lost	lost
mean	meant	meant
meet	met	met
pay	paid	paid
put	put	put
ride	rode	ridden
ring	rang	rung
run	ran	run
say	said	said
see	saw	seen
set	set	set
shake	shook	shaken
shoot	shot	shot
shrink	shrank	shrunk
sink	sank	sunk
sleep	slept	slept
speak	spoke	spoken
spend	spent	spent
spread	spread	spread
spring	sprang/sprung	sprung
stand	stood	stood
swim	swam	swum
swing	swung	swung
take	took	taken
teach	taught	taught
tear	tore	torn
tell	told	told
think	thought	thought
throw	threw	thrown
wear	wore	worn
write	wrote	written

Turn now to Assignment 8B at the end of this chapter for practice with irregular verbs.

Using *Set/Sit, Lie/Lay,* and *Rise/Raise* |8c|

These particular verbs often cause writers trouble. Does the book *lie* on the table or *lay* on the table? Do I *sit* that record on the stack or *set* it on the stack? Does the sun *rise* in the sky or *raise* in the sky? The key to using these words correctly is the ability to distinguish between transitive and intransitive verbs.

To review, if a verb is transitive, it can take an object. *Kicked* is a transitive verb, as in *Wally kicked the empty can.* Kicked what? Kicked the can. The object of the verb *kicked* is *can.* In the pairs of verbs under discussion, *lay, set,* and *raise* are transitive verbs; they take objects.

I *lay* the record on the table. [Lay *means "to put or place."*]

I *set* the record on the stack. [Set *means "to put or place."*]

I *raise* the needle off the record. [Raise *means "to lift or bring up."*]

As you might guess, if a verb cannot take an object, it is an intransitive verb. *Sit, lie,* and *rise* are intransitive verbs; they do not take objects.

I *sit* in the chair. [Sit *means "to be seated."*]

I *lie* on the bed. [Lie *means "to recline."*]

The bird *rises* into the air. [Rise *means "to go up."*]

One other complication with these pairs of verbs is that they are irregular. Here are their principal parts:

Base Form	-s Form	Present Participle Form	Past Tense Form	Past Participle Form
lie	lies	lying	lay	lain
lay	lays	laying	laid	laid
sit	sits	sitting	sat	sat
set	sets	setting	set	set
rise	rises	rising	rose	risen
raise	raises	raising	raised	raised

Finally, you should recognize that of all these verbs, the forms of *lie* and *lay* can be the most confusing. The base form of *lay* is the same as the past tense form of *lie*. And you should also be careful to distinguish between *lie* meaning "to recline" and *lie* meaning "to tell a falsehood." When used to indicate a falsehood, as in *Eric lied to his friend,* the verb is regular. Its forms are as follows:

Base Form	-s Form	Present Participle Form	Past Tense Form	Past Participle Form
lie	lies	lying	lie	lied

EXERCISE 8.3 DISTINGUISHING BETWEEN *LIE/LAY*, *SIT/SET*, AND *RISE/RAISE*

Underline the correct verb in each of the following sentences. The first one is done for you.

1. Alice sat/set her cup of tea on the drainboard.
2. After a strenuous tennis match, Dave only wanted to set/sit in an easy chair.
3. The cat had lain/laid there so long that it was stiff when it stood up.
4. Emmett couldn't remember where he'd sat/set his glass.
5. The class began to fidget because they had sat/set so long.
6. If we lie/lay the wrench here, will we remember to put it away?
7. Where is the chicken that lain/laid the golden egg?
8. I'm going to lie/lay down.
9. I'm going to lie/lay myself down.
10. Lois sat/set down at her sewing machine and sat/set the material out in front of her.
11. As the flag rose/raised, a trumpeter played "Taps."
12. The dough bubbles as it raises/rises.

VERB TENSES

> ### Student Writing Error 13: Wrong Verb Tense

Another mistake students often make with verbs is using the wrong verb tense. These writers probably have trouble deciding between some of the more complex verb tenses—perhaps they are unsure when to use present perfect and when to use present perfect progressive, for instance. If you have had rain all week, and it is still raining now, do you write "It has rained all week" or "It has been raining all week?" Questions like these are difficult for even the most experienced writers to answer. If you have ever been similarly stumped, or if your instructors have marked "wrong tense" on any of your papers, study the following material carefully. It should help you learn how to tell one tense from another and to know when to use each one.

Using the Present Tenses |8d|

By using (or not using) auxiliaries and by varying verb endings, writers tell readers exactly when things occur. If you have studied the forms that verbs can take, you have already begun to study verb tenses. As a writer, familiarity with verb tenses will allow you to convey the sequence of your thoughts or actions accurately.

We shall concentrate on the four present tenses. As you read, you may find it useful to review earlier sections discussing auxiliary verbs and the forms of regular and irregular verbs. The present tenses are illustrated using the verb *stop*.

PRESENT *stop* or *stops*

- Shows action happening at the time of the speaking or writing
- Also used for habitual action, actions likely to be true at all times, or in discussion of literary or artistic words of art

When you turn off the ignition, the car *stops*. [*habitual action*]

Your thirty seconds *stop* now. [*action happening at the time of speaking*]

PRESENT PROGRESSIVE *is stopping* or *are stopping*

- Shows ongoing action or action still happening even as it is being written or spoken about
- May also be used to indicate a scheduled event in the future

I am pushing on the brake, and you can see that the car *is stopping*. [*action happening as it is being discussed*]

The Halls *are stopping* here after dinner tomorrow night. [*action scheduled in the future*]

PRESENT PERFECT *has stopped, have stopped*

- Shows action started in the past and either completed at some unspecified time in the past or continuing into the present

The loss of wetlands *has stopped* waterfowl from breeding. [*action started in the past, with effects continuing into the present*]

I *have stopped* worrying about it. [*action started and completed in the past*]

PRESENT PERFECT PROGRESSIVE *has been stopping, have been stopping*

- Shows an ongoing action started in the past and very likely to continue into the present

Since December, the window wiper *has been stopping* whenever the rain falls hard. [*action started in the past but continuing to the present*]

For years, we *have been stopping* here for lunch. [*action started in the past and continuing to the present*]

As you can see, a knowledge of verb tenses enables you to specify a wide variety of time relationships. Turn now to Assignment 8C at the end of this chapter for practice with the present tenses.

Using the Past Tenses |8e|

The past tenses all discuss events that are over. Understanding the various relationships of these past tenses will allow you to present material in its proper time order. The past tenses are schematically presented here using the verb *start*:

SIMPLE PAST *started*

- Shows completed action

This morning, the car *started* without any trouble.

The past tense is often used in narration. If you are using the past tense to tell what happened, it is conventional to stay with the past tense throughout. Switching from past to present and back again is likely to cause confusion for your readers. Here is an example of what *not* to do:

The accident *happened* at 8:15. The yellow station wagon *comes* toward me on the right. Since the light *was* green in my direction, I *thought* the station wagon would stop. But it *doesn't*. It *comes* right at me, *swerves* at the last minute, and *hits* the front of the car. The impact *threw* me against the steering wheel. Then I *lose* consciousness. When I *woke up*, a medic *is asking* me my name.

This paragraph is more or less understandable factually. But it also communicates an implicit message: the writer has not recognized some basic grammatical errors. This message leads the reader to wonder: Was the writer in a rush? Or does he or she not know that these are mistakes? Or, worse, does the writer not care whether the writing is correct or not? In sum, the reader wonders what is wrong with the writer, instead of simply reading and understanding what has been written.

So when writing narration, choose a tense and stay with it.

PAST PROGRESSIVE *was starting, were starting*

- Shows ongoing action at an earlier time.

At that point, I *was starting* to get frustrated.

PAST PERFECT *had started*

- Shows action that occurred in the past before some other action that also happened in the past

I *had started* to worry about an hour before you arrived. [*The worry came before the arrival; both actions happened in the past*]

PAST PERFECT PROGRESSIVE *had been starting*

- Shows past action still ongoing when another past action occurred

I *had been starting* to feel restless until the boss gave me a raise.

Turn now to Assignment 8D at the end of this chapter for practice with the past tenses.

Using the Future Tenses |8f|

The future tenses discuss events that have not yet occurred. As with present and past tenses, understanding the full variety of future tenses allows writers to indicate time relationships accurately. The future tenses are presented schematically here using the verb *open*.

SIMPLE FUTURE *shall/will open*

- Shows action still to occur

The store *will open* next week.

(Note: The auxiliary *shall* is still preferred over *will* with the first person pronoun subjects *I* or *we* in most formal and academic writing, as in a sentence like *As a committee, we shall discuss each of these issues*.)

FUTURE PROGRESSIVE *shall/will be opening*

- Shows ongoing action to occur in the future

From Thanksgiving through New Year's, the store *will be opening* early.

We *shall be opening* the main auditorium at 11 A.M.

FUTURE PERFECT *shall/will have opened*

- Shows action that will be completed before some other action in the future

The store *will have opened* by the time I get back from vacation.

By this time next week, we *shall have opened* the hospital's new wing.

FUTURE PERFECT PROGRESSIVE *shall/will have been opening*

- Shows a continuing action that will be completed by some specified time in the future

  By next March 3, you *will have been opening* your new business daily for a month.

Turn now to Assignment 8E at the end of this chapter for practice with the future tenses.

Using Verb Tenses in Sequences |8g|

Writers frequently need to indicate a particular sequence of items or actions. This is often accomplished by employing dependent clauses or verbals. The simplest sequence involves actions happening at the same time: *Debbie looks at me, and I look at her.* The two actions are happening in the present. Whenever two actions happen at the same time (present, past, or future), the tenses of the verbs or verbals stay the same.

The matter gets more complicated when sentences contain verbs that express actions that happened at different times. In such complex sentences, the tense of the main verb often differs from the tense of the verbs in dependent clauses. In general, you may use whatever tenses you need in order to communicate your meaning, so long as your tense sequences stay logical and reasonable. Study the following examples.

LOGICAL SEQUENCES

simple future		simple present

He *will lend* her the money because he   *loves*   her.

future perfect		simple present

We *will have repaired* your typewriter by the time you   *arrive*   tomorrow.

ILLOGICAL SEQUENCES

simple past		simple present

We   *ate*   all the dessert by the time he *arrives.*

past perfect		simple future

I *have ridden* bicycles since before you *will walk.*

simple past		simple present

The door bell   *rang*   just after Jack *finishes* talking on the phone.

EXERCISE 8.4 USING VERB TENSES IN SEQUENCES

Read the following sentences carefully, and provide the specified information. If a sentence uses a logical sequence of tenses, put *L* on the lines provided. If the sentence uses an illogical sequence of tenses, rewrite it so that your new version is logical. You may find that you need to review the portion of this chapter that identifies the various tenses.

EXAMPLE

Catfish Hunter threw a curve even though the catcher will signal a fast ball.

main verb: threw

tense of main verb: past

dependent clause verb: will signal

tense of dependent clause verb: future

Catfish Hunter threw a curve even though the catcher signaled a fast ball.

1. Liz Claiborne had designed dresses before she designs eyewear and other accessories.

main verb: _____

tense of main verb: _____

dependent clause verb: _____

tense of dependent clause verb: _____

_____

_____

2. Dad's gift was a shirt that proved too small.

main verb: _____

tense of main verb: _____

dependent clause verb: _____

tense of dependent clause verb: _____

_____

_____

3. Mom will have left by the time you arrive.

main verb: _____

tense of main verb: _____

dependent clause verb: _____

tense of dependent clause verb: _____

_____

_____

4. The light had just changed to green when the pickup truck crumples the passenger side of my Volkswagen.

main verb: _____

tense of main verb: _____

dependent clause verb: _____

tense of dependent clause verb: _____

_____

_____

5. The soap opera had started when our power will go out.

main verb: _____

tense of main verb: _____

dependent clause verb: _____

tense of dependent clause verb: _____

_____

_____

Infinitives and participles also play an important role in communicating time relationships to readers. There are two infinitive forms: the present infinitive (the base form of the verb plus *to,* as in *to swim*) and the perfect infinitive (the past participle form of the verb plus *to have,* as in *to have appeared*). These infinitive forms are used as follows:

■ The present infinitive indicates an action occurring *at the same time as* or *later than* the main verb.

Alec and Frank like *to play* double solitaire. [*The liking and the playing occur at the same time.*]

Jane is going *to swim.* [*The going occurs first, the swimming later.*]

Lisa will decide *to hire* a specialist. [*The decision comes first, then the hiring.*]

■ The perfect infinitive indicates action occurring *earlier than* the main verb.

He was reported *to have left* his fortune to his bulldog, Jake. [*The leaving of the fortune came before the report.*]

The three participial forms each indicate a different time in relation to the main verb. The use of these participles is illustrated next.

PRESENT PARTICIPLE

■ Formed by adding *-ing* to the base form of the verb, the present participle indicates action occurring at the same time as that of the main verb.

Trying to see over the crowd, Ariel stood on her chair. [*The trying and the standing occur at the same time.*]

Seeking shelter from the hail, we ran to the porch. [*The seeking and the running occur at the same time.*]

PRESENT PERFECT PARTICIPLE

■ Formed by combining the auxiliary *having* with the past participle form, the present perfect participle indicates action occurring before that of the main verb.

Having finished her finals, she decided to take a long nap. [*The finishing of finals occurs before the decision to nap.*]

Having predicted rain, the forecaster was embarrassed by the sunshine. [*The prediction comes before the embarrassment.*]

PAST PARTICIPLE

■ The past participle indicates action occurring either before or at the same time as that of the main verb.

Surprised by the first question, I decided to move on to the next one. [*The surprise comes before the decision.*]

Flown by an expert pilot, the plane turned to a northerly course. [*The flying and the turning happen at the same time.*]

Turn now to Assignment 8F at the end of this chapter for more practice with verb tense sequence.

VOICE

Minnesota Fats pocketed the last ball with a two-cushion bank shot.
The last ball was pocketed by Minnesota Fats with a two-cushion bank shot.

If you consider those two sentences, you will see that in the first one, a person is doing something. The person is Minnesota Fats, a legendary pool player. He is the subject of that first sentence. Since Fats is performing the action, we can say that that first sentence is written in the **active voice**.

In the second sentence, the subject is not Minnesota Fats; it is the word *ball*. The verb is *was pocketed*. And in that second sentence, Minnesota Fats is the object of the preposition *by*. This is an example of the **passive voice**: something is done to the subject; the subject does not act but is instead acted upon.

All the examples used so far in this chapter to indicate tense and verb sequence are written in the active voice. The passive voice is formed by using the appropriate auxiliary (some form of *be* or *have*) plus the past participle form of the main verb. In the Minnesota Fats example, the auxiliary is *was* and the past participle form of the verb is *pocketed*. To compare active and passive forms, see the following:

	Active	*Passive*
SIMPLE PRESENT	She reads the paper.	The paper is read by her.
PRESENT PERFECT	She has read the paper.	The paper has been read by her.
SIMPLE PAST	She read the paper.	The paper was read by her.
PAST PERFECT	She had read the paper.	The paper had been read by her.
SIMPLE FUTURE	She will read the paper.	The paper will be read by her.
FUTURE PERFECT	By noon, she will have read the paper.	By noon, the paper will have been read by her.

EXERCISE 8.5 IDENTIFYING ACTIVE AND PASSIVE VOICE

Underline the main verb in each sentence, and indicate whether it is active or passive.

EXAMPLE The azalea blossoms <u>nod</u> in the wind. active

1. The next section of this report analyzes the experimental data. _____

2. The experimental data are analyzed in the next section of this report. _____

3. Suddenly, rainfall pounded on the roof over our heads. _____

4. The last apple fritter in the doughnut box was eaten by Jerry just a few minutes ago. _____

5. By this time tomorrow afternoon, they will be fishing for trout. _____

6. The wall clock downstairs says 8:05. _____

7. My paper was put in your mailbox yesterday afternoon after lunch. _____

8. My roommate put my paper in your mailbox yesterday afternoon after lunch. _____

9. Erica's purse had been returned to the lost and found. _____

10. A variety of factors contributed to the outbreak of the Civil War. _____

    In considering the merits of either active or passive voice, writers must recognize several points. Even a quick glance at the comparison chart shows that writing in the active voice produces shorter, more direct sentences. In many kinds of writing, readers appreciate this directness. Sentences in the active voice are also livelier and more vibrant.

    The difference between active and passive voice is partly a matter of emphasis. In active voice, the subject performs the action; both the performer (the subject) and the action (the verb) receive emphasis. However, in passive voice, the originator of the action is not the sentence subject. In fact, in passive voice, the originator of the action can be omitted altogether, as in this example:

    The last ball was pocketed with a two-cushion bank shot.

Here the *action* receives the emphasis; the force responsible for the action receives no mention at all. Passive construction of this sort is common and appropriate in scientific reporting. A paragraph describing experimental procedures should rightly focus on the procedures themselves rather than on the lab assistants who performed them:

> Measurements of water temperature were then taken every three minutes for one hour. These temperatures were then compared to measurements taken during phase one. . . .

But passive constructions also make it impossible for readers to learn who or what is responsible for the actions reported. Consider this example:

> The monthly rate for day care has been increased another $50.

Who is responsible for determining this increase? To whom should you complain? The passive construction of the sentence allows those responsible to remain unnamed.

EXERCISE 8.6 ANALYZING THE USES OF ACTIVE AND PASSIVE VOICE

Using your own paper, respond to the following questions. For each question, hand in a copy of your example and your analysis of it.

1. Find a one-paragraph example of writing that uses the active voice exclusively. This example could be part of a longer document and could be taken from almost any source: a newspaper, magazine, or book. Why does this piece of writing use the active voice? What would happen if this writing used the passive voice? Would the passive voice be inappropriate, and if so, why?
2. Now find a one-paragraph example of writing that uses the passive voice exclusively. This example could be part of a longer document and could be taken from almost any source: a newspaper, magazine, or book. Why does this piece of writing use the passive voice? What would happen if this writing used the active voice? Would the active voice be inappropriate, and if so, why?

- To change from active to passive, convert the object of the verb into the sentence subject.

ACTIVE   Tom chased the cat. [*Object of the verb is* cat.]

PASSIVE   The cat was chased by Tom. [Cat *has become the subject.*]

- To change from passive to active, convert the subject of the verb into a direct or indirect object and find a new subject.

PASSIVE The cake was baked for forty minutes. [Cake *is the subject.*]

ACTIVE Scott baked the cake for forty minutes. [Cake *has become the direct object, and a new subject,* Scott, *has been added.*]

EXERCISE 8.7 USING ACTIVE AND PASSIVE VOICE

Return to the two paragraphs you found and analyzed in Exercise 8.6. Applying the guidelines for converting from one voice to the other, rewrite the one that is now written in the active voice, using the passive voice. Then rewrite the other paragraph to use the active voice. You may have to make up details in order to rewrite the paragraphs; for the purposes of this exercise, that is fine. When you are done, look back at the answers to Exercise 8.6. Did your analyses hold true?

MOOD

The mood of a verb reflects how the message of that verb is conceived by its writer. If the verb is meant to express a fact or to answer a question, it takes the indicative mood. Verbs used to express commands take the imperative mood. And verbs used to express requirements, desires, suggestions, or conditions contrary to fact take the subjunctive mood.

Of these, the most common is the **indicative mood**, which is used to convey facts or answer questions. Virtually this entire workbook is written in the indicative mood. All the examples of tense and voice given earlier in this chapter are written in the indicative mood.

The second most common mood is the **imperative mood**, which is used to express commands. Many of the exercise directions in this workbook are written in the imperative mood. Such directions typically omit the sentence subject and use the base form of the verb, as in *Analyze the following sentences.* As you can see, the subject, *you,* has been left out.

The **subjunctive mood** may be used to express requirements, requests, desires, suggestions, or conditions contrary to fact. The subjective is used primarily in clauses beginning with *if, that, as if,* or *as though.* See the forms and examples that follow.

The *present subjunctive* uses the base form of the verb. The present subjunctive form of the verb *be* is simply *be.*

Will asked that he *be* excused from basketball practice. [*subjunctive expressing a desire*]

Contest rules require that you *be* present to win. [*subjunctive expressing a requirement*]

The teacher asked that one volunteer *stay* after school. [*subjunctive expressing a request*]

Note: Third person singular present subjunctive verbs—like *stay* in the third sample sentence—do not end in *-s* like third person singular verbs in other moods.

The *past subjunctive* uses the same past tense as the other moods, with the exception of the verb *be*, which uses *were* for all subjects.

If I *were* you, I would vote for the other candidate. [*subjunctive expressing a condition contrary to fact:* If I were you (but I am not you) . . .]

If Alice *were* here, she'd be talking about art. [*subjunctive expressing a condition contrary to fact:* If Alice were here (but she is not here) . . .]

The chimp scratched its head as if it *were* human. [*subjunctive expressing a condition contrary to fact:* as if it were human (but it is not human, it is a chimpanzee) . . .]

The mime artist walked the curb as though she *were walking* a tightrope. [*subjunctive expressing a condition contrary to fact:* as though she were walking a tightrope (rather than walking the curb) . . .]

Note: Since the subjunctive mood often creates a formal tone, some writers and speakers substitute the indicative mood in less formal writing or speaking situations. However, for academic writing, you should still use the subjunctive whenever required.

INFORMAL That commercial says that if I *was* a real man, I'd own a truck.

ACADEMIC That commercial implies that if I *were* a real man, I'd own a truck.

EXERCISE 8.8 IDENTIFYING VERB MOODS

Read the following short paragraph from a letter. Above each underlined verb, pencil in the mood of that verb. The first verb mood has been identified for you.

Dear Doris and Al,

indicative

We <u>were</u> pleased by your suggestion that we <u>meet</u> for several days at Long Beach this

year, and if the distance from Montana to the coast <u>were</u> even 200 miles less, such a trip to the beach would be feasible for us. Unfortunately, given the actual distance (and the fact that our motor home <u>needs</u> repair), we'll simply not be able to make the trip this summer. But <u>ask</u> the Harringtons. They <u>moved</u> to Cheney only last year. We <u>thought</u> of them because Bill Harrington always <u>speaks</u> of his love of beachcombing. Besides, Bill and Sue <u>are</u> a wonderful couple. <u>Keep</u> us posted on your plans. If we <u>were planning</u> any trip this summer, it would be to see you both.

EXERCISE 8.9 USING VERB MOODS

Using your own paper, write accurate, original sentences using the mood and verb specified. Remember, the subjunctive commonly appears in clauses beginning with *if*, *that*, *as if*, or *as though*.

EXAMPLES

a sentence using the verb *bark* in the indicative mood
Whenever another dog walks by, our Tom barks.
a sentence in which the verb *ask* is followed by a subjunctive
The personnel manager asks that you be interviewed tomorrow.

1. a sentence using *carry* in the imperative mood
2. a sentence in which the verb *insist* is followed by a subjunctive
3. a sentence in which the verb *wish* is followed by a subjunctive
4. a sentence using *climb* in the indicative mood
5. a sentence using *call* in the imperative mood

ASSIGNMENT 8A USING VERB FORMS

Using the subjects and verbs provided, write the indicated sentences.

EXAMPLE subject: *Bernie*   verb: *touch*
      sentence using a present form: *Bernie touches the soft fur.*
      sentence using the auxiliary verb *had*: *Bernie had touched a squid before.*

1. subject: *I*   verb: *walk*   sentence using a past form: _____

_____

sentence using an auxiliary verb + the present participle form: _____

_____

2. subject: *they*   verb: *ask*   sentence using a present form: _____

_____

sentence using an auxiliary verb + the past participle form: _____

_____

3. subject: *the birds*   verb: *screech*   sentence using a past form: _____

_____

sentence using an auxiliary verb + the present participle form: _____

_____

4. subject: *we*   verb: *decide*   sentence using a present form: _____

_____

sentence using the auxiliary verb *had* + the past participle form: _____

_____

5. subject: *teenagers*   verb: *consume*   sentence using a past form: _____

_____

sentence using the auxiliary verb *were* + the present participle form: _____

_____

Consulting the list of irregular verbs, write sentences as specified. Use auxiliary verbs as needed.

EXAMPLE a sentence using *they* as its main subject and the past participle form of *go* as its main verb (Remember that past participle forms are combined with auxiliary verbs.)
By the time we arrived, they had gone for supplies.

1. a sentence using *we* as its subject and the past tense form of *think* as its main verb

_____

2. a sentence using *they* as its main subject and the past form of *bring* as its main verb

_____

3. a sentence using any personal name as its main subject and the past participle

form of *become* as its main verb _____

_____

4. a sentence using *circus* as its main subject and the past participle form of *begin* as

its main verb _____

_____

5. a sentence using *I* as its main subject and the past participle form of *forget* as its

main verb _____
6. a sentence using *we* as its main subject and the past form of *draw* as its main verb

_____

7. a sentence using any appropriate noun as its subject and the past form of *drink* as

its main verb _____
8. a sentence using *they* as its subject and the past participle form of *feel* as its main

verb _____
9. a sentence using any appropriate noun as its subject and the past participle form

of *freeze* as its main verb _____

_____

10. a sentence using *I* as its main subject and the past participle form of *pass* as its

main verb _____

ASSIGNMENT 8C **USING THE PRESENT TENSES**

For each specified verb and tense, write a sentence If the verb is irregular, you may need to consult the list of irregular verbs or a good dictionary.

EXAMPLE *run,* present perfect *The new car has run every day without fail.*

1. *climb,* present progressive _____

_____

2. *marry,* present perfect progressive _____

_____

3. *discuss,* present _____

_____

4. *begin,* present progressive _____

_____

5. *tease,* present perfect _____

_____

6. *devour,* present _____

_____

7. *confuse,* present perfect progressive _____

_____

8. *lie* (tell an untruth), present progressive _____

_____

9. *sit,* present perfect _____

_____

For each specified verb and tense, write a sentence. If the verb is irregular, you may need to consult the list of irregular verbs or a good dictionary.

EXAMPLE   *swim*, past perfect progressive   *I had been swimming for years before the injury.*

1. *ride*, simple past _____

_____

2. *drink*, past perfect _____

_____

3. *steal*, past perfect _____

_____

4. *walk*, past perfect progressive _____

_____

5. *protest*, past progressive _____

_____

6. *require*, simple past _____

_____

7. *enjoy*, past perfect progressive _____

_____

8. *drive*, past progressive _____

_____

9. *sleep*, past perfect _____

_____

10. *delight*, simple past _____

_____

ASSIGNMENT 8E **USING THE FUTURE TENSES**

For each specified verb and tense, write a sentence. If the verb is irregular, you may need to consult the list of irregular verbs or a good dictionary.

EXAMPLE *swim*, future perfect   *You will have swum thirty laps by the time I wake up.*

1. *decide*, future progressive _____

_____

2. *remember*, future _____

_____

3. *compose*, future perfect _____

_____

4. *fly*, future perfect progressive _____

_____

5. *fish*, future progressive _____

_____

6. *visit*, future perfect progressive _____

_____

7. *consult*, future perfect _____

_____

8. *oppose*, future _____

9. *hike*, future perfect _____

_____

10. *celebrate*, future progressive _____

_____

Read each sentence below. If the sequence of tenses is logical, place an *L* on the first line following the sentence. If the sequence of tenses is illogical, rewrite the sentence on the lines that follow.

EXAMPLE

> When the family cat got hungry, she decides to climb the window screen and look inside.
> When the family cat got hungry, she decided to climb the window screen and look inside.

1. I had just finished spading the garden when you come out with the cold drinks.

2. On the first sunny Saturday in February, we decided to have taken a hike.

3. Surprised by winning the lottery, she decided to take a week off.

4. Before we started to have eaten dinner, we emptied the dishwasher.

5. The committee needs to have meet for an extra hour next week.

6. The evergreens began to grow where the meadow grass ended.

7. They announced the winners after we will finish dessert.

8. Mark had just stepped out of the shower when the lights started to have flickered.

9. Chaunta has surgery last month and hopes to begin training again next week.

10. Some Civil War historians would love to live in 1860.

9

Maintaining Agreement

For readers to associate subjects with verbs correctly (and thereby understand correctly what writers intend to say), writers must make sure that subjects and verbs agree in *number* (singular or plural) and in *person* (first, second, or third). Similarly, pronouns must agree with their antecedents in number, person, and in *gender* (feminine, masculine, or neuter). Lack of agreement in these word relationships will often leave readers confused and irritated. Yet errors in agreement appear twice on the list of the top twenty student writing errors. Studying the points presented in this chapter should help, if you too find agreement a difficult skill to master.

SUBJECT/VERB AGREEMENT

➤ *Student Writing Error 14: Lack of Subject-Verb Agreement*

The general rule for subject-verb agreement is simple: singular subjects take singular verbs, and plural subjects take plural verbs. Most often, you make a verb singular by adding *-s* or *-es* to the base form. See the examples that follow.

Making Verbs Agree with Third Person Singular Subjects   l9a l

In the present tense, a third person singular noun subject takes a verb ending in *-s* or *-es*. The third person pronoun subjects *he, she,* and *it* also take verbs ending in *-s* or *-es*. (Note that the verbs *be* and *have* are exceptions to this rule. See Chapter 8 for a discussion of these verbs.)

EXAMPLES

A Madras shirt fades when washed. [Shirt *is the third person singular noun subject of the verb.*]

The projectionist watches the movie. [Projectionist *is the third person singular noun subject of the verb.*]

She swims every other day. [She *is the third person singular pronoun subject of the verb.*]

These *-s* or *-es* endings are not always easy to hear in speech and are not a part of some spoken American dialects of English. However, writers using standard written English should always use these endings. (Of course noun and pronoun subjects that are not third person singular do not require an *-s* or *-es* ending. Be careful to write *we swim* and *you swim* rather than *we swims* and *you swims*, for instance.)

Maintaining Agreement When the Subject and Verb Are Separated by Other Words   19b1

Do not let words that come between subject and verb confuse subject-verb agreement. In the following example, the noun nearest the verb is *baskets* (plural). However, *baskets* is not the sentence subject; the subject is *contestant*.

RIGHT The contestant who makes the most consecutive baskets wins four free pizzas.

WRONG The contestant who makes the most consecutive baskets win four free pizzas.

In that example, a clause comes between the subject and the verb. Sometimes the intervening words are other sentence elements, such as prepositional phrases, as in this example:

RIGHT One of his bodyguards accompanies him at all times.

WRONG One of his bodyguards accompany him at all times.

Occasionally, a sentence meaning will appear to conflict with its actual grammar. This is especially true when a sentence subject is followed by a phrase beginning with *as well as, along with, together with, in addition to,* or any similar expression. In such sentences the meaning becomes plural, though grammatically the sentence subject stays singular. Here is an example:

Senator Katz, along with her aides, travels the state in a large van.

Here the grammatical subject (*Senator Katz*) is in the third person singular and so takes a singular verb (*travels*). Even though that sentence is grammatically correct, it may also sound awkward to you. To eliminate such awkwardness, some writers will simply revise the sentence in this way: *Senator Katz and her aides travel the state in a large van.* Now the subject is *Senator Katz and her aides;* this is grammatically plural and takes a plural verb, *travel.* (We shall return to such compound subjects later in this chapter.)

When proofreading to check on subject-verb agreement, reducing the sentence to only its subject and verb should make any such errors easier to spot.

The cook who baked these pizzas knows what he's doing. [cook . . . knows]

The coach, together with the team members, arrives in Salt Lake City at 9:35 P.M. [coach . . . arrives]

EXERCISE 9.1 MAINTAINING SUBJECT-VERB AGREEMENT

Read the following paragraph. Then go back and look at each sentence. Circle the sentence subject and underline the main verb. (Ignore dependent clauses.) If the sentence subject and verb do not agree, pencil in the accurate verb. The first sentence has been done for you. (*Hint:* Remember that sentence subjects cannot be the objects of prepositions.)

The Eagle Creek Trail, one of the most frequently hiked trails in the Columbia River

climbs
Gorge, climb fourteen miles into the Cascade Mountains. The trail's most striking feature

are the number of waterfalls along its length. The first of these several waterfalls are

visible from a viewpoint only a mile and a half from the trailhead. At two and a half miles,

hikers arrive at Punch Bowl Falls. Here the water continue to carve a deep pool, which

gives the falls its name. Many hikers rest here briefly. Beyond Punch Bowl Falls rise High

Bridge. This steel span crosses a narrow gorge. The creek bed is at least fifty feet below

the bridge level. The waters at this point flows through a channel only five or six feet wide. Persistent hikers eventually reach Tunnel Falls. Here the trail literally tunnel behind an otherwise impassable waterfall. Such a dramatic landscape make the Eagle Creek Trail a popular place in the summer.

Making Verbs Agree with Compound Subjects   19c1

You may well understand the general rule that singular subjects take singular verbs and plural subjects take plural verbs yet still have some difficulty deciding when a subject is singular and when it is plural. Consider this example:

Jack and Jill run up the hill.

The word *Jack* by itself is singular; so is *Jill*. Yet the sentence has the two people running up a hill. This sentence is formed around a *compound subject*; as you see from the following rule, most of the time, sentences with compound sentences take plural verbs.

- Subjects joined by *and* are usually plural and take plural verbs. However, if two or more parts of a subject form a single idea or refer to one person, those parts are considered to be singular and take a singular verb.

EXAMPLES

Jack and Jill *run* up the hill. [*Subjects joined by* and *take a plural verb.*]

Bacon and eggs is the most commonly ordered breakfast. [*Subjects combine to form a single item; thus, the verb is singular.*]

If the adjective *each* or *every* precedes a compound subject, the verb following that subject is usually singular.

EXAMPLE Each bud and flower is a sign of spring.

Now let us look at several other agreement rules.

- Compound subjects joined by *or* or *nor* take singular verbs if they are both singular, plural verbs if they are both plural.

EXAMPLES

Neither the lifeguard nor the instructor *is* responsible for providing towels. [*singular subjects, singular verb*]

Either the pool employees or the parents *are* responsible for providing towels. [*plural subjects, plural verb*]

- When one part of a subject joined by *or* or *nor* is singular and the other part is plural, the verb agrees with the part of the subject closest to it. (Common practice is to place the plural part of the subject last in these constructions, making the verb also plural.)

EXAMPLE Typically, either rain or cold temperatures *ruin* March weekends.

- When the parts of a subject differ in person, the verb agrees with the nearer subject.

EXAMPLES

Either Laura or you *were* lying.

Either you or Laura *was* lying.

Since sentences of this sort often sound awkward, writers often split the subjects, giving each its own verb: *Either Laura was lying, or you were.*

Turn now to Assignment 9A at the end of this chapter for practice with compound subject–verb agreement.

Making Verbs Agree with Collective-Noun or Indefinite-Pronoun Subjects |9d, 9e|

Collective nouns also cause some writers trouble when it comes to agreement. Such nouns (such as *family* and *team*) are singular in form even though they refer to collections of many people or things. Should such nouns be considered singular or plural? Should they take singular or plural verbs? The answers to these questions hinge on the writer's intentions.

Commonly used collective nouns are *family, team, audience, group, jury, crowd, band, class, flock,* and *committee.*

- When used as subjects, collective nouns take singular verbs when they refer to the group as a whole; they take plural verbs when they refer to parts of the group.

EXAMPLES

My family generally *eats* dinner at six o'clock. [*family as one unit: singular verb*]

That committee makes the policy decisions. [*committee as a unit: singular verb*]

My family *were* all born in the United States. [*individual family members: plural verb*]

By their nature, indefinite pronouns cause writers trouble when it comes to agreement. Often they can be used as both singular and plural, and some sound plural but are considered grammatically singular. Here is a list of pronouns that are singular in meaning and thus take singular verbs:

another	each	everything	no one	somebody
anybody	either	much	nothing	someone
anyone	everybody	neither	one	something
anything	everyone	nobody	other	

EXAMPLES

Neither of the children *enjoys* broccoli. [Of the children *is a prepositional phrase; therefore,* children *cannot function as the grammatical subject of* enjoys.]

Another of the Barlows *enters* school next year.

Something about his voice and delivery *seems* particularly convincing.

Other indefinite pronouns are always plural. These include *both, few, many, others,* and *several.*

Several of the graduates take vacations after their graduation ceremony. [*Several is plural, hence the plural verb* take.]

Still other indefinite pronouns—*all, any, enough, more, most, none,* and *some*—are singular when referring to uncountable quantities and plural when referring to countable quantities.

All of this spilled flour *makes* quite a mess. [*Flour cannot be counted; thus,* all *is considered singular.*]

All of those potholes *make* the alley a dangerous place to drive. [*Potholes can be counted; thus,* all *is considered plural.*]

Most of the votes *were cast* for Cal Henry. [*Votes can be counted; thus* most *is considered plural.*]

By 10:30, *none* of the eggnog *was left* in the bowl. [*Eggnog cannot be counted; thus,* none *is considered singular.*]

If indefinite pronouns still seem difficult, try inserting a third person pronoun after the prepositional phrase. Your choice of personal pronoun will help you determine whether the indefinite pronoun is singular or plural:

> All of this spilled flour [it] makes quite a mess.
>
> All of those potholes [they] make the alley a dangerous place to drive.
>
> Most of the votes [they] were cast for Cal Henry.
>
> By 10:30, none of the eggnog [it] was left in the bowl.

Turn now to Assignment 9B at the end of this chapter for practice with collective-noun and indefinite-pronoun subject–verb agreement.

Making Verbs Agree with Relative-Pronoun Subjects 9f

So far, the discussion of subject-verb agreement has focused mostly on simple sentences without dependent clauses. Now it is time to shift attention to dependent clauses, especially ones that are introduced by relative pronouns (*who, which,* or *that.*) Often (though not always) these relative pronouns act as subjects of the clauses they introduce.

Notice, first, that by themselves, relative pronouns are neither singular nor plural; the singular form of *who* is no different from the plural form. Thus writers must determine what the pronoun refers to in order to decide whether the verb should be singular or plural.

- Relative pronouns (*who, which, that*) used as subjects of dependent clauses take the same verb form as their antecedents, the independent clause subjects to which they refer.

EXAMPLES

> Writers who start early are likely to be successful. [*In the clause* who start early, *the subject is* who. *Since* who *refers to the plural word* writers, *the verb* start *is also plural.*]
>
> The writer who starts early is likely to be successful. [*Now* who *refers to the singular word* writer; *thus, the verb* starts *is also singular.*]
>
> Cups that hold coffee are often made of styrofoam. [*Here the dependent clause is* that hold coffee. *Since* that *acts as the subject of this clause and since it refers to the plural word* cups, *the verb* hold *takes the plural form.*]

Note that relative pronouns do not always act as the subjects of the clauses they introduce. In the sentence *The books that she wants arrive tomorrow,* for example, the relative pronoun *that* introduces the dependent clause *that she wants.* Since the subject of this clause is *she,* the verb *wants* agrees with *she* rather than with *books.* Also, when the phrase *one of* precedes the relative pronoun, take special care to determine whether the relative pronoun refers to *one* or another word. Consider these two examples:

> A. Christopher is one of those students who <u>meet</u>/meets every obligation.
>
> B. Christopher is the only one of those students who meet/<u>meets</u> every obligation.

The differences between these two sentences are subtle but important. In example A, the sentence implies that several students meet every obligation, and Christopher is one of them. In example B, the sentence quite specifically indicates that Christopher is the only student who meets every obligation. In example A, *who* refers to *students;* the verb is therefore also plural—*(students) who meet.* In example B, *who* refers to *one;* the verb is therefore also singular—*(one) who meets.*

EXERCISE 9.2 MAKING VERBS AGREE WITH RELATIVE-PRONOUN SUBJECTS

Underline the correct verb form in each of the following sentences. In each case, be ready to explain your choice.

EXAMPLE

> Tom is one of those dogs that <u>bark</u>/barks at bees or cars or the neighbor's radio. [*Many dogs bark; Tom is just one of them.*]

1. Weeks that is/are as rainy as this one make me sleepy.

2. She will ask one of the students who arrive/arrives early to help her distribute the new assignment.

3. The Gary Larson cartoons that you like/likes are posted on the bulletin board.

4. The mayor says that decisions that affect/affects us all should be decided by the city council rather than by the city manager.

5. One of the contestants who enter/enters will win a trip for two to Key West, Florida.

Making Linking Verbs Agree with Their Subjects |9g|

Here writers need only remember that verbs agree with their *subjects* and not with the complements that describe or rename those subjects.

EXAMPLES

> Her favorite breakfast is bagels and cream cheese. [*subject,* breakfast, *is singular; hence, singular verb,* is]

The committee's preference is soft drinks rather than alcoholic ones. [*subject, preference, is singular; hence, singular verb, is*]

Making Verbs Agree with Subjects That Are Plural in Form but Singular in Meaning 19h1

Words like *gymnastics, aesthetics, news,* and *politics* end in *-s* and so look plural; however, their meaning is singular. When used as subjects, such words take singular verbs.

Politics is a human constant, like death and taxes. [*politics as a human activity*]

Statistics remains a mystery to most of us. [*statistics as a mathematical science*]

Note that some of these words can be used in either a singular or a plural sense. In such cases, verb agreement depends on the meaning of the sentence.

The statistics were nonsignificant. [*statistics as numbers*]

In addition, titles of works or words named as words always take singular verbs even if those titles or words are themselves plural.

Concerns is a synonym for *worries.*

The Canterbury Tales is widely regarded as a masterpiece of poetic storytelling.

Making Verbs Agree with Subjects That Follow Them 19i1

In most English sentences, the subject precedes the verb. Occasionally, writers will change this word order to emphasize the subject (by placing it last) or to ask questions. Whenever the customary word order has been changed, remember to make sure that the verb still agrees with the subject.

| verb | | compound subject | |

Among his favorite positions were catcher and third baseman.

(The more normal word order would be *Catcher and third baseman were among his favorite positions.*)

| verb | | subject |

Near her teddy bears is a catcher's mitt.

(The more normal order here would be *A catcher's mitt is near her teddy bears.* Notice that the "normal" word order reduces the impact of this sentence.)

verb   subject
   Is   a duckbilled platypus a mammal?

(As a declarative sentence, the word order would be: *A duckbilled platypus is a mammal.*)

Writers working on rough drafts also commonly use another kind of sentence inversion. These sentences typically begin with *there,* followed by a form of the verb *be.* In such cases, the subject follows the verb. *There* never acts as the subject of a sentence.

There are many Vietnam veterans who are still haunted by the war experience. [*The verb* are *agrees with the subject* veterans.]

Stylistic note: Sentences beginning with *there are* bury their most important content in dependent clauses. A more forceful wording would be *The war experience still haunts many Vietnam veterans.*

EXERCISE 9.3 CHECKING SUBJECT-VERB AGREEMENT

Assume that the following paragraph is taken from a persuasive essay. Read the paragraph carefully, and underline the verbs. If a verb does not agree with its subject, cross out the verb and write the correct form above it. You may need to review earlier sections of this chapter. The first two verbs have been underlined for you.

Besides harming their own bodies, smokers also <u>endanger</u> the good health of people around them. Cigarette smoke, either from a smoker's exhalation or straight from the cigarette, <u>contain</u> carbon monoxide, a highly poisonous gas. Nobody appreciate breathing in poisonous gas. And it is not just the health factors that keeps people away from smokers. Even nonsmokers who do not know about carbon monoxide is usually bothered by the smoke because it makes breathing difficult. In addition, a lot of smoke in closed rooms are often irritating to the eyes. Many people is also disgusted when they smells a smoker's clothes or sees the yellow nicotine stains on a smoker's front teeth. Finally, not too many people enjoy kissing somebody whose mouth taste like an ashtray.

Turn now to Assignment 9C at the end of this chapter for more practice with subject-verb agreement.

PRONOUN-ANTECEDENT AGREEMENT

Denied the use of pronouns, writers would have to use the same nouns over and over; that would make for dull repetition. Fortunately, we can use pronouns. But we do need to be careful that every time we do so, readers understand the pronoun's antecedent. The antecedent is simply the noun to which the pronoun refers or which it replaces. Writers must make sure that both noun and pronoun agree in *gender, number,* and *person.*

EXAMPLE

The rain forced Melissa to leave her bicycle at home. [*The pronoun* her *refers to* Melissa. *The gender is feminine; the number is singular; the person is third.*]

➤ *Student Writing Error 16: Lack of Pronoun-Antecedent Agreement*

Many cases of pronoun-antecedent agreement are easy to achieve, and we may manage that agreement without giving it a thought. But some special cases often prove confusing and can give even experienced writers some difficulty. Let us look at these cases now.

Making Pronouns Agree with Compound or Collective-Noun Antecedents   19j, 9k l

Compound antecedents joined by *and* usually require plural pronouns.

EXAMPLE

It was such a hot afternoon that Beth and Jane left their coats at school. [Their *refers to* Beth and Jane.]

However, note two exceptions:

1. If a compound antecedent follows *each* or *every,* the indefinite pronoun acts as the antecedent, and the following pronoun is singular.

EXAMPLES

> Each undergrad and grad student carries his or her own student ID. [His or her *refers to the singular pronoun* each.]

> Every mother and daughter should fill out her own questionnaire. [Her *refers to the singular pronoun* every.]

2. If a compound antecedent joined by *and* refers to a single thing or person, the following pronoun is singular.

EXAMPLE

> This writer and student has achieved his success through discipline and diligence. [His *refers to one person,* this writer and student.]

- When two or more antecedents are connected by *or* or *nor,* the pronoun should agree with the part of the antecedent closest to it.

EXAMPLES

> Either one or several chapters will arrive in their folders. [*pronoun* their *agrees with* chapters]

> Neither the suitcase nor the golf clubs were recovered in their original condition. [*pronoun* their *agrees with* clubs]

(Note: In the second example, the plural noun antecedent *clubs* follows the singular noun antecedent *suitcase.* This reflects the common practice of putting the plural antecedent second, nearer the verb.)

Compound antecedents of different genders can pose problems for writers. Consider this sentence: *Either Dave or Holly will bring _____ own guitar.* What pronoun should go in the blank? Using *her* would seem to eliminate Dave; using *his* would seem to eliminate Holly. Using *their* would imply that they own one guitar jointly, and perhaps they do. But if the sentence means to indicate that both Dave and Holly own separate guitars, no single pronoun will fit in that blank. The best solution here is to rewrite the sentence: *Either Dave will bring his guitar or Holly will bring hers.*

- Collective nouns with singular meanings take singular pronouns; collective nouns with plural meanings take plural nouns.

When you are referring to a group as a single unit, use the singular pronoun. When you are referring to individual members of that group, use the plural pronoun. (Remember, collective nouns are nouns like *army, committee, family,* and *team.*)

EXAMPLES

The crowd erupted with applause as it demanded an encore. [Crowd *as a single unit takes the singular pronoun* it.]

After the encore, the crowd drifted away to their cars. [Crowd *focusing on its members is plural in meaning and takes the plural pronoun* their.]

Turn now to Assignment 9D at the end of this chapter for practice with pronoun-noun agreement.

Making Pronouns Agree with Indefinite-Pronoun Antecedents　|9|*l*|

If you have already worked through Section 9e of this chapter, you may recall that indefinite pronouns may be always singular (*anybody, each,* and *someone* are examples), always plural (*many, few, several*), or either singular or plural depending on context (*all, more, some*). Pronouns referring to indefinite pronoun antecedents must agree in number with their antecedents. See the examples that follow.

Each of the women in the bridal party wore a dress that *she* herself made. [Each *is the singular pronoun subject of this sentence.* She *is singular and refers to* each.]

Many of the visiting swimmers won *their* races. [Many *is a plural indefinite pronoun;* their *is also plural and refers to* many.]

All of the remaining sale items should be returned to *their* original storeroom locations. [*Since* all *refers to* items, *it is considered plural; hence, the plural pronoun* their.]

Not *all* of the recovered oil could be cleansed of *its* impurities. [*Here* all *refers to an uncountable quantity,* oil; *hence,* all *is considered singular.* Its, *a singular pronoun, refers to* all.]

Avoiding Sexist Pronoun Usage　|9*m*|

Indefinite pronouns such as those discussed in the preceding section often present problems of sexist usage. Consider this example:

An usher stood at the front of the movie theater and said, "If *anyone* here is a doctor, would *he* please come forward."

This sentence uses what grammarians call *the generic he* to refer to people of either sex. Though grammatically acceptable, today this usage is often criticized because it seems to exclude half of the human race. The best remedy for sexist usage is rewording:

"If *anyone* here is a doctor, would *he* or *she* please come forward."

"Will anyone who is a doctor please come forward."

Sometimes a sentence originally phrased in the singular can be rephrased in the plural, thereby allowing the use of the pronoun *they*. Thus, a sentence like *Each student must do his own homework* becomes *All students must do their own homework.*

Sometimes you will simply not know the gender of a pronoun antecedent. Consider this sentence:

Someone from the main office left *their* coat on the back of this chair.

Though the sentence avoids sexism, it inaccurately connects a singular antecedent, *someone,* with a plural pronoun, *their.* Informally, we often speak using this construction, but it should be avoided in formal or academic writing. The sentence can be revised in at least two ways:

Someone from the main office left a coat on the back of this chair.

Someone from the main office left his or her coat on the back of this chair.

Assignment 9E at the end of the chapter provides more practice in making pronouns agree with indefinite pronouns and avoiding sexist usage.

EXERCISE 9.4 MAINTAINING ACCURATE AGREEMENT

Write a paragraph (or more) that describes your ideal dinner menu. Make sure that your final version includes discussion of at least three courses of food (main course, salad, and dessert, for example). Make readers taste, see, and smell the food you describe. Try to make their mouths water.

Use your own paper for the paragraph. When you have written it, make a list showing all subjects and their verbs and all pronouns and their antecedents for each of the first five sentences of your paragraph. Make sure that all of your subjects agree with their verbs and that all of your pronouns agree with their antecedents. If any disagree, correct them and work your corrections into the final paragraph you turn in to your instructor.

SAMPLE OPENING SENTENCE

My ideal dinner begins with a plate of fresh vegetables: baby carrots that were picked that morning, washed radishes with their tops still on, sliced green pepper, and half a dozen thin rounds of cucumber.

all subjects and their verbs: *dinner/begins, that (referring to carrots)/were picked*

all pronouns and their antecedents: *that/carrots, their/radishes*

ASSIGNMENT 9A MAINTAINING AGREEMENT WITH COMPOUND SUBJECTS

Read the following sentences. Circle each subject and underline each verb. If subjects and verbs agree, write *C* on the lines. If they do not, write a corrected version.

EXAMPLE   Neither the (lawyer) nor her (clients) shows any worries about winning the case.

    Neither the lawyer nor her clients show any worries about winning the case.

1. Neither the witnesses nor the police officers was able to identify the hit-and-run

driver positively. _____

_____

2. Neither the witnesses nor the police officer were able to identify the hit-and-run

driver positively. _____

_____

3. Neither the car nor its occupants were seriously harmed. _____

_____

4. Either you or the other driver were responsible for the accident. _____

_____

5. Either the insurance company or you is going to pay for repairs. _____

_____

Below you are provided with compound subjects and base-form verbs. Use these to write a sentence in the present tense, taking particular care that subjects and verbs agree.

EXAMPLE   subject: *budding flowers and freshly cut lawns*   verb: *remind*
          Budding flowers and freshly cut lawns remind me of spring.

6. subject: *Barbara and Chris*   verb: *live* _____

_____

7. subject: *papers and midterms*   verb: *challenge* _____

_____

8. subject: *each paper and midterm*   verb: *become* _____

_____

9. subject: *my sister and confidante*   verb: *visit* _____

_____

ASSIGNMENT 9B   MAINTAINING VERB AGREEMENT WITH COLLECTIVE-NOUN OR INDEFINITE-PRONOUN SUBJECTS

In each sentence below, circle the subject and underline the main verb. Indicate whether the subject is a collective noun or an indefinite pronoun. If the subject and verb agree, write *C* on the lines that follow; if the subject and verb do not agree, rewrite the sentence so that the verb agrees with its subject.

EXAMPLE   (None) of the employees is able to substitute for you on Friday.
   Subject is an indefinite pronoun.
   None of the employees are able to substitute for you on Friday.

1. The group that rafts the Colorado River go home deeply affected by the experi-

ence. *Subject is* _____.

_____

2. Neither of these auditioners are right for the part.

Subject is _____.

_____

3. Most of those who commute use the same form of transportation every day.

Subject is _____.

_____

4. That band play a spirited rendition of "Stars and Stripes Forever."

Subject is _____.

_____

5. Some of this painting is absolutely brilliant.   *Subject is* _____.

_____

ASSIGNMENT 9C REVIEWING SUBJECT-VERB AGREEMENT

Read each sentence below. If all subjects and verbs agree, write *C* on the lines. If there are errors of agreement, rewrite the sentence on the lines provided.

1. The hands of the clock says 3:15.

   _____

2. Given her recent experience, she now agrees that alcohol is a dangerous drug.

   _____

   _____

3. Whenever it rain, I wears a coat.

   _____

4. The trains arrive daily at 2:30 and at 5:00.

   _____

5. The telephone operator who told me the arrival times were unnecessarily rude.

   _____

   _____

6. Among the great Indian chiefs are Chief Joseph of the Nez Percé.

   _____

   _____

7. One of their great hopes in the last several years have been a trip to Scotland.

   _____

   _____

8. The glaucous gull and the western gull is often found inland during the stormy winter months.

   _____

   _____

9. Rum and Coke combines to make a popular alcoholic drink.

   _____

10. Pie and ice cream have always been our favorite dessert.

_____

11. Each Saturday and Sunday morning is dedicated to sleeping late.

_____

12. Tom and Liz, who also happens to be married to each other, each wears glasses.

_____

_____

13. Neither a graphic artist nor three proofreaders has been able to improve this

poster. _____

_____

14. Either the camp leaders or the campers themselves are required to clean the mess

hall after each meal. _____

_____

15. The team is voting for team captain now.

_____

16. The presidential committee differ on the question of increased Medicare benefits.

_____

_____

17. Good news often go unreported.

_____

18. Anybody taller than six feet know it can be difficult to find clothes that fits.

_____

_____

19. It is mathematics that cause me the most trouble in college.

_____

20. The end of those last few college weeks arrives with a strange mixture of gladness

and sorrow. _____

_____

ASSIGNMENT 9D MAKING PRONOUNS AGREE WITH COMPOUND OR COLLECTIVE-NOUN ANTECEDENTS

Identify the pronouns and their antecedents in each of the sentences below. If the pronouns are used inaccurately, rewrite the sentence to correct the errors. If the sentence is correct, write _C_ on the lines provided.

EXAMPLES   Whenever Leigh and Jack go out, Shelly stays with their children.
Pronouns/antecedents: their/Leigh and Jack
C

The goat and the two sheep have cropped that pasture right down to their roots.
Pronouns/antecedents: their/pasture
The goat and the two sheep have cropped that pasture right down to its roots.

1. Deer and bobcat populations stabilized once its habitats were preserved.

Pronouns/antecedents: _____

2. By August, each gardener and homeowner is proud of their crop of squash.

Pronouns/antecedents: _____

3. Tonight either Tom or Sally will have to take the projector home in his car.

Pronouns/antecedents: _____

4. Nobody saw him, but the Anderson brothers washed Mrs. Wright's car.

Pronouns/antecedents: _____

5. Troop 381 has decided that it will take separate cars to camp and meet by the mess

hall at noon.   *Pronouns/antecedents:* _____

6. The committee has unanimously agreed to forward its recommendations.

Pronouns/antecedents: _____

7. Jenny or she called their parents with the good news.

Pronouns/antecedents: _____

_____

ASSIGNMENT 9E   **MAKING PRONOUNS AGREE WITH**
INDEFINITE PRONOUNS AND AVOIDING SEXIST USAGE

Some of the following sentences use pronouns that unnecessarily identify the gender of an antecedent and thereby seem to exclude one sex. Some sentences may also contain errors of agreement between pronouns and indefinite-pronoun antecedents. In either case, circle the incorrect or sexist pronoun and write the correct one above it. If you need to alter the antecedent, feel free to do so. If the sentence does not need revision, write a *C* next to it.

EXAMPLES
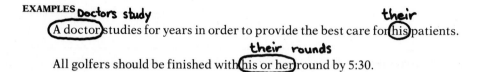

Doctors study
(A doctor) studies for years in order to provide the best care for (his) patients. *their*

their rounds
All golfers should be finished with (his or her) round by 5:30.

1. Some of those trees lose their leaves quite early in the fall.

2. Few of the postal workers finished his shift early that day.

3. A woman must consider her values and priorities before taking a new job, just as a

man must consider his.

4. Go find a nurse and ask her for a pain pill.

5. More of our first-year students change his or her majors than did so five years ago.

6. Anybody who has finished the course should receive his certificate in two weeks.

7. During the 1960s, anyone in college had to make their own decision about the

Vietnam War.

10

Using Adjectives and Adverbs

Writers use adjectives and adverbs to describe, limit, qualify, or specify. Without such modifiers, we would find it hard to say precisely what we want to say: instead of "medium rare steak," it would be just "steak"; instead of "fresh, New England–style clam chowder," it would be just "chowder." Without adjectives and adverbs, we'd not be able to do justice to the fascinating and necessary details of our lives. (Note: This chapter does not discuss verbals used as adjectives or adverbs, nor does it discuss prepositional phrases functioning as adjectives or adverbs. For discussion of these matters, see Chapter 6.)

Distinguishing Adjectives from Adverbs |10a|

Adjectives can modify nouns (*blue* marble, *desperate* client, *sleazy* proposal) and pronouns (*Stylish* and *confident,* he arrived for the trial). Some adjectives are formed by adding endings to nouns or verbs. These endings include -*al, -ive, -ish, -able, -less,* and -*ful*:

form (noun)	formal (adjective)
act (noun or verb)	active (adjective)
style (noun)	stylish (adjective)
comfort (noun)	comfortable (adjective)
rest (noun or verb)	restless (adjective)
rest (noun or verb)	restful (adjective)

Some adjectives are formed by adding the -*ly* ending (as in *lively, earthly, ghostly*). This is, however, an uncommon way to form adjectives. Regardless of how they are formed, adjectives usually answer one of these questions: *which, how many,* or *what kind*?

Adverbs modify verbs, adjectives, and other adverbs:

The cat *patiently* waited for its dinner. [*modifies verb* waited]

Phil waited for an *especially* hungry fish to take the bait. [*modifies adjective* hungry]

After dinner, the cat rested *quite* comfortably on the sofa. [*modifies adverb* comfortably]

Occasionally, adverbs modify whole clauses, as in this sentence: *Garcia said that, regrettably, he would be late.* Here, *regrettably* modifies the clause *he would be late.*

As you can see, adding *-ly* to adjectives is the most common way of forming adverbs. However, there are also quite a number of adverbs (*very* and *quite,* for example) that do not have the *-ly* ending. Other examples of these are *here, fast, there, now, then, often, soon,* and *late.* Regardless of how they are formed, adverbs usually answer one of these questions: *how, when, where,* or *to what extent*?

REVIEW

- Adjectives modify nouns or pronouns.
- Adverbs modify verbs, adjectives, other adverbs, or (occasionally) entire clauses.

EXERCISE 10.1 WRITING WITH ADJECTIVES AND ADVERBS

Use the following guidelines to help you write a paragraph, on your own paper, about a summer activity that you enjoy.

1. Identify three summertime activities you enjoy.

2. Think carefully about each of the activities you identified. Which of these three would be easiest to write about in just one paragraph?

3. What specific details about this activity will you need to include? Write phrases to answer this question, not sentences.

4. Now draft your paragraph, and lay the draft aside for a time.

5. Reread and revise your draft paragraph so that its descriptions are lively and accurate, making a special point to add more adjectives and adverbs in order to achieve this.

6. Now identify five adjectives and five adverbs from your paragraph. Copy the adjectives and adverbs on your paper below your paragraph. Indicate each word that each adjective or adverb modifies (for example, "*accurately,* an adverb modifying identify"). When you are finished, hand in your paragraph followed by the ten words identified as either adjectives or adverbs.

Using Adjectives and Adverbs after Linking Verbs |10b|

As you have seen, a word may often have both an adverbial and an adjectival form. Consider *bright,* for example. As written here, *bright* is an adjective. Adding *-ly* makes the adverb *brightly.* Partly because informal speech often does not distinguish between these two forms, writers sometimes have trouble deciding which form to use in a given sentence. The only certain way to correctly choose between *bright* and *brightly* is to determine the part of speech of the word being described. If the word is a noun or a pronoun, the modifier must be an adjective, *bright.* If the word (or phrase or clause) functions as a verb, adjective, or adverb, the modifier must be an adverb, *brightly.*

> The sun shone *brightly* through the window. [*adverb modifies the action verb* shone]
>
> The bright sun shone through the window. [*adjective modifies the noun subject* sun]

As we pointed out earlier, adverbs can often change position in a sentence without destroying its meaning.

> The sun shone *brightly* through the window.
>
> The sun shone through the window *brightly.*

Adjectives, by contrast, must usually either precede closely the nouns or pronouns they modify (*rainy* morning, *yellow* paper, and so on) or follow linking verbs. If they follow linking verbs, they are called predicate adjectives. Recall that linking verbs are various forms of the verb *be* (*is, are, was, were, will be,* and so on), as well as verbs like *look, sound, become, appear, taste, feel, seem, smell, remain,* and *prove.* In general, if you can replace a verb with some form of *be* without substantially changing the sentence meaning, the verb is probably a linking verb. Consider the sentence *The doughnuts tasted delicious.* Is the verb *tasted* a linking verb? If we substitute a past plural form of *be,* we get this sentence: *The doughnuts were delicious.* The test works; *tasted* functions here as a linking verb.

We have pursued this question because we need to know whether the word *delicious* should be an adjective or whether it should be the adverbial form *deliciously.* The rule is simple:

- Modifiers following a linking verb modify the sentence subject and must therefore be adjectives.

Here are two more examples:

CORRECT After three hours in a warm keg, the beer tastes flat.

INCORRECT After three hours in a warm keg, the beer tastes flatly.

CORRECT Sorenson felt angry that the elevator was broken again.

INCORRECT Sorenson felt angrily that the elevator was broken again.

Distinguishing between *Good* and *Well, Bad* and *Badly, Real* and *Really* |10c|

These adjectives and adverbs can cause writers trouble because common speech often blurs the distinctions between them. If you are writing dialogue or quoting someone speaking informally, you may also blur those distinctions. But if you are writing in a formal or academic setting, you should be careful to observe the distinctions outlined here.

- *Good, bad, well,* and *real* are adjectives and may follow linking verbs. (Note that *well* here means "in good health.")

  Our June weather has been *good.* [*Good describes the subject,* weather.]

  This leftover tuna smells *bad.* [*Bad describes the subject,* tuna.]

  After treatment, the patient felt *well* again. [Well *describes the subject,* patient.]

  That pearl looks *real.* [*Real describes the subject,* pearl.]

Remember that some linking verbs can also act as action verbs, as in *I looked really carefully at the fine print.* Here *looked* functions as an action verb; *carefully* is an adverb modifying *looked; really* is an adverb modifying *carefully.*

- *Well* may also function as an adverb to modify a verb, an adjective, or another adverb. (Note that when functioning as an adverb, *well* has nothing to do with health.)

  A chef for over eight years, she cooks *well.* [*Well describes how she cooks.*]

- *Badly* and *really* are adverbs and should be used to modify verbs, adjectives, or other adverbs.

  A chef for over eight years, she cooks *really* well. [Really *modifies the adverb* well.]

  They bungled that first experiment *badly.* [Badly *modifies the verb* bungled.]

EXERCISE 10.2 USING *GOOD, WELL, BAD, BADLY, REAL,* AND *REALLY*

Underline the correct adjective or adverb in each of the following sentences. Be ready to explain your choices.

EXAMPLE

A chef for over eight years, she cooks good/<u>well</u>.

1. Amanda and Henry look good/well in their tango outfits.
2. A strong introduction is real/really important in a technical report.
3. The climbers hope the weather will be good/well for tomorrow's ascent.
4. After a weekend of rest, Dan looked good/well again.
5. He painted that fence bad/badly.
6. Raising the sea chest proved real/really difficult for the divers.
7. The appraisers claimed that this desk is a real/really antique.
8. After sitting out all night on the counter, the pizza tasted bad/badly.

Turn now to Assignment 10A at the end of this chapter for more practice with adjectives and adverbs.

Using Comparative and Superlative Forms |10d|

Most adjectives and adverbs have three degree forms. The *positive* form is the simple dictionary form:

The mouse is a *small* mammal.

Alyce arrived *early*.

The *comparative* form is made either by adding the ending *-er* or by adding the intensifier *less* or *more*. The comparative form literally compares the modified thing with some other thing:

The mouse is *smaller* than the hedgehog. [*comparative form of the adjective* small]

Hank arrived *earlier*. [*comparative form of the adverb* early]

The *superlative* form is made by adding the ending *-est* or by adding the intensifier *most* or *least*. The superlative form compares the modified thing with at least two others and declares it to be the most extreme:

Of the mouse, the hedgehog, and the wildebeest, the mouse is the *smallest*. [*superlative form of the adjective* small]

Josie arrived *earliest*. [*superlative form of the adverb* early]

How do you know when to add an ending (*-er* or *-est*) and when to use an intensifier (*more, most, less, least*)? *-Er* and *-est* are used for one- and two-syllable adjectives. Longer adjectives and most adverbs use the intensifiers (*more/less, most/least*). Sometimes intensifiers are also used with the shorter adjectives; the effect in these cases is greater emphasis and formality.

Positive Form	*Comparative Form*	*Superlative Form*
tall	taller	tallest
imposing	more imposing	most imposing
cluttered	less cluttered	least cluttered

If you are not sure whether a particular adjective or adverb has *-er* and *-est* forms, look up the positive form in a college dictionary. If the *-er* and *-est* forms exist, they will be listed following the positive form.

- When comparing two things, use the comparative degree.

When speaking, informally, we are often tempted to use the superlative; however formal or academic writing normally requires the correct comparative form.

CORRECT The painting is taller than I am. [*comparison of two things: a painting's height and the speaker's height*]

INCORRECT Of woodworking and painting, painting is the most difficult. [*comparison of two things: the difficulty of painting and the difficulty of woodworking*]

CORRECT Of woodworking and painting, painting is the more difficult.

- Use the superlative degree when comparing three or more things and to indicate that the modified word is the most extreme—the largest or smallest, best or worst, most intense or least intense—of those things.

Of the three dogs we know, we like Tom the *best*.

My personal opinion is that *A Farewell to Arms* is Hemingway's *best* novel. [Hemingway wrote more than two novels.]

Now consider this example:

Elisha was least interested in art history and most interested in mathematical group theory.

Are only two things being compared here? If so, the example is incorrect as given. If Elisha is interested in several things, the sentence is technically correct as written; it is also open to misinterpretation by readers. Solution? Rewrite the sentence to clarify the terms of the comparison.

> Of all her college courses, Elisha was least interested in art history and most interested in mathematical group theory.

> Of her two courses that term, Elisha was less interested in art history and more interested in mathematical group theory.

EXERCISE 10.3 USING COMPARATIVE AND SUPERLATIVE FORMS

The sentences that follow contain various kinds of comparisons. In each case, determine what is being compared and whether or not the correct form of adjective or adverb has been used. If the sentence is correct as written, write *C* in the space after the sentence. If the sentence is incorrect as written, put *I* in the space, underline the incorrect form, and write in the correct form.

EXAMPLE   *thicker*

Compared to Pizza Gallery's crust, the Downtowner's was <u>thickest</u>. __I__

1. Three local pizza restaurants—Dumbo's, Pizza Gallery, and the Downtowner— compete for the larger share of the area's pizza business. _____

2. Of the three restaurants, only two, Dumbo's and Pizza Gallery, provide home delivery, with Dumbo's delivery time being the slowest. _____

3. Our tests show that a Dumbo's pizza took, on the average, six minutes longer to arrive than one from Pizza Gallery. _____

4. All three restaurants offered vegetarian pizzas, with the Downtowner having the fancier, most exciting version. _____

5. Overall, the biggest difference among these three restaurants was in atmosphere: the judges unanimously ruled that Dumbo's fantasyland theme made it the more enjoyable place to sit. _____

Recognizing Irregular Forms |10d1|

Note the following irregular forms for some commonly used adjectives and adverbs.

Positive	Comparative	Superlative
good	better	best
well	better	best
bad	worse	worst
ill	worse	worst
little [quantity]	less	least
little [size]	littler	littlest
many	more	most
some	more	most
much	more	most

As you can see, many comparative and superlative forms overlap. Thus, it is accurate to write *Graf played better today than she played yesterday* (*better* here functions as an adverb modifying the verb *played*), and it is also accurate to say *She feels better today than she did yesterday* (*better* here functions as a predicate adjective following the linking verb *feels* and modifying the subject *she*).

Selecting Adjectives and Adverbs When Using Comparative Forms |10d2|

REVIEW

- Adjectives modify nouns or pronouns.
- Adverbs modify verbs, adjectives, or other adverbs.

When we talk, we frequently blur the distinction between comparative adverbs and comparative adjectives. Thus, we might say, "I finished this race easier than the last one." In that sentence, *easier* is an adjective incorrectly modifying the verb *finished*. Writers should preserve the adjective-adverb distinction, making the sentence read, "I finished this race more easily than I finished the last one."

Avoiding Double Comparatives or Superlatives |10d3|

Do not use an intensifier with an *-er* or *-est* ending.

INCORRECT Jack is more smarter than I am. [*double comparative*]

CORRECT Jack is smarter than I am.

INCORRECT Helen is the most quietest student in the class. [*double superlative*]

CORRECT Helen is the quietest student in the class. [*double superlative*]

Making Comparisons Complete |10d4|

In the shared context of everyday speech, we may often make ourselves clear without completing the second half of a comparison. For example, if you and your spouse are shopping for a used car, one of you might well walk up to the fourth car you've looked at and say, "This looks better to me." Such statements are not effective in writing. The reader can only wonder, "Better than what?" The context of your shared experience with the earlier three cars would probably make that comparison clear. But in formal or academic writing (or whenever a reader or listener does not share your experience), the audience can easily misunderstand. Thus, it is important to make the terms of your comparisons absolutely straightforward.

INCORRECT   When considering capital punishment, some people argue that its deterrent effect is more important. [*more important than what?*]

CORRECT   When considering capital punishment, some people argue that its deterrent effect is more important than the moral argument against the taking of human life.

Turn now to Assignment 10B at the end of this chapter for practice with comparative and superlative forms.

ASSIGNMENT 10A IDENTIFYING AND CORRECTING ADJECTIVE-ADVERB ERRORS

Read the paragraph below. There are several errors in the usage of adverbs and adjectives. Underline those errors, and write in the correct forms. The first error has been underlined and corrected for you.

That was our tennis summer. I remember so *clearly* <u>clear</u> that the days were hot and the skies always looked cloudlessly. If the wind blew, it blew only occasional and rare. Two days after we opened a new can of balls, they'd bounce sluggish. Maybe on the first bounce they'd rise to our knees weary. Maybe they'd just lie there stupid like jellyfish. Or maybe it was we who felt tiredly. Even so, we played real good tennis. We played fierce and crazily in the three o'clock sun. That was the summer before the draft took any of us, before any of us went happy to college, before any really goodbyes. That was our tennis summer.

ASSIGNMENT 10B USING COMPARATIVE AND SUPERLATIVE FORMS

In each case below, you are given an adjective or an adverb and a specified form. Write a sentence using the specified form correctly. Make sure that your sentences distinguish appropriately between adjectives and adverbs and that the terms of any comparisons are complete.

EXAMPLES

blue, superlative form
The sky this afternoon is the bluest that I've ever seen.
sleepy, comparative form
I'm sleepier today than I was yesterday.

1. *serious*, comparative form

_____

_____

2. *seriously*, superlative form

_____

_____

3. *confusing,* comparative form

_____

_____

4. *bad,* superlative form

_____

_____

5. *well,* superlative form

_____

_____

6. *ill,* comparative form

_____

_____

7. *many,* superlative form

_____

_____

8. *hungry,* comparative form

_____

_____

9. *difficult,* comparative form

_____

_____

10. *rewarding,* superlative form

_____

_____

PART 3

Sentences: Making Conventional Choices

These questions are designed to help you, the student, decide what you need to study. (Answers are found at the back of the book.)

1. Are the pronouns in these sentences used correctly? Mark *yes* or *no*.

   a) My father asked Joe if he was needed at the store. _____

   b) During the concert, they made a lot of noise. _____

   c) In Shakespeare's *Macbeth*, he makes Macbeth's motivation clear. _____

   d) When Jack saw how much the repairs would cost, he vowed to junk the car. _____

2. Do these sentences contain any unnecessary or confusing shifts in person, number, tense, mood, subject, or voice? Mark *yes* or *no*.

   a) Everyone brought their favorite food to the class pot-luck banquet. _____

   b) Students should bring their identification cards to the library. _____

   c) To revise a paper, one should first read it yourself and then give it to someone else. _____

   d) We planned to go by bus, but then it was decided that the subway would be quicker. _____

3. Are these independent clauses correctly joined? Mark *yes* or *no*.

   a) The snow piled up, but we went to school anyway. _____

   b) Elizabeth did not like the music, she listened politely. _____

   c) My mother put the cake by an open window a bird landed on it. _____

   d) The door was closed; my brother came in anyway. _____

4. Do these examples contain sentence fragments? Mark *yes* or *no*.

   a) Some kinds of guitars sound better than others. _____

   b) I think we could get there in an hour. If we hurry. _____

5. Do these sentences use modifiers correctly? Mark *yes* or *no*.

   a) Created under conditions some might think impossible to survive, this anthology of Eskimo poems is a testament to the human spirit. _____

   b) After calling the doctor, the pills started to work. _____

   c) We will, if nothing else comes up, call our mother today. _____

6. Do these sentences have garbled grammatical structures? Mark *yes* or *no*.

   a) This book claims that in such large cities as New York and San Francisco, AIDS should be everyone's concern. _____

   b) Two days after the torrential rain, the earth seemed to come alive like never before the plants were so green. _____

   c) John owns many records, and CD player. _____

   d) Bart wanted chocolate, but Eileen orders vanilla chocolate chip, and they were all out anyway. _____

Maintaining Clear Pronoun Reference

➤ *Student Writing Error 2: Vague Pronoun Reference*

Chapter 5 discussed how you can use pronouns to help create paragraph coherence, and Chapter 7 focused on pronoun case. This chapter looks carefully at the important matter of pronoun reference. When used effectively, pronouns speed readers along; when used inaccurately or ineffectively, pronouns may actually stop the reading process by forcing readers to work backward to track down an unclear reference. Vague pronoun reference is the second most common error in student writing. This chapter should help you avoid it.

Matching Pronouns to Their Appropriate Antecedents |11a|

Sometimes writers inadvertently provide readers with two possible antecedents, as in this sentence: *Mary asked Cathy if she was responsible for the car accident.* Here, *she* could refer to Cathy or to Mary. As written, readers cannot tell for sure who may be responsible for the car accident. The writer knows the intended meaning, but readers are forced to guess.

To improve such a sentence, your first impulse may be to try to change a word or two to clarify the pronoun reference. However, this is not likely to work. On a piece of scratch paper, try to revise our sample sentence by changing just a word or two.

In most cases, a sentence like *Mary asked Cathy if she was responsible for the car accident* will need to be recast in order to clarify the pronoun reference. One solution would be to quote directly: *Mary asked Cathy, "Are you responsible for the car accident?"* or *Mary asked Cathy, "Am I responsible for the car accident?"* Here is another example:

UNCLEAR

> The drum and bugle corps accompanied the homecoming court, and Maggie thought they looked great.

REVISED

> Maggie thought the drum and bugle corps looked great accompanying the homecoming court.

Keeping Pronouns and Antecedents Close Together |11b|

Distancing pronouns from nouns also makes for difficult reading. Such separations usually force readers to stop and retrace the references. As a reader, you may remember instances of such frustration. When you discover this problem in your own prose, sometimes the best alternative is simply to repeat the original noun (thus eliminating the pronoun). If a pronoun does seem appropriate, make sure the pronoun and its antecedent are close together.

REMOTE REFERENCE

> What seems to unite the lives and careers of several seemingly disparate graduates might be called the concept of useful work. Mike B. served for two years in the Peace Corps and is now an obstetrician who spends an afternoon a week at a free clinic; Alison R. easily passed her CPA exams and now works mainly with nonprofit arts organizations. A physicist in college, Joanna K. now holds a management position in an engineering firm that specializes in the cleanup of toxic waste sites. *It* seems to unite *them* because, one way or another, their careers, while personally challenging and often monetarily rewarding, also acknowledge some obligation to society as a whole.

What does *it* refer to? If you backtrack far enough, you find that *it* refers to "the concept of useful work." You would know that only because the verb *unite* is repeated and thus serves as a pointer back to that first sentence. The most immediate referent for *them* is *toxic waste sites*—clearly not what the passage really means to say. Revising this example means repeating the original nouns.

REVISION FOR CLEARER REFERENCE

> What seems to unite the lives and careers of several seemingly disparate graduates might be called the concept of useful work. Mike B. served for two years in the Peace Corps and is now an obstetrician who spends an afternoon a week at a free clinic; Alison R. easily passed her CPA exams and now works mainly with nonprofit arts organizations. A physicist in college, Joanna K. now heads an engineering firm that specializes in the cleanup of toxic waste sites.

The concept of useful work seems to unite *these graduates* because, one way or another, their careers, while personally challenging and often monetarily rewarding, also acknowledge some obligation to society as a whole.

EXERCISE 11.1 IDENTIFYING AND REVISING CONFUSING PRONOUN USAGE

Many of the sentences that follow contain potentially confusing pronoun usage. Rewrite those sentences to clear up any such confusions. If the sentence is clear as written, write *C* on the lines.

EXAMPLE

Mary asked Cathy if she was responsible for the car accident.

REVISION

Mary asked Cathy, "Am I responsible for the car accident?"

1. During the 1988 presidential election campaign, the Dukakis-Bush debates forced him to articulate his positions.

_____

_____

2. The commission, the mayor, and the city manager agree that her management style must change.

_____

_____

3. Jack liked Alondra and was still technically going steady with Rayette; finally, he decided to ask her to the prom.

_____

_____

4. The union representative called me last night at home and asked me if I was ready to go on strike today; I told him I still wasn't sure.

_____

_____

5. When Barbara and Hank first met with the marriage counselor, he did not know how the session would go.

Checking for Troublesome Pronoun References 11c

Avoiding Vague *and* Ambiguous Use of It, This, That, *and* Which 11c1

In some situations, writers use the pronoun *this, that, which,* or *it* to refer not to a particular noun but rather to some concept or situation mentioned in an earlier clause, sentence, or paragraph. For example, look at the pronoun *that* as used in this sentence: *Grace felt tired after the racquetball game, and that is why she went to bed early.* The antecedent for *that* is not one noun. Instead, *that* refers to the entire clause *Grace felt tired after the racquetball game.*

This is but one example of **broad reference**. When carefully used, such broad reference presents few problems. However, broad reference can become problematic whenever there is the possibility for reader confusion. Writers should be particularly wary of starting sentences with *this* or *that.* Here is an example of such unclear use of broad reference:

UNCLEAR

For dinner that evening, two of us ate leftover tuna casserole, while the rest of us ate leftover salmon loaf. That must have made Jack sick. [*What does* that *refer to? Did Jack eat the tuna or the salmon loaf?*]

REVISED

For dinner that evening, two of us ate leftover tuna casserole, while the rest of us ate leftover salmon loaf. The tuna must have made Jack sick.

As a writer, you should be aware of how readers interpret references for clauses introduced by the relative pronouns *which* and *that.* The sentence *Jack drove his new truck to the dance, which his grandparents bought him* says literally that Jack's grandparents bought him a dance. Eliminating such confusion is easy: put the relative pronoun directly after the noun it modifies. Sometimes a sentence may need to be reworded: *Jack arrived at the dance driving the new truck, which his grandparents bought him.* Now *which* clearly refers to *truck.*

Finally, beware of beginning sentences with *it.* Such sentences are often unnecessarily wordy; they may also be unnecessarily vague.

WORDY

It says in the instructions that this knob adjusts the volume.

REVISED

The instructions say that this knob adjusts the volume.

WORDY

It is necessary that campers bring a sleeping bag for the overnight outing.

REVISED

Campers need to bring a sleeping bag for the overnight outing.

Turn now to Assignment 11B at the end of this chapter for practice with clear pronoun reference.

Using Who, Which, *and* That *Appropriately* |11c2|

Writers conventionally use *who, which,* and *that* in the following ways:

- *Who* refers to people and to animals with personalities or names.

EXAMPLES

Megan is the blonde girl *who* lives next door.

Charlie is the preschooler *who* likes to fly paper airplanes.

Our dog Tom is the one *who* scares the meter readers.

- *Which* refers to inanimate objects and to animals without personalities or names.

EXAMPLES

Dogs, *which* must be on leashes, are permitted in this park.

I lost my favorite mitt, *which* my father gave me on my last birthday.

- *That* can refer to animals and things as well as to anonymous persons or people treated collectively.

EXAMPLES

The beach house *that* my parents rented no longer exists.

The deer *that* has been feeding in the backyard appeared again last night.

People *that* drink and drive should be required to visit hospital emergency rooms.

Avoiding the Indefinite Use of You and They |11c3|

Sometimes, when speaking informally, we use pronouns to refer to nouns or modifiers that are implied, rather than mentioned directly. Consider this sentence: *During registration, they gave me the wrong forms.* In that sentence, *they* does not refer to any named people. Perhaps the writer doesn't know who gave out those wrong forms. The sentence should be revised to read *During registration, someone gave me the wrong forms* or *During registration, a person at the Biology Department table gave me the wrong forms.*

You is also sometimes used in this informal, vague way: *Whenever you go downtown after ten o'clock, you're taking your life in your hands.* Whom does *you* refer to? In the context of a conversation, the referent might be clear. But in academic or formal writing, clarity demands that the *you* be replaced with a more specific referent: *People who go downtown after ten o'clock risk harassment, assault, or worse.* As you can see, the informal, vague construction has been replaced by clearer phrasing; readers now know more precisely what this writer means.

The guideline here is simple: spell out your antecedents with specific nouns whenever you can.

UNCLEAR

We went to the Old World for a pint of Bellhaven and a wedge of shortbread, but they were having a concert, so we did not stay.

REVISED

We went to the Old World for a pint of Bellhaven and a wedge of shortbread, but since the pub was hosting a concert, we did not stay.

EXERCISE 11.2 USING *WHO, WHICH, THAT, YOU,* AND *THEY*

Read the following sentences, paying particular attention to pronoun usage. If the sentences use pronouns in appropriate and clear ways, write *C* on the lines. If pronouns are used in vague or inappropriate ways, revise the sentence.

EXAMPLE

Most college classes require homework. They complain about it, but they do it.

REVISION

Most college classes require homework. Students complain about it, but they do it.

EXAMPLE

The pilot whale who beached itself yesterday swam back out to sea this morning.

REVISION

The pilot whale that beached itself yesterday swam back out to sea this morning.

1. We had planned on watching *Masterpiece Theater* on Sunday evening, but since they were having transmission problems, we watched the CBS movie instead.

_____

_____

2. Parents should remember their own childhoods when setting standards for their children.

_____

_____

3. Customers which shop carefully for a used car can often make a satisfactory deal.

_____

_____

4. The Wrights expected a large crowd on Halloween night, and sure enough, they came to their door one after another.

_____

_____

5. Typing classes bore you when you're taking them, but afterward, you're glad you can type.

_____

_____

6. A dog who has been specially trained can give a blind person new mobility.

_____

_____

7. Whenever you walk into that stereo store, they come right up to you rather than letting you browse.

_____

_____

_____

Making Sure that Antecedents Are Nouns or Pronouns, Not Adjectives or Possessives |11c4|

Examine this sentence: *In Professor Ede's class, she requires weekly papers.* To whom does *she* refer? We can only assume that *she* refers to Professor Ede. Yet in that sentence, *Professor Ede's* functions as a possessive adjective modifying the noun *class.* Though the reference may be clear enough (and acceptable in conversation), many formal or academic readers will find this construction unacceptable. Remember, pronouns refer only to nouns or to other pronouns. The sentence can be revised in either of two ways:

Professor Ede requires weekly papers in her class.

In her class, Professor Ede requires weekly papers.

Here is another example:

INACCURATE

In Melville's novel *Moby Dick,* he mixes realism and symbolism.

REVISED

In *Moby Dick,* Melville mixes realism and symbolism.

Avoiding Sexist Pronoun Usage |11c5|

Avoid using *he* to refer to an entire group of people who may be of either sex.

SEXIST USAGE

A piano teacher must use all his patience when working with children.

The easiest remedy here is to switch the subject to plural:

Piano teachers must use all their patience when working with children.

For more on the question of sexist pronoun usage, see Chapter 9.

ASSIGNMENT 11A **IDENTIFYING AND REVISING VAGUE, AMBIGUOUS, OR WORDY PRONOUN USAGE**

Read the following portion of a letter written by a first-year college student to a school board member. The letter has been altered to include several kinds of pronoun errors. Underline all problematic pronouns. Then, using the space below, rewrite the letter to eliminate problems of pronoun usage.

I am a former student of Hoover High School that is now attending Valley University as a first-year student in engineering physics. Several friends which graduated in my class are also attending V.U. and are having a hard time with their classes. To graduate from high school, they took the bare minimum requirements, and they are not enough to prepare them for college. After all, most college classes build on what you have already learned. And if they don't already know the foundations, it is going to be hard to pass the class. One example is Chemistry 204. It is a class that starts off with the basics, but after two weeks, they are 200 pages into the book. Without a good high school chemistry class as background, they're lost. It is important that each school board member consider his duty to students and look into this lack of preparation. Action is needed to improve new students' chances for success in college.

Apply the directions given on the previous page to the passage reprinted below.

Once Darlene and Lester got the computer components out of boxes and onto the living room floor, then the real fun began. The instructions said on page A-2 that the short cable was supposed to plug into the C. P. U. in the back, with the other end plugging into the monitor. Unfortunately, they had no idea what a "monitor" was. To them, reading them was like reading Greek. After an hour of anger and frustration, they decided to forget it, and stacked them in the corner. Eventually, they paid a friend a free dinner to set up the system.

ASSIGNMENT 11B MAINTAINING CLEAR PRONOUN REFERENCE

Read the sentences below. If they use pronouns in clear, concise, and unambiguous ways, write *C* on the lines. Revise any sentences that use pronouns in wordy, vague, or ambiguous ways. Make sure your revision is concise, clear, and unambiguous.

EXAMPLE

When Barry discussed wages with Ted, he understood he would get a raise.

ACCEPTABLE REVISIONS

When Barry discussed wages with Ted, Barry understood Ted would get a raise.
When Barry discussed wages with Ted, Ted promised him a raise.

1. That year, when the delegates voted, they endorsed Wayne Morse.

_____

2. The picture hanging on the wall that you drew has provoked many favorable

comments. _____

3. The picture hanging on the wall that you drew has provoked many favorable

comments, even though it is peeling in places. _____

_____

4. She plans to drive her Rover over Santiam Pass, which has given her trouble in the

past. _____

5. The plumbing company placed an order with Lee Tool & Die, but it was sold before

they could fill it. _____

6. We painted over the graffiti on the fence that offended us and bordered our

parking lot. _____

_____

7. The committee discussed one proposal to raise taxes and another proposal to

freeze them; eventually, they passed it. _____

_____

_____

8. The landscape design program that you are interested in has four openings next
year; that makes it a competitive program!

_____

_____

9. Negotiators reached a settlement after fifteen weeks that included two holidays
and new provisions for vacation time.

_____

_____

10. It was said by witnesses that the car barreled around the corner that hit me and

swerved to my left. _____

_____

12

Avoiding Confusing, Ambiguous, or Unnecessary Shifts

Whenever readers notice any abrupt change or shift in what they are reading, they should also be able to recognize the reason for that change. Some changes—shifting from active to passive voice, for example—can be useful, even necessary. But sometimes writers make inadvertent shifts that only serve to confuse readers. This chapter focuses on such inadvertent or confusing shifts.

Identifying and Revising Confusing Shifts in Tense 112a

➤ *Student Writing Error 10: Shift in Verb Tense*

As Chapter 8 discussed, writers use verb tenses to identify time relationships; for example, *After I go* (present tense) *to the bank, I will pay* (future) *you back*. Here the sentence meaning makes the shift in verb tense clear and necessary.

However, sometimes writers carelessly or inadvertently shift tenses. It is hard for readers to make sense of the sentences these shifts yield. To avoid such confusion, keep verb tenses consistent unless there is clear reason to do otherwise. Consider these examples:

CONFUSING TENSE SHIFT

past	*present*	*future*

After I studied chemistry and go to the bank, I will pay you back.

REVISED

present	present	future

After I study chemistry and go to the bank, I will pay you back.

Besides paying attention to verb tenses within sentences, writers should make sure that verb tenses are consistent from sentence to sentence.

CONFUSING TENSE SHIFT

First she set up her camera. Then she walked entirely around the table with its plate of fettuccine. Finally, she adds a scattering of sliced olives, adjusts the lights, checked the exposure, and began to take the pictures that were scheduled to appear in the Sunday food section of the paper.

REVISION

(Note that the past tense has been used throughout.)

First, she set up her camera. Then she walked entirely around the table with its plate of fettucine. Finally, she added a scattering of sliced olives, adjusted the lights, checked the exposure, and began to take the pictures that were scheduled to appear in the Sunday food section of the paper.

Note: When referring to events in literary works, use the present tense:

In *Portrait of a Lady,* Isabel Archer *marries* Gilbert Osmond.

EXERCISE 12.1 IDENTIFYING AND REVISING CONFUSING SHIFTS IN TENSE

Read the five sentences that follow. Underline the verbs. If the sentence is correct as written, write *C* on the lines. If the sentence needs revising to eliminate confusing tense shifts, rewrite the sentence on the lines.

EXAMPLE

The barn swallows return about the same time that school recessed for spring break.

REVISION

The barn swallows return about the same time that school recesses for spring break.

1. Ann measures the flour and poured it into the bowl.

2. We paint the inside wall Friday, work in the garden on Saturday, and went to the

beach on Sunday. _____

_____

3. Jack swims like a fish and eats like a pig.

_____

4. The winds, which were blowing at almost gale force, capsize the rubber raft just as
it reached the mouth of the river.

_____

_____

5. Sleeping late on Saturday morning is an indulgence that we've earned after work-

ing hard all week. _____

_____

**Read the following paragraph. Underline all the verbs. Then revise the paragraph so
that the verb tenses are consistent and sensible. Pencil in your changes above the
offending verbs.**

The accident, which occurs on Bellfountain Road at approximately 11:30 Saturday

night, left four people injured and resulted in the death of one cow belonging to Homer

Groenur. According to Mr. Groenur, the cow will wander out onto the road through a

vandalized part of his pasture fence and settled onto the warm pavement for the night.

Said Mr. Groenur, "The pavement holds the day's heat, you know. They like to lie there if

they can. It's like a big hot water bottle to them." Police said tire marks indicate that the

Subaru was swerving in an attempt to miss the cow. _____

Identifying and Revising Confusing Shifts in Mood and Voice I 12b, 12c I

As discussed in Chapter 8, writers use verbs in any of three moods: the
indicative (to report facts or opinions), the imperative (to convey orders or
instructions), and the subjunctive (to state wishes or conditions contrary to

fact). Shifting from one mood to another without good reason will confuse your content and your readers. Here is an example:

CONFUSING SHIFT

subjunctive

My car repair company always requests that a customer *call* for a service

indicative

appointment, then *brings* the car in promptly at eight o'clock.

REVISION ELIMINATING SHIFT

subjunctive

My car repair company always requests that a customer *call* for a service

subjunctive

appointment, then *bring* the car in promptly at eight o'clock.

Writers may also make unnecessary shifts in verb voice. You already know that verbs may be in either the active voice (*Our dog Freckles chases cars*) or the passive voice (*Cars are chased by our dog Freckles*). Sometimes, shifting from passive to active (or vice versa) is justified and useful, as in this sentence: *Professor Emberson asked* (active) *for the papers, and as they were being passed* (passive) *forward, he gave* (active) *the new assignment.* Switching voices here keeps the sentence focused on Professor Emberson's actions, not on the actions of his students.

However, sometimes such shifts are unnecessary (and potentially confusing whenever the agent of the action goes unnamed). Here are some examples:

CONFUSING SHIFT

active   *passive*

Lisa *called* the children, and the groceries *were brought* to her.

REVISION ELIMINATING SHIFT

active   *active*

Lisa *called* the children, and they *brought* her the groceries.

UNNECESSARY SHIFT

passive	*active*

After the minutes *were read* by Harry, he *turned* to the first item on the agenda.

REVISION ELIMINATING SHIFT

active	*active*

After Harry *read* the minutes, he *turned* to the first item on the agenda.

Turn now to Assignment 12A at the end of this chapter for practice in revising shifts in mood and voice.

Identifying and Revising Unnecessary Shifts in Person and Number |12d|

➤ *Student Writing Error 11: Shift in Pronoun or Point of View*

Writers should not shift between first person (*I, we*), second person (*you*), and third person (*she, he, it, one, they*) unless there is good reason to do so. Be particularly careful about such shifts inside a sentence.

UNNECESSARY SHIFT

One ought to be careful about excessive alcohol consumption, especially if *you* plan to drive. [*The sentence begins with the third person* one *but ends with the second person* you.]

REVISIONS ELIMINATING SHIFT

One ought to be careful about excessive alcohol consumption, especially if one plans to drive. [*consistently third person*]

You should be careful about drinking too much, especially if you plan to drive. [*consistently second person*]

Remember that *you* should not be used in a vague or indefinite way. (For more on the vague or indefinite use of *you*, see Chapter 11.) Perhaps the clearest solution lies in replacing the problematic pronoun with a noun:

Adults ought to be careful about excessive alcohol consumption, especially if they plan to drive.

Here is another example:

UNNECESSARY SHIFT

Golfers should try the new course, but you should beware of those long holes on the back nine. [*Here* you *is being used as an incorrect substitute for* they.]

REVISION ELIMINATING SHIFT

Golfers should try the new course, but they should beware of those long holes on the back nine.

Shifts from singular to plural (or vice versa) can also be confusing: *Last night the Nashville Cable Network presented a new country singer* (singular), *and they* (plural) *were a big hit!* To whom does *they* refer? The sentence should read: *Last night the Nashville Cable Network presented a new country singer, and she* (or *he*) *was a big hit!* As you can see, many shifts in person and number are actually problems with pronoun-antecedent agreement (for more on such agreement, see Chapter 9).

EXERCISE 12.2 IDENTIFYING AND REVISING CONFUSING SHIFTS IN PERSON AND NUMBER

Many of the following sentences contain unnecessary shifts in person and number. Rewrite these sentences to eliminate those unnecessary (and potentially confusing) shifts. If a sentence is accurate as written, write *C* on the lines.

EXAMPLE

Zoo patrons should be sure to visit the aviary, and you shouldn't miss the elephant house, either.

_____ Zoo patrons should be sure to visit the aviary, and they shouldn't miss the elephant house, either.

1. If one visits the local art museum, you will find on display recent prints by Greg Pfarr.

_____

_____

2. Sea anemones thrive in coastal tidepools, but it cannot survive outside the water for very long.

_____

_____

3. When amateur photographers take pictures, he or she often enjoys the activity as much as the finished prints.

_____

_____

4. Lewis and Clark both kept journals, even though they wrote under less than ideal conditions.

_____

_____

5. A weekend runner is a prime candidate for running-related injuries, especially if they get no exercise during the week.

_____

_____

6. Tourists should be aware that road crews are busy on Highway 34, and a driver should expect some delay at the Oglesby Bridge construction site.

_____

_____

_____

7. Whenever newspaper carriers go on vacation, you should make sure that you have arranged for a substitute to take over your route in your absence.

_____

_____

_____

Avoiding Shifts between Direct and Indirect Discourse |12e|

Shifts from direct discourse to indirect discourse occur when writers move from direct quotation to paraphrasing in the same sentence. Such movement often results in odd shifts in tense. Consider this example:

> In her wonderful book *West with the Night*, the aviator Beryl Markham writes that her plane seemed alive, and "to me she speaks."

Here the problem occurs after the word *writes*: her plane *seemed* (past) *alive, and "to me she speaks"* (present). This is one example of a shift from indirect discourse (paraphrase) to direct discourse (quotation). That shift has made for a difference in tenses (past to present) and a difference in person (third person pronoun *her* to first person pronoun *me*). In such situations, writers need to choose one or the other—direct quotation or paraphrase.

DIRECT DISCOURSE (QUOTATION)

> In her wonderful book *West with the Night*, the aviator Beryl Markham writes of her plane, "To me she is alive and to me she speaks."

INDIRECT DISCOURSE (PARAPHRASE)

> In her wonderful book *West with the Night*, the aviator Beryl Markham writes that she knew her plane so well that it seemed alive and even spoke to her.

Notice that indirect discourse uses no quotation marks (for more on the use of quotation marks, see Chapter 31).

EXERCISE 12.3 AVOIDING SHIFTS BETWEEN DIRECT AND INDIRECT DISCOURSE

Find four printed sentences (or short groups of sentences) that you find interesting. Use these four sentences to write four of your own. In two of your sentences, directly quote your sources (direct discourse). In the other two, use paraphrase (indirect discourse). Make sure that you do not use both quotation and paraphrase in the same sentence. Use your own paper for this exercise. Follow the format of the examples.

EXAMPLES

> *Source sentence:* "To me she is alive and to me she speaks."
> *Origin: West with the Night* by Beryl Markham.
> *Discussion using direct discourse:* In her wonderful book *West with the Night*, the aviator Beryl Markham writes of her plane, "To me she is alive and to me she speaks."

Source sentence: "Suppose you tell me about it, from the beginning, and then we'll know what needs doing."
Origin: The Maltese Falcon by Dashiell Hammett
Discussion using indirect discourse: The Maltese Falcon begins with Sam Spade asking a client to tell her story.

Avoiding Shifts in Tone and Diction |12f|

Writers establish a relationship with readers based on the tone they set in their writing. In part, **tone** is based on the goal a writer has for a particular piece of writing. If you want readers to laugh, you try to set a humorous, lighthearted tone. If you want readers to think about some idea or experience, you try to set a more serious, perhaps reflective tone. The tone of a textbook should be straightforward without being stuffy. A workbook should be deliberate and trustworthy. You are not likely to find in this book (except by way of example) a sentence like *OK, you mules, listen up!* A book written entirely that way, with a hostile and arrogant tone, would be a novelty for a few paragraphs; after that, the tone would simply be annoying.

Diction refers to word choices and to the overall level of formality or technicality that writing possesses. For our purposes, we can identify four levels of diction: *formal,* which is appropriate for many kinds of academic writing; *technical,* which is appropriate for scientific and research writing; *informal,* which is the language of normal talk and may be appropriate for personal essays; and *slang,* which is usually the language of banter between close friends. (For more on diction and tone, see Chapters 25 and 26.)

SLANG We stuffed that rig until it near croaked.

INFORMAL We loaded that truck until the springs groaned.

FORMAL We loaded the truck with the largest possible cargo.

TECHNICAL The vehicle was loaded 112 pounds in excess of its maximum recommended weight.

Shifts in tone and diction can be sources of richness and surprise. However, when inappropriately used, such shifts may indicate that a writer is inexperienced or perhaps not entirely in control of what is being written. In general, when we talk, we mix levels of diction without creating problems. Body language and facial expression help us to do so. But readers, who have access only to sentences on a page, must be convinced that any shifts in tone or diction are controlled and purposeful.

[*211*]

MIXED TONE AND DICTION OF ACTUAL SPEECH

Whoa there! Hold it! This is my land and you have no permission to drive all over it willy-nilly with total impunity and rank disregard for native plant species.

CONSISTENT TONE AND DICTION OF A WRITTEN COMPLAINT

When I came upon Mr. Jones, he was behind the wheel of a Jeep stuck up to its back axle in the middle of a field. It happens that this field contains one of the few remaining undisturbed populations of a rare species of wild rose. I spoke with Mr. Jones, registering my complaint at his behavior and at his obvious disregard for the ecology of the area. I indicated that I would not allow any more four-wheel-drive vehicles on my property.

EXERCISE 12.4 AVOIDING SHIFTS IN TONE AND DICTION

Each of the following five sentences is identified as written with a particular kind of diction. Using your own paper, rewrite each sentence using the diction indicated.

EXAMPLE

Some jerkwater salesman sold me an empty box! (slang; write an informal version)
An out-of-town salesman sold me an empty box.

1. Careful observation that leads to the reviewing of a seam before it unravels will prevent nine times as much sewing at a later date. (formal; write an informal version)
2. This is really going to bum you out, but your mother busted an artery in her head and it bled all over in there. (informal/slang; write a more formal version)
3. We spent one heck of a long afternoon in that teeny room looking through a one-way glass and watching chickens to see if they could remember which color button to peck at so as to get some of those food pellets. (informal; write a technical version)
4. In the event of unseasonable precipitation, employees are instructed to activate these toggle switches in order to deploy the large canvas awning, thereby covering the exhibition of watercolors. (inappropriately formal; write an appropriately informal version)

Read the following paragraph carefully. You will find that most of it employs a reasonably formal, informative tone and level of diction. Underline any sentences or phrases that strike you as inappropriate in tone or diction. Then, on your own paper, rewrite the paragraph so that its tone is consistently appropriate.

Anyone interested in writing for publication should be aware of the existence of "vanity presses." Listen folks, these guys and gals are out to empty your wallet! Such companies are incorporated for the sole purpose of printing books *at the expense of their authors.*

Such "publishers" do not provide any advance money against future royalties. In fact, vanity press publishers make no bones about the fact that they make no monetary investment in any book. Rather, the author (that's you, bucko!) provides the moola up front. You either send the check or they sit on your manuscript. Even advance payment from an author is no guarantee that a printed book will receive the kind of attention authors seek. The fact is, many bookstores assume that these books are turkeys and won't stock them. Many authors who've paid for vanity press publiction end up with hundreds of books in their garages or basements. Such authors often feel both cheated and degraded.

EXERCISE 12.5 RECOGNIZING AND REVISING INAPPROPRIATE, UNNECESSARY, OR CONFUSING SHIFTS

The following passage contains several unnecessary shifts of the kind discussed in this chapter. Read the passage carefully, and underline any shifts you believe unnecessary or confusing. Then, on your own paper, rewrite the passage to eliminate these shifts.

Employees ought to follow these company guidelines whenever dealing with customers:

First, if you can't understand what some bozo is saying, you shouldn't say, "Huh?" Say instead, "Pardon me"or "I'm sorry." If one is receiving a phone order, say, "We seem to have a bad connection; could you repeat that please?"

Second, if one believes a customer's choice of apparel is inappropriate, one should not register disapproval. You ain't there to raise folks' fashion consciousness; you're there to provide courteous service.

Third, if you are sick and could not come to work that day, he or she should have called the store manager. One employee went home early before they told anyone. That was wrong too. Such absences result in customers who feel neglected and other employees who felt frustrated because of your absence on the sales floor.

Fourth, if you were obligated by store policy to say no to some big spender, follow your no with a yes. For example, if you say that a credit purchase has not been approved, make sure you said that the store welcomed personal checks, or say, "We will gladly set this merchandise aside for you."

Following these four guidelines will help ensure that customers returned to our stores. And repeat customers (and solid sales figures) made for a stable and remunerative employer-employee relationship.

ASSIGNMENT 12A IDENTIFYING AND REVISING CONFUSING OR UNNECESSARY SHIFTS IN MOOD AND VOICE

Read the following sentences. Underline the verbs, and pay particular attention to any shifts in mood or voice. If those shifts appear unnecessary or confusing, rewrite the sentence. If a sentence is clear and well written in its original form, write *C* on the lines. If a sentence unnecessarily employs both the active and the passive voice, convert the passive verbs to active. See the examples in the text of this chapter, as well as those provided here.

EXAMPLES

Ms. MacNaught read the plans carefully, and they were approved by her. [*unnecessary shift from active to passive*]
Ms. MacNaught read the plans carefully, and she approved them.

The dinner was prepared and was delivered by Fast Catering Co. [*no shift here*]
C

On race day, drive slowly and you should be careful of the competitors. [*unnecessary shift from imperative to indicative*]
On race day, drive slowly and be careful of the competitors.

1. The chair asked that Marj report the subcommittee's finding and presents its recommendations.

_____

2. The roses were gathered by Lionel, and then he arranged them.

_____

3. The graduate school requires that a master's student pass exams and defends his or her thesis.

_____

4. Before you leave tonight, water the plants and you should lock the doors.

_____

5. The construction company delivered lumber Monday afternoon, and the wiring and plumbing materials were delivered by them later in the week.

_____

_____

6. Say no to their request, but you should say it tactfully.

_____

7. Holiday traffic congested the freeway and delayed the wedding party's arrival by over an hour.

_____

_____

8. The credit company asks that an applicant fill out an application and returns it within fourteen days.

_____

_____

9. The invitation suggests that Tanya brings roller skates and arrive at two o'clock.

_____

_____

10. If Alysha were to become president and if Callie was elected treasurer, we would celebrate with a dinner out.

_____

_____

13

Identifying and Revising Comma Splices and Fused Sentences

Most of the time, when we write sentences, we are careful to punctuate them so that each contains only one independent clause (sometimes together with one or more dependent clauses). To review briefly, an independent clause contains a subject and a verb, and it can stand alone as a sentence. (For further review of clauses, see Chapter 6.)

Suppose that you are writing about summer visits to your grandmother's. During brainstorming, you jot down some of your memories about her lilacs. Then, based on those notes, you might write several separate sentences:

One of the things I particularly recall about those visits is Grandma's lilacs.

They had been planted right underneath the kitchen window by the door.

Grandma always kept that window open.

I remember the fragrance of those flowers filling the room.

I remember the light filtering through those green leaves.

As a writer, you might also want to combine some of those sentences. For example, the fact of the open window is inseparable from the scent of the flower clusters. One way to do justice to that immediacy is to combine two independent clauses in one sentence, like this:

Grandma always kept that kitchen window open; the fragrance of those flowers filled the room.

That sentence is really two sentences packed together. A semicolon links them.

➤ Student Writing Errors 8 and 18: Comma Splice and Fused Sentence

Using a semicolon is just one acceptable way to link independent clauses (you will see other options as this chapter progresses). But there are two incorrect ways to link independent clauses, and they are discussed below. This chapter will present several options for revising them.

Avoid Comma Splices When commas are used to join two independent clauses, the result is a **comma splice** (two independent clauses "spliced together" with a comma). Although this construction is occasionally used in journalism and literature, most readers and academicians view comma splices as errors. So do not use a comma to link two independent clauses.

COMMA SPLICE

Grandma always kept that kitchen window open, the fragrance of those flowers filled the room.

Avoid Fused Sentences In a **fused sentence** (sometimes also called a run-on), two independent clauses have been put side by side ("fused") without any punctuation whatsoever; this is incorrect and confusing to readers.

FUSED SENTENCE

Grandma always kept that kitchen window open the fragrance of those flowers filled the room.

Separating Independent Clauses into Two Sentences 13a

The simplest way to revise comma splices or fused sentences is to separate the independent clauses and punctuate them as two sentences.

COMMA SPLICE

Czeslaw Milosz is widely recognized as one of the finest poets of the twentieth century, his *Collected Poems* was issued in 1988.

FUSED SENTENCE

Czeslaw Milosz is widely recognized as one of the finest poets of the twentieth century his *Collected Poems* was issued in 1988.

CORRECTED SENTENCE

Czeslaw Milosz is widely recognized as one of the finest poets of the twentieth century. His *Collected Poems* was issued in 1988.

Revising by making each independent clause a sentence emphasizes the separateness of content in each sentence.

Linking Independent Clauses with a Semicolon |13b|

Comma splices or fused sentences may also be revised by inserting a semicolon as the sole punctuation between the two independent clauses. Using a semicolon in this way suggests not only a grammatical balance but also a balance between the independent clauses, showing that they carry equal importance.

COMMA SPLICE

When they met in 1988, the Democrats gathered in Atlanta for their nominating convention, the Republicans called their faithful together in New Orleans.

FUSED SENTENCE

When they met in 1988, the Democrats gathered in Atlanta for their nominating convention the Republicans called their faithful together in New Orleans.

CORRECTED SENTENCE

When they met in 1988, the Democrats gathered in Atlanta for their nominating convention; the Republicans called their faithful together in New Orleans.

Linking independent clauses with semicolons also allows you to set two ideas side by side in the same sentence. There are many possible effects to be gained from doing this. Primarily, you tell your reader that the two ideas are very closely related but that you are counting on your reader to understand the relationship without spelling it out. Here are two examples:

I won't be able to meet you at noon today; I have an appointment at the Financial Aid office. [*cause-effect relationship implied*]

They danced all night; they wanted to dance forever. [*the action; the impulse behind it*]

EXERCISE 13.1 IDENTIFYING AND REVISING COMMA SPLICES AND FUSED SENTENCES BY SEPARATING INDEPENDENT CLAUSES OR BY LINKING THEM WITH A SEMICOLON

Read the sentences that follow. Identify comma splices with *CS*, fused sentences with *F*, and correct sentences with *C*. Revise the comma splices and fused sentences either by making the independent clauses separate sentences or by using a semicolon to link them. *Be ready to explain your choice.* Pencil in your revisions in the spaces above the sentences.

EXAMPLE

___F___ An unusual thunderstorm dumped over a half an inch of rain in less than an hour several area roads were flooded when drains were unable to carry the water away.

_____ **1.** Georgia O'Keeffe's stunning use of color helped make her one of America's great painters forsaking the art world of large cities, she lived much of her life painting landscapes in desert New Mexico.

_____ **2.** Fashion designing demands a rigorous knowledge of fabric, of the human form, and of changing taste, it also demands daring, intuition, and an eagerness to set fashion rather than follow it.

_____ **3.** Usually, we do not question the time slots that television programmers give to their shows we seem perfectly willing to absorb the routine tragedies of the evening news while we eat lasagna or macaroni and cheese.

_____ **4.** Burglary and car theft continue to be a major problem in many larger cities and towns, added prison space, unfortunately, does not deal with the unemployment, drug addiction, or lack of education that experts often cite as causes of such crime.

_____ **5.** A short-wave radio can bring listeners programs in a variety of languages broadcast from locations as widely separate as South Africa, Britain, Germany, Latin America, Canada, and Japan.

Linking Independent Clauses with Commas and Coordinating Conjunctions |13c|

You can also link two independent clauses using a comma and a coordinating conjunction. There are seven coordinating conjunctions: *and, but, for, nor, or, so, yet.* To link independent clauses using one of these conjunctions, place the comma after the first clause, and follow this comma with the coordinating conjunction:

[Independent clause], [coordinating conjunction] [independent clause]

Following this diagram, we can revise *Margaret felt like she might sneeze. She reached for a Kleenex* to read *Margaret felt like she might sneeze, and she reached for a Kleenex.*

Linking independent clauses using a comma and a coordinating conjunction is the best way to show a specific relationship between independent clauses. *And* and *or* indicate continuation; *but* and *yet* indicate opposition; *for, so,* and *because* indicate cause and effect. As the following two examples show, the choice of a coordinating conjunction can make a considerable difference in sentence meaning:

> Maria felt somewhat uncomfortable, *for* she was the first guest to arrive at the party. [*Maria is uncomfortable because she is the first guest.*]

> Maria felt somewhat uncomfortable, *yet* she was the first guest to arrive at the party. [*Maria is uncomfortable but arrives first despite this feeling.*]

EXERCISE 13.2 LINKING INDEPENDENT CLAUSES WITH COMMAS AND COORDINATING CONJUNCTIONS

In each of the cases that follow, two sentences are provided. Join the two sentences using a comma and an appropriate coordinating conjunction. Write these directly above the place where they should go. Reread each resulting compound sentence to make sure it sounds right to you.

EXAMPLE

No biography of Shakespeare was written during his lifetime. Scholars continue to *,and*

puzzle over his identity.

1. The rhododendrons and daffodils bloomed early. April turned out to be unseasonably warm.

2. Jack's employee evaluation was mostly positive. He was laid off due to a shortage of orders.

3. Susan was reading Amos Tutuola's *Palm-Wine Drinkard*. She thought it a very strange book.

4. Maybe we should plan on discussing this tomorrow at the staff meeting. Maybe we should call a special meeting that would include the other working group.

5. Alice was concerned that her chemistry books were overdue. The due date stamped in the back told her she still had two days to return them.

Linking Independent Clauses with Semicolons and Conjunctive Adverbs or Transitional Phrases

So far in this chapter, you have seen how to join independent clauses using semicolons and using commas with coordinating conjunctions. A third method is available to you as a writer: using semicolons with conjunctive adverbs or transitional phrases. A list of conjunctive adverbs is provided; both conjunctive adverbs and transitional phrases function in the same ways and require the same punctuation. Here is an example:

The test was a difficult one; *however,* Jason did well.

Note that a comma follows the conjunctive adverb *however.*

	[conjunctive adverb]		
[Independent clause];	or	,	[independent clause]
	[transitional phrase]		

Here is a list of commonly used conjunctive adverbs:

also	finally	indeed	nevertheless	subsequently
anyway	furthermore	instead	next	then
besides	however	meanwhile	otherwise	therefore
consequently	incidentally	moreover	still	thus

Here is a list of commonly used transitional phrases:

after all	for example	in fact
as a result	in other words	on the other hand
even so	in addition	

Linking independent clauses using a semicolon and a conjunctive adverb (or transitional phrase) followed by a comma allows you to specify relationships and to vary tone.

That Simm's Grocery had to raise its coffee prices shouldn't surprise us; *after all,* Mr. Simm's prices have gone up too. [After all *indicates a cause-and-effect relationship; the tone is informal.*]

Karen was a fine golfer; *in fact,* she once shot a hole-in-one. [In fact *indicates that an example follows; the tone is more formal.*]

Common usage sometimes omits the comma following some conjunctive adverbs or transitional phrases. If you are a native speaker, you can probably hear the pause that usually follows a transitional phrase such as *in addition* or conjunctive adverbs such as *incidentally* or *besides*. Conjunctive adverbs like *then* and *thus* require less of a pause, encouraging writers to omit the comma. For more on the use of commas, see Chapter 27.

EXERCISE 13.3 LINKING INDEPENDENT CLAUSES WITH SEMICOLONS AND CONJUNCTIVE ADVERBS OR TRANSITIONAL PHRASES

In each of the following cases, two sentences are provided. Join the two sentences using a semicolon and an appropriate conjunctive adverb or transitional phrase. Write these directly above the place where they should go. Reread each resulting sentence to make sure it sounds right to you.

EXAMPLE

Students returning to school after years at home or in the work force are often nervous
           ; nonetheless
about the transition. With good academic counseling and with good support at home, most

succeed.

1. The sign urged that those of you who partake of alcoholic beverages refrain from

the operation of your automobiles. If you drink, don't drive.

2. No rains fell in Iowa for over six weeks. Grain and corn farmers suffered significant losses.

3. With all the traveling we do, we couldn't possibly own a dog. The apartment rules

forbid pets.

4. One month she can't talk or even sit up herself. She's standing wobbly-legged

against the furniture and calling, "Ma, Ma."

5. Biographers agree that writing the novel *Moby Dick* caused Melville considerable

pain and difficulty. Some argue that it provoked a mental and physical collapse.

Distinguishing between Coordinating Conjunctions and Conjunctive
Adverbs or Transitional Phrases ❘13c1❘

At this point, joining two independent clauses may begin to look confusing. After all, you use a comma with a coordinating conjunction, but you use a semicolon with a conjunctive adverb or transitional phrase. How can you tell when to use a comma and when to use a semicolon? Consider the earlier example with Jason and his test. The sentence looks like this using a semicolon and conjunctive adverb:

> The test was a difficult one; *however,* Jason did well.

Using a comma and a coordinating conjunction, the sentence looks like this:

> The test was a difficult one, *but* Jason did well.

Here is one method that will help you see a difference between coordinating conjunctions (such as *and, or, nor,* and *but*) and conjunctive adverbs (such as *however, thus, nevertheless,* and *also*): coordinating conjunctions cannot be moved around in the sentence; conjunctive adverbs can. If we move the conjunctive adverb, the sentence still makes sense:

> The test was a difficult one; Jason, however, did well.

If we move the coordinating conjunction, the sentence does not make sense:

> The test was a difficult one, Jason but did well.

Turn now to Assignment 13B at the end of this chapter for more practice in joining independent clauses.

Recasting Two Independent Clauses as a Single Independent Clause ❘13d❘

Sometimes two independent clauses may be revised to make just one independent clause. When such revision is possible, the new version is generally shorter and more direct. Consider the following set of examples.

FUSED SENTENCE

> The word *education* is an elusive one it often means different things to different individuals.

COMMA SPLICE

> The word *education* is an elusive one, it often means different things to different individuals.

Faced with either incorrect sentence, a writer must decide on a revision that retains his or her original intention and reflects accurate punctuation. By now, you should be aware of several ways to link these independent clauses; here is a way to combine them to form one independent clause:

> An elusive word, *education* often means different things to different individuals.

In that revision, the first independent clause has been reduced to an appositive phrase modifying *education*. The resulting sentence is certainly more concise and more forceful. Is the shorter, more concise version necessarily better? That is a question of style. However, often the most concise statement does carry the greatest impact.

Recasting One of Two Independent Clauses as a Dependent Clause   13e

Chapter 6 discusses the role of dependent clauses and provides a list of subordinating conjunctions. To review, a dependent clause is introduced by some subordinating word and contains a subject and a verb but cannot stand on its own as a sentence. Here are two ways to revise the earlier example using a dependent clause; the subordinating word in the first case is *since*; in the second case, it is *which*.

> Since the word *education* is an elusive one, it often means different things to different individuals.

> The word *education*, which is an elusive one, often means different things to different individuals.

Turn now to Assignment 13C at the end of this chapter for practice in recasting clauses.

Can Independent Clauses Ever Be Joined Using Commas?

In working to avoid comma splices and fused sentences, you should now be aware of several options for their revision. Sometimes, however, writers can join independent clauses using commas. We shall explain these exceptions briefly.

Three (or More) Independent Clauses in a Series   Suppose that you have a set of directions to convey. There are three parts to these directions: *Crumple the paper, lay the wood, and then light the fire.* Or suppose that you want to describe a traffic jam at Ninth and Monroe: *The bicyclist slowed to make a left turn, the Dodge swerved to avoid the bicyclist, and a garbage truck plowed into the Dodge.* These two sentences are both punctuated correctly, even though they appear to break the rules.

What these sentences have in common is that they come in three distinct parts, three independent clauses. Because they are independent clauses in at least a three-part series, they follow different rules—the ones for punctuation of a series, explained in Chapter 27.

Note that placing three independent clauses in one sentence makes for interesting effects. In the first example, the directions are terse and therefore more easily remembered. In the second example, the cause-effect relationships are clearer than they might otherwise be. The quickness of the sentence also begins to mimic the speed at which the accident actually occurred.

Reversed Emphasis Clauses (Negative, Then Positive)   In this kind of sentence, the opening independent clause has a negative emphasis, and the second clause reverses that emphasis. Such independent clauses are appropriately joined by a comma. *The spectators didn't just cheer, they exploded!* In sentences such as this one, the *not* clause leaves readers wondering what did happen. The second clause delivers this information quickly. Caution: Do not reverse the emphasis in a sentence like this one. If you do, the result is a comma splice: *The spectators exploded, they didn't just cheer.*

Using Commas with Quotations   When writers quote speakers, the result is often a sentence within a sentence: *"We'll plan on seeing the late show," she said.* In such sentences, a comma correctly joins two independent clauses: the quotation and *she said.*

ASSIGNMENT 13A REVISING COMMA SPLICES AND FUSED SENTENCES

Read the following passage, and underline all comma splices and fused sentences (remember the exceptions). Then use the space below to rewrite the passage. You may choose to continue to link independent clauses, or you may choose to punctuate them as separate sentences. You may add coordinating conjunctions, conjunctive adverbs, or transitional phrases as you wish. You may revise using dependent clauses or by converting two independent clauses into one. Make sure that your revised paragraph is grammatically correct and punctuated accurately. For each comma splice or fused sentence you rewrite, be ready to explain the reason for the particular revision you choose.

Perhaps the most striking fact about people is that they make things. When early October arrives, swallows migrate dogs get heavier coats snakes go into a kind of hibernation people knit themselves caps. People without caps and people with too many caps get together and invent the set of promises we call money. Having invented money, people pay other people to make parkas and slickers or they use money to buy kits and make these things themselves. Rain pelts down deer seek the densest cover they can find people build houses with roofs. When cats get cold, they curl into tight little balls. People invent insulation or they pay sheep ranchers to provide the wool that's made into warm shirts. When caribou get hungry, they have no choice but to seek a new range. When people get hungry, they don't move eventually they invent pizza. They figure out how to cure olives they figure out how to make thick bread crusts, they experiment with anchovies and pineapple they invent beer. Indeed, people are makers.

ASSIGNMENT 13B DISTINGUISHING BETWEEN COORDINATING CONJUNCTIONS AND CONJUNCTIVE ADVERBS OR TRANSITIONAL PHRASES

Each question below presents you with a pair of sentences. Combine them as indicated using either a comma and a coordinating conjunction or a semicolon, a conjunctive adverb (or transitional phrase), and a comma. You may wish to review the lists of coordinating conjunctions, conjunctive adverbs, and transitional phrases.

EXAMPLE

> The Russian processing ship remained stationary on the horizon. Several Russian trawlers fished for hake. (Combine using an appropriate conjunctive adverb.)
> The Russian processing ship remained stationary on the horizon; meanwhile, several Russian trawlers fished for hake.

1. The birds were singing. The sunlight shone through the slats of the bedroom's venetian blinds. (Combine using an appropriate coordinating conjunction.)

_____

_____

2. She awoke feeling unusually optimistic. She felt like she might sing out loud. (Combine using an appropriate transitional phrase.)

_____

_____

3. My diet plan says I can eat four ounces of fish for dinner. I could choose the same amount of chicken. (Combine using an appropriate coordinating conjunction.)

_____

_____

4. Deer are curious animals. They will often run a short distance, stop, and look back. (Combine using an appropriate conjunctive adverb.)

_____

_____

5. The sun rises early on a June morning. The chorus of robins and bluebirds and sparrows starts even earlier. (Combine using an appropriate conjunctive adverb.)

_____

_____

6. For a long time, childhood had seemed distant, forgotten. That morning, standing at the window and hearing geese, she remembered a little girl held by her father, both of them looking up. (Combine using a coordinating conjunction, a conjunctive adverb, or a transitional phrase.)

_____

_____

_____

_____

Read the following sentences, paying particular attention to how they combine independent clauses. If a sentence is correct as written, write _C_ on the lines. If a sentence is incorrect as written, rewrite it on the lines provided. Make sure your revision uses an appropriate coordinating conjunction, conjunctive adverb, or transitional phrase. Make sure your revision is also punctuated accurately.

EXAMPLE

> He could hear traffic noise behind him he could see the white-capped Pacific in front of him.
> He could hear traffic noise behind him; however, he could see the white-capped Pacific in front of him.

7. Salal grows in dense, green bushes; but, when it blooms, the dainty blossoms are no larger than your smallest fingernail.

_____

_____

8. The softwood lumber industry provides significant jobs for many workers in Louisiana and neighboring states as well as for northwestern states such as Washington, even so, some U.S. jobs are lost when the logs are exported overseas.

_____

_____

_____

_____

9. Rattan furniture is constructed when the materials are wet and pliable; yet those same materials prove both tough and durable once they have dried.

_____

_____

10. The leading economic indicators all registered modest drops yesterday hence the stock market dropped in today's trading.

_____

_____

11. The Academy Awards telecast is often criticized as boring and too long, however it consistently garners high ratings.

_____

_____

ASSIGNMENT 13C REVISING COMMA SPLICES AND FUSED SENTENCES BY USING DEPENDENT CLAUSES OR BY MAKING TWO INDEPENDENT CLAUSES INTO ONE INDEPENDENT CLAUSE

Each case below features a comma splice or a fused sentence. Revise the incorrect sentence in two ways: (A) by making one of the independent clauses a dependent clause, and (B) by converting the two independent clauses to one independent clause.

EXAMPLE

Twentieth-century studies courses carry three units of credit they fulfill the requirements for electives in humanities.

A. REVISION USING A DEPENDENT AND AN INDEPENDENT CLAUSE

Twentieth-century studies courses, which carry three units of credit, fulfill the requirements for electives in humanities.

B. REVISION USING A SINGLE INDEPENDENT CLAUSE

With three units of credit, twentieth-century studies courses fulfill the requirements for electives in humanities.

1. The College of Education receives applications from more individuals than it can admit the college carefully screens all applications.

A. _____

_____

_____

B. _____

_____

2. The committee discussed the zoning variance for thirty minutes, the variance was then approved on a 5–3 vote.

A. _____

_____

B. _____

_____

3. The governor is a Democrat he has decided not to attend the national nominating convention this year.

A. _____

_____

B. _____

_____

4. Computer technology changes rapidly however few businesses can afford to take advantage of every new advance.

A. _____

_____

B. _____

_____

5. Breakfast consisted of fresh strawberries, homemade biscuits, and scrambled eggs, it was served promptly at 9 A.M.

A. _____

_____

B. _____

_____

14

Recognizing and Revising Sentence Fragments

A sentence fragment is some part of a sentence (often a phrase or a subordinate clause) that has been punctuated so that it looks like a sentence. Such fragments begin with a capital letter and end with a period. What is wrong with a sentence fragment? When readers see what *looks* like a sentence, they expect the full meaning that a sentence provides. Fragments often appear in advertising and in literature, but in academic prose they are normally considered errors.

➤ Student Writing Error 12: Sentence Fragments

An occasional sentence fragment may tell readers that the writer has not proofread carefully. Frequent sentence fragments suggest that the writer is not fully aware of what constitutes a grammatical sentence. Many college writers have trouble with sentence fragments. This chapter discusses how to recognize fragments and how to revise them.

Sentence fragments often occur as a result of the way we think. We write something and put a period at the end of that thought. Then we remember something to add, so we add it. The result might look something like this: *Holly and Anne have definite opinions on education. And the experience to back them up.* There is nothing at all wrong with writing this in a rough draft; the writer's error here is in failing to recognize and correct the fragment before turning in the final draft. It should read *Holly and Anne have definite opinions on education and the experience to back them up.*

Perhaps the easiest way to detect sentence fragments is to read your writing backward, from the last sentence of a paragraph to the first. Reading in this way will alert you to your own punctuation.

Recognizing and Revising Phrase Fragments   **|14a|**

The kinds of phrases that are most often punctuated as fragments are listed here. For a review of these phrases, see Chapter 6.

Verbal Phrases   Verbal phrases are made from verbs but function as nouns or adjectives or adverbs; verbal phrases often include objects or modifiers. Infinitives (*to confuse*), present participles (*confusing*), past participles (*confused*), and gerunds (*confusing*) are all verbals.

FRAGMENT

The team lined up in punt formation. *To confuse their opponents.* [*infinitive fragment*]

REVISION

The team lined up in punt formation to confuse their opponents.

FRAGMENT

Confused by the fake punt. The opposing team allowed our halfback to score. [*participle fragment*]

REVISION

Confused by the fake punt, the opposing team allowed our halfback to score.

FRAGMENT

Confusing your opponents. Is one strategy for successful football. [*gerund subject separated from its verb, resulting in two fragments*]

REVISION

Confusing your opponents is one strategy for successful football.

Prepositional Phrases   Prepositional phrases are composed of prepositions and their objects and associated words. Such phrases do not include subjects or finite verbs. Prepositional phrases by themselves are not sentences.

FRAGMENT

With the color of these walls. I think we ought to choose a different rug.

REVISION

With the color of these walls, I think we ought to choose a different rug.

FRAGMENT

Meet me at 4:30. *Inside the hotel lobby.*

REVISION

Meet me at 4:30 inside the hotel lobby.

Noun Phrases   Noun phrases are formed around nouns together with any adjectives, phrases, or clauses that modify the nouns. Lacking finite verbs, noun phrases frequently appear before fragments containing verbs but no subjects.

FRAGMENT

The children who are whining in the upstairs apartment. Should be disciplined by their parents. [*two fragments*]

REVISION

The children who are whining in the upstairs apartment should be disciplined by their parents.

FRAGMENT

The jumper that Donna outgrew last spring. Has been sent to Aunt Lucille for her kids to wear. [*two fragments*]

REVISION

The jumper that Donna outgrew last spring has been sent to Aunt Lucille for her kids to wear.

Appositive Phrases   Appositive phrases consist of nouns with their modifiers. These phrases rename (or describe) other nouns. Appositive phrases by themselves are not sentences.

FRAGMENT

All Sunday afternoon, the two of them followed Arnold Palmer. *One of the most famous professional golfers in the world.* [*Note that this appositive phrase has two prepositional phrases embedded in it.*]

REVISION

All Sunday afternoon, the two of them followed Arnold Palmer, one of the most famous professional golfers in the world.

FRAGMENT

On the day of William Faulkner's burial, everything else stopped in Oxford, Mississippi. *Faulkner's hometown.*

REVISION

On the day of William Faulkner's burial, everything else stopped in his hometown of Oxford, Mississippi.

As the examples show, eliminating sentence fragments is easy and can be accomplished in either of two ways: build a new sentence to express the fragment's meaning or combine the fragment with a sentence next to it.

EXERCISE 14.1 IDENTIFYING AND REVISING PHRASE FRAGMENTS

Several of the short passages that follow contain phrase fragments. Read each passage sentence by sentence from the end. Underline the fragments. Then revise the passage so that it contains only complete sentences. If the passage is correct as printed, write *C* beside the number of that passage. Use your own paper for this exercise.

EXAMPLE

The rhododendrons bloomed like orchids. Outside her window. As she typed, she could see them. Some of the blooms. Were a deep vermilion. Others were the pale, off-white color. Of piano keys.

REVISION

The rhododendrons bloomed like orchids outside her window. As she typed, she could see them. Some of the blooms were a deep vermilion. Others were the pale, off-white color of piano keys.

1. He was surprised at how the countryside changed. In just a few miles. The car dealerships and fast-food restaurants were replaced by rolling pasture. Enclosed by electrified fences.

2. When a woman is considering abortion, she ought to seek counseling. From family members, from her clergy, and from qualified social workers. She ought to talk candidly and at length. With the father. Certainly an interested party. Above all, she ought to listen. To her own conscience, then make her own decision.

3. Dancing in the rain was something Gene Kelly did in a movie. Called *Singing in the Rain.* It probably wasn't actually raining. During the filming. More likely, the movie crew rigged a rain machine over the set.

4. Designing advertising posters and brochures is great experience. It's particularly useful for journalism majors. Journalism 406 provides just such experience.

5. The committee has spent the last several days carefully reviewing your proposal. To extend the deadline for completion of your degree requirements. We are happy to be able to tell you that an extension has been granted. Your requirements must now be completed. By August of this year.

Recognizing and Revising Compound-Predicate Fragments |14b|

"Compound predicate" is a technical way of saying "two verbs." A compound-predicate fragment is produced when the second of the verbs (plus any phrases or modifiers) is punctuated as a sentence; such fragments lack subjects. Since compound verbs are typically linked with words such as *then, but, and,* and *or,* compound-predicate fragments often begin with these words. Remember, however, that the key to a compound-predicate fragment is the absence of a subject; many perfectly good sentences (with subjects and verbs) also begin with *then, but, and,* and *or.*

ACCEPTABLE SENTENCES

Julie ate her lunch. Then she began studying for a midterm.

COMPOUND-PREDICATE FRAGMENT

Julie ate her lunch. *Then began studying for a midterm.* [*The fragment lacks a subject.*]

As we said earlier, revising such nonsentences involves either combining the fragment with a nearby sentence or building a new sentence to express the fragment's meaning.

ACCEPTABLE REVISIONS

Julie ate her lunch and then began studying for a midterm.

Julie ate her lunch. Afterward, she began studying for her test.

Recognizing and Revising Dependent-Clause Fragments |14c|

Dependent clauses begin with words called *subordinators.* These words signal to readers that the sentence contains at least one independent clause as well as the dependent (or subordinate) clause. When readers cannot find that independent clause, the result is at least momentary confusion. In such cases, the writer's real message is this: *I didn't catch this fragment.*

A wide variety of words operate as subordinators. They include relative pronouns (such as *who, which,* and *that*) and subordinating conjunctions (among them *after, although, because, before, even if, if, in order that, once, since, though, unless, until, when, where,* and *while*). For more complete lists of relative pronouns and subordinating conjunctions, see Chapter 6.

FRAGMENT

We shouldn't forget. That we all have days that seem dark and endless.

REVISION

We shouldn't forget that we all have days that seem dark and endless.

Since dependent-clause fragments are sometimes long, their length alone may make them seem like sentences. These are often the hardest fragments to catch.

FRAGMENT

> *After I arrived at the airport and found that the plane was late leaving Phoenix and would not depart for another hour.* I decided to buy a magazine at the newsstand.

REVISION

> After I arrived at the airport and found that the plane was late leaving Phoenix and would not depart for another hour, I decided to buy a magazine at the newsstand.

EXERCISE 14.2   IDENTIFYING AND REVISING COMPOUND-PREDICATE FRAGMENTS AND DEPENDENT-CLAUSE FRAGMENTS

Read the following brief paragraphs, and underline any sentence fragments. Then revise the paragraphs to eliminate the fragments. Write your revision on a separate page.

Community residents will have their final say tonight. When the city council convenes a special hearing on the proposed Sylvan Green Development Project. The project has already received preliminary approval from the council. The development proposal calls for the construction of two anchor stores in its first phase. And specifies widening McKean Boulevard to accommodate increased traffic. The developers, who have already invested over $300,000 in architectural fees and permits. Argue that all city zoning requirements have been met. Local residents and developers have clashed at two earlier meetings.

According to opposition leaders, residents worry. That nighttime deliveries might cause considerable noise. And those opposed have also voiced concern over increased traffic at the school crosswalk at Oak and Fifty-sixth. When the hearing convenes tonight at 7:30 in Council Chambers. Those opposed to the development promise fireworks.

Using Fragments Sparingly for Special Effect

There are times when writers do use sentence fragments for particular stylistic reasons. Two guidelines are crucial here: writers must be certain that they are entirely aware of sentence-building rules before purposely using stylistic sentence fragments, and writers must be certain that their readers will not object to the use of such fragments. Many teachers and readers of academic prose look upon the use of *any* incomplete sentence as a sentence fragment. If your teachers or readers object to the use of stylistic sentence fragments, do not use them.

Stylistic fragments do function in some predictable ways. The four uses listed here may appear in informal prose but almost never in more formal academic prose.

Fragments in Dialogue People often speak in fragments. When such speech is faithfully reproduced on the page, the result is often a sentence fragment.

> "Really?"
>
> "Yes. Right there in line for the movie."

Fragments as Commands Commands typically omit the sentence subject.

> Turn right at Glen Ridge, then left on Ponderosa.
>
> Pick up some orange soda when you go to the store.

(See Chapter 8 for further discussion of commands and the imperative mood.)

Fragments in Answer to Questions When questions are followed immediately by answers, repeating information presented in the questions often seems unnecessary. This is particularly so in informal writing.

> When will I be home? After the test.
>
> Which ingredient should be added now? The melted butter.

Fragments as Exclamations By definition, exclamations are not complete sentences.

> That home run traveled over 450 feet. Amazing!
>
> The model wore a swimsuit that cost over a million dollars. Incredible!

Writers occasionally use sentence fragments in other situations, particularly when describing or telling a story. Award-winning writer Barry Lopez uses fragments rarely but effectively. Here is an excerpt from his book *Arctic Dreams*; the fragments have been underlined.

> It was still dark, and I thought it might be raining lightly. I pushed back the tent flap. <u>A storm-driven sky moving swiftly across the face of a gibbous moon.</u> Perhaps it would clear by dawn. The ticking sound was not rain, only the wind. <u>A storm, bound for somewhere else.</u>

This paragraph occurs on page 152; by this time, Lopez has amply proved his credentials as a writer.

EXERCISE 14.3   IDENTIFYING AND REVISING SENTENCE FRAGMENTS

Read the following passage on test taking. You will notice several sentence fragments. Underline every fragment you find. Then, on your own paper, revise the passage. You may combine or rearrange sentences in any way you see fit, so long as you retain the original content. You need not eliminate every single fragment; if you decide to keep a fragment, copy it after your revision. Then briefly explain that decision.

How people take tests says something. About them as people. Some individuals worry. And do nothing but worry. They don't reread, they don't review their notes, and they don't discuss major issues with classmates. After all this, they may still be surprised. When the test day arrives and they aren't prepared. Other people worry, but they put that worry to work. These individuals use their worry. As motivation to make study plans. In addition to reviewing notes and doing some selective rereading. These students might also try to anticipate test questions. And then construct appropriate answers. In effect, they take practice tests. Still another group of people don't worry at all. They don't take tests seriously. And probably don't spend much time in preparation. The most naturally gifted in this group. May still do reasonably well on tests. However, even the most naturally gifted may be cheating themselves. If they don't study. As my grandma used to say, "If you've never worked hard, how do you know how hard you can work?"

15

Recognizing and Revising Misplaced, Disruptive, and Dangling Modifiers

➤ *Student Writing Error 19: Dangling or Misplaced Modifiers*

This chapter discusses another common writing error: dangling or misplaced modifiers. Curing this problem depends first on becoming knowledgeable about it. Once knowledgeable, you should be able to identify such modifiers by carefully rereading your draft. (For background on the use of modifiers, see Chapters 10 and 17.)

Identifying and Revising Misplaced Modifiers |15a|

Writers use modifiers to add detail. The sentence *We had a great weekend* becomes more interesting when it is made specific: *We had a great weekend waterskiing behind the Lakowskis' blue Chris Craft.* Notice that as readers we expect modifiers to be positioned next to the words they modify; we cannot move modifiers around in the sentence without creating confusion (or outright gibberish): *We Lakowskis had a blue weekend waterskiing behind the great Chris Craft.* Here is another example:

MISPLACED MODIFIERS

Boiling and foamy, we stood at the viewpoint and watched the surf. [*As now positioned,* boiling *and* foamy *modify* we.]

CORRECTED

We stood at the viewpoint and watched the boiling and foamy surf.

Limiting modifiers always come before the words they modify. Here is a list of such words: *almost, even, hardly, just, merely, nearly, scarcely, simply.* Repositioning a limiting modifier can result in an entirely new meaning.

Only crocuses bloom in March. [*The one flowering plant in March is the crocus.*]

Crocuses *only bloom* in March. [*Crocuses are only blooming, not growing, adding leaves, etc.*]

Crocuses bloom *only in March.* [*Crocuses bloom only during March, not in February or April.*]

EXERCISE 15.1 IDENTIFYING AND REVISING MISPLACED MODIFIERS

Each of the following sentences contains a misplaced modifier. Underline it, and use an arrow to indicate its proper placement in the sentence.

EXAMPLE

Only Just Woolens sells yarn and related knitting supplies.

1. Barking, the chain link fence restrained the dog.
2. The computer system almost cost $1,000, but Michelle paid it in monthly installments.
3. The sign said this: "Only at St. Anthony's, services are held on Sundays at 9:15 A.M."
4. Even the weather surprised the meteorologist.
5. Campers may play various games if it rains indoors.
6. The directions said to shut *on* the light inadvertently when we left the room.
7. Most days are warm enough nearly for swimming before lunch.

Misplaced Phrases and Clauses

The placement of phrases and dependent clauses follows the same general guideline as that for single-word modifiers: place the phrase or dependent clause adjacent to the word (or words) it modifies. (For a review of phrases and clauses, see Chapter 6.)

MISPLACED PREPOSITIONAL PHRASE

In the refrigerator, Amelia Bedelia chilled the wine. [*implies that Amelia Bedelia herself is in the refrigerator*]

REVISION

Amelia Bedelia chilled the wine *in the refrigerator.*

MISPLACED PARTICIPIAL PHRASES

Newly washed and tumbled dry, the kids put on their play clothes. [*implies that the kids have been washed and tumbled dry*]

The warm sun felt good on her legs *streaming through the windows.* [*implies that legs are streaming through the windows*]

REVISIONS

The kids put on their *newly washed and tumbled-dry* play clothes.

The warm sun *streaming through the windows* felt good on her legs.

MISPLACED DEPENDENT CLAUSES

The tennis racket was no good to anyone *that was broken during the last match.*

People should stay away from pet stores *who are allergic to cat hair.*

REVISIONS

The tennis racket *that was broken during the last match* was no good to anyone.

People *who are allergic to cat hair* should stay away from pet stores.

Squinting Modifiers

Consider this sentence: *People who swim frequently will improve their physical condition.* Look at that word *frequently.* Does the sentence refer to people who swim often? Or does the sentence mean that improvement occurs frequently? That word *frequently* is called a squinting modifier—it looks in two directions. Because of its placement in the sentence, it could modify two separate things. The reader has no way of knowing which meaning was intended.

Revising sentences with squinting modifiers is easy if you are the writer. The revision involves repositioning the squinting modifier, as in the following sentences:

People who frequently swim will improve their physical condition.

People who swim will frequently improve their physical condition.

Squinting modifiers may also be phrases or clauses. Here is an example:

SQUINTING MODIFIER

The commission promised *at its final meeting* to make its recommendations public.

REVISIONS

At its final meeting, the commission promised to make its recommendations public.

The commission promised to make its recommendations public *at its final meeting.*

EXERCISE 15.2 IDENTIFYING AND REVISING SQUINTING MODIFIERS

Read each of the following sentences carefully. Underline any squinting modifiers you find. Then circle the two words or groups of words the writer might have wanted the squinting modifier to modify. If the sentence is clear as written, write *C* in the margin next to it.

EXAMPLE

Rita thought after the meeting she would like to go home.

1. Employees entering this area routinely are required to wear safety gear.

2. The defendant promised during the trial he would obey the judge's instructions.

3. Margie felt often Jack was considerate and good with the children.

4. The renters promised faithfully to honor the conditions of the lease.

5. People frequently argue about the role of U.S. troops overseas.

On a separate sheet of paper, rewrite each sentence with a squinting modifier twice: once to make the modifier modify only the first section of the sentence that you have circled, and a second time to make it modify only the second part that you have circled. After each pair of rewritten sentences, write a brief explanation of how they differ in meaning.

EXAMPLES

After the meeting, Rita thought she would like to go home. [*The meeting was already over when Rita thought about going home.*]

Rita thought she would like to go home after the meeting. [*Rita is thinking beforehand that she will want to go home when the meeting has finished.*]

Identifying and Revising Disruptive Modifiers |15b|

Disruptive modifiers interrupt, disrupt, or obscure the normal connections between parts of a grammatical structure or sentence. These disruptive placements cause readers to lose their grasp of the structure of the sentence; often they will have to reread the sentence many times to understand what it was meant to say. Here is an example:

Rico felt *after eating two chicken breasts, a baked potato, a tossed salad, and strawberry shortcake* full.

Revise such a sentence by repositioning the modifiers:

After eating two chicken breasts, a baked potato, a tossed salad, and strawberry shortcake, Rico felt full.

Here are several other examples:

DISRUPTIVE PLACEMENTS

In the next several months, Lynn hopes to *despite her busy schedule of entertaining* maintain her diet and actually lose weight. [*phrase splits the infinitive* to maintain]

A red-tail hawk will, *if it has nothing else to do and if the weather is right,* spend most of an afternoon soaring high over the landscape. [*clause placed within a verb phrase*]

The faculty grievance board, *although it had not done so in over three years,* ruled in favor of several students who claimed they had been graded unfairly. [*clause separates subject from verb*]

She sang *in her first public concert* a selection of traditional folk songs and ballads. [*phrase placed between the subject and its object*]

REVISIONS

In the next several months, Lynn hopes to maintain her diet and actually lose weight *despite her busy schedule of entertaining.*

If it has nothing else to do and if the weather is right, a red-tail hawk will spend most of an afternoon soaring high over the landscape.

Although it had not done so in over three years, the faculty grievance board ruled in favor of several students who claimed they had been graded unfairly.

In her first public concert, she sang a selection of traditional folk songs and ballads.

Note that all the disruptive modifiers in these examples are relatively long phrases or clauses. In some cases, single-word modifiers may effectively be inserted inside verb phrases, as in this example:

These days, employers who ask their personnel to move will *often* pay for the cost of the move.

Try shifting the word *often* to a position outside the verb phrase. In a sentence such as this one, shifting the modifier results in a new meaning.

Inserting a single-word modifier between *to* and the verb in an infinitive phrase may also be acceptable in some writing situations:

To *almost* succeed is better than to *utterly* fail.

However, some academic readers will object to such split-infinitive constructions. In such cases, revise the sentence to eliminate the infinitives:

Near success is better than utter failure.

Turn now to Assignment 15A at the end of this chapter for practice in correcting disruptive modifiers.

Identifying and Revising Dangling Modifiers |15c|

When writers use modifiers without giving them anything to modify, those modifiers just "dangle"; they are not attached to anything. Consider the sentence *After swimming for an hour, lunch was delayed.* That sentence literally says that lunch swam for an hour and was delayed. Lunches can be delayed, but they cannot swim. So the initial phrase *After swimming for an hour* is a dangling modifier. The only solution is a revision that gives the phrase something or someone to modify. That something or someone must follow the comma after the modifying phrase itself: *After swimming for an hour, the team found that lunch was delayed.*

Dangling phrases may often lead to unintended comic effects.

DANGLING PHRASES

Singing in the shower, the water suddenly turned cold.

Dressed and ready for the dance, her car would not start.

REVISIONS

> Singing in the shower, he felt the water suddenly turn cold.

> Dressed and ready for the dance, she found that her car wouldn't start.

Opening phrases as in these examples always modify the word directly after the comma.

Dangling phrases and dangling clauses are similar in appearance and in effect. A dangling clause is a clause that has not been completely presented; the subject or verb (or sometimes both) has been left out. (Such clauses are examples of elliptical structures. For more on careful, effective use of elliptical structures, see section 16c in Chapter 16.) In effect, a dangling clause looks like a dangling phrase; you can tell it is a dangling clause because it opens with a subordinating word (*while, after, whenever,* etc.). Turning that phrase into a complete clause is another way of clarifying sentence meaning.

DANGLING CLAUSES

> *While singing in the shower,* the water suddenly turned cold.

> *Whenever driving,* your seat belt should be fastened.

COMPLETE CLAUSES

> *While I was singing in the shower,* the water suddenly turned cold.

> *Whenever you are driving,* your seat belt should be fastened.

EXERCISE 15.3 IDENTIFYING AND REVISING DANGLING MODIFIERS

Read the following passage, paying particular attention to phrase and clause modifiers. Underline any dangling phrases or clauses. Make a list of all the modifiers you have underlined and explain briefly why they are inaccurately used. Then rewrite the passage to clarify its content. Use your own paper for this exercise.

When stricken by spring fever, the results may be disastrous.[1] Although not fatal, this disease can lead to loss of productivity.[2] Consulting authorities, the specific symptoms include lassitude, a lack of motivation, an eagerness to spend long hours prone under sunlight, and an unwillingness to concentrate.[3] Enduring hard winters, spring fever is a particular problem.[4] Once May arrives, New Yorkers have been known to leave their offices as early as 1 P.M. on Friday afternoons.[5] Happy at the return of good weather and hoping for good luck, "Gone Fishing" signs appear in midwestern shop windows.[6] Dotting the skies over Albuquerque, tourists admire hot-air balloons.[7] Actually, spring fever means trouble only to the manufacturers of small wading pools for children.[8] Though pleased by the avalanche of orders, factory buildings hum night and day to meet the demand.[9]

ASSIGNMENT 15A IDENTIFYING AND REVISING DISRUPTIVE AND DANGLING MODIFIERS

Underline any dangling or disruptive modifiers (phrases or clauses) you find in each of the sentences below. Then revise the sentence so that it reads smoothly and clearly. If the sentence is fine as written, write _C_ on the line.

EXAMPLES

She sang in her first public concert a selection of traditional folk songs and ballads.
In her first public concert, she sang a selection of traditional folk songs and ballads.

Winded and tired, the race seemed endless.
Winded and tired, he felt the race would never end.

1. Fresh fish, although more expensive and sometimes hard to locate, tastes better than fish that has been frozen. _____

_____

2. After years playing chess the game got boring. _____

_____

3. Aliceann decided to after a particularly bad week both at work and at home visit her sister for the weekend. _____

_____

4. Looking both ways, the traffic was too heavy to cross the street safely. _____

_____

5. Eating his lunch, his stomach began to growl. _____

_____

6. John Davidson in _The Music Man_, which opened last night, got rave reviews.

_____

_____

7. Now that she is eleven and believes her parents know virtually nothing, Melissa has decided that the telephone is her best friend. _____

_____

_____

8. Happy and no longer tired, the finish line appeared at last at the bottom of the hill.

_____

_____

9. Before jogging regularly, a good pair of running shoes should be purchased.

_____

_____

10. The candidate gave following a dinner of fried chicken, peas, and mashed potatoes a speech supporting the president's foreign policies. _____

_____

_____

Maintaining Consistent and Complete Grammatical Structures

Making Grammatical Patterns Consistent |16a|

A sophisticated sentence often packs quite a bit of information between its initial capital letter and its ending period. Such sentences depend on a variety of phrases and clauses to carry all that meaning. Given the wide variety of possible sentence structures available to us as writers, it is no wonder that occasionally we begin a sentence one way and end it quite another. For instance, read this sentence aloud:

> White House officials said that in most deportation cases require a more thorough investigation than many illegal aliens cannot afford.

The sentence begins clearly enough: "White House officials said that . . . ." The word *that* signals a dependent clause, and as readers we expect to find a subject and verb for that clause. Instead, we find a prepositional phrase beginning with *in*. Since all prepositions take nouns (or phrases or clauses acting as nouns) as their objects, as readers we look for the object—*in* what? "Deportation cases" looks like it could be the object of *in*, except that this same noun phrase acts as a subject for the verb *require*. We know that the same noun cannot act as both the object of a preposition and the subject of a verb. Clearly, the grammatical pattern of this sentence is garbled. Here are three possible revisions for it:

> White House officials said that most deportation cases require a more thorough investigation than many illegal aliens can afford.

> White House officials said that most deportation cases require a thorough investigation, which many illegal aliens cannot afford.

> White House officials said that in most deportation cases, a thorough investigation is required—something most illegal aliens cannot afford.

Here is another example of a sentence that mixes grammatical patterns:

> As compact discs rapidly replace cassette tapes are going to become obsolete.

Here, the phrase *cassette tapes* tries to do two things at once: to act as the object of the verb *replace* and as the subject of the verb *are going*. The result is a confusing sentence. Once the grammatical problem has been isolated, the revision is relatively easy:

> As compact discs rapidly replace cassette tapes, the latter are going to become obsolete.

Sometimes straightening out a garbled sentence requires substantial rewording:

> The increasing popularity of compact discs will make cassette tapes obsolete.

Turn now to Assignment 16B at the end of this chapter for practice in identifying and revising garbled sentences.

Matching Subjects and Predicates |16b|

Writers also need to make sure that subjects and their predicates are carefully and accurately matched. If they are not, the result is **faulty predication**. Faulty predication occurs most frequently in sentences with the verb *be*.

FAULTY

> The most important *qualification* is *applicants* with experience. [*This sentence literally says that a qualification is applicants.*]

REVISED

> The most important *qualification* for applicants is *experience*.

Faulty predication can also occur when writers allow themselves to be confused by words coming between the subject and the verb.

FAULTY

The clock with the black hands circled regularly.

REVISED

The clock's black hands circled regularly.

The clock had black hands, which circled regularly.

Sometimes faulty predication is really the result of incomplete thinking. Consider this sentence: *The elevation of Mt. Hood claimed several lives last summer.* Is this faulty? Yes, it is faulty because a mountain's *elevation* cannot *do* anything. We can arrive at a grammatically correct revision by simply dropping any mention of elevation: *Mt. Hood claimed several lives last summer.* However, this revision sacrifices some of what the writer wanted to say. The real question is this: what is it about the mountain's elevation that is important? Posing that question may lead to this revision: *Blizzard conditions at the 10,000-foot level of Mt. Hood caused the death of several climbers last summer.*

Finally, writers need to be careful of sentences built on *is when, is where,* or *the reason is because* constructions. A sentence like *Your watch is where you left it* makes perfect sense. However, a sentence like *Recess is where all the children play kickball* incorrectly turns recess into a place. Possible revisions include *At recess, all the children play kickball* or *Recess is the time when all the children play kickball.* A definition must have a noun or noun phrase on both sides of the verb *be.* Neither *when* nor *where* is a noun.

Sentences structured around *the reason is because* are redundant. The word *because* simply repeats the meaning of the phrase *the reason is.* Chances are, either *because* or *the reason is* can be eliminated.

REPETITIVE

The reason I ate the potato chips is because I was hungry.

REVISED

I ate the potato chips because I was hungry.

The reason I ate potato chips was that I was hungry.

EXERCISE 16.1 MATCHING SUBJECTS AND PREDICATES

Read the following passage. Underline any sentences with faulty or unnecessarily wordy predication. Work on revising the passage to make it clearer. Add or clarify

content if you feel that will make for a clearer final version. Use your own paper for this exercise. (To make classroom discussion easier, the sentences have been numbered.)

The reason people can recognize a smooth collie is because they look like collies but when they're full grown their hair is short.[1] Smooth collies are where they have the same general build as their hairier cousins (called rough collies) and the same long noses.[2] But probably their most important characteristic is where like other collies they have great dispositions.[3] The nature of collies will accept abuse that would snarl or even bite.[4] Small children can sit on collies or hold their paws as if shaking hands just like people.[5] Collies will even tolerate someone playing with their food.[6] Actually, collies are so lovable to hurt or tease them.[7] They're loyal, and they're so excited to see you in the morning that their brown eyes make you glad you got out of bed.[8] Collies are also superior intelligence.[9]

Using Elliptical Structures Carefully |16c|

When a sentence repeats a structure, it is often acceptable to omit repeated words *so long as the repeated words are identical to those found earlier in the sentence.* In the examples that follow, the italicized word or words are identical, and the ones in parentheses can be omitted.

Beth *owns* quite a few books, and Jane (*owns*) just as many.

Canon manufactures copiers *for the* home and (*for the*) office.

Remember, the omitted words must be identical, not just similar. Here is an example of an inappropriate omission:

Phil's native talents are obvious, and his paper wonderful.

To be accurate and grammatical, the sentence must be revised to read this way:

Phil's native talents are obvious, and his paper *is* wonderful.

Even if the verbs are identical, they should be retained whenever the sentence substantially changes its meaning as it goes along. In the next example, the italicized words are identical, but none of them should be omitted.

Will *wanted to* see a science fiction movie, Melanie *wanted to* see a romance, and Brian *wanted to* stay home.

EXERCISE 16.2 USING ELLIPTICAL STRUCTURES CAREFULLY

Read the following sentences. If a sentence omits words that should be included or if it repeats words that could be omitted, revise the sentence on the lines provided.

EXAMPLES

> Will wanted to see a science fiction movie, Melanie wanted to see a romance movie, and Aaron stay home.
>
> Will wanted to see a science fiction movie, Melanie wanted to see a romance, and Aaron wanted to stay home.

> Cathie arrived first, and Katie arrived ten minutes later.
> Cathy arrived first, and Katie ten minutes later.

1. Jaime gets along well with Cecilia and Don with Barbara but not Bev.

_____

2. We could clearly hear Radio Moscow yesterday, but less today.

_____

3. During the summer, Ben plays softball on Tuesdays, he plays tennis on Wednesdays, and he plays soccer on Thursdays.

_____

4. Harold decided to take a nap, Michael decided to study for his chemistry test, and Susan to take a book back to the library.

_____

_____

5. The car's exterior is blue, but the seats black vinyl.

_____

_____

Checking for Inadvertent Omissions |16d|

Virtually every writer working on a rough draft is liable to leave out a word or phrase from time to time. Usually, the writer is capable of correcting these errors once they are identified. How does a writer identify such errors? You can ask others to check a final draft for you; another pair of eyes can often see omissions that you have unconsciously read into your draft. (Ask for help in identifying your errors, but do not let others correct them. Instead, learn from those errors: keep a personal editing checklist. For more on the personal editing checklist, see Chapter 3.)

Read your draft aloud. Read it backward, one sentence at a time, starting at the end. Concentrate on each word and consciously keep your eyes from going too far ahead. Learning to read this way takes practice, but it can help you catch omissions and may also help you detect spelling errors.

Checking Comparisons for Completeness, Consistency, and Clarity |16e|

Writers can also get into trouble with incomplete or carelessly phrased comparisons. Above all, comparisons must grammatically and logically compare items, qualities, or things that are comparable. As Chapter 10 discusses, the informality of speech and shared experience often allows people to form careless or incomplete comparisons with little confusion or loss of meaning. However, in formal or academic writing, readers expect both logic and completeness. Look carefully at the following examples.

INCOMPLETE   Fast food tastes better. [*better than what?*]

ILLOGICAL   Fast food tastes better than cooking. [*compares taste with an action*]

REVISED   Fast food tastes better than his cooking tastes.

ILLOGICAL/INCOMPLETE   This clam chowder is thicker and creamier than last week.

REVISED   This clam chowder is thicker and creamier than the chowder we cooked last week.

ILLOGICAL/INCOMPLETE   Bobbie Ann Mason's novel differs from Tim O'Briens. [*The omission of an apostrophe makes this sentence seem to compare a novel to a person.*]

REVISED   Bobbie Ann Mason's novel differs from Tim O'Brien's.

    Bobbie Ann Mason's novel differs from the one by Tim O'Brien.

Turn now to Assignment 16C at the end of this chapter for practice with comparisons.

ASSIGNMENT 16A RECOGNIZING AND REVISING GARBLED PROSE

Read the following passage carefully. Look for omissions, incomplete comparisons, and any garbled or blurred pattern sentences, underlining any that you find. In the space below, revise the passage to clarify its content.

Writers familiar with word processing programs have a variety of skills literally their fingertips.[1] Such writers can move paragraphs or sentences from one part of paper to another.[2] They can revise sentences or whole passages without that having to retype the entire document.[3] They can experiment with the sizes of the margins italic or boldface type.[4] Some printers are even equipped with adjustable pitch changes the number of characters can be printed on one line.[5] In short, word processing programs make revisions easy and no excuse for failing to revise.[6] For all of these reasons, writers who use computers are often considered more productive by employers.[7]

Read the following sentences aloud. If a sentence reads clearly and correctly, write a C on the lines. If the sentence sounds garbled and confusing, revise the sentence and write your revision on the lines provided.

EXAMPLE

Allergies on an average spring day you will find many people suffering.
On an average spring day, you will find many people suffering from allergies.

1. The newspaper said that instead of beginning at 8:30, the sale would not open its

doors until 9:30. _____

_____

2. On average, the rain here falls at a rate of 50% higher than east of the mountains.

_____

_____

3. Before we reorganized the books were stacked on those shelves reached as high as

the ceiling. _____

_____

4. I was stretched out on the grass, and the clouds looked like animals.

_____

5. Not only was the tape dispenser empty, and the light bulb had burned out.

_____

_____

6. Most electric coffeepots come equipped with a thermostat that shutting off the

electricity when the pot boils dry. _____

_____

7. To find the financial aid office is on the third floor of the administration building.

_____

_____

ASSIGNMENT 16C CHECKING FOR INADVERTENT OMISSIONS AND FOR INCOMPLETE COMPARISONS

Read the sentences below, checking carefully for any omissions or faulty comparisons. If a sentence needs revising, write your new version on the lines provided. Add new content as necessary. If the sentence is accurate and acceptable as written, write *C* on the lines.

> The small-screen color television is more expensive.
> The small-screen color television is more expensive than the 19-inch black-and-white model. _____

1. Her play in today's match was better than yesterday. _____

_____

2. If we can believe the newspaper, the weather in San Francisco yesterday was the

same as New York. _____

_____

_____

3. The firewood was stacked neatly in wooden rack by the back door. _____

_____

4. This piano is in better tune. _____

_____

5. Titled *Straight on till Morning,* Mary Lovell's biography chronicles the life times

of Beryl Markham. _____

_____

_____

6. The Rambo movies appeal to a different audience than *Bambi.*

_____

_____

7. These days, summer boredom seems worse twelve-year-olds than it does for young

children or for teenagers. _____

_____

_____

8. The Department of Environmental Quality claims that its pollution readings for

this month are worse than last month. _____

_____

_____

9. On particularly hot days, the railroad crossing gates descend and block traffic
even though there is no train in sight.

_____

_____

10. The Vietnam War caused considerable controversy at home; Americans generally

supported World War II. _____

_____

_____

PART

Sentences: Making Stylistic Choices

These questions are designed to help you, the student, decide what you need to study. (Answers are found at the back of the book.)

1. Can the following sentences be revised to be more concise? Answer yes or no.
   a. Contemporary rock groups performing now frequently make use of synthesizers.

   _____

   b. The election did not resolve anything. _____

2. Underline the coordinating conjunctions in the following sentences.
   a. Siberian huskies have thick fur so they will never be cold in the winter. _____

   b. Usually Carolyn is never late but this time she missed her train. _____

3. Can a subordinate clause ever stand on its own? Answer yes or no. _____
4. Underline the subordinate clauses in the following sentences.
   a. When the rain started, Jocylen and I took shelter in a book store.
   b. The man who gave me this watch seemed to be desperate.
   c. Carolyn was late even though she left an hour early.

5. Do the following sentences use parallel structures correctly? Answer yes or no.
   a. We will carry the fight for the ERA into the schools, the churches, and into the legislatures. _____
   b. It is better to remain silent and to have people take you for a fool than to speak and to remove all doubt. _____
   c. Hard work, long nights in the library, and constantly revising your essays will guarantee you good grades. _____

6. Identify any of these stylistic weaknesses in the following sentences: passive verbs, wordiness, weak verbs. If none of these weaknesses are present, mark a *C* next to the sentence.
   a. It is necessary that everyone arrive at the ticket booth at the same time. _____
   b. Pianists often wrestle with the technically treacherous passages of Bach's *Goldberg Variations.* _____
   c. Although the bronze and the silver medals were won by the other team, the gold was won by us. _____

   d. Today the weather was bad. _____

   e. My paper topic was approved by my history teacher. _____

Constructing Effective Sentences

Emphasizing Main Ideas |17a|

Using Opening and Closing Positions for Emphasis |17a1|

Effective writing takes advantage of all we know about how readers read and remember what we write. For example, we know that readers tend to remember what we say last. This holds true for an essay, and it holds true for individual sentences. Here is a set of sample sentences; notice that the ending position is held by a different idea each time, resulting in a different emphasis each time.

David lost six pounds following his diet this week.

This week, David lost six pounds following his diet.

Following his diet this week, David lost six pounds.

The first example stresses time; it comes from a paragraph discussing the time David needed to lose weight. The second example stresses his diet; it comes from a paragraph focusing on the diet itself. The third sentence stresses the number of pounds lost; it comes from a paragraph emphasizing David's achievement.

As a writer, you can use sentence order to create emphasis. The results may not seem to make much difference in a single sentence, but used over the course of an entire essay, careful ordering of sentences can make the difference between merely competent writing and truly effective writing.

Using Climactic Order |17a2|

Sentences using climactic order present their ideas—usually three or more—in a sequence of increasing importance, power, or drama. Sometimes, this sequence also corresponds to a normal time sequence:

> Position your food in the center of the tray, program the microwave, and then push the button and wait for the bell.

Violating this normal time sequence lessens impact and may lead to confusion:

> Push the button after you have programmed the microwave and positioned your food in the center of the tray, then wait for the bell.

Sometimes, climactic order has nothing to do with time and everything to do with intensity:

> Prison inmates face routine boredom, long separations from family and friends, and the very real risk of violence at the hands of other prisoners.

To revise sentences to take advantage of climactic order, first look for any sentences that present a series of ideas or actions. Look closely at the series to determine the least important idea or action; this one should come first. Position the remaining ideas or actions so that they proceed from lesser importance to greater importance, ending with the most important (or dramatic or powerful) idea or action.

Three ideas were presented in our last sample sentence. Arranging them from least terrible to most terrible yielded the most dramatic sentence.

Turn now to Assignment 17A at the end of this chapter for practice in using climactic order.

Being Concise |17b|

As we write sentences for a rough draft, we are thinking hard about what we want to say; we are struggling with ideas and words. A rough draft about capital punishment might contain a sentence like this one: *It is true that the question of capital punishment is a complicated one because it involves a moral decision.* Getting this idea down on paper for the first time is itself an accomplishment. If you have written that sentence, you have begun to realize what you think and how you feel about capital punishment. We write rough drafts in large part precisely to make such realizations.

However, rough drafts need revising to clarify both their content (expanding sometimes, cutting at other times) and their expression. Clarifying expression means rewriting sentences to make their meanings as clear and straightforward as they can be. In short, part of revision involves examining the wording of each sentence.

In the rough draft sentence we were just discussing, revision could begin with cutting *It is true that.* This kind of opening helps a writer get something on paper, but these four words add nothing to the meaning of the sentence. In addition, such a sentence buries its main points in a relative clause beginning with *that.* Cutting the opening leaves *The question of capital punishment is a complicated one because it involves a moral decision.* Can it be tightened further? *Capital punishment is a complicated question because it involves a moral decision.* Now this sentence has two parts connected with *because.* If we can figure out a way to combine those two parts, we will have an even more concise sentence. Notice that the idea of a question is repeated in the word *decision.* Noticing that gives us a final revision: *Capital punishment is a complicated moral question.*

You can identify sentences that contain redundant material by carefully rereading your draft, looking for sentences that say the same thing twice. Here are some additional examples:

REDUNDANT: Contemporary poets writing now use rhyme more sparingly than did the poets of the '40s and '50s. [*By definition, contemporary poets must be writing now.*]

REVISED: Contemporary poets use rhyme more sparingly than did the poets of the '40s and '50s.

REDUNDANT: A synthetic and artificially produced material made from oil, polyester now shows up in everything from clothing to ropes to seat cushions. [*If the material is produced from oil, it must be both synthetic and artificial.*]

REVISED: Produced from oil, polyester now shows up in everything from clothing to ropes to seat cushions.

Certain common expressions are always redundant: *few in number, large in size, combine together, continue on, continue to remain, repeat again, red in color,* and *free gift.*

A number of phrases that may sound "official" are actually simply redundant. In almost every case, these phrases can be replaced with simpler ones, resulting in more concise, less pompous prose.

Redundant	Concise
at the present time	now, today
at that point in time	then
in the event that	if
general consensus of opinion	consensus
exhibits a tendency to	tends

Finally, you should be careful in your use of all-purpose modifiers such as *absolutely, definitely, really, very, quite, literally, great, awfully, fine, weird, major, central,* and *important.* Standing alone, such modifiers mean almost nothing:

> We definitely had an absolutely and quite literally great time at the beach.

A sentence like this one, although it sounds very emphatic, does not give readers much real information; only the writer has any idea as to what really happened at the beach to make the experience so wonderful.

Turn now to Assignment 17B at the end of this chapter for practice in being concise.

EXERCISE 17.1 REVISING WORDY PROSE

Read the following passage, paying particular attention to any sentences that seem to you unnecessarily wordy. Work on a revision of the passage, and copy your best version onto a separate sheet of paper to hand in to your instructor. By way of example, a revision of the first sentence follows the passage.

If I think back to the time of the 1950s when I was a child, a mere youngster, I can see again in my mind's eye and remember the look of Portland's trolley cars. Their parallel tracks or iron wheel guides crisscrossed downtown streets, boulevards, and byways (but not alleys), and their overhead wires mirrored the tracks. The cars I remember were mostly quiet, as were all trolley cars. They made a distinctive humming noise that was much quieter than any bus or auto or internal combustion engine. The trolley cars I remember were also run down inside and decrepit, with paint red in color and peeling and with seats oozing cotton stuffing or padding. Perhaps because the cars themselves were in sorry shape, it always seemed that the riders were in similar condition. Of the riders I remember from that point in time, a few continue to remain in memory: some of them were drunk, some just rambled to themselves, and some just needed showers. For a small child of perhaps four or five years in age, riding in a trolley car was an experience that produced an interesting mixture of fear and excitement. The fear was of those other passengers: Would they simply continue to remain dozing peacefully? Would they stand up raving? Would they hurt or do violence to children? The excitement came from experiencing something unfamiliar, something new, something unpredictable.

REVISED FIRST SENTENCE

If I think back to my childhood in the 1950s, I can remember Portland's trolley cars.

ASSIGNMENT 17A   USING CLIMACTIC ORDER

Revise the following sentences so that they use climactic order.

EXAMPLE   Skiing is expensive and time-consuming, but it is also a lot of fun, which I never knew because I had not tried it.

REVISION   Because I had never tried to ski, I was surprised to find that, although expensive and time-consuming, it is a lot of fun.

1. Coast Guard personnel conduct boating safety classes, must sometimes risk their own lives to save others, and routinely monitor emergency radio channels.

_____

_____

2. John Kennedy became president after being elected to Congress and after distinguished service as a PT boat commander during World War II.

_____

_____

3. Jamaica produces many crops, including sugarcane (its most important farm product), citrus fruits, bananas, and allspice. _____

_____

4. Most agree that Martin Luther King's career as a civil rights leader reached its high point when he addressed over 200,000 protesters at the Washington Monument in August 1963; King helped to establish the Southern Christian Leadership Conference in 1957 and became its first president that same year.

_____

_____

_____

_____

_____

_____

ASSIGNMENT 17B **BEING CONCISE**

The sentences below are all either redundant or plagued by all-purpose modifiers. Rewrite each sentence so that it is concise. If you must supply content (instead of all-purpose modifiers), do so.

EXAMPLES We definitely had an absolutely and quite literally great time at the beach.

The condominium salesperson repeated again that the unsold units were few in number and that we would receive a free gift for taking a tour of the grounds.

REVISIONS The sunny weather and temperatures in the mid-seventies made for an enjoyable weekend at the beach.

The condominium salesperson told us that only a few unsold units remained, and he promised us a gift for taking a tour of the grounds.

1. At the present time, it is true and continues to remain the case that welfare reform

is a really major, central, and important issue. _____

_____

2. It is believed by many experts who have studied this problem that workers who labor on graveyard shifts exhibit a tendency to commit more errors then workers commit during the shift during the day. _____

_____

3. Aaron requested of me and asked that in the event that he could not return to the campus by 9 A.M., at that point in time I ought to turn in his paper for him.

_____

_____

4. It is true that the sandwich that you made tasted really great.

_____

5. The consensus of agreement that we have reached as a result of our discussions is that the paper originally scheduled on the calendar to be turned in on Monday will

now be due on the following Friday thereafter. _____

_____

_____

18

Creating Coordinate and Subordinate Structures

Using Coordination to Relate Equal Ideas |18a|

Consider these two sentences:

> The sun shone.
>
> The sky was a clear, deep blue.

Each sentence is a short independent clause: each has a subject and a verb, and each can stand alone. If you wished to combine those two sentences, you could use **coordination** to do so, joining the two sentences with *and, or, but, nor, yet, for,* or *so*. These words are called coordinating conjunctions. (For more on conjunctions, see Chapter 6.) Given the two sentences we started with, the most likely choice for an appropriate coordinating conjunction would be *and*. The two sentences combined using *and* would look like this:

> The sun shone, and the sky was a clear, deep blue.

The key to understanding sentence coordination is this: both halves of the sentence are grammatically equal; both are independent clauses.

Coordination can be used to convey accumulation (using *and, or,* or *nor*), contrast (using *but* or *yet*), and cause and effect (using *for* and *so*). Examples of each follow; the coordinating conjunctions joining the clauses are underlined.

ACCUMULATION We were caught in the rain without an umbrella, <u>and</u> there wasn't one bus or taxi in sight.

CONTRAST   Yesterday was hot and steamy, <u>but</u> today a cool wind has made the apartment more comfortable.

CAUSE AND EFFECT   The geography test had me worried, <u>so</u> I studied in the library for two hours after lunch.

When two sentences are joined by a coordinating conjunction, the proper punctuation is a comma preceding the conjunction. Notice that in each example above, the underlined coordinating conjunction is preceded by a comma. (Two independent clauses may also be linked using a semicolon; see Chapter 13.)

Coordinating conjunctions can also join phrases or nouns:

I've packed my dress shoes <u>and</u> clean shirts. [And *joins two nouns with their modifiers.*]

That order should be ready in the morning <u>or</u> in the early afternoon. [Or *joins two prepositional phrases.*]

Turn now to Assignment 18A at the end of this chapter for practice with coordination.

Using Subordination to Distinguish Main Ideas |18b|

The two simple sentences *The sun shone* and *The sky was a clear, deep blue* can also be combined using **subordination**:

<u>While the sun shone</u>, the sky was a clear, deep blue.

The underlined portion of the sentence is a subordinate clause; it contains a subject and a verb, but it cannot stand alone as a sentence (*While the sun shone* is a sentence fragment). Reading that subordinate clause, readers expect an independent clause to follow it. Hence, the independent clause almost always gets more emphasis. In addition, this subordinate clause limits the independent clause, suggesting that only while the sun shone was the sky a clear, deep blue.

Consider the following pair of sentences, one using coordination and the other using subordination. Note that the coordinate structure produces two sentence halves of roughly equal importance. The subordinate structure, by contrast, clearly emphasizes the meaning in the independent clause.

COORDINATE STRUCTURE   The sprinkler has been running for forty-five minutes, yet the water has penetrated only an inch. [*roughly equal emphasis, making the terms of the contrast separate and clear*]

SUBORDINATE STRUCTURE Although the sprinkler has been running for forty-five minutes, the water has penetrated only an inch. [*emphasizes the minimal water penetration*]

Most subordinate clauses begin with subordinating conjunctions such as *when, since, because, if, although, unless, whenever, often, before, while, after, as,* and *until* (see also Chapter 6). Subordinate clauses can also be introduced by the pronouns *who, which,* and *that.* Occasionally these words are omitted altogether.

> *Unless* we decide otherwise, we'll meet you at Silver Creek State Park at noon.
>
> The woman *who* sold me this sweater seemed to be about Debbie's size.
>
> The pizza *that* you ordered tasted delicious.

Subordination and coordination can often be found in the same sentence:

> Although clouds gathered and darkened in the west, we decided to go ahead with the family picnic. [*A subordinate clause opens this sentence; inside the subordinate clause,* and *joins compound verbs. Note that the subordinate structure gives emphasis to the picnic.*]

Notice again how different the emphasis becomes when the other half of the sentence is subordinated:

> As we prepared to go ahead with the picnic, clouds gathered and darkened in the west. [*The emphasis here is on the worsening weather.*]

We have so far discussed only subordinate clauses, but verbals and prepositional phrases are also subordinate structures. Minor ideas can often be included in such structures.

> Linc bicycled to work, his front tire hit a patch of black ice, and he fell. [*coordinate independent clauses*]
>
> As Linc bicycled to work, his front tire hit a patch of black ice, and he fell. [*subordinate clause followed by two coordinate independent clauses*]
>
> As Link bicycled to work, his front tire hit a patch of black ice, causing him to fall. [*subordinate clause followed by independent clause followed by verbal*]

For more on the use of these subordinate structures, see Chapter 6.

Turn now to Assignment 18B at the end of this chapter for practice with subordination.

Using Coordination and Subordination for Special Effect |18a1, 18b1|

Imagine overhearing this complaint from the eleven-year-old in the apartment below you: *I've cleaned my room, and I've put away my laundry and Callie's, and I cooked breakfast this morning, and I cleaned the dishes, and I just finished fixing Tory's bicycle, and now you want me to go to the store?* That eleven-year-old speaker is using coordination for a very particular effect. The accumulation of independent clauses makes the final question *(and now you want me to go to the store?)* seem like an injustice. Writers can use the same technique, though sparingly. Whenever you pile independent clause on independent clause, the result will be emphatic.

Writers can also use repeated subordination to achieve special effects. Consider this sentence: *When you're a chemistry major who hates chemistry, when you're just barely scoring well enough to pass your chemistry classes, when you'd rather spend more time on your psychology class than on any chemistry class, maybe it's time to think hard about changing majors.* In this sentence, the accumulation of conditions makes the sentence's conclusion seem true and undeniable. That repetition also adds a note of sarcasm to the word *maybe.*

The kind of repetition we have been talking about here is a matter of style. Such repetition adds emphasis whenever it is used, but if used too often, its effectiveness diminishes.

EXERCISE 18.1 USING COORDINATION AND SUBORDINATION FOR SPECIAL EFFECT

On a separate sheet of paper, compose two sentences using repeated coordination and two sentences using repeated subordination. Then find one published example of either repeated coordination or repeated subordination and copy out the sentence(s) using it. Be sure to note down the writer of your example as well as its place and date of publication. (College readers and anthologies of essays are good sources of examples, as are college handbooks and newsmagazines.)

ASSIGNMENT 18A USING COORDINATION

Use coordination to combine each pair of simple sentences. Make sure the resulting sentence is properly punctuated. Do not use the same conjunction more than once.

EXAMPLE

The geography test had me worried. I studied for two hours in the library.
The geography test had me worried, so I studied in the library for two hours after lunch.

1. Georgeann wanted higher grades on her written work. She studied to improve her spelling.

_____

_____

2. During the storm, we heard tree trunks snap. We saw the weird, blue light of electrical transformers as they shorted out.

_____

_____

3. The sun did not come out today. The rain never stopped.

_____

_____

4. Karen thought she would have trouble with the math class. She earned an A on the last test.

_____

_____

5. Saturday we will have spaghetti for dinner. We may have beef stroganoff.

_____

_____

For each of the five cases below, combine the given simple sentences by making one of the sentences a subordinate clause. (More than one correct answer is possible for each sentence.)

EXAMPLE

The woman sold me a sweater. She seemed to be about Debbie's size.
The woman who sold me this sweater seemed to be about Debbie's size.

1. You gave me a computer disk. The disk was the wrong size.

_____

_____

2. Students make decisions about careers. Students should think about what makes them happy as well as about what will make them wealthy.

_____

_____

_____

3. Reggie was sick with a cold last week. He turned his paper in on time.

_____

_____

4. Guido came along with his Ferrari and his Italian accent. Emily and John were a hot item.

_____

_____

5. Greg's works were featured for three weeks at the Guistina Gallery. His works include both paintings and drawings.

_____

_____

_____

Creating and Maintaining Parallel Structures

Why do we remember (and use) maxims, or clichés, like *A bird in the hand is worth two in the bush* or *Take it or leave it* or *Red sky at morning, sailors take warning; red sky at night, sailors delight*? We use such succinct sayings because they are easy to remember, and they are easy to remember because they are constructed using grammatically parallel structures. The diagrams below illustrate this further.

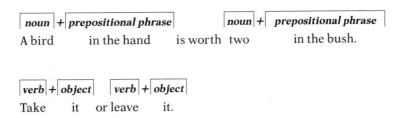

The success of clichés is ultimately their downfall. Clichés are so successful at summarizing or crystalizing experience that they tend to reduce all experience to a set of premade sentences and phrases.

As a writer, you ought to be wary of clichés, but you ought to be aware of the effectiveness of the parallel constructions they use. Sentences can employ parallel words, parallel phrases, or parallel clauses. Such constructions can make prose more concise, more graceful, and more readable. Many writers also carry parallel structures from sentence to sentence to create tighter, more emphatic passages. (Assignment 19B offers samples of such parallelism.)

Using Parallel Structures in a Series |19a|

Listing items in groups of three is one common parallel construction:

> We should order a bottle of Alpine Riesling to go with the <u>salad</u>, <u>fish</u>, and fresh <u>vegetable</u>.

Notice that all three of the underlined words are nouns. By the time readers have read *salad, fish, and* . . . , the parallel structure has led them to expect that third noun.

Occasionally, however, writers unconsciously or inadvertently break this pattern of expectation, resulting in confusion for readers:

> We should order a bottle of Alpine Riesling to go with the salad, fish, and we will have to think about dessert.

The confusion may not be particularly dramatic if it occurs only once. However, if writers consistently misuse parallel structures in a series, readers (particularly academic readers) will react with frustration and impatience. Here is a revision that is both grammatical and logical:

> We should order a bottle of Alpine Riesling to go with the salad and fish. We will have to think about dessert later.

Using Parallel Structures with Pairs |19b|

Consider this sentence:

> After work, I might stop by to see my mother, or grocery shopping is something that I need to do too.

Because the two independent clauses in this sentence follow different constructions, the reader may think that in the second clause, the writer is changing the subject. When clauses are parallel, however, it is clear that they present versions of a single idea—in this case, the writer's two options for what to do after work.

To make such a sentence parallel, repeat the same grammatical structure in both parts of the sentence; often, you will be able to repeat the same words:

> After work, *I might* stop by to see my mother, or *I might* go grocery shopping.

Notice that the coordinating conjunction *or* joins the two parts of the sentence. Other coordinating conjunctions may serve the same function.

Some parallel structures are nested inside pairs of correlative conjunctions such as *either . . . or, both . . . and, neither . . . nor,* or *not only . . . but also.* When such correlative conjunctions are used, the structures following each conjunction must be grammatically parallel.

NONPARALLEL

Either I will take a nap, or going swimming would be nice.

PARALLEL

Either I will take a nap, or I will swim.

Including All Necessary Words in Parallel Constructions |19c|

You have seen this example, but look at it once more:

> After work, *I might* stop by to see my mother, or *I might* go grocery shopping.

Suppose that you decided to omit the second *I might,* figuring that such repetition might be unnecessary. The resulting sentence would then read this way:

> After work, I might stop by to see my mother or go grocery shopping.

Remember that *or* is a coordinating conjunction; it joins similar words, phrases, or clauses. But what is *or* joining in the example? *Mother* is the object of the infinitive *to see.* The phrasing *mother or* leads readers to expect a compound object. But the sentence does not provide a compound object. Thus, leaving out *I might* may mislead readers.

In short, be careful about omitting repeated words in parallel constructions; include repeated words whenever necessary to assure clear and grammatically correct sentences. This is particularly important in formal or academic prose.

Turn now to Assignment 19A at the end of this chapter for practice with parallel structures.

EXERCISE 19.1 USING PARALLEL STRUCTURES IN REVISION

Read the passage that follows, paying particular attention to any sentences that could use parallel structures but do not. Remember that sometimes combining sentences will yield useful parallel structures. Underline any sentences that you would want to revise to make their structures parallel. Revise the passage, and copy your best ver-

sion on a separate page to hand in to your instructor. The sentences are numbered for easy reference.

When faced with the task of moving from one town to another, we decided to save money by tackling the entire job ourselves.[1] We quickly discovered that moving was not fun—it was working hard.[2] The physical work was tiring enough, but we had more trouble with the decision making.[3] Should we sell Aunt Maude's needlepoint pillow with the moth hole, or should it be lovingly packed in a box?[4] Occasionally we agreed on such things, but more often our opinions did not coincide.[5] Then we either continued packing in a tense silence, or some joke would defuse the situation.[6]

Through trial and making mistakes, we discovered that the heaviest items should go into the smallest containers.[7] Thus, books went into the smallest boxes; mid-size boxes held small lamps (minus the shades), and shoes.[8] And the biggest boxes bulged with the lightest goods, such as clothing, bedding, or what came from the linen closet.[9] We also learned that not only must all boxes be carefully packed, stacking is important.[10] Small, heavy boxes crush those which are large and airy.[11] But neither careful packing nor an adequate job of stacking could tell us exactly what was inside an unlabeled box.[12]

EXERCISE 19.2 ANALYZING PARALLEL STRUCTURES AND THEIR EFFECTS

Below are two sample passages, each presented in three different versions. Some versions employ parallel structures; others do not. On your own paper, indicate whether each version uses parallel structures, and, in one or two sentences, describe how the effect of each version on the reader differs from the effects of the other two versions. Do not be concerned with which version is better but with the impressions or feelings each conveys.

1. **a)** To Rita, Ed was a real catch; to her parents, he was an aimless drifter.
    b) To Rita, Ed was a real catch. An aimless drifter is what he seemed like to her parents.
    c) Either Ed was a real catch, which is what Rita thought, or he was just an aimless drifter, which is what Rita's parents thought.
2. **a)** Joe wants a big house and a fast car. Joe wants nice landscaping and a built-in swimming pool. Joe wants a lot of things.
    b) Joe wants a big house, a fast car, nice landscaping, and a built-in swimming pool; Joe wants a lot of things.
    c) Joe wants a big house. You should see the car he wants to buy. Nice landscaping is important to him, too. After he has all of that, the next thing on his list of things to buy is a built-in swimming pool. An awful lot of things is what Joe wants.

ASSIGNMENT 19A USING PARALLEL STRUCTURES

Read the sentences below. If the sentence employs accurate parallel structures, underline these structures and write "structures parallel" on the lines provided. If the sentence does not employ accurate parallel structures, write an accurately parallel revision on the line. Do not worry if your revision changes the content of the original; the idea is to write sentences with accurately parallel structures.

EXAMPLES

Some kids love reading, and for others it's soccer that they love.
Some kids love reading, and others love soccer. _____

Take it or leave it. _____
structures parallel _____

1. Mason preferred to do his own landscaping, his own roofing, and install the carpet

himself. _____

_____

2. This company not only designs and manufactures superior hardware, it also provides first-class customer service.

_____

_____

3. On a clear day, you can see west to the Pacific Ocean, the Three Sisters mountains in the east, and north to Mount Hood.

_____

_____

4. The firefighters asked for calm and that spectators remain a safe distance away.

_____

_____

5. This week, senators may vote on child care legislation, or after the upcoming

holiday recess. _____

_____

6. Comprehensive health insurance, making sure everyone kept their jobs, and the right to strike—those were the union's main demands.

_____

_____

_____

7. The road wound down out of heavily forested mountains, through pastureland, and then you come to the city.

_____

_____

8. She ate cold pizza for breakfast, and lobster was what she ate at dinner. _____

_____

9. I'm not swayed by candidate A with his fiery rhetoric, nor by candidate B with his impossible promises.

_____

_____

10. Some of the bloodiest fighting of World War I occurred at the Somme River, just as lots of people landing on the beaches at Normandy were killed during World War II.

_____

_____

_____

20

Varying Sentence Structures

Varying Sentence Lengths 20a

The length of a sentence has a strong effect on its message and its impact. Short sentences express simple, almost childlike assertions: *I want ice cream* or *This blanket's mine.* Short sentences tend to be blunt and forceful. Sometimes, they crystallize complex thought or emotion: *Live free or die* or *The buck stops here.*

In contrast, longer sentences tend to depict fully the complications and complexities of experience. Notice how this longer sentence accommodates two conflicting possibilities and then resolves them: *On the one hand, I'm fond of roast beef because it reminds me of Saturday dinners when I was a kid; on the other hand, my doctor encourages me to avoid red meat: I'll order the fish.*

When should you use short sentences? When should you use long sentences? You learn to make such choices for yourself. But you begin by noting what happens when different stylistic choices are made:

SHORT-SENTENCE VERSION   Live free or die.

LONG-SENTENCE VERSION   If we as people do not live under a government that allows us the basic freedom of choice, we ought to fight for that freedom of choice, just as we would fight for life itself; we ought to fight for that freedom even if it means giving our lives.

The short example is a fine rallying cry. It is easy to remember. The long-sentence version is far more complicated; it cannot be easily remembered. But it does carry its own kind of careful persuasion.

SHORT-SENTENCE VERSION I'm fond of roast beef. It reminds me of Saturday dinners. I was a kid then. I went to the doctor not long ago. She did some tests. She says I should change my diet by avoiding red meat. So I'll order fish.

LONG-SENTENCE VERSION On the one hand, I'm fond of roast beef because it reminds me of Saturday dinners when I was a kid; on the other hand, my doctor says to avoid red meat: I'll order the fish.

The short-sentence version is grammatically correct. However, it is also choppy and sounds scattered and confusing. The long, one-sentence version is clearer because its structure and punctuation help us to understand the relationships among all those independent clauses. As a result, readers have an easier time following the writer's thought. The long-sentence version unites content and form; it is a much better choice.

Choosing what you feel is the most appropriate length for each sentence you write is a good way to begin thinking about varying your sentences. Even when you have done so, however, you may find that all of your sentences have ended up at about the same length. This is because thinking about sentence lengths is sometimes not enough. If this happens to you, try selecting some of the sentences and revising them to be of a noticeably different length, even if you think this will not make them better. Many times, we stick with one version of a sentence or paragraph simply because we have not fully explored the alternatives and therefore do not realize how they might improve what we have written. This sort of experimentation will usually lead you to a more effective version than you had thought was possible.

Turn now to Assignment 20A at the end of this chapter for practice in varying sentence lengths.

Varying Sentence Openings |20b|

If you are writing to hold readers' attention, you will probably want to vary your sentence openings as well as their lengths. Such variety will add interest and pizazz to your writing. Read this passage:

The first afternoon and evening was sunny and hot. We ate dinner in a meadow overlooking the Pacific, and we watched the sun set. It was almost every shade of orange, red, and purple going down. We went to bed expecting good weather. It rained that night. We woke up in the morning and tried to make pancakes while staying warm in our sleeping bags. Some of the batter spilled onto the sleeping bags. The spill made an unpleasant mess.

What you have just read is part of a narrative of a camping trip. Every single sentence starts with a simple subject and is immediately followed by its verb. The passage carries some interest simply due to its details. But it conveys a pretty boring trip overall. Why? Because its sentences all begin the same way.

Here are three ways to vary sentence openings:

- Begin with single word transitions. (For more on transitions, see Chapter 5.)

    Afterward, we discussed the difficulties of being a single parent.

    Hence, the board has approved your design.

- Begin with prepositional, verbal, or absolute phrases. (For further discussion of these phrases, see Chapter 6.)

    Before dawn, the mountain etches its silhouette against the sky.

    Talking around the clock, negotiators finally reached a settlement.

    Our business concluded, we decided to go out to lunch.

- Begin with a subordinate clause. (For more on subordinate clauses, see Chapter 18.)

    Although we could not understand the ancient script, we thoroughly enjoyed seeing an original copy of the Magna Charta.

    Once Valerie had become a vegetarian, the thought of a medium-rare steak no longer tempted her.

EXERCISE 20.1 IDENTIFYING VARIOUS SENTENCE OPENINGS

Compare the following passage to the version that appears on page 282. Underline any new or changed material, and number it as (1) a single-word transition, (2) a prepositional, verbal, or absolute phrase, or (3) a subordinate clause. As an example, the first change has been underlined and identified for you.

(3)

<u>Because that first afternoon and evening was sunny and hot</u>, we ate dinner in a meadow overlooking the Pacific, and as we ate, we watched the sun set. It was almost every shade of orange, red, and purple going down. After such a brilliant sunset, we went to bed expecting good weather. Unfortunately, it rained that night. Disappointed only a little bit, we woke up in the morning and tried to make pancakes while staying warm in our

sleeping bags. Because we were clumsy and maybe still a little sleepy, some of the batter

spilled onto the sleeping bags. As you can imagine, this made for an unpleasant mess.

EXERCISE 20.2 REVISING PROSE BY VARYING SENTENCE LENGTHS AND SENTENCE OPENINGS

Revise the following passage by varying sentence lengths and by varying sentence openings. You may combine or recombine sentences; you may add new content. Make sure that your final version is smoother than the original version. Copy your final version on a separate sheet of paper.

Land use issues are important. We don't often pay attention to them. We do pay attention when a developer decides to change the character of our neighborhood. Our family knows about this because the field behind our house has been slated for clearing, grading, and construction. Our kids have played there for years. A new shopping center will be built. That means cars, noise. It could mean new shops and a better local selection of goods. It might mean a fancy new restaurant or two. Sometimes, we think the development is a good idea. It will benefit the community and provide jobs. Sometimes, we don't want that field to change. The whole family goes to planning commission hearings. We listen to the developer. We listen to our neighbors. Land use isn't some foggy, distant issue anymore. It's as close as our backyard.

Varying Sentence Types |20c|

Are there other ways to vary your prose, making it more vibrant and lively? Certainly. Though most of the sentences you write in formal or academic situations will be declarative, you may also be able to use an occasional question, command, or exclamation. Such sentences change the routine for readers and keep them interested. Beginning a paragraph with a question (as this one does) is but one way to add such variety.

This chapter has already discussed variety in sentence lengths and openings; it is only a small step from that discussion to a larger discussion of grammatical sentence types. Here is a brief review of those types; you ought to be able to use all of them in your own writing.

- Simple (one independent clause)

  Some people go to college to obtain a good job.

- Compound (two or more independent clauses)

  Some people go to college to obtain a good job, but others go to gain an understanding of their values and beliefs.

- Complex (a subordinate clause and an independent clause)

  Whereas some people go to college to obtain a good job, others go to gain an understanding of their values and beliefs.

- Compound-complex (a combination of multiple subordinate and/or independent clauses)

  Whereas some people go to college to obtain a good job and others go to gain an understanding of their values and beliefs, a significant number go to meet people with similar interests.

Two other kinds of sentences provide variety: periodic and cumulative sentences. **Periodic sentences** save their main idea (usually expressed in an independent clause) for the end of the sentence, often using several phrases or dependent clauses to build up to the independent clause.

  For job training, for fostering an understanding of values and beliefs, for meeting other people with similar interests, for drama or forestry or philosophy, for waking yourself up—a college campus is the place.

In contrast, **cumulative sentences** begin with the main idea (again usually in an independent clause), following with several phrases or dependent clauses.

  A college campus is a place for job training, for fostering an understanding of values and beliefs, for meeting others with similar interests, for drama or forestry or philosophy, for waking yourself up.

EXERCISE 20.3 ADDING SENTENCE VARIETY

Use your own paper to freewrite on the topic of why you, personally, are in school. What brought you to college? What is keeping you here? What are your goals? If these are somewhat confusing questions to you, talk about why they are confusing. Write quickly and freely, and do not censor yourself. Do not worry about spelling or grammar. Try to fill at least two-thirds of a page.

When you have finished, reread and revise your freewriting. Your goal is to produce at least two clear and coherent paragraphs using at least *five* of the seven sentence types identified as follows:

1. simple sentence
2. compound sentence
3. complex sentence

4. compound-complex sentence
5. periodic sentence
6. cumulative sentence
7. interrogative, imperative, or exclamatory sentence

Copy your final version onto another sheet of paper, placing the number corresponding to the appropriate type after each sentence. Every sentence in your final version should have a number after it.

ASSIGNMENT 20A WRITING SENTENCES OF VARYING LENGTHS

Revise each of the following sentences as specified. Be ready to discuss the differences of meaning and emphasis between the original and your revision.

EXAMPLES

Since we've lost two games already and since this week's opponent has lost only one game, you can see that it's really important that we come out on top. (Summarize in a short sentence.)
We need to win!

It was Sunday afternoon. The sun was shining. The hammock was in the backyard. It was a perfect day for resting in the hammock. (Combine into one long sentence.)
That sunny Sunday afternoon was perfect for resting in the hammock in the backyard.

1. You should stop playing or looking at the gravel or doing whatever you're doing out there in the street because a large dump truck is coming. (Summarize in a short sentence.)

_____

_____

2. First you strip off the original finish, then complete any rough sanding, then smooth all of the table's exposed surfaces with fine steel wool, and then apply the new finish. (Break into several short sentences.)

_____

_____

_____

3. Some people have trouble with math. Often they say they study and study. Then they take the test. They are usually disappointed with the results. (Combine into one smooth sentence.)

_____

_____

_____

4. Persistence pays. (Write a longer single sentence version that emphasizes the importance of persistence.)

_____

_____

_____

5. The clam chowder is good. The clam chowder is thick. Clam chowder and French bread make a good meal. Sometimes, they go well with a glass of Riesling. The clam chowder is served on Fridays. It's served at lunchtime. (Combine into one or two smooth sentences.)

_____

_____

_____

_____

21

Creating Memorable Prose

The best prose accomplishes two difficult tasks: it embodies what its writer wished to say, and it moves readers to feelings, action, or agreement exactly as the writer intended. Such prose depends on a writer's sincerity and commitment, but it just as surely depends on stylistic principles that all can learn.

Choosing Strong Verbs |21a|

Strong verbs convey their meaning in precise and unmistakable terms. Consider these three ways of saying basically the same thing:

The gulls *were flying* into the wind.

The gulls *flew* into the wind.

The gulls *hovered and soared* into the wind.

The last example here is the strongest; the verbs *hovered* and *soared* convey most precisely and vividly the actual motion of gulls in the air. All three examples are grammatically correct, but only the final one conveys any real sense of motion or grace.

Unlike the action verbs *hover* and *soar*, verbs formed from *be, do,* and *have* carry no sense of specific movement. Because these verbs can work in almost any sentence, they frequently crop up in rough drafts. Notice how sentences with these weak verbs can be revised to produce more vibrant prose:

WEAK The traffic downtown today was bad.

REVISED Heavy traffic clogged downtown streets today.

[*289*]

WEAK   We had a two-mile run this morning in P.E.

REVISED   We jogged and sweated through a two-mile run this morning in P.E.

Sentences beginning with *It is* or *There are* also tend to clutter rough drafts; after all, almost anything can follow *It is.* Combing through your rough draft to revise such sentences will almost always result in stronger prose. See how the following examples have been strengthened by revision:

WEAK   There is fog outside that obscures our view of Seal Rock.

REVISED   The fog outside obscures our view of Seal Rock.

WEAK   There are many comedians who perform to conquer their shyness.

REVISED   Many comedians perform to conquer their shyness.

Changing Nouns to Verbs |21a2|

Much contemporary writing depends unnecessarily on noun-heavy prose, which sounds pompous and self-important. Consider this sentence:

Our research department has a consistent involvement in the development of new products.

What is wrong here? The sentence is grammatically correct but is crammed full of weighty nouns around the bland verb *has.* If you find yourself writing such stuffy sentences, revise them by changing nouns and noun phrases into verbs. For example, the entire concept expressed by *has a consistent involvement in the development of* can be conveyed by the single, vivid verb *develops*:

Our research department develops new products.

Here is another example:

WORDY AND STUFFY   For this job, *the requirement* of the Occupational Safety and Health Administration *is* that men be clean-shaven.

REVISED   For this job, the Occupational Safety and Health Administration *requires* that men be clean-shaven.

Turn now to Assignment 21A at the end of this chapter for practice with strong verbs.

Choosing between Active and Passive Voice |21b|

Consider these two ways of describing the same event:

ACTIVE VOICE On the deck of the USS *Missouri,* Douglas MacArthur signed the peace treaty ending World War II in the Pacific.

PASSIVE VOICE The peace treaty ending World War II in the Pacific was signed by General Douglas MacArthur on the deck of the USS *Missouri.*

As you can see, active voice focuses readers' attention on somebody or something performing an action: subject *(General Douglas MacArthur),* action verb *(signed).* In contrast, passive voice focuses attention on whatever receives the action *(the peace treaty).*

Recognizing these different emphases is another key to writing memorable prose. Weak prose often overuses the passive voice, choosing it even when there is no good reason to do so. In practice, most academic prose uses the active voice, while much scientific reporting uses the passive voice.

ACTIVE Maxine Kumin's poems often illuminate New England life. [*Here, the subject,* poems, *performs the action,* illuminate.]

PASSIVE Temperatures were recorded for a thirty-minute period. [*Here, the action,* were recorded, *is performed by an unnamed agent.*]

Notice that in the active voice, the subject performs the action of the verb. In the passive voice, the performer of the action may not be named at all.

Here is one way to help you choose between the active and the passive voice. First, write the sentence in the active voice: *The committee reviewed all proposals.* Now, determine the subject (the performer of the action), the verb, and the direct object of the verb:

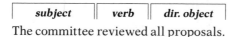

| subject | verb | dir. object |

The committee reviewed all proposals.

If you wish to emphasize the subject and the action performed, keep the sentence in the active voice. If you wish to emphasize the direct object (the receiver of the action), use the passive. Notice that in the passive voice, the direct object *(all proposals)* becomes the sentence subject: *All proposals were reviewed by the committee.* The active voice emphasizes the committee and what it did; the passive voice emphasizes the proposals and what was done to them.

Finally, if you have no good reason to use the passive voice, it is probably better to choose the active voice.

Turn now to Assignment 21B at the end of this chapter for practice with the active and the passive voice.

Creating Special Effects |21c|

Repetition of particular sounds, words, phrases, or grammatical structures can result in memorable prose. Here is an exasperated parent using repetition to underscore the urgency of a required action:

> Before you turn on the television, before you leave to play baseball or ride your skateboard, before you call anyone on the telephone, before you so much as think of what you are going to do next, you must clear the floor of your dirty clothes and put them in the hamper.

That sentence repeats similar items to achieve its emphasis; another effect may be achieved with sentences that operate on the principle of contrast.

> When I was a youngster, I ate everything in sight and never gained weight; now, everything I eat gathers at my waist and will not go away.

The emphasis in this sentence is the difference between the past and the present. The tension in such contrast sentences makes them interesting.

Writers can also achieve special emphasis by changing the normal word order in a sentence. Most English sentences follow the subject→verb→object word order. Changing that order invariably calls attention to the sentence.

NORMAL ORDER   This painting reminds me of my father.

INVERTED ORDER   My father—this painting reminds me of him.

NORMAL ORDER   A deer stood less than ten feet away.

INVERTED ORDER   Less than ten feet away stood a deer.

Notice that in each case, the normal word order seems matter-of-fact, whereas the inverted order tends to convey an emotional overtone.

The special effects described in this section should be used sparingly and judiciously. Such techniques work only because their rarity makes them stand out.

Turn now to Assignment 21C for practice with special effects. Then proceed to Assignment 21D to review the styling techniques covered in Part 4 (Chapters 17–21).

ASSIGNMENT 21A REVISING BY CHOOSING STRONGER VERBS

Weak verbs and unnecessarily wordy constructions plague the following sentences. Revise the sentences by substituting stronger verbs.

EXAMPLES

It is necessary that the cast arrive for rehearsal at 6 P.M.
The cast must arrive for rehearsal at 6 P.M.

A large amount of electrical energy is a requirement for aluminum production.
Aluminum production requires a large amount of electrical energy.

1. The murder mystery on television was so boring that I fell asleep.

_____

2. There were many parents in the parking lot waiting to pick up their children.

_____

3. In many cities, gang activities are a threat to neighborhood stability.

_____

4. It is said by most political cartoonists that a candidate's looks are more important than a candidate's positions on the issues.

_____

_____

5. There were over 36,000 fans to watch the Cubs defeat the Mets in the first night baseball game at Chicago's Wrigley Field.

_____

_____

6. The personal lives of actors and actresses are of interest to many of their fans.

_____

7. A requirement of many computer programs is at least 256 kilobytes of memory.

_____

Identify the following sentences as either active or passive. Then note the intended emphasis of each. If the original version accomplishes that emphasis, write *OK*. If the original version does not accomplish that emphasis, rewrite the sentence by changing its voice.

EXAMPLES

My supervisor approved your memo.

Sentence is <u>active</u>. Intended emphasis: the memo

The memo was approved by my supervisor.

The weather forecast was given as the last news item.

Sentence is <u>passive</u>. Intended emphasis: the weekend news anchor

The weekend news anchor gave the weather forecast as her last news item.

Kenyan coffee is grown in Africa.

Sentence is <u>passive</u>. Intended emphasis: the coffee

    OK

1. A gold medal was won by U.S. skier Bill Johnson.

Sentence is _____. Intended emphasis: U.S. skier Bill Johnson

2. Dogs and cats are frequently disturbed by the explosions of July 4 fireworks.

Sentence is _____. Intended emphasis: dogs and cats

3. You are hereby summoned to appear in Traffic Court on July 21 at 10 A.M.

Sentence is _____. Intended emphasis: the City of New York

4. In summer, soaring red-tail hawks are often seen by us high over the meadows.

Sentence is _____. Intended emphasis: we

5. In the next eight minutes, seismographers recorded five aftershocks.

Sentence is _____. Intended emphasis: the aftershocks

ASSIGNMENT 21C COMPOSING SENTENCES THAT USE SPECIAL EFFECTS

The chapter identifies three kinds of sentences using structures that create special effects. One kind uses repetition, the second uses contrast, and the third uses inverted word order. For this exercise, compose a sentence of each kind. An example of each kind of sentence is given.

EXAMPLE OF REPETITION   Once I sweep out the garage, once I mow the lawn, once I wash and vacuum the car, once I pick up my sweater at the cleaner's, once I balance the checkbook and pay the bills, I will have all that free time to write letters to friends.

YOUR EXAMPLE OF REPETITION

1. _____

_____

_____

_____

EXAMPLE OF CONTRAST   We began the project full of energy and enthusiasm; we finished weary and relieved that it was over.

YOUR EXAMPLE OF CONTRAST

2. _____

_____

_____

_____

EXAMPLE OF INVERTED WORD ORDER   A handy, even indispensable tool is the computer.

YOUR EXAMPLE OF INVERTED WORD ORDER

3. _____

_____

_____

_____

Using any of the structures and revision suggestions covered in Chapters 17–21, revise the following short passages to create what you feel is more varied, interesting, effective prose. You may want to write partial revisions on the passages themselves, before beginning work on the lines provided below.

1. I got off the bus. I looked for my keys. They were not in my backpack. They were not in my pocket. I remembered locking the door after me in the morning. I could not figure out where they were now. I went to the door. There were no lights on in the apartment. I rang the doorbell. My roommates were not home. I had a sinking feeling. I was locked out.

_____

_____

_____

_____

_____

2. It is really true that there is no such thing as a bargain in this day and age that we are living in now. Products are bought by people who have not got the time that is needed to be careful, smart shoppers. They are busy all the time, and money is no object to them, so high prices are perpetuated by the merchants, who after all cannot be blamed if they want to make a profit.

_____

_____

_____

_____

_____

_____

PART 5

Selecting Effective Words

These questions are designed to help you, the student, decide what you need to study. (Answers are found at the back of the book.) First, find and correct any misspellings in the following sentences.

1. Their always telling us when they're going to have us over.
2. Harold definately never eats desert.
3. He herd the bells ringing, then he developped a headache.
4. During the rein of Queen Elizabeth I, many famous righters lived and dyed.
5. The Reagan administration concluded a nucular arms reduction treatey.

Use your dictionary to answer the following questions.

6. What is the origin of the word *adjudicate*? _____

7. What does *dementia praecox* mean? _____

8. Give at least two synonyms for *tendency*. _____

9. How many meanings does *revolution* have? _____

Respond to these questions about roots and suffixes.

10. Find two words for each of the following roots:

    a) *bio* = life (Gr.) _____

    b) *jur* or *jus* = law (Lat.) _____

11. What suffix indicates an *adverb*? _____

12. What are three suffixes indicating adjectives? _____

Underline any words in the following sentences that seem incorrectly used or inappropriate within the context. Write in the correct word if there is an error; write *C* if there is none.

13. Woody Allen eludes to T.S. Eliot in his short stories. _____

14. The stink of baking apples was wonderfully appetizing. _____

15. I am continuously being interrupted by a continual stream of memos and phone calls. _____

16. This wine complements the meal perfectly. _____

Mark an *X* next to any of the following sentences that use language that is inappropriate for a college essay.

17. My research into the effect of television on babies requires tons of statistics.
18. Feminism and Marxim are two critical approaches frequently employed by contemporary literary critics.
19. Anyone who has studied this author's work in detail can see that he's just wrong.

22

Mastering Spelling

At some time or another, every writer makes spelling errors; such errors occur more frequently than any other kind. However, you can become a better speller. All it takes is time and effort on your part.

Spelling Tip 1: Change Your Writing Habits

As you draft, underline every word that you are not sure how to spell, even if you believe you have remembered it correctly. Later, look up all the underlined words at once. It is easy, once you have written a word and gone on to something else, to forget that you may have misspelled it; underlining as you go will help you remember to check. You can look up words in any standard dictionary (see Chapter 23 for advice on how to use a dictionary). Finally, if you are composing on a word processor, you may be able to make use of a spell checker. These programs are helpful in spotting *some* misspellings, but they are not a substitute for careful proofreading of your own work. For example, a spell checker will not catch typographical errors like *form* for *from* or *king* for *kind*, nor will it know that you have written *herd* instead of *heard* or *loose* instead of *lose* because these misspellings spell words that are correct in other contexts.

Spelling Tip 2: Learn to Proofread for Spelling Errors

A final proofreading of anything you have written is essential if you want to catch your own spelling errors. The best way is to proofread sentence by sentence from the end to the beginning. Underline any questionable word as you go along. Pay little attention to content; force your eyes to study each single word.

EXERCISE 22.1 NOTING SPELLING UNCERTAINTIES AS YOU WRITE AND PROOFREADING FOR MISSPELLINGS

On your own paper, freewrite quickly and nonstop on the topic of diet and health. Begin by copying this opening: *When I think about diet and health, I think about . . . .* **Finish that sentence and keep right on going. Do not worry about grammatical correctness. If you are concerned about the spelling of particular words, simply underline those words and go on.**

Once you have finished freewriting, proofread your work sentence by sentence, starting with the last sentence and working toward the first. Underline any words you think may be misspelled. Then look them up, correct them, and make a list of your corrections.

Spelling Tip 3: Master Commonly Misspelled Words |22a|

Research on college writing by the authors of *The St. Martin's Handbook* has identified the fifty most commonly misspelled words. Chances are that at least a few of these words give you trouble too. Here is the list:

1. their/there/they're	18. through	35. business, -es
2. too/to	19. until	36. dependent
3. a lot	20. where	37. every day
4. noticeable	21. successful, -ly	38. may be
5. receive, -d, -s	22. truly	39. occasion, -s
6. lose	23. argument, -s	40. occurrences
7. your/you're	24. experience, -s	41. woman
8. an/and	25. environment	42. all right
9. develop, -s	26. exercise, -s, -ing	43. apparent, -ly
10. definitely	27. necessary	44. categories
11. than/then	28. sense	45. final, -ly
12. believe, -d, -s	29. therefore	46. immediate, -ly
13. occurred	30. accept, -ed	47. roommate, -s
14. affect, -s	31. heroes	48. against
15. cannot	32. professor	49. before
16. separate	33. accept, -ed	50. beginning
17. success	34. without	

EXERCISE 22.2 REVIEWING COMMONLY MISSPELLED WORDS

Reread the list of commonly mispelled words. Identify from the list five words that have given you trouble in the past. Indicate how you misspelled the word, and then use that word (correctly spelled) in a sentence. Use your own paper for this exercise.

EXAMPLE

Word: apparently
In the past, I've misspelled this word by adding an extra *r*.
Sentence: *After checking her purse, Elvira said, "Apparently, I forgot the grocery list."*

Spelling Tip 4: Recognize Homonyms and Similarly Confusing Words |22b|

Many words have the same sound but different spellings and meanings. *Deer* are wild animals; *dear* often begins a letter. *Cereal* is a breakfast food; *serial* is a magazine or journal. Other words sound so nearly similar that they are often confused. Here is a list of homonyms and frequently confused words; familiarizing yourself with the words in this list may help you become more sensitive to this kind of spelling problem.

advice/advise	dairy/diary	passed/past
allusion/illusion	desert/dessert	peace/piece
are/our	device/devise	personal/personnel
bare/bear	die/dye	plain/plane
berth/birth	elicit/illicit	principal/principle
board/bored	eminent/immanent/imminent	quiet/quite
brake/break	fair/fare	rain/rein/reign
breath/breathe	forth/fourth	right/rite/write
buy/by	hear/here	road/rode
capital/capitol	heard/herd	seen/scene
choose/chose	heroin/heroine	stationary/stationery
cite/sight/site	know/no	threw/through/
coarse/course	later/latter	thorough
complement/compliment	lead/led	waist/waste
conscience/conscious	loose/lose	weak/week
council/counsel	meat/meet	wear/where/were

Spelling Tip 5: Be Wary of Spelling According to Pronunciation |22c|

Spelling words according to their sounds often leads to trouble (consider a word like *enough*). Even when words are spelled as they sound, sometimes we mispronounce them (and so misspell them). We may say "reconize" when we mean "recognize," and we may carry the inaccurate pronunciation over onto the page. Here are some additional examples; in each case, the correct spelling is italicized.

nucular *nuclear*	strickly *strictly*	wich *which*
goverment *government*	artic *arctic*	suppose *supposed*
use to *used to*	liberry *library*	

EXERCISE 22.3 DISTINGUISHING BETWEEN HOMONYMS AND OTHER SIMILAR-SOUNDING WORDS

Five pairs of words are given below. For each word, write a sentence that uses the word correctly. Use your own paper for this exercise.

EXAMPLE

a. witch   b. which
a. The wicked witch wore ruby slippers.
b. I cannot decide which one of these movies to rent tonight.

1. a. lose   b. loose
2. a. conscience   b. conscious
3. a. descent   b. dissent
4. a. accept   b. except
5. a. ladder   b. latter

Now choose five other pairs of troublesome words (refer to the words listed in the text if necessary). Use each word correctly in a sentence. Make the best use of this part of the exercise by selecting words that you know you tend to confuse.

Spelling Tip 6: Recognize Words with More than One Form |22b1|

In some instances, terms may be written as two words or combined to make a single word, depending on the intended meaning. Here is a list of commonly confused terms; check your dictionary for differences in meaning.

| all ready/already | every day/everyday | may be/maybe |
| all ways/always | every one/everyone | no body/nobody |

Writers also commonly misspell *a lot* and *all right*: these words are never combined. *Cannot*, in contrast, is always spelled as one word.

Spelling Tip 7: Note Unpronounced Letters or Syllables and Unstressed Vowels |22c|

To remember the spelling of words with unpronounced or unstressed letters or syllables, try to picture them in your mind. Or, create an alternate pronunciation that allows you to hear every letter and syllable. For example, remember *drastically* by saying to yourself "dras-tic-al-ly"; similarly, *Wednesday* becomes "Wed-nes-day." Here is a list of frequently misspelled words of this kind, with their unpronounced or unstressed letters or syl-lables italicized:

candidate	foreign	probably
condemn	government	quantity
different	interest	restaurant
drastically	marriage	Wednesday
February	muscle	

Words like *definite* contain unstressed vowels, making it hard to hear whether or not the last syllable should be spelled *-ite* or *-ate*. Sometimes, picturing the word will help; remembering a related word (like *define*) should help you locate *definite* in the dictionary.

Spelling Tip 8: Take Advantage of Spelling Rules |22d|

- *I* before *e*, except after *c* or when sounded like "ay" as in *neighbor* and *weigh*.
  i before *e*: *achieve, believe, grief, friend, piece, relieve*
  except after *c*: *receive, ceiling, deceit*
  or when sounded like "ay": *neighbor, weigh, sleigh, inveigh, heinous, their*
  EXCEPTIONS: *either, neither, foreign, forfeit, height, leisure, efficient, seize, seizure, weird, science, ancient, nonpareil, conscience*

Adding Prefixes and Suffixes |22d2, 22d3|

(Prefixes and suffixes are defined in section 24d.)

- When attaching a prefix, merely add it; do not change the spelling of the original word.
  contaminate + prefix *de-* = *decontaminate*
  moral + prefix *a-* = *amoral*
  spell + prefix *mis-* = *misspell*
- To add a suffix for a word ending in silent *e*, keep the *e* if the suffix begins with a consonant; drop the *e* if the suffix begins with a vowel.
  snare + *-ing* (suffix begins with vowel; drop *e*) = *snaring*
  care + *-ful* (suffix begins with consonant; keep *e*) = *careful*
  EXCEPTIONS: *acreage, mileage, judgment*

The silent final *e* is retained after a soft *c* (*service* + *-able* = *serviceable*) or soft *g* (*courage* + *-ous* = *courageous*). Sometimes, the silent *e* is dropped when it is preceded by another vowel: in *true* + *-ly*, the silent *e* is preceded by the vowel *u*; hence, *true* + *-ly* = *truly*. The *e* is also retained occasionally to prevent confusion with other words (*dye* + *-ing* = *dyeing*).

- When adding *-ally* or *-ly*, use *-ally* if the word ends in *ic*; use *-ly* if the word does not end in *ic*.
  basic + *-ally* = *basically*
  slow + *-ly* = *slowly*
  EXCEPTION: *public* + *-ly* = *publicly*

EXERCISE 22.4 USING RULES FOR *I* BEFORE *E* AND FOR SOME SUFFIXES

Read the following five sentences carefully. Circle any misspelled words you find, and write the correct spelling above each misspelling.

EXAMPLE   *Basically proceeds*   *neighbor's*
      (Basicly) (procedes) of the fund-raising activities will be used to rebuild the (nieghbor's) house.

1. A carful analysis of the situation indicates that niether party has recieved a

paycheck for last week.

2. Friends can usualally help overcome greif.

3. Children sometimes have trouble shareing toys or treating each other diplomaticly.

4. Haveing the ceiling fixed has been a big relief.

5. Paco is a couragous goalie who truely enjoys playing soccer.

- When adding a suffix to a word ending in *y*, keep the *y* when it follows a vowel and whenever adding *-ing*; change the *y* to *i* when the *y* follows a consonant.
  play + -ful (*y* follows vowel; keep *y*) = *playful*
  play + -ing (adding *-ing*; keep *y*) = *playing*
  beauty + -ful (*y* follows consonant; change *y* to *i*) = *beautiful*
  beauty + -fy (*y* follows consonant; change *y* to *i*) = *beautify*
  beautify + -ing (adding *-ing*; keep *y*) = *beautifying*
  EXCEPTIONS: Keep the *y* in some one-syllable base words: *shy + -er = shyer.* Change the *y* to *i* in some one-syllable base words: *day + -ly = daily.* Keep the *y* if the base word is a proper name: *Kennedy + esque = Kennedyesque.*

Sometimes, adding a suffix means doubling the final consonant of a word (*pin + -ed = pinned*), and sometimes, it does not (*shower + -ed = showered*). Knowing when to double or not depends on your ability to identify the number of syllables in a word and your ability to hear where the stress falls when a word is pronounced correctly.

- When adding suffixes to words of one syllable that end in consonants, double the final consonant only when a single vowel precedes that final consonant.
  pin + -ing (final consonant preceded by single vowel; double consonant) = *pinning*

> *flip* + *-ed* (final consonant preceded by single vowel; double consonant) = *flipped*
>
> *stream* + *-er* (final consonant preceded by two vowels; do not double) = *streamer*
>
> *curl* + *-ing* (final consonant preceded by consonant; do not double) = *curling*

- In words of more than one syllable, double the final consonant when a single vowel precedes the final consonant *and* the sounded stress falls on the last syllable of the original word once the suffix has been added.

> *recall* + *-ed* (final consonant preceded by consonant; do not double) = *recalled*
>
> *begin* + *-er* (final consonant preceded by single vowel, and sounded stress falls on last syllable of original word once suffix is added; double final consonant) = *beginner*
>
> *invent* + *-ing* (final consonant preceded by consonant; do not double) = *inventing*

EXERCISE 22.5 USING ADDITIONAL SUFFIX RULES

Based on the suffix rules just discussed, determine the proper spelling of the following new words and state the rule you applied. Use your own paper for this exercise.

EXAMPLE *coin* + *-ed*

> Correct spelling: coined
> Rule: In words of one syllable, double the final consonant only when a single vowel precedes the final consonant.

1. *employ* + *-er*
2. *conduct* + *-ing*
3. *refer* + *-ing*
4. *study* + *-ed*
5. *control* + *-able*

Adding the Endings *-sede, -ceed, and -cede*

The ending pronounced "seed" can be spelled in three ways.

- *-sede:* The only word in which this occurs is *supersede.*
- *-ceed:* The only words in which this occurs are *exceed, proceed,* and *succeed.*
- *-cede:* The ending pronounced "seed" is spelled this way in all other English words.

Forming Plurals

- Form the plurals of most nouns by adding *-s*, as in *papers, clouds, dimes.*
- Form the plurals of nouns ending in *s, ch, sh,* or *x* by adding *-es*, as in *churches, bosses, telexes.*

- Form the plurals of nouns ending in *y* by changing the *y* to *i* and adding *-es*, as in *countries* (from *country*), *luxuries* (from *luxury*), *scarcities* (from *scarcity*).
- Form the plurals of nouns ending in *f* or *fe* by changing the *f* or *fe* to *v* and then adding *-es*, as in *leaves* (from *leaf*), *thieves* (from *thief*), *loaves* (from *loaf*). (Note: Verbs ending in *s, ch, sh,* or *x* form their third-person singular in the same way, as in *Shirley cashes a check.*)
- Form the plurals of nouns ending in *o* by adding *-s* if the *o* is preceded by a vowel (as in *radios*) or by adding *-es* if the *o* is preceded by a consonant (as in *potatoes* or *heroes* (exceptions: *sopranos, pros, pianos, hippos, pimentos*).

Some words taken from other languages use the plurals from those languages: *phenomenon/phenomena, datum/data, medium/media, locus/loci, radius/radii.*

Spelling Tip 9: Use a Personal Spelling Chart

Spelling errors are not deliberate errors: no one sets out to use inaccurate spelling. Constructing, using, and evaluating the data from a personal spelling chart will help you to see the pattern of your particular spelling problems. Once you know the pattern, you will be able to identify the specific kinds of words that give you trouble. You can then begin to anticipate which words you will need to underline (either during drafting or proofreading) and then look up. And you will also be able to concentrate on learning the appropriate rules.

The form for a personal spelling chart is as follows:

	Word (Spelled Correctly)	Inaccurate Version	Letters or Syllables Involved	Type of Misspelling
1.	due	do	o/ue	homonym
2.	receiving	recieving	ei/ie	letter reversal
3.	response	reponse	s	missing letter
4.	nastiest	nastyest	i/y	suffix rule
5.	supreme	supream	e/ea	long vowel sound
6.	language	langauge	au/ua	letter reversal
7.	flue	flew	ue/ew	homonym
8.	definite	definate	i/a	unstressed vowel
9.	snoring	snoreing	e	suffix rule
10.	compiling	compilling	l	suffix rule

If such words as the ten listed here appeared on your own spelling chart, you would be able to see that homonyms, letter reversals, and suffix rules consistently cause trouble. Keep such a chart over the course of a term, and you will see patterns in the errors you make. Armed with such knowledge, you will become an even more effective proofreader of your own writing.

ASSIGNMENT 22A   CONSTRUCTING A PERSONAL SPELLING CHART

Following the format just given, begin your own personal spelling chart. Use anything you have written recently (the draft you produced in Exercise 22.1, for instance, or a letter or a list). Find and list at least ten words you have misspelled, and fill out the other three columns of the chart for each of those words. If your draft does not contain ten misspellings, complete your chart with words you have misspelled in the past. Finally, identify and list any misspelling patterns you see in your chart—what kinds of words should you look at more carefully the next time you are proofreading your writing for spelling errors?

Word (Spelled Correctly)	Inaccurate Version	Letters or Syllables Involved	Type of Misspelling

Proofread the following passage. Underline any misspelled words or words you do not know how to spell. Check all of them and then, in the space provided below, write out a list of the misspellings you found and the correct spelling of each.

Constructing any thing takes knowlege, time, and patients. Wether you are sewwing a dress, desining a cabinet, or useing your culinery skills to make a grate omelet, chances are that your product will not be prefect the first time. So plan on makeing that first dress for youself and giving the second one as a gift; plan on staying at the workbench longer than you woud like and on hanging that first cabanet in the garage; and plan on consumeing that first omelet in privite. In this way, your expectted mistakes hurt no one. Keepping your patience, maintaning high stanards, controling your tempter—these things aren't easy. However, if you can make mistakes and lern from them, your work will improove and so wil your one estimateion of your talence.

23

Using Dictionaries

Writers use dictionaries the way carpenters use hammers and cooks use pots and pans—as indispensable tools. Chances are that you have used dictionaries in the past and that you have some sort of dictionary available to you. If you are purchasing a dictionary, choose one of the hardback "college" dictionaries. Among the most popular and well designed are the *American Heritage Dictionary* (published by Random House) and *Webster's Ninth New Collegiate Dictionary* (published by Merriam-Webster, Inc.). Both are also available in paperback editions.

Using the Standard Dictionary Entry |23a|

Dictionaries help writers check spelling, meaning, and syllabic divisions, as well as a variety of other things. Suppose that you are working on a rough draft and quoting a sentence from a speaker who said, "That should appeal to the *hoypoloy*." You underline *hoypoloy* because you are unsure of its spelling; besides, you want to look up that word because it is unfamiliar to you.

In revising, you come upon *hoypoloy* and decide to look it up. How do you look up a word that you have never seen before? First, figure out the letter combinations that could produce the word's opening sound. The first syllable could be spelled *hoy* (as in *boy*) or *hoi* (as in *noise*). Using a hardbound college dictionary, you look first under *hoy* but find nothing. Looking under *hoi*, however, does give you the entry. The word (really a phrase, as it turns out) appears this way: **hoi pol•loi**. Now you know how to spell the term and how to divide its syllables. The phrase means "the general populace; the masses." So in effect, your speaker was saying, "That should appeal to the masses."

Dictionary entries vary slightly from publisher to publisher and may provide as many as a dozen separate kinds of information. Most entries will include at least the first six of the following items.

1. *Spelling,* including alternate spellings, if they exist
2. *Word division,* with syllables separated by bars or dots, showing where to break a word at the end of a line
3. *Pronunciation,* including alternate pronunciations, if any (Keys indicating the sounds of the phonetic respellings are typically found in a dictionary's front matter and along the bottom margin of every page.)
4. *Grammatical functions and irregular forms,* including plurals of nouns, principal parts of verbs, and comparative and superlative forms of adjectives and adverbs
5. *Etymology,* the language and words that the word comes from (Knowing a word's origin can help writers choose appropriately among several words that mean roughly the same thing.)
6. *Meanings,* usually given in order of either development or frequency of use
7. *Examples* of the word in the context of a phrase or sentence
8. *Usage labels and notes* telling readers that some or all meanings of a word may not be appropriate in certain contexts (For example, the meaning of the word *mart,* "a fair," might carry the usage label *archaic* to indicate that this meaning is no longer in common use. Other common usage labels include *obs.,* meaning obsolete; *colloq.* or *coll.,* meaning colloquial; *informal*; and *slang.*)
9. *Field labels,* indicating that a word has a specialized meaning in a particular field of knowledge
10. *Synonyms and antonyms*
11. *Related words* and their grammatical functions
12. *Idioms,* conventional phrases in which the word appears and their meanings

Figure 2 (opposite) shows the *American Heritage Dictionary*'s entry for the word *compose.*

EXERCISE 23.1 CONSULTING BASIC DICTIONARY ENTRIES

For each of the following words, consult a hardbound college dictionary to confirm spelling and to determine syllabic divisions. Some of the words may be spelled incorrectly; consider possible variants before you give up! On your own paper, write the correctly spelled word, placing asterisks between the syllables. At the top of your paper, indicate the name of the dictionary you are using.

EXAMPLE disterbution   *dis*tri*bu*tion*

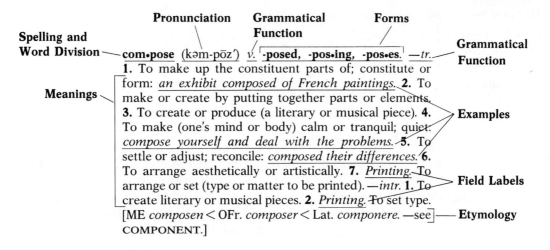

Figure 2   A Standard Dictionary Entry

1. precede
2. hors d'eourve
3. prestigeous
4. inviegle
5. pin-head
6. manikin
7. necesary
8. meadiate
9. accuterment

Now find two or three synonyms for each of the following words.

EXAMPLE fair   *just, equitable, impartial*

10. material
11. demand
12. illuminate
13. way
14. angry
15. word
16. bothered
17. place
18. chilly

Finally, look up the following words. For each word, write out each pronunciation provided, indicate the grammatical functions, and briefly summarize all meanings. Note that many words have more than one meaning. Follow the format of the example.

EXAMPLE conduct

> Pronunciations: *kən duct' (v.), kon' duct (n.)*
> Grammatical Function Labels: *v.—tr. (transitive verb), n. (noun)*
> Meanings: *(v.) to direct the course of, lead, or manage; (n.) the way a person acts, behavior, management*

19. concrete	24. advertisement
20. delegate	25. advocate
21. animate	26. recluse
22. interest	27. amortize
23. converse	

Distinguishing among Dictionaries |23*b*|

Unabridged (uncondensed) dictionaries typically contain more than twice the entries of their shorter "college" cousins. Often multivolumed and quite expensive, unabridged dictionaries are most easily found in libraries. The most famous unabridged dictionary is the *Oxford English Dictionary*, often referred to simply by its initials, *OED*. An *OED* entry provides a complete historical account of a word, indicating not just its spelling but also the evolution of its meaning.

Consulting Specialized Dictionaries |23*c*|

In addition to general-use abridged and unabridged dictionaries, many dictionaries are designed for specific uses. *Longman's Dictionary of American English* provides considerable grammatical and usage information not often found in other dictionaries. For example, this dictionary identifies nouns as countable (*dime* is a countable noun) or uncountable (*honesty* is an uncountable noun). Nonnative speakers find this dictionary particularly helpful.

Probably the most commonly used of the special dictionaries is the thesaurus. Providing word synonyms and antonyms, a thesaurus can help a writer choose the precise word for a particular context. Under *anger*, for example, writers might find *rage, resentment, annoyance*, and *pique*.

Other special dictionaries include various "spelling dictionaries" (entries are common misspellings, followed by correct spellings) and various thematic dictionaries (for example, a dictionary of musical terms or a dictionary of American slang). Your library and campus bookstore probably have a wide selection of such reference aids.

Finally, there are dictionaries of usage that address the appropriate use of specific words. Is it possible, for example, for something to be *more unique* than something else: can one movie director be *more unique* than another? That is a usage question. Among the better-known usage dictionaries are H. W. Fowler's *Dictionary of Modern English Usage*, Bergen and Cornelia Evans's *Dictionary of Contemporary American Usage*, and Margaret M. Bryant's *Current American Usage*.

EXERCISE 23.2 USING A THESAURUS

Use a thesaurus to find five synonyms for each of the italicized words in the phrases that follow. If you do not own a thesaurus, your reference librarian should be able to help you find one. List the synonyms on a separate sheet of paper, and be ready to discuss the shades of meaning that distinguish one synonym from another.

EXAMPLE a *savvy* politician

Synonyms: *shrewd, perceptive, wise, understanding, experienced*

1. to *satiate* her hunger for knowledge
2. to *reject* all bids for the construction project
3. an *obscure* Amazonian tribe
4. to *pacify* an angry boss
5. the *strength* of her argument

EXERCISE 23.3 USING THE LIBRARY'S SPECIAL DICTIONARIES

At your local library, find special dictionaries in the reference area (ask your reference librarian for help if you need it). Select three of them. For each, on your own paper, provide the types of information shown in the example below.

EXAMPLE

Title: *The Oxford Dictionary of English Christian Names*
Author or Editor: E. G. Withycombe, ed.
Publisher: Oxford University Press
Year of Publication: 1977
Information Provided: 310 pages of first names together with their meanings and origins
Sample Entry (from p. 235): OSWIN (m): Old English *Oswin*, compound of *os* 'a god' and *wine* 'friend.' It remained in use until the 14th C. and was occasionally revived in the 19th C.

Next, consulting a dictionary of usage, briefly answer the following questions. Indicate the name, all authors or editors, and the publisher of the dictionary you consult.

EXAMPLE

What is the difference, if any, between *further* and *farther*?

Fowler's *Modern English Usage* says that *farther* is now common only where distance is concerned. *Further* "has gained a virtual monopoly of the sense of *moreover*, both alone and in the compound *furthermore*."

A Dictionary of Modern English Usage, by H. W. Fowler, 2nd ed., revised by Sir Ernest Gowers. New York: Oxford University Press (paperback), 1983, p. 190.

1. What is the difference between *libel* and *slander*?
2. Is it permissable to *allude* to someone by name?
3. What is the difference between *mendacity* and *mendicity*?

24

Enriching Vocabulary

Recognizing Word Roots |24c|

Most words possess long histories; before they became the English words we recognize, they may have been French (*ensign,* for example) or German (*night,* for example). Most English words come from Latin and Greek. Thus, the Latin words for mother (*mater*) and father (*pater*) are the **root words** (or simply *roots*) for *maternal* and *paternal,* respectively.

Readers familiar with the most common Latin and Greek roots often find that they can determine the meaning of an unfamiliar word. Thus, if you know the Greek roots *-biblio-* (meaning "book") and *-phil-* (meaning "love"), you can figure out that a *bibliophile* is a book collector—someone who loves books.

Here is a list of some common Latin and Greek roots:

Root	*Meaning and Typical English Words*
-audi- (L)	to hear: *audible, auditorium*
-bene- (L)	good, well: *benevolent, benefit*
-bio- (G)	life: *biology, biography*
-duc-, -duct- (L)	to lead or make: *induct, conducive*
-gen- (G)	race, kind: *gene, genealogy*
-geo- (G)	earth: *geologist*
-graph- (G)	to write: *graphic, biography*
-jur-, -jus- (L)	law: *justice, jury*
-log-, -logo- (G)	word, thought: *logical, biology*
-luc- (L)	light: *translucent*
-manu- (L)	hand: *manufacture*
-mit-, -mis- (L)	to send: *mission, submit*
-path- (G)	to feel, to suffer: *empathy*
-phil- (G)	love: *philosopher, bibliophile*
-photo- (G)	light: *photograph, telephoto*

-port- (L)	to carry: *portable, transport*
-psych- (G)	soul: *psychology*
-scrib-, -script- (L)	to write: *scribble, inscribe*
-sent-, -sens- (L)	to feel: *sensitive, sentiment*
-tele- (G)	far away: *telegraph, telepathy*
-terr- (L)	earth, ground: *territory*
-therm- (G)	heat: *thermometer, thermal*
-vac- (L)	empty: *evacuate, vacuum*
-vid-, -vis- (L)	to see: *envision, video*

EXERCISE 24.1 USING WORD ROOTS

One word is missing from each of the following sentences. Each missing word is formed using one of the roots in the list just given. Complete each sentence by writing in the correct word.

EXAMPLE

> People who wear glasses or contact lenses would not possess 20/20 <u>vision</u> without these seeing aids.

1. Before agreeing to make a movie, a director will want to read a _____.

2. A _____ is literally an example of "writing with light."

3. Narrow tires are suitable for bicycling on flat ground; fat tires are better on

bumpy _____.

4. A book of writing about a person's life is called a _____.

5. Hand labor is also called _____ labor.

6. Literally, a _____ is someone who "thinks about the soul."

7. The phenomenon that lets people see things from far away is called

_____.

EXERCISE 24.2 COMPOSING USING WORD ROOTS

On a separate sheet of paper, write sentences that use at least a dozen of the roots listed on pages 316–317. If you can use more than one root in a sentence, do so. After each sentence, list the roots and meanings used in that sentence.

EXAMPLE

> They decided to photograph some of the territory.
> Roots: -photo- (light), -graph- (to write), -terr- (ground)

Recognizing Prefixes and Suffixes |24d|

Sets of letters attached to the front of a root word are called **prefixes**, and sets of letters following a root word are called **suffixes**. Prefixes act like modifiers, altering the original meaning, whereas suffixes typically change the word's part of speech.

Knowing the meaning of a particular prefix or suffix can help you puzzle out an unfamiliar variation of a familiar word. Suppose that you know that *practice* means, in general, to do something, as in *to practice medicine*. Then *malpractice* must mean "wrong-practice," a wrong action. The following lists provide the meanings of some commonly used prefixes and suffixes. (Note: In some cases, these lists will show the same meaning for more than one prefix or suffix. Unfortunately, these prefixes and suffixes are *not* interchangeable: we say *hemisphere* but not *semisphere*, *bicycle* but not *dicycle*. If you are in doubt about the prefixes that can be attached to a specific noun, consult a good college dictionary by looking under the prefix. If you are in doubt about suffixes, consult your dictionary by looking under the word itself.)

Prefixes Indicating Negation or Opposition

a-, an-	without, not: *amoral, anemia*
anti-, contra-	against: *antidote, contradict*
de-	from, take from: *decontaminate, deduct*
dis-	apart, away: *disappear*
il-, im-, in-, ir-	not: *illogical, immature, inconclusive, irrelevant*
mal-, mis-	wrong, bad: *maladjusted, misjudge*
non-, un-	not: *nonsense, unfortunate*

Prefixes Indicating Quantity

semi-, hemi-	half: *semicircle, hemisphere*
uni-, mono-	one, single: *unicycle, monotone*
bi-, di-	two: *bicycle, dichotomy*
tri-	three: *tripod, triplicate*
omni-	all: *omnivorous, omnipotent*
poly-	many: *polysyllabic*
milli-	thousand: *millimeter*

Prefixes Indicating Time and Space

ante-, pre-	before: *antechamber, prejudice*
circum-	around: *circumnavigate*

[*317*]

Selecting Effective Words

co-, col-, com-, con-, cor-	with: *coequal, collaborate, commiserate, construct, correlate*
e-, ex-	out of: *emit, exhale*
hyper-	over, more than: *hyperventilate*
hypo-	under, less than: *hypodermic*
inter-	between: *interrupt, intercoastal*
mega-	large, enlarge: *megaphone*
micro-	tiny: *microscope*
neo-	recent, new: *neoconservative, neonatal*
post-	after: *postscript*
re-	again, back: *rewind*
sub-	under, below: *submarine*
super-	over, above: *superscript*
syn-	at the same time: *synchronize*
trans-	across, over: *transmit*

Suffixes Indicating Nouns

Words ending with these suffixes are always nouns.

-acy	state or condition of: *piracy, democracy*
-al	act of: *refusal*
-ance, -ence	state or quality of: *maintenance*
-dom	place or state of being: *fiefdom, freedom*
-er, -or	one who: *trainer, investor*
-ism	doctrine or belief: *Catholicism*
-ist	one who: *soloist*
-ment	condition of: *entertainment*
-ness	state of being: *cleanliness*
-ship	position held: *professorship*
-sion, -tion	state of being or action: *confusion, constitution*

Suffixes Indicating Verbs

-ate	cause to be: *regulate*
-en	cause to be or become: *enliven*
-ify, -fy	make or cause to be: *amplify*
-ize	make, give, or cause to become: *popularize*

Suffix Indicating Adverbs

-ly	way or manner: *slowly*

Suffixes Indicating Adjectives

-able, -ible	capable of: *assumable, edible*
-al, -ial	pertaining to: *regional, proverbial*
-ful	having a notable quality of: *colorful*

-ious, -ous	of or characterized by: *nutritious, famous*
-ish, -ive	having the quality of: *clownish, conductive*
-less	without, free of: *relentless*

Analyzing the Contexts of New Words |24e1|

Knowing roots, prefixes, and suffixes will certainly help you determine the meanings of new words. But even if a word is entirely unknown to you, the words around it will give you clues about its meaning. We call those clues **context**. Consider the following sentence: *The clown's long face and lugubrious manner brought laughs from the crowd.* Whatever *lugubrious* means, it has something to do with laughter and with a long face. In fact, the *American Heritage Dictionary* says it means "mournful or doleful, especially to a ludicrous degree."

EXERCISE 24.3 DETERMINING MEANING FROM CONTEXT

Find a passage in a book or magazine containing words with which you are not familiar (ask your instructor for help in choosing one if you have trouble). Read until you have found eight words that you do not know. On a separate page, copy each word and write what you think it means, based on the context, or what you can understand about the passage. Then look up the words in your dictionary to see how close you came to the correct meanings.

Becoming an Active Reader |24e2|

Here are four suggestions to help you become a more active reader and thus build your vocabulary.

- *Increase the amount of time you spend on pleasure reading.* Do not confine reading to schoolwork; save some time for reading material that interests *you*— newsmagazines, general science magazines, specialty sport or craft magazines. If you do not read a daily newspaper, start doing so. Read novels or biographies. Even the busiest schedule can accommodate twenty minutes a day for such reading.
- *Pay conscious attention to word choices in addition to content.* Reading in this way will inevitably slow your reading speed somewhat, but part of your purpose is to increase the number of words you recognize and can use.
- *Underline or otherwise note any word not entirely known to you.* You may be able to guess at some of the words you note from their context; others may be entirely baffling.
- *Copy new words into a vocabulary journal.* Make sure that your entry contains space for a brief definition and for a sentence using the word correctly. There is no need to complete the entries as you read. Simply enter the words; then, once

you have finished reading, use a dictionary to check definitions and to help you write sample sentences. Here is a typical entry:

Word	Definition	Use
obdurate	hardened, unyielding	The tenants were obdurate in their decision to resist eviction.

Note that you are doing considerably more than simply consulting a dictionary; you are writing definitions and composing examples. Keeping such a journal during a time when you are also required to do considerable writing will increase your working vocabulary. Remember, reading and writing go hand in glove: to increase your writing vocabulary, you need to be reading and writing.

EXERCISE 24.4 USING PREFIXES AND SUFFIXES

Drawing from the prefixes listed in this chapter and the list of common roots in this exercise, construct five new words. If you are not sure your word is in fact an English word, consult your dictionary. Write the words on a separate page, and indicate the literal meaning and the common meaning. Then use the word in a short sentence. See the example following the list of common roots. (Number your words from 1 to 5.)

Common Roots and Meanings

-dict-, say	-phon-, sound	-vid-, -vis-, see
-vene-, come	-graph-, write	-duct-, lead
-scrib-, write	-ped-, foot	-mit-, -mis-, send

EXAMPLE transmit Literal meaning: *across + send* Common meaning: *to send across*
Sentence: *A radio tower transmits radio waves.*

Attach an appropriate noun suffix to each of the following root words. Then write two sentences. Use the original word in the first sentence. Use the new word in the second sentence. Consult your dictionary as necessary.

EXAMPLE king *Henry VIII is a famous British king.*
kingdom
The daily changing of the guard reminds Britons that they still live in a kingdom.

6. operate **7.** false **8.** friend

Add an appropriate verb or adjective suffix to each of the root words that follow. Then follow the instructions given for 6–8.

9. broad **10.** suspense **11.** pass

Understanding Diction

Choosing Appropriate Language |25a|

Choosing appropriate **diction** for college essays means choosing vocabulary and grammar that will be recognized and readily understood by your intended readers. In addition to avoiding regionalisms and dialects, college prose tends to avoid colloquial language and slang. Colloquial language (*snooze, ain't, nukes*) is informal; slang (*groady, def, rad*) is both informal and often understandable only to a few. The unconscious or haphazard use of either slang or colloquial language in college writing suggests that the writer has not really thought hard about what is being said to whom. Colloquial language or slang thus undermines an essay's credibility.

One colloquial term, *a lot*, deserves special mention, for it appears frequently in college essays. Not only is it too colloquial for most situations, but *a lot* is also glaringly imprecise: *A lot of people agreed with Paine's views.* Is *a lot* a vocal minority, a bare majority, or near unanimity? See how using *a lot* can frustrate readers? Whenever you find *a lot* in your own rough drafts, ask yourself what you really mean; then substitute clearer, more accurate phrasing.

Denotation and Connotation |25b|

Consider the word *blue*. The denotative (literal, most straightforward) meaning of *blue* is a particular color. Choosing a word that does not say what was really intended is a denotative error. The writer who says *The government was disposed in a bloodless coup* probably means *The government was deposed in a bloodless coup.* Using *disposed* instead of *deposed* is a denotative error.

Connotative meanings result from associations around words or phrases. *Country club* has meanings far beyond a club located in the country. *Coun-*

[*321*]

try club also connotes luxury, wealth, and exclusivity. Sometimes a connotative meaning can overpower any literal or denotative meaning. It is entirely reasonable for a writer to rely on the connotative meaning of *country club* and write *Although he'd lost everything, he kept up his country club lifestyle.*

Connotative meanings are often all that separate one synonym from another. *Stink, stench, fragrance, odor, scent,* and *aroma* all involve smell. However, unpleasant associations are attached to the words *stink* and *stench. Odor* and *scent* are more neutral, and *aroma* and *fragrance* are most often positive. Thus, a coffee commercial is quite right to praise the coffee's *aroma* but would hurt its own cause by referring to the coffee's *stink.*

Connotative meanings can become particularly tricky whenever you are writing to persuade. Consider the connotative differences between *hasten* and *stampede* or between *plan* and *conspiracy.* As you can see, some connotative meanings can indicate judgments; a wrong word choice in an argumentative essay may be all it takes to convince a reader that the writer is not being fair-minded.

Writers often make denotative or connotative errors when they use words they do not entirely understand; virtually every writer makes errors of these sorts sooner or later. After all, if writers restricted themselves only to words they were sure of, they would never grow as writers. This means being willing to reach for new words when you write a rough draft and willing to check those words by consulting a dictionary or by consulting with readers and other writers.

Turn now to Assignments 25A and 25B at the end of this chapter for practice with denotation and connotation.

Balancing General and Specific Diction |25c|

General words refer to or identify categories, classes, or groups of things. *Tree, book, house, emotion*—these are general words. *Elm, hymnal, bungalow,* and *anger* are more specific words. Most good writing balances general and specific words to make its content clear. Imagine the span from general to specific as a continuum:

General →	*Less General* →	*More Specific* →	*Quite Specific*
plant	flower	rose	tropicana rose
writing	poem	American poem	"Stopping by Woods on a Snowy Evening"

Weak writing often depends too heavily on one end of the continuum. For example, some writers forget that they are writing to readers who do not yet share their experiences or ideas. The result is prose full of summarization and judgment. Here are three sentences long on general and abstract diction but short on specifics: *That ride is scary. The equipment looks old, and the ride operators seem oblivious to safety concerns. We got in, and before we could feel comfortable, the first car started moving.*

These sentences give readers emotion (*scary*) and judgment (*equipment looks old, operators . . . oblivious to safety concerns*). The only people named, *the ride operators,* are shown in only the most general terms. Readers do not get to see any of the sensory information that yields the feeling *scary* except *looks old.* Do the words *looks old* mean that the equipment needs a paint job, that it has bent supporting rods, or that it has missing or very rusty bolts? What is it about those ride operators that makes them "oblivious to safety concerns"? What exactly do those ride operators look like? What do they do (or not do)? Presumably, the writer of the passage could easily answer these questions. By not answering them, the passage actually excludes the reader from the experience it seeks to describe.

Writers can also err in the direction of too many specifics, particularly if they are presented in what seems like random fashion. College essays should provide readers with both a general context and the specifics to illustrate it; the general statements raise questions, and the specific statements answer those questions:

GENERAL:

> Tenants complain that their apartments are decrepit and unsanitary. [*Readers' questions: What have the tenants complained about? What are the apartments really like?*]

SPECIFIC:

> Tenants complain repeatedly by phone and by letter that their windows will not seal and some of the window panes are cracked and loose so that the rooms are drafty, and the older tenants especially find their health jeopardized. They complain that the oil heater has been malfunctioning for months and has never been properly fixed; that the bathroom plumbing leaks consistently whether you shower, use the sink, or flush the toilet; . . . [*Readers will wish that this writer would get to the point.*]

GENERAL + SPECIFIC:

> Tenants complain that their apartments are decrepit and unsanitary, with windows that will not seal, heaters that have never been repaired, and bathroom plumbing that leaks every time it is used. In an effort to force the owner to make repairs, tenants have filed a suit in county court.

EXERCISE 25.1 BALANCING GENERAL AND SPECIFIC DICTION IN A PARAGRAPH

Using your own paper, follow these steps for writing a paragraph that uses both general and specific diction.

1. Select a topic from the following list.

    a) One aspect of what it is like to return to school after time away
    b) One indicator that should suggest to a student that it is time to change majors
    c) One aspect of the difficulty of moving to a new place
    d) One aspect of the joy of being a brother, sister, aunt, or uncle
    e) One memory, one fear, or one pet peeve

2. Brainstorm, freewrite, and make notes. Do not censor yourself. Save these notes and turn them in with your final draft.
3. Complete a rough draft; save it and turn it in stapled to your final draft.
4. Revise, paying special attention to an appropriate mix of general and specific diction.
5. Write your final version. Hand it in along with earlier notes and drafts.

Turn now to Assignment 25C for practice in choosing appropriate diction for college writing.

ASSIGNMENT 25A CHECKING FOR DENOTATIVE ERRORS

Read each of the following sentences, looking for denotative errors. Underline every error that you find, and write the incorrect word at the bottom of the page. When you have read all ten sentences, examine each error to determine the word intended. Write the correct word in the blank following each sentence. If there are no denotative errors in the sentence, write *C* in the blank. The first sentence has been done for you as an example. (Note: all of the correct words are to be found in the list you create at the bottom of the page.)

1. Your <u>conscious</u> would tell you that dishonesty is not the best policy.

conscience _____

2. A rabbit's foot or similar talisman gives some people the allusion of security.

_____

3. Despite the witnesses' reluctance, he did finally provide a disposition.

_____

4. Conscientious employees typically expect promotions and regular increases in compensation. _____

5. Now that our analyses are complete, you can expect our confidential purport by the end of this month. _____

6. When emergency personnel arrived, the victim was conscience and alert.

_____

7. Encyclopedias often feature both biographical and geographical entries.

_____

8. The main report of the memo deals with staffing levels for the following year.

_____

9. One literary illusion in this poem may be referring to Frost's "After Apple Picking." _____

10. The consumption of squash somehow goes against my native deposition.

_____

ASSIGNMENT 25B **UNDERSTANDING CONNOTATIVE MEANINGS**

Write a sentence that accurately uses the connotations associated with each word in the following pairs of similar words. If you are unsure of the connotations of a particular word, check a good dictionary.

EXAMPLE

dance: *Fred Astaire and Ginger Rogers danced in several movies.*
motion: *In motion, a hummingbird's wings are a blur.*

1. crazy: _____

_____

psychotic: _____

_____

2. cheap: _____

_____

a bargain: _____

_____

3. spry: _____

_____

nimble: _____

_____

4. destruction: _____

_____

disposal: _____

_____

5. imitation: _____

_____

forgery: _____

_____

The sentences that follow contain words with strongly judgmental connotative meanings. Underline these words; then revise the sentence to make it sound more neutral.

EXAMPLE

> The current NRA <u>scheme</u> appeals to patriotism as a <u>smokescreen to obscure the real issue</u> of gun control.
> *The current NRA position appeals to patriotism rather than responding directly to gun control proposals.*

6. News media crackpots claim that their news reports are fair and impartial.

_____

_____

7. Pro-choice sympathizers keep screaming that a ban on abortion would drive abortion out of hospitals and into back alleys.

_____

_____

8. A mob of protesters appeared, yelling and jabbing their signs in the air.

_____

_____

9. Liberals keep whining about the bums, the crazies, and the lazy.

_____

_____

10. Only recently have ladies landed a seat on the Supreme Court.

_____

_____

[*327*]

ASSIGNMENT 25C CHOOSING LANGUAGE APPROPRIATE TO COLLEGE ESSAYS

The sentences below contain various regional, colloquial, or slang terms. Revise the sentences to make them more acceptable for college essays.

EXAMPLE

Some Soviet and American nukes have been junked in compliance with recent treaties. *Some Soviet and American nuclear weapons have been destroyed in compliance with recent treaties.*

1. Moby Dick's humongous size was matched only by Ahab's obsessive desire to wipe him out.

_____

_____

2. Some grunts in Vietnam were accused of freaking out and wasting innocent civilians.

_____

_____

3. This essay will trash Mr. Buckley's goofy argument.

_____

4. Every election year, public service announcements urge us all to boogie on down to our respective polling places and make our preferences known.

_____

_____

_____

5. James Agee's most famous novel, *A Death in the Family*, focuses on a young boy and on what happens after his old man croaks in a car wreck.

_____

_____

_____

26

Establishing Tone

How would you describe the comics page of your newspaper? Perhaps you would use words like *amusing, irreverent,* even *silly.* In contrast, you might use words like *serious* or *earnest* to describe the editorial page. The overall impression that writing makes is its **tone**; the tone of the comics page is quite different from that of the editorial page. Writers create tone by analyzing and working with a variety of factors: the writer-audience relationship, the writer's purpose, and the writer's own relationship to the topic.

Considering Purpose and Appealing to Your Audience   l26a, 26bl

If you have ever thought to yourself, *how do I want this to sound?* or *how do I want readers to think of me?* you have mulled over the question of tone. (For more on audience considerations in essay writing, see Chapter 2.) Writers make decisions influencing tone almost continuously; through experiment and conscious decision making, you can control the tone of what you write. Use these questions to help in that process:

1. Of all the people likely to read this, who will need the most background? (In general, the more information writer and reader share, the more informal the tone. The more you need to explain or persuade, the more formal the tone.)
2. What sorts of word choices will this reader expect? What kinds of words might offend this reader?
3. What sort of response do I want from readers—laughter, agreement, specific action (such as writing a letter of support)? What tone will encourage this response?
4. What dominant impression do I want to create?

EXERCISE 26.1 VARYING TONE TO FIT YOUR AUDIENCE

Your dinner at a local sit-down restaurant kept you up all night with various physical symptoms (you decide what you ordered and what physical symptoms resulted). Using your own paper, write a complaint letter to the manager of the restaurant. In your letter, explain when and what you ate at the restaurant, and what symptoms you suffered. Be specific and detailed. End your letter by requesting a refund equal to the cost of your meal. Write this letter in a tone that will compel the manager to take you seriously but will not be considered offensive.

Next, write a letter to one of your best friends and tell that person about your meal. Be as formal or informal as you would normally be in writing to a close friend.

Avoiding Offensive Language |26b1|

Most of the time, readers pay attention to the content of writing rather than to the actual word choices. However, insulting or offensive language will stop readers, provoking anger and encouraging those readers to quit reading. The key to avoiding offensive language is simply to remember that your readers are human beings who expect just what you do: courteous, respectful treatment.

Treat readers as members of the human community. Do not use words that deride race, ethnic background, sexual orientation, or religious creed. People who use such terms (even without malicious intent) identify themselves as bigoted and self-righteous.

Know your audience. Are people over sixty-five offended at the term *senior citizen*? If so, and if you use the term, you may unknowingly alienate your readers. If you are unsure about the appropriateness of a given term, find out if respected journals or magazines use it; if they do, you are probably safe to do so as well.

Use language that is free of gender bias. Do not refer to women in belittling or sexist terms. *Girls* have not yet reached puberty; the term is not appropriate for *women*. Use identifiers that include both sexes: *mail carrier* rather than *mailman*, *police officer* rather than *policeman*. The term *Ms.* is now generally accepted as the counterpart to *Mr.* Avoid using *he* to refer to both sexes; recast such a sentence in the plural. Rather than *When on duty, a firefighter should wear his uniform*, say *When on duty, firefighters should wear their uniforms.*

Avoid the vulgar, obscene, and profane. Vulgar words carry a social taboo that severely limits their use. Obscene words usually refer to sexual or excretory functions in nonclinical, disparaging ways. Profane words imply extreme criticism of or lack of respect for God. Vulgar, obscene, or profane language is usually spoken in anger or for purposes of derision, and it is rarely appropriate in college writing.

EXERCISE 26.2 INCREASING YOUR AWARENESS OF APPROPRIATE
AND INAPPROPRIATE LANGUAGE

Describe one experience you have had with offensive language, whether you used it yourself or had it used against you. Discuss the language itself, the reason it was used, and its effect in that particular instance. Your classmates are your audience for this discussion; select a tone appropriate to them. Begin by writing *When I think of offensive language, I think of . . . .* Finish that sentence and keep writing for at least ten minutes; write quickly, and do not worry about errors. Revise as many times as you like, paying particular attention to your tone: be sure it is appropriate to your readers and will not offend them. Hand in all your drafts with your final revision.

Using Figurative Language |26b2|

Figurative language helps writers communicate tone to readers. Often, figurative language also plays a crucial role in understanding a writer's meaning and content. For example, few of us would really grasp the force of an ocean wave hitting a rocky outcropping if that force were expressed simply as "extreme." But we can quite readily understand the statement that such waves hit with the impact of a truck driven into a brick wall at eighty miles per hour. That comparison is one type of figurative language.

Using Metaphors, Similes, and Analogies

Metaphors claim that one thing *is* another: *The Beatles were the Sixties.*

Similes claim that one thing *is like* another, and they make the comparison obvious by including the words *like, as,* or *as if: The ball rolled toward the hole as if drawn by a magnet.*

Metaphors and similes appear inside single sentences. **Analogies** extend the comparison to several sentences:

> Looked at in these ways, capital punishment amounts to state-sponsored murder. After all, capital punishment is the premeditated taking of another life. Like the act of a murderer, capital punishment argues that human beings have the right to deny life; it argues that human beings know how and when to exercise this right.

Metaphors, similes, and analogies help us look at things in surprising, interesting new ways. Instead of saying *We were all bored watching that movie,* a writer might say *Consider* Shoot 'Em Up III *a sleeping pill.* Metaphors such as that one carry considerable punch. Of course, no movie can actually be a sleeping pill. What the writer means is that both movie and sleeping pill have the same effect. But the use of metaphor turns an unremarkable thought into a fresh, amusing statement, the tone of which is very different from *We were all bored watching that movie.*

Avoid Dead, Bad, or Mixed Metaphors. **Dead metaphors** are clichés: *crazy as a loon, good as gold, hat in hand.* Such metaphors are used so often that they risk making readers bored. Using too many dead metaphors tells readers that the writer lacks imagination.

Bad metaphors compare things so unlike that the dissimilarity is puzzling. *She sang like new wallpaper.* Does wallpaper sing (in any sense of the word *sing*)? What in fact does the statement mean? Further explanation might rescue the metaphor, but why stretch the comparison when another metaphor might be far more effective?

Mixed metaphors combine several comparisons in ways that create confusion or unintentional humor: *As our local economy continues to heat up this fall, we've got to get down to brass tacks and make sure we squeeze out a drop for everyone.* Such sentences are mildly amusing, but the joke comes at the expense of the writer. Revising such sentences requires making the terms of comparison consistent: *As our local economy continues to heat up, we want to make sure that everyone feels warmer.*

Using Other Figures of Speech

If you want to comment on your friend's new Hawaiian shirt, you might say, "I could hear that shirt a block away." Shirts do not really shout, yet your listeners understand your meaning. By giving human qualities or capabilities to something that does not really possess them, you have personified that shirt. Such **personification** gives vibrancy to what would otherwise be flat writing: "That shirt is colorful."

Suppose that you are looking at the same shirt and you want to exaggerate in a different way. You might say (or write), "That shirt simply drips color." This deliberate exaggeration is called **hyperbole**. On the other hand, deliberate understatement, or **litotes**, involves defining something by stressing what it is not, as in "A meal at the diner was *not* a gourmet affair."

Irony is the term for a statement that clearly means the opposite of what it says, as in "Wow, that is one drab shirt." **Sarcasm** is a bitter or mocking form of irony, as in, "Sure, Richard, that shirt is perfect for my sister's church wedding." Note that both irony and sarcasm depend on the audience's ability to recognize that the actual meaning is different from what is being said. In short, both irony and sarcasm depend on context. If the audience misses the irony or sarcasm, the writer has not sufficiently established the context.

Writers may also refer to the cultural knowledge they share with readers. Such **allusions** include references to history, literature, the Bible, current events, or common wisdom. Saying "That shirt must be the exact opposite of Yeats's connemara cloth" is to allude to the poem "The Fisherman" by William Butler Yeats. Schoolchildren with "sharpened No. 2s" is a reference to pencils. Make sure readers understand your allusions; if your audience has never heard of William Butler Yeats, your allusion may seem pompous or simply puzzling.

EXERCISE 26.3 IDENTIFYING AND USING FIGURATIVE LANGUAGE

Most of the sentences that follow contain some figurative language. In the space provided, identify the type of figurative language each sentence uses. If a sentence contains no figurative language, write *none* in the space.

EXAMPLE

By the end of her summation, Ms. Ashford had the jury following her as an orchestra follows a conductor. <u>simile</u>

1. The lawn cried out for water. _____

2. It's well written, but it's not exactly "To be, or not to be." _____

3. Producing broccoli, carrots, lettuce, cucumbers, even corn—the tiny garden was a produce section all by itself. _____

4. I will have to go for days without sleep in order to read all these employee evaluations. _____

5. The old radio hummed like a swarm of bees. _____

6. A whip cracking in the wind, the flag stood out, taut and rippling. _____

7. Oh, yes, I absolutely love my trips to the dentist. _____

8. "It is not cold," said the weather forecaster when announcing the temperature of 101 degrees. _____

9. With these rains and high winds and bolts of lightning, why it's exactly the "sure-fire suntan weather" the brochure described, isn't it? _____

10. Like huge matchsticks on the horizon, the tinder-dry pines flared one by one as the flames reached them. _____

Now, on your own paper, write sentences to illustrate each of the figures of speech you have identified in this exercise (eight altogether).

Avoiding Clichés and Stock Phrases Phrases like *true blue, quick as a wink, slow as molasses in January,* and *scarce as hen's teeth* are clichés. Such phrases have been overused to the point that they have lost their original sparkle or wit. Similarly, we all know quite a number of stock phrases, all of them predictable. Here are several: *beyond the shadow of a doubt, have a nice day, dyed in the wool, climb the ladder of success, explore new horizons, have a sneaking suspicion, flagrant violations, unexpected development, raging fire.* Like clichés, stock phrases have become so commonplace that readers will find them boring and will quickly lose interest in your writing if you use them often.

EXERCISE 26.4 INCREASING SENSITIVITY TO THE USE OF CLICHÉS AND STOCK PHRASES

Thirteen examples of clichés or stock phrases were just given in the text. Add seven more to the list; then write three or four paragraphs that include as many of these examples as possible. Finally, comment on the writing you have just done. Do you like it? Do you think readers would?

Using the Appropriate Level of Language |26c|

When we speak about levels of language, we acknowledge the differences between the writing of a hastily written note to a roommate and the writing of a job application letter. We shall discuss three levels of language: familiar, informal, and formal. Most college writing uses the formal level, but you should also be able to recognize and use the other levels.

Familiar Language |26c1|

Familiar language—the language of nicknames, nonstandard grammar, regionalisms, slang, and sentence fragments—is almost exclusively spoken. It is sometimes the language of special groups; for instance, armed forces personnel serving in Vietnam had an intricate "second language" unique to that time and place. "In country" was their term for South Vietnam; "the world" was everywhere else, but especially the United States.

Consider this bit of talk:

> Skoochies we hit about nine. Dead. Nothing. Tried Eighty-second but too many blue lights. Makes ya nervous, ya know. And Jimmy wanting to crash. So we bailed out.

Translated into more formal language, it might read like this:

> We arrived at Skoochies, a dance club, about 9 P.M. Since the dance floor was virtually empty, we decided to try driving up and down Eighty-second Avenue. When we got there, we noticed several police cars. Just seeing police cars made us nervous. All this time, Jimmy kept saying that what he wanted to do was go home and sleep. With nothing more to do, we finally did just go home.

Although the first version is terse and somewhat dramatic, not everyone will be able to follow it. The second, more formal version is admittedly less exciting, but it is also more understandable to more readers. In fact, familiar language appears in print almost exclusively in the pages of fiction, in song lyrics, and in personal letters or diaries. Since familiar language excludes anyone not within its circle of intimacy, it is rarely appropriate for college writing.

Informal Language |26c2|

The use of informal language still implies a fairly close relationship between writer and reader: we use informal language for much of our everyday conversation. Informal language typically includes contractions (*won't*) rather than full phrasings (*will not*), abbreviations (*L.A.* instead of *Los Angeles*), colloquialisms (*a bunch* rather than *several*), and the regular use of the first person pronoun *I*.

Some college writing situations appropriately call for informal language. An assignment to write a play review written for a college newspaper might stipulate college students as its audience. That review will probably be more informal than an essay examining the dramatic structure of Shakespeare's *Romeo and Juliet*. When in doubt about the appropriate tone for a given piece of writing, consult the person who has assigned the writing and/or your readers.

EXERCISE 26.5 IDENTIFYING FAMILIAR AND INFORMAL LANGUAGE

Read the passage that follows. What characteristics would lead you to describe the passage as familiar or informal? Underline any particular words or phrases that reflect these characteristics. Then write a paragraph discussing these characteristics, using brief quotations to illustrate your points. Do you believe that the passage would be appropriate as college writing? Why or why not?

I mean, well, pardon me but the people against McDougal are just wrong. Maybe they're airheads or something because I mean he's a nice guy. Straight arrow. He's so sincere. Look, all you have to do is watch the guy. Look at the tube, that cable channel. He's on there all the time. Besides, he's cool on jobs. Wants bigger bucks even for the yucko ones. Heck, my little sis works at a burger joint—she gets peanuts, $3.25, and she has to fork over for her own uniform. I heard him talkin' about it once—wages, I mean—and the guy *knows*. Even over the tube you could tell. He got all loud and sweaty and the crowd cheerin' and all, then Benjy my stupid brother comes in and zaps it over to Mr. Rogers.

Formal Language |26c3|

Formal language establishes a courteous, friendly relationship with readers without being fanatical or chummy. It avoids slang, regionalisms, and nonstandard grammar, and it uses contractions sparingly. Since writers using formal language usually wish to maintain an objective and impersonal stance toward their topic, they tend to avoid the use of *I*. This is not a matter of modesty so much as it is a wish to focus readers' attention on the subject at hand rather than on the writers themselves.

There are notable exceptions to this tendency; reviews, narratives, and personal essays may all use formal language *and* speak in the first person. If you have a question about a particular college writing assignment and the use of *I*, ask your teacher.

Formal language is typically the language of explanation. It should be specific, often literal, and may include description, brief narratives, or quotations. Even within formal language, there is room for considerable variation. For example, the explanations in this text should be formal enough to be understandable to a wide variety of readers, yet not so formal that they seem stuffy or coldly impersonal.

Writing Formal Language Some college writers feel uncomfortable using formal language. One strategy here is to write formally from the very beginning of the writing process. Use formal language as you make notes. Try freewriting using formal language, and use that same language as you complete a rough draft and begin to revise.

Or you could postpone the question of language level until you have completed notetaking, brainstorming, and drafting. Writing a review, you might begin freewriting this way:

> I think this movie was dull, boring, and visually a yawner. For one thing, the lead actor was really miscast. For another thing, all the camera angles were the ones you'd expect, and besides, the story kept jumping around. It was really confusing. . . .

This writer will consider tone only at the revision stage. At this stage, he or she may decide to focus on the movie itself and so eliminate the use of *I*. The writer might also realize that readers need more explanation of *dull*, *boring*, and *visually a yawner*; these terms may also seem too informal and may actually encourage readers to conclude that the review itself is offhand or rushed. Thus, the freewriting might be revised in this way: *Due to miscasting of the leading actor, uninspired camera work, and a confused and confusing story,* Sherlock *is a disappointment. . . .*

Getting used to writing formal language may take some time. But the effort is worth it. Once comfortable writing in formal language, you will feel confident that you can handle virtually any writing challenge, from a letter to a friend to a job application letter or a sales presentation.

EXERCISE 26.6 REVISING FAMILIAR AND INFORMAL LANGUAGE

Using your own paper, revise the passage you examined in Exercise 26.5 so that it consistently uses formal language to establish a tone appropriate to college writing. Begin by revising the first sentence as follows:

Opponents of the gubernatorial candidate McDougal do not have solid grounds for argument.

Using Technical Language and Neologisms and Avoiding Jargon |26c5|

Since virtually every specialty has its own vocabulary, technical language is often employed with other formal language. When professional or technical writing is aimed at other professionals, this specialized vocabulary permits both brevity and precision. In fact, technical language causes trouble only when it is aimed at readers who do not understand it. Finding such language, we might call it **jargon**, which is simply technical language used with the wrong set of readers. If your subject is technical and you are writing for an educated but nontechnical audience, much of your success will depend on your ability to anticipate which terms will cause readers problems and to explain those terms quickly and clearly.

Neologisms are literally "new (*neo*) words (*logos*)"—words that have not yet found their way into dictionaries. Such terms often come from the sciences; *software* was a neologism a few years ago. Some writers now use *wetware* to refer to the brain and its function. *Olliedolatry* was a term coined by a *Wall Street Journal* reporter to describe the public's brief worship of Colonel Oliver North in the summer of 1987. As you can see, some neologisms perform useful tasks. Some become words in standard usage; some disappear. Others, however, become overused (*interface* is an example) or are used to create a false or unnecessary sense of importance.

When coupled with pretentious diction, the result can be unintentionally comic: *Formal deaccession of duplicate library materials and the transfer of those materials to private ownership will commence Saturday, August 15, at 9:00 A.M.* Note that both this sentence's vocabulary and its structure cause problems. The vocabulary here is unnecessarily technical (*deaccession*) and elevated (*commence*); the structure is unnecessarily lengthy. Here is a better version: *The library's sale of duplicate books begins Saturday, August 15, at 9:00 A.M.*

EXERCISE 26.7 ANALYZING THE USE OF TECHNICAL LANGUAGE

Analyze the following passage, paying particular attention to its use of technical language. Assume that the passage is intended for the widest possible audience of college readers. Does the passage use language that will puzzle or confuse this audience? Write your analysis in a brief paragraph that itself uses the formal language appropriate to college writing. Use your own paper for this exercise.

In 1988, the sophistication of desktop publishing software could be measured by how such software handled kerning. Some software packages adopted the strategy of consciously deleting any mention of this complicated aspect of typography. Others provided fixed kerning for a limited number of common combinations. However, the most sophisticated (and expensive) versions of this software combined WYSIWYG capabilities with the ability to custom-kern any letter combinations, thus avoiding the "widows and orphans" that plagued lesser software products.

PART

6

Understanding Punctuation Conventions

These questions are designed to help you, the student, decide what to study. Correct the punctuation in the following sentences. If the punctuation is already correct, write a *C* next to the sentence.

1. Even though all of their friends thought Susan and Adam shared much they did not like each other in the slightest.
2. Gina, who is my father's cousin lives in Florence.
3. The china was, totally ruined in the dishwasher.
4. The poems of Wallace Stevens are difficult at first, however, upon further reading their greatness becomes evident.
5. The restaurant advertised for all sorts of positions; short-order cook, busboys, waiters, and bartenders.
6. Whereas Bartholomew kept calling the library a "bookhouse;" I referred to it as "the house of naps."
7. "When are we going to eat?" Marisa asked
8. T S Eliot entitled his first major poem "The Love Song of J Alfred Prufrock."
9. "Can working with a computer really improve one's writing," they asked.
10. Just as Richard passed through customs, a guard shouted "Stop!".
11. When I read the judges decision, I decided that they had not paid sufficient attention to the defenses arguments.
12. Mother does not care what the critics say, she just doesnt want to see that movie.
13. The symphony will be broadcast at eight oclock tomorrow night.
14. The dog kept a close watch on anyone who went near its supper dish.
15. I did not know that this bicycle was their's.
16. I did not know that Anne was coming with us this evening, Peter said.
17. "Eileen said that her job was "very taxing,"" Vincent reported.
18. "Cold and windy", the weather report said.
19. The police officer said that the robbers 'are now in custody.'
20. In Elizabeth Bishop's poem "Crusoe in England," she retells Defoe's novel "Robinson Crusoe."
21. A very wise person once said that there are only two types of literature; good and bad.
22. Although the wine was very good (sixty dollars worth of good), the rest of the meal was terrible.

27

Using Commas

Commas allow writers both to link sentence elements and to separate them. Since commas have such a dual function, their use can puzzle even the most accomplished writers. Part of the difficulty writers have with commas lies in the fact that sometimes commas are required, other times they might be "optional" (depending on the writer's intention), and sometimes they simply do not belong. And writers do have difficulty with commas: five of the top twenty errors deal with inaccurate comma usage! This chapter will begin by discussing sentence structures that regularly use commas. If you need to review the basics of sentence grammar, see Chapter 6.

➤ *Student Writing Error 1: No comma after introductory expression.*

Using Commas after Introductory Elements |27a|

[Introductory element], [rest of sentence].

A comma regularly follows an introductory element in a sentence, thus separating it from the main clause. The introductory element may be a word, phrase, or adverb clause. Do not be fooled by the relative length of an adverb clause compared to the main clause: *Once we have the fire net positioned under the window, you jump!* Here are other examples:

Moreover, we will refuse to pay. [*introductory word*]

To prevent polio, children receive an oral vaccine. [*introductory phrase*]

Their rooms clean and ready for inspection, the sisters decided to play gin rummy. [*introductory phrase*]

Since Town and Country Realtors helped us sell our house, we have recommended them to other sellers. [*introductory adverb clause*]

EXCEPTIONS

If the introductory element is short and easily understood without a comma, the comma may be omitted: *While I was waiting I stirred the soup.* If the introductory element is followed by inverted word order (verb before subject), the comma is not used: *From the back of the car came a series of giggles.*

EXERCISE 27.1 USING COMMAS AFTER INTRODUCTORY ELEMENTS

Some of the sentences in the following paragraph lack commas between introductory elements and whatever follows. Insert commas where necessary, and circle the commas you add. The first comma has been added and circled for you. For each comma you add (or decide not to add), be ready to discuss your decision.

Since its introduction by Parker Brothers in 1935, Monopoly has taught several generations its unique version of American capitalism. In this game of wish fulfillment everyone starts with ready cash. Decision making is reduced to a roll of the dice. And wonder of wonders nobody works. Instead game players simply wait to arrive again at Go in order to collect another $200. Besides a life of leisure Monopoly players come to expect remarkably depressed real estate prices. For instance the Mediterranean Avenue property still sells for only $60.

➤ *Student Writing Error 3: Missing comma in compound sentence.*

Using Commas in Compound Sentences |27b|

[Independent clause], coordinating conjunction + [independent clause].

Commas routinely appear before coordinating conjunctions (*and, but, or, for, nor, so, yet*), which join two independent clauses. (See Chapter 6 for a review of independent clauses.) Be careful to use both the comma and the coordinating conjunction; leaving out the conjunction will result in a comma splice.

The garage light burned faithfully for days, <u>but</u> it burned out in one big flash this morning.

Writers may also choose to join independent clauses using semicolons. These are the only correct ways to join two independent clauses:

1. [Independent clause], coordinating conjunction + [independent clause].
2. [Independent clause]; [independent clause].

Joining independent clauses only with commas is acceptable in just one case: when there are three (or more) such clauses in a series.

EXAMPLE

> We walked the dog, Jane came home after her night at Rachel's, Beth and Will played in the tree house, and we spent the hot afternoon being lazy.

Note that in this kind of sentence, commas can effectively separate clauses only when they are not used in other ways. *I went home, he saw I was calm, happy, and smiling, and he became calm and happy, too* is a confusing sentence. It is clearer when punctuated this way: *I went home; he saw that I was calm, happy, and smiling; and he became calm and happy, too.*

Turn now to Assignment 27A at the end of this chapter for practice in using commas with independent clauses.

➤ Student Writing Error 5: No comma with nonrestrictive modifier.

Using Commas to Set Off Nonrestrictive Elements |27c|

Suppose that you have been conducting a study of men and women who are substantially overweight. Some of your results indicate that a large percentage of these individuals also suffers from low self-esteem. In your report, do you write *Men and women, who are substantially overweight, tend to suffer from low self-esteem* or *Men and women who are substantially overweight tend to suffer from low self-esteem*? The only difference between the two sentences is a set of commas.

Here is the relevant guideline: If you mean *only* men and women who are substantially overweight, you want a **restrictive modifier**. In this case, use no commas. Leaving commas out restricts (or limits) the general category of men and women to a specific number within that group.

If you do use commas, you are saying that the information between the commas is of secondary importance; furthermore, the information between the commas does not restrict the original noun—it is a **nonrestrictive modifier.** Here are some examples:

> All children who are taller than four feet may ride on the Scrambler. [*Restrictive, hence no commas; the sentence means* only *children taller than four feet.*]

The Deschutes, a popular rafting river, winds its way north through Central Oregon. [*Nonrestrictive, hence commas used; the information between the commas is secondary information. Note that the sentence keeps its main meaning even if we drop the information between the commas.*]

The candidate who seems most genuine and trustworthy will get my vote.

Employees, whether they be male or female, must conform to company safety regulations regarding hair length.

Walter Mondale was the first presidential candidate to select a woman, Geraldine Ferraro, as a running mate.

Note that an adjective clause that begins with *that* is always restrictive and is not set off by commas. An adjective clause beginning with *which* may be either restrictive or nonrestrictive; however, some writers prefer to use *which* only for nonrestrictive clauses.

The sculpture that she entered in the competition won first place. [*Restrictive clause introduced by* that; *hence no commas used.*]

Crime and Punishment, which I have only started, is said to be the greatest novel in Russian literature. [*Nonrestrictive clause introduced by* which; *hence commas used.*]

To summarize: Use commas to set off secondary information. Omit commas to restrict or limit.

EXERCISE 27.2   USING COMMAS TO SET OFF NONRESTRICTIVE, SECONDARY INFORMATION

The following sentences contain information that is either secondary (nonrestrictive) or restrictive. Read each sentence carefully and add commas as needed. Underline the secondary or restrictive element in each sentence. On the line provided, indicate whether the information you have underlined is secondary or restrictive, and indicate whether or not you have added commas.

EXAMPLES

The candidate <u>who seems most genuine and trustworthy</u> will get my vote.
restrictive; no commas added

Our firewood, <u>maple and fir</u>, should last us through the winter.
secondary; commas added

1. The girl wearing the striped swimsuit is my daughter.

___

2. We were asked to bring fruit preferably some kind of melon to the picnic.

___

3. MTV which is carried locally on Channel 29 features the newest in music videos.

___

4. Trout that measure less than six inches must be released.

___

5. Razor clams which have grown increasingly rare in recent years still make the best clam chowder.

___

➤ *Student Writing Error 15: Missing series comma.*

Using Commas to Separate Items in a Series |27d|

Commas are routinely used to separate three or more words, phrases, or clauses in a series. Here are some examples:

> Our order was for three boxes of computer paper, two boxes of typing ribbons, a stapler, and four rolls of tape. [*four parallel items*]

> During the heat wave, some people bought air conditioners, others settled for fans, and some just drank glass after glass of iced tea. [*introductory element set off by a comma, then three parallel clauses*]

When the items in a series are long and complex or when they contain commas of their own, use semicolons rather than commas to separate them. For examples, see Chapter 28.

Coordinate adjectives are also separated by commas. Coordinate adjectives are adjectives that can be placed in any order in front of the noun they modify. In *Her straight, long drive took a large bounce and rolled another five yards, straight* and *long* are coordinate adjectives; their order can be switched without changing the meaning of the sentence: *Her long, straight drive took a large bounce and rolled another five yards.*

If two adjectives are not coordinate, they should be left unpunctuated: *Ellen is an accomplished free-lance ad writer.* In that sentence, *accomplished, free-lance,* and *ad* are all adjectives modifying the noun *writer.*

However, changing the order of these adjectives plays havoc with the sentence's meaning: *Ellen is an ad accomplished free-lance writer.* Since these adjectives are not coordinate, no commas are used.

Turn now to Assignment 27B at the end of this chapter for practice in using commas with coordinate adjectives and series.

Using Commas to Set Off Interjections, Direct Address, Contrasting Elements, Parenthetical and Transitional Expressions, Tag Questions, and Parts of Dates, Addresses, Titles, and Numbers |27e, 27f|

Interjections and words used in direct address are routinely set off by commas.

INTERJECTIONS

Well, this is an interesting turn of events.

Oh my, it is hot today!

DIRECT ADDRESS

Beth, go give your dog some exercise.

Now, ladies and gentlemen, let us bow our heads.

Writers may also use commas to set off contrasting elements in a sentence.

CONTRASTING ELEMENTS

Her days were numbered, but not her hopes.

Available credit, not ready cash, determines a consumer's purchasing power.

Parenthetical expressions are defined as relatively unimportant supplementary information or comments by the writer. Transitional expressions include conjunctive adverbs like *however* and *furthermore*. Parenthetical or transitional expressions are always set off by commas.

PARENTHETICAL OR TRANSITIONAL EXPRESSIONS

That watercolor over the couch is, by the way, an original Mulvey.

The picture near the stereo, however, is only a reproduction.

A question that follows a statement and calls that statement into doubt is called a tag question. Use a comma to separate such a question from the rest of the sentence.

TAG QUESTION

You ordered your hot dog with chili and onions, didn't you?

Commas also routinely separate parts of dates, addresses and place names, titles, and numbers.

DATES

She was born on Tuesday, July 31, 1952.

When only a month and year are given, the comma is omitted, as in *August 1987 was an unusually warm month.*

ADDRESSES AND PLACE NAMES

He said he grew up in Malta, Montana.

Her mailing address is Azalea House, 12856 S.W. Jackson St., Cairo, Texas 66731. [*Note that no comma is used in street numbers or between state and ZIP code.*]

TITLES AND NUMBERS

Martin Luther King, Jr., was one of the twentieth century's greatest orators.

Danielle Smith, M.D., performed the surgery.

Their smooth collie stands two feet, nine inches at the shoulder.

She thinks Philomath's population is about 7,500. [*Note: the comma is sometimes omitted in four-digit numbers but is always used in numbers from 10,000 up.*]

Turn now to Assignment 27C at the end of this chapter for practice with special uses of commas.

Using Commas with Quotations |27g|

Use commas to set off quotations from words that introduce or explain those quotations. A comma following a quotation always goes inside the quotation marks.

"Autobiography," said Claude Simon, "is the most fictional of forms."

EXCEPTIONS

Do not use a comma after a question mark or an exclamation point.

"Are you planning to take the 6:05 train?" he asked.

Understanding Punctuation Conventions

Do not use a comma when a quotation is introduced by *that*.

The writer of Ecclesiastes concludes that "all is vanity."

Do not use a comma when quoted material in a sentence is both preceded and followed by other material.

His repetitions of "Please don't panic" failed to calm the crowd.

Do not use a comma before a paraphrase.

Mary Louise said that she would read the report this week.

EXERCISE 27.3 USING COMMAS WITH QUOTATIONS

Add needed commas to the following sentences using quotations. Circle the commas you add. Cross out any unnecessary commas.

EXAMPLE

"Showers tomorrow, with a high near 50," said the forecaster.

1. Beth said "Can we go to Beasley's after dinner?"

2. "Few Americans" she said "are able to understand the history of conflict in Northern Ireland."

3. People who say, "Trust me on this" always make me suspicious.

4. Lyndon Johnson appeared in a nationally televised address to declare that, he would not seek reelection.

5. "Yesterday" he said, "I disagreed with you. But after my experience today, I have changed my mind."

Using Commas to Prevent Misunderstanding   27h

Sometimes using commas will make difficult sentences easier to read, as in these examples:

They strutted in in matching tuxedos and top hats.
They strutted in, in matching tuxedos and top hats.

Shortly after the rock concert began in earnest.
Shortly after, the rock concert began in earnest.

Realize that sometimes the way to cure punctuation problems is to re-write the sentence. The awkwardness of *They strutted in, in matching tuxedos and top hats* can be relieved by revising the sentence to read *They strutted in wearing matching tuxedos and top hats.* The fact that a sentence is accurately punctuated does not necessarily mean that it is well written.

➤ Student Writing Error 17: Unnecessary comma with restrictive modifier.

Omitting Unnecessary Commas with Restrictive Elements |27i1|

Sometimes using too many commas causes readers confusion. In fact, nowhere is correct usage more important than in sentences with restrictive elements. Commas incorrectly used in such situations will radically alter sentence meaning. Consider this sentence, asking yourself whether its punctuation is accurate:

Candidates, who were selected as the five finalists, were to be interviewed beginning Monday of next week.

Now examine this grammatically identical sentence:

Candidates, who ranged in age from 22 to 60, were to be interviewed beginning Monday of next week.

Only one of these two sentences is accurately punctuated. Which one? Remember the guidelines:

1. Omit commas when your intent is to restrict or limit.
2. Use commas to set off secondary, nonessential information.

Clearly, the sentence specifying the five finalists means *only* those five candidates. Thus, that first sentence should not have any commas at all: *Candidates who were selected as the five finalists were to be interviewed beginning Monday of next week.*

Turn now to Assignment 27D at the end of this chapter for practice in punctuating restrictive and nonrestrictive elements.

Omitting Commas between Subjects and Verbs and between Verbs and Objects |27i2|

Misused commas confuse readers by failing to stick to predictable patterns. Look at these sentences with misplaced commas:

The Avery Square shopping mall, will be advertising heavily during November.

Dolphins, are a joy to watch.

The Forest Service representative said, that fire crews were being flown in from Nevada and Arizona.

Satellite photographs now form, the basis for most weather forecasts.

In the first two sentences, commas unnecessarily and incorrectly separate subjects from verbs. In the last two, commas unnecessarily and incorrectly separate verbs from objects. These commas distract readers from content; they also identify the writer as either careless or uneducated. The rule is simple: never use a single comma to separate subjects, verbs, or objects. A *pair* of commas may be used to enclose appropriate words, phrases, or clauses.

INCORRECT Running two miles every other day, helps keep me fit. [*No comma needed between subject and verb.*]

CORRECT Running two miles every other day helps keep me fit. [*Gerund phrase as subject; no comma between subject and verb.*]

CORRECT Running two miles every other day, which is what Mavis does, helps keep her fit. [*Pair of commas correctly used to set off nonrestrictive information.*]

INCORRECT Alan decided, his father loved him. [*No comma needed between verb and object.*]

CORRECT Alan decided his father loved him.

CORRECT Alan decided, however, his father did love him. [*Pair of commas set off however.*]

EXERCISE 27.4 OMITTING COMMAS BETWEEN SUBJECTS AND VERBS AND BETWEEN VERBS AND OBJECTS

In the following passage, some sentences are punctuated correctly and some are not. Read each sentence carefully, paying close attention to the use of commas. Put an X through any misplaced commas. In all cases, be ready to explain your decisions.

Consider, the wonders of wood heat. The old adage is that wood heat warms you twice: once when you chop it, and once when it's burned. At our house, it seems like heating with wood provides, all sorts of warmth. Since we own neither truck nor chain saw, the first heat we get from wood, comes with the joy of stacking it. Stacking begins as soon as the wood-lot truck leaves. The process, neither intricate nor requiring excessive intelligence, involves about 120 minutes of steady movement, from woodpile in the driveway to wood stack in the garage.

Checking for Other Unnecessary Commas |27i3, 27i4|

- Do not use commas before or after coordinating conjunctions used in compound constructions. (The common coordinating conjunctions are *and, or, but, nor, for, so,* and *yet*.)

INCORRECT   Jack, and Jill went up the hill.

CORRECT   Jack and Jill went up the hill.   [*compound subject*]

INCORRECT   Jack fell down, and broke his crown.

CORRECT   Jack fell down and broke his crown.   [*compound verb*]

CORRECT   Jack fell down and broke his crown, and Jill came tumbling after.   [*comma* + and *joining two independent clauses*]

- Do not use commas to set off nonparenthetical phrases

INCORRECT   She raced, to first base, with plenty of time to spare.

CORRECT   She raced to first base with plenty of time to spare.

INCORRECT   I loved, eating tuna sandwiches, every day for lunch.

CORRECT   I loved eating tuna sandwiches every day for lunch.

- Do not use commas after the last item in a series or before the first.

INCORRECT   Tonight at Papa's we ordered a pizza with, mushrooms, sausage, and green pepper.

INCORRECT   Tonight at Papa's we ordered, a mushroom, sausage, and green pepper, pizza.

CORRECT   Tonight at Papa's we ordered a pizza with mushrooms, sausage, and green pepper.

- Do not use a comma before an opening parenthesis.

INCORRECT   Portland's Pacific Coast League, (PCL) baseball team is the Beavers.

CORRECT   The Portland Beavers are members of baseball's Pacific Coast League (PCL).

If a phrase set off by commas includes a parenthetical comment, the final comma comes after the closing parenthesis, as in *If you live in Athens (the one in Georgia), chances are that you know the University of Georgia.*

Turn now to Assignments 27E and 27F at the end of this chapter for practice in recognizing when to omit commas.

ASSIGNMENT 27A   USING COMMAS TO JOIN INDEPENDENT CLAUSES

Study each of the five sentences below. If commas are needed for accurate punctuation, insert them. Circle any comma you add. On the lines provided, indicate a grammatic representation of each sentence.

EXAMPLE

Before we leave for home*,*Alison needs to make sure the windows are tightly latched*,*
and Jed needs to empty the refrigerator.
[Introductory element], [independent clause], and [independent clause].

1. Although we are not finished discussing this material the bell will ring soon so let
me give you the assignment for tomorrow.

_____

_____

2. New York's subway station mosaics are true works of art and we feel strongly that
they ought to be preserved.

_____

_____

3. The Boundary Lakes area of Michigan boasts many miles of hiking trails and quiet

water. _____

_____

4. Dad will not allow you to drive his car nor will I tell you where he hides the keys.

_____

_____

5. It's 98 degrees here on the porch and the rest of the family is complaining about the
heat yet I like it.

_____

_____

The sentences below contain coordinate adjectives, noncoordinate adjectives, and items in series. Add commas where needed, and circle any commas you add. On the lines provided, indicate all reasons for any commas you add. If the sentence contains any noncoordinate adjectives, copy them on the lines provided.

EXAMPLE

> Jane arrived carrying a doll, a lollipop, and a large crayon picture she had drawn.
> items in a series; noncoordinate adjectives: *large, crayon*

1. Beth has worn her blue Campfire hat almost nonstop since she arrived home from

camp. _____

_____

2. We're confronted with continuing drought a possible labor strike and the highest rate of bankruptcies in two decades.

_____

_____

3. The blackberry pie smelled delicious looked absolutely inviting and tasted divine.

_____

_____

4. The Alsea River bridge is a dramatic functional example of design that combines

beauty and utility. _____

_____

5. My father drank the beer I saved the bottles and wrote the notes and on the way home we'd throw them all off the stern end of the Columbia River ferry.

_____

_____

Compose your own sentences as directed below. For subject matter, think of the room in which you normally eat your meals. Make sure each sentence you write is punctuated correctly.

Write a sentence with coordinate adjectives and noncoordinate adjectives. Underline the noncoordinate adjectives.

The table is covered by a <u>pale blue</u> cloth fringed with intricate, expensive lace.

6. Write a sentence with noncoordinate adjectives. Underline them.

_____

_____

7. Write a sentence with three parallel clauses. Circle any commas in the sentence.

_____

_____

8. Write a sentence with coordinate adjectives. Circle any commas in the sentence.

_____

_____

9. Write a sentence with only two items in a series. Circle any commas in the sentence.

_____

_____

10. Write a sentence with coordinate adjectives and noncoordinate adjectives. Underline the noncoordinate adjectives.

_____

_____

ASSIGNMENT 27C USING COMMAS WITH INTERJECTIONS, DIRECT ADDRESS, CONTRASTING ELEMENTS, PARENTHETICAL AND TRANSITIONAL EXPRESSIONS, TAG QUESTIONS, AND PARTS OF DATES, ADDRESSES, TITLES, AND NUMBERS

Write sentences incorporating the elements specified in each case. Make sure that your sentences use commas correctly, both for the specified elements and anywhere else they may be necessary. In each case, be ready to discuss your comma usage.

EXAMPLE

Write a sentence that includes a city and a state.

Nike, Inc., is headquartered in Portland, Oregon.

1. Write a sentence that includes contrasting elements.

_____

_____

2. Write a sentence that includes a number greater than ten thousand.

_____

_____

3. Write a sentence that includes a month and year only.

_____

_____

4. Write a sentence that includes a mailing address and ZIP code.

_____

_____

5. Write a sentence that includes an interjection.

_____

_____

Add needed commas to the sentences below, and circle the commas you add.

EXAMPLE   We were married on Sept. 11Ⓞ1971.

6. Bill could you read over the third paragraph and tell me what it says to you?

7. Laura Williams M.D. can be found in office 228 on the second floor.

8. Now we stitch the seam right?

9. Last year I am sorry to say six elms had to be destroyed due to Dutch elm disease.

10. Your rough draft is due Friday October 28.

NAME _____ DATE _____

ASSIGNMENT 27D **DISTINGUISHING BETWEEN RESTRICTIVE AND NONRESTRICTIVE SENTENCE ELEMENTS**

Underline the restrictive or nonrestrictive elements in each of the following sentences. Indicate whether the material you have underlined is restrictive or nonrestrictive. Punctuate the sentence correctly, and circle any commas you add.

EXAMPLES

The lab technician reports that the blood tests⊙which were performed yesterday⊙were negative. <u>nonrestrictive</u>

The lab technician reports that the blood tests <u>that were performed yesterday</u> were negative. <u>restrictive</u>

1. Pit bulls which have been mistreated by their owners are often hostile to anyone who gets too close. _____

2. The furniture marked down for this special sale is going fast. _____

3. The evacuees some with only the clothes on their backs prepared to spend the night inside the high school gym. _____

4. The Dave Smith who is an accomplished poet and teacher lives in Richmond, Virginia. _____

5. Health care administration a field that has grown in recent years often attracts some of the best and brightest talents. _____

[*357*]

Cross out any unnecessary commas in the following sentences. If a sentence is correct as shown, write *C* next to its number.

EXAMPLE

> For twenty-six straight days, the high temperature in Salt Like City **✗** reached over ninety degrees.

1. During midsummer one year, (on the fourth of July, in fact) snow fell in Missoula.

2. Nothing smells more delicious, than a field of ripe strawberries waiting to be picked.

3. Raspberries make, for great pies, and, sweet jelly.

4. Jim runs ten miles every other day, and he says he feels strong, healthy, and fit.

5. Two lanes (usually those on the far left side of the pool), are routinely reserved for lap swimming.

6. Any list of living, well-respected poets would have to include Rich, Levertov, Kinnell, and Warren, (the granddaddy of them all).

ASSIGNMENT 27F USING COMMAS CORRECTLY

The following sentences are punctuated correctly. Combine or revise each according to the specific directions. Make sure your new version is punctuated accurately.

EXAMPLE My father graduated from Portland's Washington High School in 1933. (Revise so that the sentence begins *In 1933 . . .*)
In 1933, my father graduated from Portland's Washington High School.

1. Carpentry requires patience, as does needlework. (Revise so that the sentence

subjects are *carpentry* and *needlework*.) _____

_____

2. Designing your own clothes is not as hard as some people think. Designing your own clothes can be quite rewarding. (Combine into one sentence containing second-

ary, nonrestrictive information.) _____

_____

3. Some writers like to read a bit before writing. Some writers make copious notes to themselves. Some writers are too terrified to do anything. Some writers just sit down and start writing whatever comes to mind. (Combine into one sentence with multiple

independent clauses.) _____

_____

_____

4. You wake up in Los Angeles. You look out the window. It's so clear that you under-stand why everyone moved here. This happens on those rare April mornings after a heavy rain. (Combine into one sentence with an introductory element followed by

several independent clauses.) _____

_____

_____

5. These orientation classes are designed for transfer students only. These orienta-tion classes begin Monday morning at 9. (Revise to a single sentence containing re-

strictive information.) _____

_____

[*359*]

On the lines provided, combine each of the following groups of sentences into one sentence of connected independent clauses. Join the independent clauses by using commas and appropriate coordinating conjunctions. Use pronouns as necessary.

EXAMPLE   Hay fever season has arrived. We had better buy more Kleenex.
Hay fever season has arrived, so we had better buy more Kleenex.

6. The typewriter is fast. The typewriter produces professional-looking documents.

_____

7. The typewriter is fast. The typewriter produces professional-looking documents. I

still prefer to handwrite my memos. _____

_____

8. We have confirmed our reservations. We have taken the dog to the neighbors'. The

car is packed. Let's go. _____

_____

9. Eglantine tripped going down the stairs. She did not lose consciousness.

_____

10. You love golf. You enjoy the companionship. You admire the lush landscape. You

play maybe once a year. _____

_____

28

Using Semicolons

Using Semicolons to Link Independent Clauses |28a|

Powerful effects can sometimes be achieved by juxtaposing more than one idea inside a single sentence. Chapter 27 discussed the use of a comma plus a coordinating conjunction to link two independent clauses. Using coordinating conjunctions allows you to indicate the relationship between the two independent clauses. Semicolons can also be used to link independent clauses, resulting in compound, complex, or compound-complex sentences. Linking independent clauses with semicolons often makes for succinct, even blunt prose. (For more on this topic, see Chapter 13.) Here are two correct examples:

> Karen votes for a movie, so we are going to a movie. [*comma + coordinating conjunction* so *indicating cause and effect*]

> Karen votes for a movie; we are going to a movie. [*semicolon linking the two independent clauses and resulting in a blunt, direct statement.*]

Remember that when joining two independent clauses, a comma *cannot* substitute for a semicolon; if a comma is used, it must be followed by a co-ordinating conjunction.

Semicolons are also used to link independent clauses when the second clause opens with a conjunctive adverb or a transitional phrase:

> I know starting early means I will accomplish more; however, 5:30 in the morning is just too early.

> We can expect afternoon temperatures to be cooler today; after all, it is midmorning, and the sun has yet to burn off the fog.

REVIEW

Common conjunctive adverbs include *also, anyway, besides, finally, furthermore, hence, however, indeed, meanwhile, moreover, nevertheless, otherwise, still, then, therefore,* and *thus.* Common transitional phrases include *after all, as a result, at any rate, even so, for example, in addition, in fact, in other words, on the contrary,* and *on the other hand.*

Remember that semicolons separate *sentences.* The last example given can also be accurately punctuated as follows: *We can expect afternoon temperatures to be cooler today. After all, it is midmorning, and the sun has yet to burn off the fog.*

Do not use semicolons to separate a dependent clause from an independent clause.

INACCURATE

While we were walking the dog after dinner; the moon rose.

We were up until after 2 last night; because our group project is due this afternoon.

CORRECTED

While we were walking the dog after dinner, the moon rose.

We were up until after 2 last night because our group project is due this afternoon.

or

Because our group project is due this afternoon, we were up until after 2 last night.

Turn now to Assignment 28A at the end of this chapter for practice in linking independent clauses.

Using Semicolons to Separate Items in a Series |28*b*|

Besides joining what would otherwise be complete sentences, semicolons have only one other use: to separate complex items in a series. Recall from Chapter 27 that commas are used in this way too. Use semicolons whenever one or more of the items you are listing includes commas already.

Pitcher, catcher, short stop; goalie, center, right wing; tackle, quarterback, end—these are positions in baseball, hockey, and football. [*Here commas separate the individual positions, with semicolons separating the groups of positions.*]

In the attic of one rental house, we discovered a yellowed, still readable newspaper from 1945; a wicker, two-wheeled baby carriage; and fifty-five cents' worth of buffalo head nickels. [*Here commas are used as part of the identification of items, with semicolons used to separate the items themselves.*]

As you can see, the semicolons in the preceding sentences serve the useful function of separating items. Those sentences require semicolons; commas used in place of the semicolons would be confusing to readers.

Remember to use a colon, not a semicolon, to *introduce* a series, as in this example: *The buffet featured several kinds of fruit: apples, pears, kiwis, mangoes, and persimmons.* For more on colon usage, see Chapter 32.

Semicolons and Style

Knowing the rules of semicolon usage presents writers with new choices: should I join two independent clauses, or punctuate them as separate sentences? One thing is certain: the use of too many sentences joined with semicolons results in dull, formally repetitious prose. Using too many semicolons also deprives the writer of the clarity that dependent clauses can afford. *I see it has begun to rain; I'll turn off the sprinklers* is grammatically accurate, but its full meaning depends on readers' willingness and ability to see the connection between the two independent clauses. Subordinating one clause to the other spells out the cause-and-effect relationship between the observation and the action: *Since it is raining, I'll turn off the sprinklers.*

In general, joining sentences with semicolons should produce some obvious and positive benefit. If you join two or more sentences with semicolons, you ought to be able to point to the resulting benefit.

EXERCISE 28.1 REVISING USING SEMICOLONS

Some of the sentences in the passage that follows are punctuated inaccurately. Others may be accurate in their punctuation, but you may not feel the current version to be the most effective one. Edit the passage, making whatever minor revisions you feel necessary. Copy your best version on your own paper, and make sure that your version is punctuated accurately. Also make sure that your revised version uses semicolons in at least three instances. Finally, underline your changes.

Recovering alcoholics are some of the nicest people you'd ever want to meet, unfortunately, they also tell some of the saddest, most distressing stories. Many of them come from alcoholic families maybe the father was a functional, low-profile drinker for years; maybe the mother drank during the day and locked her own kids out of the house because she couldn't stand their noise; maybe the kids also suffered from sexual abuse or other physical violence; when these kids reached adulthood, they hid their hurt in a bottle. Some of them didn't wait for adulthood. Some drank right along with their parents.

Untreated alcoholics believe they have every reason to drink. Through treatment, however, they come to learn that no reason is a good enough reason for them to drink. For the alcoholic, that beer or wine or gin makes every problem worse, without fail, excessive, compulsive drinking creates new problems. Staying clean and sober doesn't do away with the alcoholic's problems; it does eliminate one pressing, overpowering difficulty, the sober alcoholic then has at least the opportunity to deal with other problems. Recovery isn't easy. Recovery is never complete. But with family support and the help of organizations like Alcoholics Anonymous, people do dry out, families do get better.

Using Semicolons with Other Punctuation |28e|

Occasionally, you may want to use semicolons with quotation marks, parentheses, or abbreviations. The following examples show you how to handle these situations.

Semicolons and Quotation Marks Semicolons are normally placed outside any quotation marks.

> Sometimes the British hesitate to speak in the first person, saying "one" rather than "I"; most Americans say "I" without giving it a thought.

Semicolons and Parentheses Semicolons are placed after and outside parentheses. Semicolons never precede parentheses.

> The actress was nominated for an Academy Award (her third nomination in three years); this year she may win.

Semicolons and Abbreviations When a semicolon follows an abbreviation using a period, use both the period and the semicolon.

> The unwanted package arrived C.O.D.; I politely refused to pay the charges.

ASSIGNMENT 28A USING SEMICOLONS TO LINK INDEPENDENT CLAUSES

Carefully check the punctuation in the following sentences. If the punctuation is accurate, write *C* on the lines provided. If it is inaccurate, write a corrected version.

EXAMPLE   The unwanted package arrived C.O.D., I politely refused to pay the charges.
The unwanted package arrived C.O.D.; I politely refused to pay the charges. _____

1. The traffic safety office has mailed out forms to request parking stickers; completed forms are due back by October 1. _____

_____

2. My current work-study job ends in two weeks. I'll need to find a new position; starting next term. _____

_____

3. Please save your questions for the end of the presentation; if you don't understand.

_____

4. For four glorious but underpaid weeks; I'll be working in Yosemite this summer.

_____

5. Swinging the door open quietly; the two police officers surprised a young burglar as he worked; to disconnect the cable wire from the Tuckers' color television.

_____

_____

6. The invitation distinctly said R.S.V.P., even so, we lost the invitation and never properly responded. _____

_____

7. Monday's U.S. Open tennis tournament was rained out, however, play is scheduled to resume Tuesday. _____

_____

8. Oak burns slowly and makes a hot fire; fir splits easily and makes superior

kindling. _____

9. Raspberries, which are my favorite fresh fruit, ripen in late June and early July in

addition, some years there's a later, smaller crop in September. _____

_____

_____

Use a semicolon and whatever other punctuation is required to combine each of the following sets of brief sentences into one longer sentence. You may revise the sentences slightly as needed. Make sure that your new sentence is punctuated correctly.

EXAMPLE   We walked the dog after dinner. The moon rose. The moon shone round and white as a bone china saucer.

While we were walking the dog after dinner, the moon rose; it shone round and white as a bone china saucer.

10. A replacement key for your office costs $10. You might lose your office key. Lost keys are sometimes turned in at the front security desk.

_____

_____

11. Some people think of wallpaper hanging as a do-it-yourself project. We tried wallpaper hanging. We think of wallpaper hanging as a project for professionals only.

_____

_____

12. I'll meet your train at the downtown station. Look for the woman under a dark blue umbrella. I'll also be carrying a tan briefcase.

_____

_____

13. There are fewer drive-in theaters than there once were. The Canyon Drive-in, for

example, has been demolished for a shopping mall. _____

_____

29

Using End Punctuation

Read this paragraph:

Without periods and the spaces that conventionally follow them, readers would have no ready way of recognizing the end of a sentence instead of being able to read quickly and effortlessly, we would all be required to slow down and continually ask ourselves whether or not the words we have just read constitute a complete sentence in short, we would be analyzing the form of the writing as well as trying to grasp its content; we would be doing two things at once chances are we would not be entirely successful with either task the end result would be frustration and an unwillingness to read

Now go back and reread the paragraph, putting in a period every time you think you have come to the end of a sentence. Does reading the paragraph feel easier and more comfortable now?

Using Periods |29a|

Using periods correctly makes life easier on your readers. It is not a complex skill to master. A period should end any sentence that is not a question or an exclamation.

I expect your essays on Tuesday. [*statement*]

Turn in your essays on Tuesday. [*mild command*]

Periods are often used with direct quotations, even if the quoted material is a question: *"Are you going home now?" she asked.* However, if the sentence is turned around, the question mark alone is sufficient; no period is necessary: *She asked me, "Are you going home now?"*

Some abbreviations also use periods:

Ms.	A.M.	etc.	Dr.	D.D.S.	B.C.	M.S.
Mr.	P.M.	et al.	Ph.D.	R.N.	A.D.	C.O.D.
Jr.	Mrs.	ibid.	M.D.	C.P.A.	M.A.	f.o.b.

See Chapter 34 for more on abbreviations.

Using Question Marks |29b|

Sentences that ask direct questions end with question marks. Sentences that report questions (that is, sentences that contain indirect questions) end with periods. Note the differences.

DIRECT QUESTION Did you air out the house after the exterminators were finished?

INDIRECT QUESTION I was wondering if you aired out the house after the exterminators were finished.

When quotation marks are used with direct questions, the order in which sentence elements are presented makes a difference.

I said, "What time will the exterminators leave?" [*Here the quoted question ends the sentence. In this case, the question mark is the sentence's end punctuation.*]

Did I just say, "Be there or be square"? [*Here the question mark applies to the whole sentence and so goes outside the quoted material.*]

Did I just say, "What time will the exterminators leave?" [*Here both the sentence itself and the quoted material are questions. A second question mark does* not *follow the quotation marks.*]

Writers also use question marks between questions in a series, even when the questions do not form separate sentences.

Is that dog a collie? a Labrador retriever? what?

Turn now to Assignment 29A at the end of this chapter for practice with end punctuation.

Using Exclamation Points |29c|

Exclamation points close emphatic and emotional statements. Using too many exclamation points is like being the boy who cried wolf; after a while, nobody listens. Sparingly used, however, exclamation points can indicate subtle differences in tone or meaning. Suppose that you have just given someone an expensive present in a small box. This someone opens the wrappings, looks at what is inside, and says only one word. This word could be punctuated three ways: *"Oh."* or *"Oh?"* or *"Oh!"* Which punctuation would indicate the most positive response?

Exclamation points are not followed by commas or periods. When part of a direct quotation, the exclamation point goes inside the quotation marks, as in *"Oh!"*

When informed that she had won the lottery, all Erin Johannsen could do was scream over and over, "I can't believe it! I can't believe it!"

The border guard yelled, "Halt!"

"Halt!" yelled the border guard.

EXERCISE 29.2 PROOFREADING AND REVISING END-PUNCTUATION ERRORS

Proofread the following passage for errors with end punctuation (periods, question marks, and exclamation points). Add needed end punctuation, and make sure that every new sentence begins with a capital letter. Cross out any punctuation that should not be there. If you are not sure whether to use periods with particular abbreviations, consult your dictionary.

Most people think of jogging as a solitary activity I'll grant that most of the time it is exactly that. But occasionally something unusual happens. Once a Winnebago with strange license plates swerved across the center line and stopped right in front of me? I swerved too, trying not to break stride, only to hear a rather shrill voice yell "Wait a minute, honey hey we need to talk to you. I stopped I can't help it if my parents taught me to be polite "Son," the driver said, "we're touring the USA, and I'm afraid we're just a little bit lost". As it turned out, they were looking for an address in the southeastern part of town; however, they were driving around on streets all clearly labeled as northwest they never noticed (or at least never acknowledged) that I was beet red in the face, sweaty, and scowling. I suppose they figured they were being polite too.

Another time a kid with a flat bicycle tire ran along beside me for twenty yards or so saying "Mister, you got ten dollars I can borrow. My tire's flat you got a dime so I can call my mama." He didn't notice that my jogging shorts had no pockets. Of course, when I got home and told my kids about the bicycle rider's plight, they could hardly believe it "Did that guy really expect you to have ten dollars, one asked? And said the other, "Did he really think you'd give it to him even if you had it"? All I could do was answer with a shrug. I hadn't taken the requests too seriously. I'd been too busy trying to breathe on a regular basis.

ASSIGNMENT 29A IDENTIFYING AND CORRECTING END-PUNCTUATION ERRORS

Some of the following sentences use question marks correctly, but many do not. Proofread each sentence. If the printed version is accurate, write _C_ on the lines provided. If the printed version needs correction, copy the sentence with corrected punctuation on the lines.

EXAMPLE

> Can you please pick up your room before I lose my temper.
> Can you please pick up your room before I lose my temper? _____

1. Didn't I say? "Either clean up your room, or there'll be no desserts after dinner?"

_____

_____

2. Was it in sixth grade that we studied United States history or fifth grade? _____

_____

3. If you're not sure which bus to ride, just ask the driver if the bus is going to the Raleigh Hills area.

_____

_____

4. "Have you heard the one about the tourist and the barber," he asked. _____

_____

5. Did you just say, "What time is it?"?

_____

6. "Yes, I asked you what time it was?"

_____

7. "Katie, did Beth invite you over after school" she asked?

_____

8. "Have you arranged for a substitute so that we can go to the ball game tonight?"

asked Aaron. _____

_____

9. My opponent has posed an interesting question: "Should the United States *ever* engage in the covert overthrow of a foreign government."? _____

_____

_____

10. Displaying uncommon impatience, she hollered, "Why is our food so slow?"

_____

_____

11. What, exactly, do you want!

_____

12. What do you mean coming in here and telling me to leave the room.

_____

30

Using Apostrophes

➤ *Student Writing Error 9: Missing possessive apostrophe*

Using Apostrophes to Signal Possession |30a|

An apostrophe plus *-s* at the end of a singular noun says that whatever follows the *'s* either belongs to the noun, is part of the noun, or was made by the noun.

Raymond*'s* bicycle [*the bicycle belonging to Raymond*]

the judge*'s* decision [*the decision made by the judge*]

the album*'s* cover [*the cover that is part of the album*]

Keats*'s* poems [*the poems written by Keats*]

As you can see, the possessive of a singular noun is formed by adding *'s*. This rule also holds true for acronyms (words formed by several first initials) and for indefinite pronouns. With titles or compound (multiword) nouns, the *'s* follows the last word. Note that the rule applies even if the noun ends in *-s* (as in *Keats's*).

ACRONYM NASA*'s* performance record [*the record belonging to NASA*]

INDEFINITE PRONOUN everyone*'s* choice [*the choice made by everyone*]

MULTIWORD NOUN her father-in-law*'s* car [*the car belonging to her father-in-law*]

TITLE the transportation secretary*'s* speech. [*the speech made by the transportation secretary*]

What about plural nouns? Many plural nouns end in *-s* or *-es*. To form the possessive of plural nouns ending in *-s* or *-es*, simply add the apostrophe. With plural nouns that do not end in *-s* or *-es* such as *children*, add *'s* as you would for any singular noun.

> Walking along the rocky shoreline, we could see the *seals'* faces. [*the faces of more than one seal*]

> The *children's* room is here at the end of the hall. [*the room belonging to the children.*]

Suppose that you wish to indicate joint ownership. The boat belonging to Mo and Ann would be referred to as *Mo and Ann's boat.* To indicate joint ownership, add *'s* only to the last noun. Suppose both Mo and Ann own their own boats. Then both of their names would carry apostrophes, as in *Mo's and Ann's boats are entered in the race on Saturday.*

Since missing or misused possessive apostrophes occur frequently, re-reading your draft to look for such errors is a good idea. As you reread, watch for any nouns ending in *-s.* Is the noun meant to show ownership or possession? If so, it needs an apostrophe.

Finally, remember that possessive pronouns—*my, your, his, her, its, our(s), your(s), their(s),* and *whose*—are already possessive; they do not need apostrophes. *The stolen bicycles were ours.* (not *our's*).

➤ Student Writing Error 20: It's/its confusion.

Remember, *its* is a possessive pronoun, as in *The bird watched its nest fall to the ground. It's* is a contraction for *it is,* as in *It's nearly time for lunch.* To check for this error in your own writing, reread your draft, paying particular attention to every use of *its* or *it's.* Use the apostrophe to indicate *it is;* use *its* to show possession. (In academic writing, it is best not to use contractions at all.)

Turn now to Assignment 30A at the end of this chapter for practice with indicating possession.

Using Apostrophes to Form Contractions |30*b*|

We also use apostrophes to form contractions, which are usually two words shortened to one. Some common contractions are listed below.

Full Form	*Contraction*	*Full Form*	*Contraction*
are not	aren't	let us	let's
cannot	can't	she had, she would	she'd
could not	couldn't	she had, she is	she's

did not	didn't	she will	she'll
do not	don't	there has, there is	there's
he had, he would	he'd	was not	wasn't
he had, he is	he's	were not	weren't
he will	he'll	who has, who is	who's
I am	I'm	will not	won't
I had, I would	I'd	would not	wouldn't
I have	I've	you are	you're
I will	I'll	you have	you've
is not	isn't	you will	you'll
it has, it is	it's		

Note that certain contractions sound identical to other words—*whose/ who's, theirs/there's, lets/let's, its/it's*—though they have quite separate meanings. Using the wrong spelling in a particular sentence is a common error; in fact, confusing *its* and *it's* is one of the top twenty errors found in student writing (see section 30a). The only sure cure is careful proofreading.

Apostrophes are also used in some common phrases to signal that letters or numbers have been left out. Thus *of the clock* becomes *o'clock* and *class of 1989* becomes *class of '89*. Occasionally, writers trying to create the sound of spoken dialects will also use apostrophes to signal omitted letters. Thus, *suppose* might become *s'pose*, or *probably* might be written *prob'ly*.

Contractions result in more informal prose; full forms make prose somewhat more formal and precise. Using contractions in formal situations will sometimes create an inappropriate tone. Here is an example:

> In order to keep a clean, safe working area, employees'll be responsible for seeing that scrap materials are discarded and tools properly stored.

Here the informality of the contraction seems to conflict with the seriousness of the responsibility discussed; the full form would be more appropriate. Some contractions are so informal (or incorrect) that they should not appear in college writing. These contractions include *ain't, who's ever* (for *whoever is*), and *'nother*. (For a fuller discussion of formal and informal tone, see Chapter 26).

Turn now to Assignment 30B at the end of this chapter for practice with contractions.

Using Apostrophes to Form the Plural of Numbers, Letters, Symbols, and Words Referred to as Words **I**30c**I**

An apostrophe plus *-s* is used to form the plural of numbers, letters, typographical symbols, and words used as words.

Plural Numbers   All my psychology test scores have been in the 90's.

Plural Letters Young children sometimes confuse *b*'s and *d*'s.

(Note that letters of the alphabet referred to as letters are either underlined or set in italics.).

Plural Typographical Symbols When I looked at the page I was typing, all the $'s were 4's.

Plural Words Referred to as Words Every one of her *separate*'s was spelled incorrectly.

(Note that words referred to as words are either underlined or set in italics.)

The plural of years can be written either with or without the apostrophe; ask your instructor which form to use, and make sure you are consistent.

EXAMPLE

The 1990's will see a rise in the number of high school students.

The 1990s will see a rise in the number of high school students

ASSIGNMENT 30A   USING APOSTROPHES TO SIGNAL POSSESSION

The following sentences contain material in parentheses. Incorporate that material, using apostrophes correctly.

EXAMPLE   Several buildings (designed by Frank Lloyd Wright) are still used as private residences.

Several of Frank Lloyd Wright's buildings are still used as private residences.

1. The guy wires (belonging to the antenna) were snapped by the wind.

_____

2. (The dresses belonging to your children) look very pretty.

_____

3. The poster (advertising the Oregon Coast Music Festival) hung on his wall.

_____

4. The finish (belonging to the piano) was cracked and peeling.

_____

5. Let's order another box of ribbons (that our typewriters use).

_____

6. (The poster made by Sean and the poster made by Demelza) have both been chosen as winners.

_____

7. It sounds like your muffler (which is part of your station wagon) needs to be replaced.

_____

8. (The finish that belongs to it) was scratched in the accident.

_____

9. (The choices of all participating voters) have been made.

_____

10. (The paper belonging to me) was turned in on time.

_____

11. (It is) an important decision.

_____

12. Yes, I think (that is) (the coat belonging to him) over there on the chair. _____

_____

USING APOSTROPHES TO CREATE CONTRACTIONS

Read each sentence below. If the sentence uses contractions, rewrite it so that it uses full forms. If the sentence uses full forms, rewrite it so that it uses contractions. Correct any improperly used contractions. Think about the sentence's meaning and its probable context. Then indicate which of the two forms of the sentence you consider more appropriate by placing an _X_ next to it.

EXAMPLE

In the unlikely event of any accidental injury to your child, medical personnel'll be available immediately.

In the unlikely event of any accidental injury to your child, medical personnel will be available immediately. **X** _____

1. Should not we have stopped at Dairy Mart for more milk?

_____

2. You have been listening to several folks as they have described how the United Way has helped them; now will you not please take out your checkbooks and help your neighbors?

_____

_____

_____

3. That guy who's been giving you a ride after work called about nine o'clock.

_____

_____

4. Some critics argue that Anne Tyler'll be remembered as one of the best novelists of

the '80s. _____

_____

5. The clothes I am washing now did not really get too dirty.

_____

6. For the test you'll be takin' on Monday, your required to have a pencil with a No. 2

lead. _____

_____

7. The judge'll be available to meet with you once court adjourns.

_____

8. The distributor informs me that you're order has not received it's required approval from the business office.

_____

_____

9. Who's ever responsible for an accident has the legal obligation to compensate any

injured parties. _____

_____

10. You've been told over and over that you shouldn't play in the street.

_____

The following passage contains numerous errors involving apostrophes. Circle any errors you find, and pencil in your corrections in the spaces between lines.

With the end of summer, college students begin to think about registration for the new term, course schedule booklets become hot items, and the rumor mill churns into operation. Whose had whom in which classes? Hows so and so in history? How many As did so and so give in psychology last term? Anyone heard how many 121s there'll be? Hallways buzz and the tables in the student union fill up once more. All over campus, department secretaries patience wears thin even as they politely answer question's about adding or dropping classes, changing majors, and so forth. Faculty members offices echo with the sound of typewriters or computer printers. Meanwhile, the bookstores lines stretch back from the cash registers all the way to the next years calendars, which are already on sale. Returning student's sometimes find its not possible to walk across campus without running into an old acquaintance. They keep "Hows it going?" and "What's up?" at the ready.

By late November, the elms dont rustle; theyre bare. Maybe its even snowed already. Snow or not, much of the terms earlier anticipation has been replaced by some quite specific challenges: the paper due tomorrow, the necessary B on the next test (after two Cs and a C−), the P.E. classes required 20 laps. But in August or September, all thats in the future. The sun shines, the summers moneys in the bank, and everyone secretly believes that again this term the registrars computer will be friendly.

31

Using Quotation Marks

Using Quotation Marks to Signal Direct Quotation |31a|

In our culture at least, words have a status similar to that of personal property; thus, we use double quotation marks to signal the reproduction of someone else's exact words. Doing so also helps ensure that readers understand accurately who said what.

> "I vote for eating breakfast out this morning," she said.

Use single quotation marks to enclose a quotation within a quotation:

> "Mother says she feels 'a little better' this morning," James said.

Remember that quotation marks, whether single or double, identify someone else's *exact words*; when paraphrasing, do not use quotation marks.

Paraphrase No quotation marks:

> Lisa said that she thought it would be a good idea for me to speak to the accountants' organization.

Direct Quotation Quotation marks required:

> Lisa said, "You know, I think it would be good for you to speak to the accountants' organization."

Using Quotation Marks with Other Punctuation |31f|

Quotation marks are almost always used with other punctuation marks. Commas and colons are often (but not always) used to introduce quoted material. In general, a comma or a colon is used whenever there is a perceptible pause or interruption separating the writer's words from the quoted words. Verbs describing speech are frequently set off by commas, especially if the quoted material is a complete sentence.

Quotation Marks with Periods and Commas Periods and commas always go inside the quotation marks.

> The Coast Guard officer called the rescue "routine."
>
> "For Eastern Oregon, it should be fair but quite cold tonight," said the radio announcer. [*comma used to set off quotation from the verb* said]
>
> Martha said that she "wouldn't be caught dead in that place." [*no comma because quote is only part of a sentence*]
>
> "If you go in there," he threatened, "I'll walk away and you'll never see me again." [*commas used to set off material that interrupts the quoted material*]

Quotation Marks with Colons and Semicolons Colons and semicolons go outside the quotation marks.

> Mr. Ono smiled and said, "I have brought you one example": there before us was a watermelon almost the size of an oil drum.
>
> The cowboy said, "Smile when you say that"; he reached for his gun as he spoke.

Quotation Marks with Question Marks, Exclamation Points, and Dashes
These punctuation marks go inside when they are part of the quotation; they go outside when they are not part of the quotation.

> "Jack! Wait!" [*Exclamation is part of the meaning of the quoted material; thus, the exclamation point goes inside the quotation marks.*]
>
> Who was it who said, "There's a sucker born every minute"? [*The quotation itself is a statement. However, the entire sentence is a question. Hence, the question mark punctuates the sentence and is placed outside quotation marks.*]
>
> Frankie called after her, "Wait! I need—" but she was already gone. [*The dash here indicates that Frankie stopped abruptly.*]

Quotation Marks with Apostrophes The quotation marks follow the 's.

> I distinctly recall Luigi saying, "We'll meet after work at Pizza Bill's."

Finally, footnote numbers and parenthetical citations always go outside quotation marks.

A Note about Capitalization Capitalize the first quoted word when that word begins a completely quoted sentence set off by a comma or colon.

> The Coast Guard officer called the rescue "routine." [*not a sentence, not set off: not capitalized*]

> She said, "If he offers me a promotion, I'll accept a transfer." [*complete sentence, set off by a comma: capitalized*]

> Vern predicted that "if we get rain tomorrow, we will be able to contain this fire." [*incomplete sentence, not set off: not capitalized*]

Turn now to Assignment 31A at the end of this chapter for practice with direct quotation.

Quoting Longer Prose Passages |31a1|

If you use quoted material as part of an essay or an argument and that quoted material runs only four lines or less, use quotation marks and incorporate the quoted material as part of your paragraph. Quoted material that runs longer than four lines should be indented ten spaces from the left margin, without quotation marks. (Indented quotations are also known as block quotations.) When material from another speaker or source appears inside a block quotation, use double quotation marks. When quoted material runs to more than one paragraph, indent the first line of each new paragraph an additional three spaces. When typing, double-space block quotations, just like the rest of your paper. (Note: these guidelines follow the style set by the Modern Language Association. For other styles and further information on using quotations, see Chapters 39–41.)

EXAMPLE

```
        Lacking visitors due to the heavy storms and unable to journey to town
    for the same reason, Thoreau says he was forced to imagine his company.
    That is precisely what he does:
                For human society I was obliged to conjure up the former
            occupants of these woods.  Within the memory of many of my
            townsmen the road near which my house stands resounded with the
            laughter and gossip of inhabitants, and the woods which border it
            were notched and dotted here and there with their little gardens
            and dwellings. . . . (Walden and "Civil Disobedience" 172)
```

Quoting Poetry |31a2|

The guidelines regarding indentation of quoted material hold true for poetry as well as for prose: four lines or less may (using appropriate quotation marks) be incorporated into the body of your essay, and more than four lines should be indented without using quotation marks. When quoted within quotation marks, a slash mark (with a space on each side of it) is used to indicate the end of a line. Here, for example, are the opening two lines of the early American Anne Bradstreet's poem "In Memory of My Dear Grandchild Anne Bradstreet Who Deceased June 20, 1669, Being Three Years and Seven Months Old": "With troubled heart and trembling hand I write, / The heavens have changed to sorrow my delight." Because line breaks in a poem are often as important as the punctuation and the actual words, you must not omit the slash marks.

When quoting more than four lines in a block quotation, make sure that you accurately reproduce all the line breaks, indentations, capitalizations, and stanza breaks of the original.

EXERCISE 31.1 VARYING QUOTATION FORMAT ACCORDING TO LENGTH

Find a poem that you particularly like. Read the poem and decide on the one or two lines you like best. Use a sentence or two to introduce those lines, and then quote them. Punctuate your writing and your quotation accurately. Type your work, double-spaced, or write it out carefully on your own paper.

EXAMPLE

> Andrew Marvell's "To His Coy Mistress" is one of the few poems that
> I have memorized. My favorite lines come at the very end: "Thus, though
> we cannot make our sun / Stand still, yet we will make him run."

Find a paragraph in this book that is longer than five lines and has been helpful to you. Introduce the paragraph by telling why it has been helpful; then quote the paragraph itself. Make sure that your block quotation follows the guidelines set forth in this chapter. Make sure that your introduction to the quotation indicates the original page number of your quoted material. Type your work, double-spaced, or write it out carefully on your own paper.

Using Quotation Marks to Signal Dialogue |31b|

When writing dialogue, start a new paragraph to indicate a change of speaker. Sometimes these paragraph shifts will be the only indication readers need:

> "You're going," he said as though it were a fact.
> "Yes." Her voice was quiet but firm.
> "And you believe you ought to have the Ferrari and the Picasso?"

"It was my money that bought them."

"So it was," he said. "So it was."

To signal that a single speech covers several paragraphs, use quotation marks at the beginning of the speech, at the beginning of every new paragraph continuing this speech, and at the end of the speech. The omission of quotation marks at the end of a paragraph signals to readers that the same speaker continues speaking in the new paragraph.

EXERCISE 31.2 USING QUOTATION MARKS TO SIGNAL DIALOGUE

Using your own paper, write a short (one to two pages) fictional sketch that features dialogue between two characters. Use quotation marks accurately, and use new paragraphs to indicate the shift from one speaker to the other.

Using Quotation Marks to Signal Titles and Definitions |31c|

Titles

Use quotation marks to identify titles that are parts of larger works, such as titles of individual poems, short stories, articles, chapters, and essays. In contrast, full collections of poems, short stories, articles, and essays should be either underlined or italicized (for more on underlining and the use of italics, see Chapter 35). Songs and individual episodes of television or radio shows are also identified by quotation marks.

Song Bing Crosby's "White Christmas" gets radio airplay every December.

Television Episode John Cleese appears tonight in a *Cheers* episode titled "Simon Says."

(Note that the television series title is underlined or italicized.)

Short Story Tim O'Brien's "Quantum Jumps" later became part of his third novel.

Essay "Loren Eiseley, Student of Time," an essay by Erleen Christiansen, was published in 1987.

Poem In Elizabeth Bishop's poem, "The Waiting Room," the speaker is an adult remembering herself as a young girl.

Chapter This chapter is titled "Using Quotation Marks."

Note that titles are often used as appositives (as in the "Poem" example). In such cases, the quotation follows the same punctuation conventions as any other appositive; that is, the appositive is set off with commas.

Identifying Definitions

Writers also use quotation marks to indicate definitions.

> The word *radical* originally meant "root."

> *Forte* comes from the Latin and originally meant "strong" or "brave."

(Note that words used as words are italicized.)

Using Quotation Marks to Signal Irony or Coinages |31d|

Writers may also use quotation marks sparingly to indicate irony or skepticism. Using quotation marks in these ways is akin to using exclamation points. Such punctuation works only when used prudently and rarely.

> Our "dinner date" turned out to be a fifteen-minute stop at a hamburger drive-in.

> The "appetizers" at that restaurant are so rich and delicious that they really make a meal in themselves.

Used carelessly, quotation marks may actually communicate a meaning directly opposed to that of the words alone. For example, most readers will interpret the following example as ironic rather than emphatically sincere: *I "love" your mother's creamed broccoli.* For emphasis, use italics or underline:

> I *love* your mother's creamed broccoli.

Quotation marks are also used to signal the invention of a new word or the use of an old word in an entirely new context. Here is an example:

> Computer companies occasionally announce new software only to discontinue its development later; some people call such software "vaporware."

When titles normally set off by quotation marks appear inside other quoted material, use single quotation marks to indicate the title:

> What Professor Smith said was, "If you'd read Richard Hugo's 'Glen Uig,' you'd know that not all of his poems focus on shame or degradation."

Turn now to Assignments 31B and 31C at the end of this chapter for practice with quotation marks.

ASSIGNMENT 31A   USING QUOTATION MARKS TO SIGNAL DIRECT QUOTATION

Copy the sentences below, using quotation marks each time someone else's exact words are being used. Make sure that you use quotation marks with other punctuation marks correctly.

EXAMPLE

Your phone's ringing! yelled Phil from the end of the hall.

"Your phone's ringing!" yelled Phil from the end of the hall.

1. Ultimately, our differences with management may result in the need to strike; the crowd shifted uneasily at those words.

_____

_____

2. I'm going outside for some fresh air, said Barb as she put on her sweater, but I'll only be a few minutes.

_____

_____

3. Has everyone been informed that Ms. Jenkins said, For the duration of these training seminars, there will be no absences?

_____

_____

4. I could not believe the condition of my hometown, he wrote.

_____

_____

5. Emerson didn't say Consistency is the hobgoblin of little minds; he said, A foolish consistency is the hobgoblin of little minds.

_____

_____

Read the following sentences. On the line, identify the quotation as either direct or indirect. Add quotation marks as needed.

It was the American revolutionary Patrick Henry who said, "Give me liberty or give me death." <u>direct</u>

6. Through his publicist, Michael Jackson said that he was pleased at the support his Japanese fans had shown him. _____

7. After a tornado ripped through her house, a tearful Indiana woman said We're here today only because God held us in his hand; that's all I can say. _____

8. Call me Ishmael is the first sentence of Herman Melville's *Moby Dick.* _____

9. Most people like to characterize themselves as open-minded and flexible enough to change when the circumstances demand. _____

10. The county employment office's annual summary states that the current unemployment rate is 37% lower than it was five years ago. _____

ASSIGNMENT 31B USING QUOTATION MARKS CORRECTLY

Proofread the following sentences for correct use of quotation marks. If the sentence is correct, write *C* on the lines provided. If the sentence needs to be repunctuated, copy the sentence and punctuate it accurately. Should you need a review, the first section of this chapter discusses the use of quotation marks with other punctuation.

EXAMPLE

"Under Stars and The Ritual of Memories" remain two of my favorite Tess Gallagher poems.

"Under Stars" and "The Ritual of Memories" remain two of my favorite Tess Gallagher poems.

1. Listen," screamed the television character, if you say I'm going to leave you" one more time, I'll ask you to leave!

_____

_____

2. Loren Eiseley's essay "The Judgment of the Birds deserves its place in the anthologies.

_____

_____

3. The episode I enjoyed most,' she said, was the one titled "Atomic Shakespeare; it was inventive and funny.

_____

_____

4. 'Buddhist Economics is not a chapter title you'll find in too many college textbooks.'

_____

_____

5. "As I was telling you, he sat there in his library, sipped his drink, and said, I find it delightfully reassuring to live among all these words."

_____

_____

6. "Who but the British," the guide remarked, "would knit 'sweaters' for their tea-pots?"

_____

_____

7. "Did I tell you," he said, that when Cary got here, the first thing she asked was 'Well, are the hills alive with the sound of music"?

_____

_____

_____

8. The opening line of her parody read, "It was Pee-wee Herman who said 'Give me liberty, but not bad breath.

_____

_____

9. When it came to family pets, the exterminators' contract specifically denied any responsibility for their safety.

_____

_____

_____

10. The medical report came to this conclusion: "Patients who 'take responsibility for their own recovery' do indeed recover faster than those who see themselves as victims passively accepting treatment."

_____

_____

_____

_____

ASSIGNMENT 31C IDENTIFYING AND CORRECTING ERRORS WITH QUOTATION MARKS

Below is the final draft of a brief essay. Read it first. Then proofread it for errors involving quotation marks. Place a check in the left margin beside any line that needs correction. Cross out whatever should not be there; add whatever should. If some portion of the essay needs repositioning, indicate that in the margin.

One of the best-kept secrets about poetry is that reading it can be a wonderful, benign addiction. Poems, like anything else handmade, reflect their makers; they are as strange, exotic, thought-provoking, and beautiful as people. Who can deny a rush of adrenaline at taking a deep breath (a really deep breath) and saying (almost singing) some of the most gorgeous sounds in English: "Now as I was young and easy under the apple boughs / About the lilting house and happy as the grass was green, / The night above the dingle starry, / Time let me hail and climb /

       Golden in the heydays of his eyes,

    And honoured among wagons I was prince of the apple towns

    And once below a time I lordly had the trees and leaves

        Trail with daisies and barley

      Down the rivers of the windfall light.''

So goes the opening stanza of Dylan Thomas's Fern Hill. Skeptics might say "Even if we grant that the language of Fern Hill is indeed gorgeous, as you say, it is also virtually impossible to follow.

Ah, pity the skeptics; they have an adversarial relationship with the world. Fern Hill is difficult only for readers who ask that it transmit its content as a newspaper does. Newspapers are read for their information. They're written to be read easily, quickly. The sentences are short, and individually they are forgettable. Who recalls last week's headlines? In contrast, Poetry, said Ezra Pound, is news that stays news.

The truth is, Fern Hill is made to be read slowly and even inquisitively. How, after all, can a house be called "lilting"? The word has more to do with song than with architecture. Could someone have been singing? How happy is happy as the grass was green? It's as happy as the night is starry. Is the pun on heydays (hay days) intentional? What can it mean to be prince of the apple towns? Could apple towns be rows of apple trees--an orchard? Does that tie in with the "windfall" of the last line?

And what does this add up to? Doesn't it add up to an intensity of feeling that makes the experience ours even though it's not? We don't know that farm, except we do. We've seen the imaginations of children;

we've seen how they become queens or kings of their bedrooms, their toys, their dolls. The speaker in Fern Hill is prince of it all. The speaker owned that farm, that time, and owns it still.

What about the odd shape of Fern Hill on the page? Why insist on such an arrangement? Why is the second stanza arranged identically to the first? And how is it that Thomas could ensure that the first line of the second stanza contains precisely the same number of syllables as the first line of the first stanza? The same correspondence is true for the second lines of each stanza, and the third lines, and so on until the fifth stanza, which changes the pattern somewhat. What astonishing union of content and form are we looking at here?

Actually, Fern Hill is childhood distilled; all the frustrations and angers have been boiled away. What's left is an awe-inspiring precision of language and feeling. What's left is the exhilaration of childhood as time in the Garden of Eden, 'it was all / Shining, it was Adam and maiden, / The sky gathered again / And the sun grew round that very day.' If poems are indeed an addiction, they must be the very best kind.

32

Using Other Punctuation Marks

Using Parentheses |32a|

Writers use parentheses to set off supplementary information. Such information may be only a word or two or may form an entire sentence. Whatever this information may be, readers will view it as less important than the rest of the sentence. Any sentence containing parenthetical information should be grammatically complete and clear without the material in parentheses. Here are some examples of sentences containing parenthetical information:

> Walt Disney's movie *Alice in Wonderland* (1951) remains a bright, weird tale even on television's small screen.

> Stock analysts refer to IBM (International Business Machines) as a blue chip stock.

> Just as I rounded the corner (and I could tell something smelled funny), I saw flames licking at the Whittleseys' garage.

Occasionally, writers will place quite important information in parentheses. These writers count on the surprise value such information yields. Here is an example:

> The taxi driver was finally persuaded (by means of $600) that the damage to his back seat could be repaired after all.

As with exclamation points and quotation marks used for irony, parenthetical explanations or additions should be used carefully. The following sentence makes two tactical errors. It contains too much parenthetical information, and that information is crucial, not supplementary:

> Employees (by which is here meant all employed half-time or less) are not expected to resume work (that is, should not be physically present on company premises) until the last Monday of this month (when it is expected that line repairs will be complete).

Revising such a sentence may involve writing several smaller sentences. In this way, each important idea receives its due attention from readers:

> Part-time employees (half-time or less) should plan to return to work on the last Monday of this month. Line repairs should be completed by that time. Until then, we ask these employees to remain off company premises in order to allow repairs to proceed.

The second version is only a little bit longer, but it is quite a bit clearer.

Writers use parentheses in only one other way: to set off numbered or lettered items.

> Once you have finished dinner, I want you to (1) clear your place, (2) take a shower and wash your hair, and (3) give your old dog a walk before it gets too dark.

End punctuation goes outside the parentheses unless the parenthetical material is a separate and complete sentence.

> Geri says she is smart because she has ESP (whatever that is).

> We will meet at the lodge at noon. (Remember your sack lunch.)

When needed, commas follow closing parentheses; commas are never used before a parenthesis.

> If we decide to climb Mount Rainer (or any of the Alaskan peaks), we will do so only with an experienced guide.

Using Brackets   I32bI

Writers use brackets in two quite specialized ways.

1. To set off a parenthetical element within an already parenthesized passage:

> Some books we read as children (like Oliver Butterworth's *Enormous Egg* [Boston: Atlantic–Little, Brown, 1956]) we now read to our own children.

2. To insert explanatory words or comments into a quoted passage:

> Then she turned and said, "Will you [meaning my father] be joining us for dinner?"

In sentences like the one just given, readers attribute the bracketed material to the author of the sentence, not to the person who is quoted. (If your typewriter or computer lacks bracket keys, it is acceptable to write brackets in by hand.)

EXERCISE 32.1 USING PARENTHESES AND BRACKETS

Some of the five sentences that follow confuse parentheses and brackets. If a sentence uses these punctuation marks correctly, write *C* in the margin next to it. If the sentence uses these punctuation marks incorrectly, write in the necessary corrections.

EXAMPLE

"I think he [**X**Robinson Jeffers**X**] thought of people as wild, passionate, and usually not very rational or altruistic," Alfred said. (Note: Assume that the name did not form part of the quotation and was inserted by the writer reporting this opinion.)

1. That mantel clock [made in Germany in 1888] has been in the family since my father's grandmother brought it over with her in 1901.

2. Either [1] we propose our modifications now, or (2) we wait for the final set of engineering results and risk a production failure.

3. "Your presentation (which was, by the way, cogently argued) impressed several members of the committee." (Assume that the same speaker said all of these words.)

4. Touring Hearst Castle [in San Simeon, California] gives you an idea of how America's rich and famous once lived.

5. "Her book [*Out of Africa*] is to me both an astonishment and a delight." (Assume that the title has been inserted and was not part of the original quotation.)

EXERCISE 32.2 REVISING TO ENSURE CORRECT USE OF PARENTHESES

In each of the two passages that follow, parentheses have been overused or used inappropriately. Using your own paper, rewrite each passage so that parentheses are used sparingly and appropriately, making sure that crucial information does not appear in parentheses.

1. *Where in the World Is Carmen Sandiego?* (an ever-popular and hard-to-stock game program) has just arrived on our shelves. This program (it runs on any of the various PC's manufactured by IBM) teaches gameplayers world geography (including such things as the various national currencies and flags, as well as the locations of major cities and rivers). This moderately priced program (so popular that new shipments sell out in days) is marketed by Broderbund Software Co. (San Rafael, California).

2. Our car was approaching the intersection from the west (we were arguing about which movie we were going to see, so maybe we weren't paying close attention) when somebody (maybe Judy, who was driving) yelled "No!" Just seconds after that (I think by then Judy had begun to swerve right to try to get out of the way), the station wagon hit our front end behind the wheel (the left one). As metal crunched and we spun around, it all seemed to be happening in slow motion.

Using Dashes |32c|

Dashes may be used singly or in pairs. A single dash indicates a sudden change or contrast; occasionally, the single dash can be used repeatedly to mimic the breathlessness or fragmentary quality of thought or speech. (To type a dash, hit the hyphen key twice, leaving no spaces between the dash and the words on either side of it.)

EXAMPLES

We'll meet you at nine at Woodstock's for pizza—if Rob's aging Buick can get us there. [*single dash used to signal sudden change or contrast*]

I—wait—*no*—don't shoot—I'll tell you—I'll tell you what you want to know. [*single dash used repeatedly to mimic the breathlessness or fragmentary quality of thought or speech*]

Writers use dashes in pairs to set off material from the rest of the sentence. You may recall that commas and parentheses also set off material from the rest of the sentence. What are the differences here? The contrast with parentheses is one of emphasis. Parenthetical information is almost always considered to be of lesser importance than the information contained in the rest of the sentence. Dashes, by contrast, tend to emphasize the material they enclose. In the first of the following sentences, the writer is trying to downplay John Glenn's fame; in the second, the intent is to make that fame an integral part of the sentence's meaning.

> As a boy, I lived next door to John Glenn (the former astronaut who was later a U.S. senator) and mowed his lawn every Saturday. [*parentheses used to minimize*]

> As a boy, I lived next door to John Glenn—the former astronaut who was later a U.S. senator—and mowed his lawn every Saturday. [*dashes used to emphasize*]

The difference may be lost on cursory readers. However, as a writer, you ought to be able to see that these two sentences do not communicate quite the same thing.

Could commas be substituted for either the dashes or the parentheses in the two sentences just discussed? Yes. A writer using commas would be neither emphasizing nor minimizing. (For more on comma usage, see Chapter 27.)

Writers also use dashes whenever it is necessary to set off a list from the rest of the sentence. Since commas separate items in the list, dashes must be used to set off the entire list.

> Graceful, athletic, intense—Dorothy Hamill was a joy to watch on the ice.

> That hamburger patty had everything on it—tomato, mustard, mayo, romaine lettuce, thin-sliced cucumber, and onion rings so thick that they formed a kind of wall to contain everything else—except maybe the kitchen sink.

Finally, if the material inside the dashes is a question or an exclamation, the appropriate punctuation mark precedes the final dash.

> Mr. Swift's argument is—who can dispute this?—both cunning and abhorrent.

Turn now to Assignment 32A at the end of this chapter for practice in using dashes.

Using Colons |32d|

Used correctly, colons actively contribute to sentence meaning. A colon says that whatever follows will be an example or an explanation of what has just been said.

EXAMPLES

> The registrar's computer has given me four classes: Introduction to Biology, Composition, History of American Thought, and Fitness Aerobics.

The district attorney's announcement was entirely unexpected: two highly regarded local doctors had been indicted on fraud charges.

When a colon is used to introduce an example or an explanation, it should follow a grammatically complete independent clause. The colon should *not* separate a verb or preposition from its object, nor should a colon follow *especially, including,* or *such as.*

INCORRECT

Lisa's book is: readable, intelligent, and useful. [*Colon separates verb and subject complement.*]

CORRECT

Lisa's book is readable, intelligent, and useful. [*No colon is needed.*]

Reviewers agree that Lisa's book possesses these traits: readability, intelligence, and usefulness. [*Colon follows a grammatically complete independent clause.*]

INCORRECT

Paul Cook has published several novels, including: *Halo* and *Tintagel.*

CORRECT

Paul Cook has published several novels, including *Halo* and *Tintagel.*

INCORRECT

Nearly Normals makes its Swiss-melt sandwich with: Swiss cheese, sautéed mushrooms, and lettuce, all grilled between two slices of dark rye bread.

CORRECT

Nearly Normals makes its Swiss-melt sandwich with Swiss cheese, sautéed mushrooms, and lettuce, all grilled between two slices of dark rye bread.

Colons are also frequently used in the following ways:

Following Parts of Memos
To: Dean Wilkins
From: Robert Frank

After Salutations
Dear Scholarship Committee:

To Separate Hours, Minutes, and Seconds

Class begins promptly at 8:30.
The seismograph indicates that the earthquake began at 2:15:36 A.M.

To Separate Biblical Chapters and Verses

We learned about Noah in Genesis 5:28.

To Separate Titles and Subtitles

Eileen Simpson's *Poets in Their Youth: A Memoir* re-creates a dozen or so years (the forties and early fifties) that readers and critics now recognize as a pivotal time for American poetry in this century.

To Separate Volumes and Page Numbers

Check the *Encyclopaedia Britannica* 3:187. [*volume 3, page 187*]

To Separate Items in Bibliographic Entries

Simpson, Eileen. *Poets in Their Youth: A Memoir.* New York: Random House, 1982. [*Colon separates title from subtitle and place of publication from publisher.*]

Will, George. "A Liberal's Waiting Game." *Newsweek* 16 March 1987:82. [*Colon separates the year from the page numbers.*]

Turn now to Assignment 32B at the end of this chapter for practice in using colons.

Using Slashes |32e|

Use slashes in any of these three ways:

1. To signal line divisions in quotations of poetry that run four lines or less
2. To separate terms that are equally applicable
3. To indicate numeric fractions

To Indicate Line Divisions in Poetry Quotations of Less than Four Lines

The opening lines of Thomas Campion's "I Care Not for These Ladies" go like this: "I care not for these ladies, / That must be wooed and prayed: / Give me kind Amaryllis, / The wanton country maid." [*Leave a space before and after the slash. Use two slashes to show a stanza break.*]

To Separate Equally Applicable Terms

This form must be signed by the applicant's parent/legal guardian. [*no space before or after the slash.*]

To Indicate Numeric Fractions

The baby measured 20 3/4 inches. [*no space before or after the slash*]

Using Ellipses |32f|

Writers use ellipses—three dots, equally spaced—to let readers know that something has been left out. Ellipses show omissions in the middle of a sentence. Ellipses plus a period (four dots in all) are used when, in the middle of a quoted passage, the writer has omitted the end of a sentence, the beginning of a succeeding sentence, or one or more complete sentences.

EXAMPLES

Ellen wrote, ". . . I really do love him." [*Ellen's full sentence read, "Even though I've only known him for three weeks, I really do love him."*]

Reynaldo wrote, "I love her very much. . . ." [*Reynaldo's full sentence read, "I love her very much, even though I've only known her for three weeks." Four ellipsis points are used in the quoted sentence: the first is the sentence's period, and the next three indicate ellipsis. Note that the quotation marks follow the final point without any intervening space.*]

"Before we leave for the beach, . . . make sure the downstairs door is locked." [*The entire sentence reads, "Before we leave for the beach, I'll make sure the windows are closed, and you make sure the downstairs door is locked."*]

"This Sunday we'll cut the wood. . . . And next Sunday, we'll be able to have a fire in the fireplace." [*The original passage reads, "This Sunday we'll cut the wood. We'll have the chimney cleaned during the week. And next Sunday, we'll be able to have a fire in the fireplace." The first point is the first sentence's period. The three ellipsis points then follow.*]

As a writer, you are obliged to preserve the tone and meaning of your sources. When you use ellipses, make sure that your shortened version does not distort the original in spirit or content.

Ellipses may also be used to signal a pause or hesitation. This usage occurs most often in dialogue, but it may also appear in unquoted prose.

EXAMPLES

Fidelity . . . She was saying the word over and over to herself, as though it might have a taste, as though by saying it over and over, she could determine what it meant to her.

"Billy . . . Billy . . . Billy . . ." Someone was calling him. Someone far away was looking for him and calling his name.

ASSIGNMENT 32A USING DASHES

Read the sentences below, paying particular attention to the use of dashes. If the sentence is acceptable as written, write *C* on the lines. If the sentence needs revising, write your revision on the lines. Make sure your revision uses dashes correctly. Be ready to explain your reasoning.

EXAMPLE

> Hamburg today the largest city—and busiest port—in West Germany—has twice risen from the ashes of fire and destruction.
> Hamburg—today the largest city and busiest port in West Germany—has twice risen from the ashes of fire and destruction.

1. Few recognize the name Sarah Josepha Hale many know her poem titled—"Mary Had a Little Lamb."

_____

_____

2. Several kinds of lace among them Alencon, Honiton, and Maltese—take their names from their place of origin.

_____

_____

3. We'll send a postcard when we arrive in International Falls if we remember.

_____

_____

4. Their sophistication, their perceptual abilities, even how they feel about themselves children's pictures can tells us much—about the children who drew them.

_____

_____

5. Your papers should be finished the deadline is Friday at noon and placed in the envelope on Professor Cook's office door.

_____

_____

Combine each group of short sentences, using dashes appropriately as needed.

Chicago's Sears Tower contains 110 stories. It rises to a height of almost 1,500 feet. It measures 104 feet taller than New York's World Trade Center. It is the world's tallest building.

Rising some 1,500 feet, containing 110 stories, and measuring 104 feet taller than New York's World Trade Center—Chicago's Sears Tower is the world's tallest building.

6. Paul Klee was a renowned graphic artist, painter, and art theorist. He died some fifty years ago. He remains an influential presence for contemporary artists.

7. Parents should act like parents. They should not act like squabbling children.

8. Twice Knoxville served as Tennessee's state capital. This occurred from 1796 to 1812 and again from 1817 to 1818.

9. Renata Scotto is famous. She is an opera singer. She was born in Italy. She is still remembered for her debut in Milan in 1953. She is particularly recognized today for her performances of Puccini's *Madame Butterfly*.

10. You should escape your troubles. You should travel without ever leaving your chair. You should save your money. You should visit your local library. You should read.

ASSIGNMENT 32B USING COLONS

Combine the following sentences, using colons in each one. There may be more than one way to combine these sentences; for this exercise, however, make sure that your versions use colons.

EXAMPLE

Check the *Encyclopaedia Britannica.* The volume to check is volume 3. The page number is 187.
Check the *Encylcopaedia Britannica* 3:187. _____

1. You're supposed to bring the condiments. You ought to bring mustard, catsup, pickle relish, dill pickles, and mayonnaise. _____

_____

2. Bill's decision was a difficult one, but he stuck to it. Bill quit smoking for good.

_____

3. Ellen Gilchrist has a fourth book. It is titled *Drunk with Love.* It is subtitled *A Book of Stories.* _____

4. I like the Book of Proverbs. I especially like Chapter 12. I especially like verse 8 in that chapter. _____

5. Troop 415 packed what seemed like a ton of gear into the van. They packed four tents, a dozen sleeping bags, three propane stoves (with propane bottles), food for two nights, ropes, craft projects, and the troop flag. _____

_____

_____

Read each of the sentences below, paying particular attention to the use of colons. If the sentence is punctuated accurately, write *C* on the lines. If the sentence needs revising, write your revision on the lines. Make sure your revision uses colons correctly.

> Advertisers assume that we all want to be: beautiful, protected, stylish, and trendy.
> Advertisers assume that we all want to be beautiful, protected, stylish, and trendy.

6. Leonid Telyatnikov has done something he hopes no one else will have to do he has: commanded a fire crew attempting to extinguish a nuclear reactor fire.

_____

_____

_____

7. Recognized as perhaps the nation's best prison newspaper, the *Prison Mirror* of Stillwater, Minnesota, publishes articles on: stress management, the alternatives to execution, smoking, and education.

_____

_____

_____

8. The list of John Huston's movie credits includes: *Moby Dick, Prizzi's Honor, The Maltese Falcon,* and *The African Queen.*

_____

_____

_____

9. Lucille Boone Berry, a genuine descendant of Daniel Boone, suffered a fate that seems right out of the history books: when she was a young girl, her father and brother rode out hunting one day and never returned.

_____

_____

_____

10. Every American city has its own streets lit by signs proclaiming: "Jesus Saves" and littered with the bodies, brown bags, and empty bottles of human beings.

_____

_____

_____

11. We ask that you come to the test equipped with the following. At least two number 2 sharpened pencils, erasers, two bluebooks, and scrap paper.

_____

_____

_____

12. Let me just tell you this, he will not come because he disapproves of the entire outing.

_____

_____

13. I am: annoyed, exasperated, sorely tried, and: fed up.

_____

The following passage is taken from *Machine Dreams* by Jayne Anne Philips (New York: Dutton/Seymour Lawrence, 1984). In this passage, a daughter is remembering the first winter after the death of her mother. Read the passage. Then copy it, leaving out the underlined portions. Make sure you use ellipses accurately.

That winter, my breath caught each time I heard a sigh of heat from the register in the hall. Small, silly things. I did sometimes talk to her in my mind, and answered myself with memories of things she'd said or particular details. An hour before her death, I'd given her a drink of water from a teaspoon. Months afterward, I felt us frozen in that instant, the spoon at her mouth. She was semiconscious and I had the feeling, as the wetness touched her lips, that I was only taking care of things—the house, the rooms, her body. Then or later, I wasn't aware of any anger toward her, or even toward the disease. But there was so much sadness, and constant measuring up (17–18).

PART

Understanding Mechanical Conventions

These questions are designed to help you, the student, decide what to study. Correct any mistakes in capitalization, abbreviation, use of numbers, use of italics, or hyphenation that you find in the following sentences. If there are no mistakes, mark a *C* next to the sentence.

1. we will be going to Northwestern France in two weeks.
2. These books—They all cost under a dollar—are available inside.
3. Michael Dukakis, governor of Massachusetts, ran for president.
4. We used to live on First Avenue, but then we moved uptown.
5. A common misconception among students is that the renaissance was man-centered whereas the middle ages were God-centered.
6. Anne Fisher is a doctor and an M.D.
7. First Kay got her B.A., then she decided to become a social worker so she applied for an M.S.
8. Boethius composed the *Consolation of Philosophy* somewhere between 480 and 524 AD.
9. Whenever you go to Jane's Bakery, you must take a #.
10. My parents live in Cal., but I now go to school in Ariz.
11. 6 people came to hear the lecture.
12. He has about 10,000 records.
13. The *Hebrew Bible*, the *Gospels*, and the *Koran* are all sacred books.
14. Stephen Greenblatt's chapter on "King Lear," "Shakespeare and the Exorcists," appears in his book "Shakespearean Negotiations."
15. Roland Petit's ballet, *Notre Dame de Paris*, will be performed next week.
16. Every night I tune my radio to NPR and listen to *New Sounds*.
17. Spenser's epic, *The Fairie Queene*, begins "in medias res," in the middle of things.
18. In the Renaissance, "poetry" did not just mean verse, but all fiction.
19. "Annie Hall" is my favorite Woody Allen film.
20. Although Beethoven wrote many works for piano, his Moonlight Sonata is the best-known.
21. We depend upon oil for approximately seventy-five percent of our energy.
22. Although they said that it would be cloud-less, it rained all afternoon.
23. He was always such a happy-go-lucky person.
24. None of the television stations had better-coverage of the election.
25. Only one-third of the class showed up today.
26. This anthology contains poetry from eighteenth- and nineteenth-century manuscripts.

33

Using Capitals

Using Capitals for the First Word in a Sentence and in Poetry |33a|

Capitalization depends almost entirely on convention—the customary habits writers follow and readers expect. One of the oldest of these conventions is the capitalizing of the first letter of the opening word in a sentence. This holds true for quoted material as well as for your own words. Every sentence on this page provides you with an example of this capitalization convention.

Here is an example of a quoted sentence appearing inside another. The first word of the sentence is capitalized; so is the first word of the quoted sentence:

Mark yelled, "Will you be in early tomorrow?"

When a sentence follows a colon, capitalization is optional. Either version of the following sentence is acceptable:

Writers speculate that Lindbergh's aerial tour of the United States contributed to his interest in conservation: he [*or* He] saw firsthand the still unspoiled beauty of his country.

If your sentence contains a sentence set off by dashes or parentheses, the sentence inside the dashes or parentheses does *not* begin with a capital letter. Here is an example:

All requests—please keep them to one page—should be on Jennifer's desk by noon Friday.

When writing or typing a letter, capitalize proper names and the first word of the salutation (*My dear Angela*) and the closing (*Very truly yours*). For more on letter forms, see Chapter 44.

Finally, if you are quoting lines of poetry, follow the poet's wishes when it comes to capitalization. If the poet capitalizes the first letter of every line, follow suit. If the poet has chosen not to capitalize the first letter of every line, again, follow suit.

EXERCISE 33.1 USING CAPITALIZATION FOR THE FIRST WORD OF A NEW SENTENCE

The following passage sometimes uses capitalization incorrectly. Capitalize any words that should be capitalized, and substitute lowercase letters where necessary. Make your revisions in the spaces above the lines.

Basically, she was shy.[1] as a child, she had always been quite a bit shorter than her classmates, Leading to a certain amount of teasing.[2] Sometimes the teasing was quite severe—Once a dozen or more of her fifth-grade class had circled her, chanting "you're short, you're short, you're short."[3] when the playground monitor broke up the circle, She was on her knees in the middle of the group, tears on her face, Her hands held tight over her ears.[4] "no, no, no, no."[5] She'd been screaming, trying to outshout her tormentors.[6]

Then, in eighth grade, finally she grew: she grew six inches in six months, she gained fifteen pounds, and the teasing stopped.[7] her classmates quickly forgot about it, but she did not forget.[8] for years, she had to teach herself to join the group.[9] She had to persuade herself that she would be accepted, not teased.[10] How do I know this?[11] i am that girl, or rather she is a part of me.[12] And if I am no longer shy, It is because I have worked hard.[13] I don't want to forget those experiences.[14] I do want to keep them in perspective, To learn from them rather than be victimized by them.[15]

Using Capitals for Proper Nouns and Proper Adjectives | 33b|

Whenever you name specific persons, places, or objects, those names should be capitalized. For example, in the sentence *Marilyn lives in New*

York, it is accurate to capitalize both the *M* in *Marilyn* and the *N* and *Y* in *New York* because both are proper names.

Proper adjectives (made from proper nouns) are also capitalized. Thus the adjective *New Yorker* (made from the proper noun) is capitalized in the sentence *Marilyn is a New Yorker.*

When a title precedes a name, in effect becoming part of the name, both are capitalized, as in *Aunt Bernie, Grandma Berry, Senator Kennedy,* and *Police Chief Harrington.* However, when these titles follow the name or are used instead of the name, the titles are not capitalized. The only exception here is for very high officials, such as *president* or *prime minister;* these titles are sometimes capitalized even when used alone.

EXAMPLES

Senator Kennedy	Edward Kennedy, senator from Massachusetts
Police Chief Harrington	Penny Harrington, the police chief
Aunt Bernie	Bernardine Matusek, my aunt
the Prime Minister	Margaret Thatcher, Prime Minister of Great Britain

The names of products, corporations, and businesses are also capitalized, as in *First Interstate Bank; American Express; Floating Point, Inc.; Wheaties;* and *Campbell's Soup.*

Specific geographic sites and formations are capitalized, as in *Patterson Falls, Fifth Avenue, Europe, the Flatiron Building*, and *the Great Salt Lake.* Note that although the articles *the, an,* and *a* usually accompany proper names or proper adjectives, they are not normally capitalized.

Common nouns like *road, brook*, and *avenue* are capitalized only when they form part of a proper name or an address. The same is true of directional words like *west* and *southeast*.

Southeast Missouri State University	the southeast corner
Ponderosa Road	the road to town
Fairhaven Brook	the rocky brook

Consider this sentence: *The Waterfall at Alsea falls forms the focus for a Picnic Ground and an overnight camping area.* Should all the underlined words be capitalized? Should other words be capitalized? *Waterfall* is not part of a proper name; hence it should not be capitalized. *Alsea* is part of a proper name, so its capitalization is correct. *Falls* is also part of the proper name, so it should be capitalized. *Picnic ground* is a generic identification; hence, it should not be capitalized. Thus, the sentence should really look like this: *The waterfall at Alsea Falls forms the focus for a picnic ground and an overnight camping area.*

EXERCISE 33.2 USING CAPITALS FOR PROPER NOUNS AND PROPER ADJECTIVES

Words are underlined in each of the sentences that follow. Analyze how each underlined word is used, and decide whether it should be capitalized. Then rewrite each sentence so that it uses capitalization accurately. Write your analyses and your revised sentences on a separate sheet of paper.

1. Columbia, <u>south</u> Carolina, lies on the <u>Congaree</u> <u>river</u> and boasts a <u>Population</u> of nearly 100,000.
2. <u>Screen</u> <u>Actress</u> and later <u>Princess</u> of <u>Monaco</u>, Grace Kelly died when her car (which was headed <u>North</u>) left the road and plunged down an embankment.
3. Salt Lake City <u>Business</u> <u>leaders</u> consider <u>american</u> <u>express</u> one of the <u>City's</u> most important corporations.

Turn now to Assignment 33A at the end of this chapter for more practice with capitalization.

Many other names and titles are also routinely capitalized. Here are some examples.

Days of the Week, Months, and Holidays

Monday   October   Columbus Day   Easter   Ramadan   Passover

Historical Events, Movements, and Periods

the Civil War   the Victorian Era   the Battle of Hastings

Government or Public Offices, Institutions, and Departments

West Slope Water District   the U.S. Senate   the Commerce Department

Organizations, Associations, and Their Members

United Auto Workers   Rotarians   The Crazy 8's   the League of Women Voters

Races, Nationalities, and Languages

Hispanic   Filipino   Dutch   Haitian   Arabic   Russian

(Note: The terms *black* and *white* are not usually capitalized when used to refer to race.)

Religions and Their Adherents

Judaism/Jews   Protestantism/Protestants   Hinduism/Hindus
Islam/Muslims, Moslems   Buddhism/Buddhists

Sacred Persons, Places, or Things

Allah	Rama	the Koran	the Angel Moroni
God	Jesus	the Bible (*but* biblical)	Saint Peter's Basilica

Trade Names

IBM Pepsi Bartles & Jaymes Charmin

Some trade names have become generic and hence are not usually capitalized; an example is *aspirin*. When in doubt about a trade name, consult a dictionary.

Academic Units, Colleges, Departments, and Courses

College of Mechanical Engineering Department of Art Writing 121

Do not capitalize the name of a subject area unless it is a language: *I was bumped from both psychology and French.* The name of a specific course is capitalized, as in *Writing 121.*

Using Capitals for Titles of Works 133c

Important words in the titles of books, articles, essays, poems, songs, paintings, musical and dance compositions, films, plays, short stories, documents, and television series are capitalized:

Interview with the Vampire	"How I Found My Runaway Husband"
"A Modest Proposal"	"Ode on a Grecian Urn"
"A Hard Day's Night"	*The Peaceable Kingdom*
Great Mass in C Minor, K. 427	*Swan Lake*
The Big Chill	*Death of a Salesman*
"The Lottery"	Treaty of Versailles
I Love Lucy	

As in the case of poetry, an author or artist will occasionally decide not to capitalize the title of a work—the poet e. e. cummings made a stylistic statement by avoiding capitalization in most of his works, for instance. Another example is the television series *thirtysomething*. Always check to see how the title of a work is capitalized in its original form and follow that styling when in doubt.

A and *an* are not capitalized unless they are the first word of the title itself. *The* is not capitalized when it is the first word in a magazine or newspaper title, even if it is part of the title itself. Prepositions, conjunctions, and possessive pronouns that are under five letters long are not capitalized unless they are the first or last words in the title. Remember to capitalize the titles of your own works as well as others'.

[**413**]

Using Capitals for the Pronoun *I* and the Interjection *O* |33d|

The first person pronoun *I* is routinely capitalized whenever it is used. *O* is an old and stylized version of the word *oh*.

> Whenever I feel sad at her being gone, I try to remember what the pastor said: "And remember, O ye of little faith, that justice and mercy shall attend thee at the end of thy days. . . ."

Checking for Unnecessary Capitals |33e|

Inexperienced writers sometimes punctuate sentences almost solely according to the thought process that produced them: any pause in the process produces a punctuation mark (usually a comma), and a long pause produces a period. These writers then capitalize the first word of the "new sentence." The results might look something like this:

> Any discussion of the death penalty, makes me uncomfortable. Because it goes against everything I believe. Namely, that life is sacred and no government has the right to kill.

In such instances, writers cannot correct their punctuation until they are able to distinguish between sentences and fragments. For review in this area, see Chapter 14. Accurately punctuated (and only slightly rewritten), the same passage looks like this:

> Any discussion of the death penalty makes me uncomfortable because the death penalty goes against everything I believe. In my opinion, life is sacred, and no government has the right to kill.

Overall, good writers recognize that capitalization is not a matter of style or emphasis. Capitalizing for emphasis, as in "The test subjects did NOT respond as we had predicted" is not helpful to readers or appropriate in most writing. Capitalization is, rather, a matter of following generally accepted conventions. Some of the most common capitalization errors are detailed here.

- Seasons, academic terms, and academic years are not capitalized.

spring   fall quarter   summer semester   junior year

- Compass directions are not capitalized unless they refer to the accepted name of a geographic area of the United States.

The wind blew fitfully from the southeast.

The West was hit by an unseasonably early frost.

- Diseases and medical terms are not capitalized unless a proper noun is part of the name.

German measles   measles   Tourette's syndrome   strep throat

- The names of family relationships are not capitalized unless they substitute for a proper name.

My father took me to my first circus when I was six.

I asked Father if he would buy me cotton candy.

The letter said my uncle had had open-heart surgery.

The letter said Uncle Herman had had open-heart surgery.

Worrying about capitalization too early in the writing process can distract you from concentrating on what you want to say. Try saving such concerns for proofreading—usually the last stage of the writing process. Here is a capitalization checklist you can use as you proofread.

- Are the following words capitalized?

    proper nouns and adjectives
    names of people, places, events, institutions, products, and businesses
    titles of works of art, music, and literature

- Have capitals been used incorrectly for any of these words?

    season   family relations
    compass directions   medical terms

Turn now to Assignment 33B at the end of this chapter for more practice with capitalization.

EXERCISE 33.3 MORE PRACTICE WITH CAPITALIZING PROPER NOUNS AND PROPER ADJECTIVES

Some italicized words in the following sentences are capitalized; others are not. Analyze how each italicized word is used, and briefly note that analysis as shown below. Then rewrite the sentence so that it uses capitalization accurately.

EXAMPLE

That *Botany* 201 *class* looks tough, but not as tough as *french* or *physics*.

Botany title of actual class; capitalize

class not part of a title; do not capitalize

french name of a language; capitalize

physics not the title of a specific course; do not capitalize

Revision: *That Botany 201 class looks tough, but not as tough as French or physics.*

1. Many nonnatives are surprised by the rent *Landlords* typically charge for *A New York Apartment.*

2. *The Division Of* Language and Literature is happy to announce that it is the recipient of a grant from the United States Department of *education.*

3. Cub *scouts,* Rotarians, members of the *league* of Women Voters, and *Members* of various fraternities and *Sororities* joined forces yesterday to publicize the need for more blood donations.

4. Since *Flag* Day falls on *a saturday* this *year,* the actual observance will be reserved for the following Monday.

5. The *biblical* injunction to *honor* one's parents is echoed in *the koran* and can also be found in the *various* sayings attributed to *Confucius.*

ASSIGNMENT 33A **REVISING FOR CORRECT CAPITALIZATION**

In the following sentences, if capitalization is used correctly, write *C* on the lines provided. If a sentence needs revising, write your new version on the lines.

EXAMPLE

In 1987, philadelphia's Independence hall was the site of numerous festivities celebrating the American Form of Government.

In 1987, Philadelphia's Independence Hall was the site of numerous festivities celebrating the American form of government.

1. If you turn West on Northwest Walnut Street, you won't miss Hoover school.

_____

_____

2. The Senator strode forward, shook the President's hand, and said, "Mr. President, I support your latest tax proposals."

_____

_____

3. Some wealthy Business Executives resign their posts in order to seek new challenges in Business or Education.

_____

_____

4. Architects have commented favorably on designs for The First Bank Tower, which will eventually be built on the Northwest corner of Fifth street and Alder avenue.

_____

_____

_____

5. The cemetery at Arlington, Virginia, was established during the civil war and is also the Site of Arlington House, a memorial to Robert E. Lee.

_____

_____

_____

Often the most difficult part of proofreading is focusing on matters of correctness rather than content. Below you will find a frankly obnoxious letter posing as a job application. Do not pay attention to what this letter says. (This writer is confused about correct business letter style and format, among other things. For instruction on writing business letters, see Chapter 44.) Instead, focus on identifying and revising any capitalization errors. Read the letter, underline any word that uses capitalization incorrectly, and write your correction in the space between lines. The first such correction has been made for you.

2000 <u>n.e.</u> main st.   **N.E.**

mist, Oregon 97979

january 2, 1989

Acme Trading co.

43561 Shaniko lane

Vanport, oregon 97777

My dear Friends at Acme Trading,

Are You looking for a Self-starter—somOne who can Get the Job Done? I have had over

Two Years of retail experience working for Waterbeds, Waterbeds, & waterbeds, Inc.

During one Summer, I sold over six new complete packages. I sold waterbeds as Halitosis

cures, Bunion relievers, and—o yes!—headache destroyers (so long as the head of the bed

was facing West). I could sell a waterbed to the ghost of my Mother's grandmother. I could

sell ice cubes on Sundays in Winter in new England. All of this convinces me that i AM

Management Material; your trainee program sounds perfect for me. Give Me the chance,

and I'll get YOU the results you want.

Very Truly YOURS,

34

Using Abbreviations and Numbers

ABBREVIATIONS

Abbreviating Personal and Professional Titles |34*a*|

In general, the more common the personal or professional title, the more often it is abbreviated. And two abbreviations—*Ms.* and *Mrs.*—are always abbreviated; they have no expanded, full form.

- Abbreviate certain personal titles when used with proper names. Some titles appear before the name:

Ms. Barbara Hogg   Mr. Gregory Pfarr   Rev. John Dennis
Dr. Errett Hummel   St. Theresa of Avila

Other titles follow the name:

Alan Palmer, D.D.S.   Suzanne Clark, Ph.D.   Hank Williams, Jr.

Use *Ms.* as the common title for women, just as *Mr.* is the common title for men. In current usage, neither of these terms relates to an individual's marital status. Substitute *Miss* or *Mrs.* only when you know that a particular woman prefers it.

Other religious, military, academic, and government titles may be abbreviated whenever they precede a full name; if they appear before only the last name, the title should be written in full. Furthermore, these titles cannot be abbreviated when they are used without names.

Sen. Nancy Kassebaum *or* Senator Kassebaum
Rev. David Olivier *or* Reverend Olivier
Prof. Laura Rice-Sayre *or* Professor Rice-Sayre

INCORRECT

My Dr. said the lab test results would be ready Wednesday.

CORRECT

My doctor said the lab test results would be ready Wednesday.

Spell out *Reverend* and *Honorable* whenever they are used with *the* and precede an individual's name, as in *the Reverend John Dennis.*

Be careful not to be redundant: *Dr. Suzanne Clark, Ph.D.* literally means "Doctor Suzanne Clark, Doctor of Philosophy." That is saying "Doctor" one time more than is necessary.

The abbreviations for educational degrees are commonly used whether attached to particular people or not.

B.A. (Bachelor of Arts)   B.S. (Bachelor of Science)
M.A. (Master of Arts)   M.S. (Master of Science)
Ph.D. (Doctor of Philosophy)

EXAMPLE

He is finishing his M.A. work this spring.

Remember that abbreviations should not be confusing. If your readers will not recognize an abbreviation, use the full form. If your context makes it likely that readers will be confused by abbreviations, do not use them. For example, *M.S.* commonly means the educational degree Master of Science; however, *MS* is also commonly used to mean the disease multiple sclerosis. Using both abbreviations in a single document may confuse and frustrate readers.

EXERCISE 34.1 USING ABBREVIATIONS FOR PERSONAL AND PROFESSIONAL TITLES

Proofread the following sentences for errors in the use of abbreviations. If the sentence is correct as written, write *C* after it. If the sentence needs revision, make your correction above the line.

EXAMPLES

general

The World War II invasion of Normandy was led by a Gen. who never went into politics: Omar Bradley.

Mr. Greg Pfarr's paintings have been selected to appear in many juried art shows across the nation. *C*

1. Some graduate students believe that a Ph.D. automatically leads to a good job.

2. The Rev. Eammon O'Conner led the singing, but Fr. McDill gave the sermon.

3. Thursday's presentation will feature Dr. JoAnne Trow, Ph.D.

4. Sir Thomas More, now recognized as a St., was an English statesman.

5. The profs. in the Spanish Department decided to establish a composition prize.

Using Abbreviations with Numerals | 34b |

Some abbreviations—for example, *F* for *Fahrenheit* and A.M. for *ante meridiem* ("before noon")—should be used only when preceded by numbers, as in *75°F* or *6:45 A.M.* In general, these abbreviations deal with units of measure—temperature, size, quantity, time, and the like.

Abbreviation	Meaning	Example of Use
B.C.	before Christ	399 B.C.
A.D.	*anno Domini*, Latin for "year of our Lord"	A.D. 49
A.M.	*ante meridiem*, Latin for "before noon"	11:15 A.M.
P.M.	*post meridiem*, Latin for "after noon"	9:00 P.M.
r.p.m. *or* rpm	revolutions per minute	2,000 r.p.m. *or* rpm
m.p.h. *or* mph	miles per hour	55 m.p.h. *or* mph
F	Fahrenheit scale	212°F
C	Celsius scale	100°C

Writers traditionally capitalize *B.C.* and *A.D.* but use lowercase letters for *a.m.* and *p.m.* Printers and publishers often use small capitals for all four of these abbreviations.

The common symbols on the top line of your typewriter are also abbreviations. With the exception of the dollar sign ($), which is allowable in

[421]

formal writing so long as it is followed by a number, none of the other symbols should be part of formal essay prose. (Graphs, charts, and other modes of visual presentation sometimes do employ some of these abbreviations in captions or identifications, but such charts or graphs are typically parts of memos or technical reports, not essays.)

EXERCISE 34.2 USING ABBREVIATIONS WITH NUMERALS

Read each sentence. If it uses unacceptable abbreviations, underline these abbreviations and write out the full versions on the lines provided. If the sentence as written is correct and acceptable in formal prose, write *C* on the lines.

EXAMPLE

The individual with the winning <u>#</u> will receive an annual income in excess of $60,000 <u>+</u>

a contract to appear in lottery advertising. <u>number, plus</u> _____

1. We estimate that four workers will be required @ a rate of $21.00 per hour.

_____

2. The airlines report one A.M. flight leaving on Tuesday.

_____

3. Approximately seventy-two% of those polled agreed that religious beliefs were an

important part of their lives. _____

4. The earthquake destroyed several downtown buildings, ruptured water & gas

mains, and left hundreds homeless. _____

5. @ the current rate of interest, your total payment of principal + interest would =

$792.25 per month. _____

6. Confucius lived at the time we would now identify as 500 B.C.

_____

7. The $ that you requested has been approved by the grants committee.

_____

8. The $450.00 that you requested has been approved by the grants committee.

_____

9. Traveling at the mph you indicate, that type of aircraft usually stalls.

Using Acronyms and Other Initial Abbreviations |34c|

Countries, companies, and a variety of other organizations regularly shorten their own names to initials. The National Broadcasting Company advertises and identifies itself as NBC; Mothers Against Drunk Driving regularly refers to itself as MADD. MADD is an example of an **acronym**—a set of initials that form a pronounceable word. NBC, by contrast, is simply a set of initials that do not form a pronounceable word. Sets of initials and acronyms are typically written in capital letters and without periods separating them. (If you are unsure about the use of periods in a particular abbreviation, consult your dictionary.)

How can you know whether or not an organization's name can be shortened? Two factors should guide you here. If the organization itself uses initials or an acronym, chances are that you may acceptably do so as well. Examples here would include IBM and AFL-CIO. Be sure that your readers will recognize any initials or acronyms you use. For example, the initials COLA probably suggest a soft drink to most people. Only a very few readers (those involved in labor-management contracts) may recognize those initials as standing for *cost-of-living adjustment.*

When in doubt, write the name or title in full and enclose the initials or the acronym in parentheses immediately following the title.

In the 1950s and early 1960s, doctors commonly prescribed the drug diethylstilbestrol (DES) for pregnant women. However, it was not until the late 1970s that researchers discovered its dangers for female children. Since 1973, over 70,000 "DES babies" have been diagnosed with cervical cancer.

Here is a short list of common acronyms and initial abbreviations:

Nations

USSR   Union of Soviet Socialist Republics
UK   United Kingdom

Corporations

AT&T* American Telephone and Telegraph
UPI   United Press International

*This is one of the few instances where an ampersand (&) is acceptable in college writing.

Organizations

OAS   Organization of American States
UN   United Nations
NASA   National Aeronautics and Space Administration
ACLU   American Civil Liberties Union

Scientific or Technical Terms

DNA   deoxyribonucleic acid
ROM   read-only memory
AIDS   acquired immune deficiency syndrome
ABM   antiballistic missile

EXERCISE 34.3 USING ACRONYMS AND INITIAL ABBREVIATIONS

Identify five abbreviations or acronyms beyond those just given. Give the abbreviation or acronym, spell it out, and use the abbreviation or acronym in a sentence. Then identify an audience that would recognize the abbreviation or acronym and identify another audience that might not recognize it. Use your own paper, and follow the format of the example.

EXAMPLE

Abbreviation/Acronym: DWI
Long form: driving while intoxicated
Sample sentence: Jack was cited for his third DWI offense.
Audience that will recognize this abbreviation/acronym: anyone in the criminal justice system
Audience that might not recognize this abbreviation/acronym: anyone not familiar with law enforcement, drunk driving, or alcohol abuse

Checking for Inappropriate Abbreviations |34d|

In composing notes, rough drafts, informal letters, and the like, writers will often abbreviate in order to write quickly. Such abbreviations can be quite helpful, but they should generally not appear in the final draft of a college essay.

- Units of measure should be spelled out, not abbreviated.

  Our smooth collie weighs ninety-two pounds. [*not* 92 lbs.]

  Deke's Harley gets over fifty miles to the gallon. [*not* 50 m.p.g.]

- Names of days, months, and holidays should be spelled out.

   Sunday turned out warm and cloudless. [*not* Sun.]

   October 21 was our first day of heavy rain. [*not* Oct. 21]

- Geographic names should be spelled out.

   New York boasts several major-league sports teams. [*not* N.Y.]

   The Columbia River empties into the Pacific at Astoria, Oregon. [*not* Col. R., *not* Astoria, OR]

- Academic subjects should be spelled out.

   Psychology and economics are proving to be my most difficult subjects this term. [*not* Psych. and econ.]

   Chemistry laboratory sections are scheduled in the afternoons. [*not* Chem. lab sections]

- Divisions of written works should be spelled out.

   One of the most famous chapters in *Moby Dick* is Chapter 32, "Cetology." [*not* chs., *not* Ch. 32]

   Those twelve or so pages begin on page 116. [*not* p. 116]

- Company names should be spelled out exactly as used by the company itself. Use *Co., Inc., Ltd.,* and the ampersand only when used by the company itself.

   Arrowood Book Company is a small, regional publisher of literary titles. [*not* Arrowood Bk. Co.]

- Informal Latin abbreviations should be written out in English. These include *etc.* ("and so forth"), *i.e.* ("that is"), *cf.* ("compare"), *e.g.* ("for example"), *et al.* ("and others"), and *N.B.* ("note well"). Note that some Latin abbreviations are still used when writers cite sources; see Chapter 41.

   She recommended conservative investments—for example, utility stocks and time deposits. [*not* e.g.]

   Michael Stoops and other advocates for the homeless gathered in Washington to lobby for progressive legislation. [*not* Michael Stoops *et al.*]

Turn now to Assignment 34A at the end of this chapter for practice with abbreviations.

NUMBERS

Writing Numbers |34e, 34f, 34g, 34h|

Suppose that you are writing about the time of day, weight loss plans, or the costs of various products, services, or programs. Should you spell out the numbers you use, or should you use numerals?

The conventions vary from discipline to discipline. For instance, most scientific or technical journals stipulate that numbers be identified with numerals rather than spelled out in letters. Journalists follow their own set of conventions. College essay writing typically follows a different set of conventions. We present these formal essay conventions here.

- Spell out numbers that can be expressed in one or two words.

  None of the fifty-eight people on board were injured yesterday when a commercial jet made an unscheduled landing outside Pittsburgh.

- Use numerals when an amount cannot be expressed in one or two words.

  With an average paid attendance of 44,258, the football program will have no trouble meeting its budget this year.

- Spell out any number that begins a sentence.

  Fifty-eight people escaped injury yesterday when a commercial jet made an unscheduled landing outside Pittsburgh.

If a particularly large or cumbersome number begins a sentence, consider recasting the sentence so that the number appears later.

  Four thousand two hundred and sixteen people passed through the turnstiles at the Philomath Rodeo last July.

  The Philomath Rodeo attracted a crowd of 4,216 last July.

- When several numbers appear in one sentence, be consistent: either use numerals in every case, or spell out every number. If a number opens the sentence, either spell it out or rewrite the sentence.

This week we served 157 patrons, which is 30 more than last week.

This week we served one hundred and fifty-seven patrons, which is thirty more than last week.

- Use numerals for street addresses, exact amounts of money, days and dates, exact times of day, statistics and scores, measurements, decimals, fractions, percentages, pages and divisions of written works, and identification numbers.

1515 Main Street	302 Fifth Street, S.E.*
$34.95	October 16, 1948
3:35 P.M.	a median score of 66
Patriots won, 21–14	9.7
5,280 feet	50%, 50 percent
7 5/8	Chapter 60
pages 44–50	account number 0461

Spell out hours followed by *o'clock*, as in *nine o'clock*. Note that this expression is used with whole numbers only (not, for example, 7:30 o'clock).

Turn now to Assignment 34B at the end of this chapter for practice with writing numbers.

*Note that both numerals and spelled out numbers are necessary here in order to avoid confusion.

ASSIGNMENT 34A **AVOIDING THE MISUSE OR OVERUSE OF ABBREVIATIONS**

Read the following sentences. Underline all abbreviations, and determine whether or not these abbreviations are appropriate for college essay writing. If the abbreviations are appropriate, leave the sentences alone. If the abbreviations are inappropriate, write in the acceptable forms above the abbreviations. You may need to review earlier portions of this chapter.

EXAMPLE

for example

She recommended conservative investments—e.g., utility stocks and time deposits.

1. Blind Lemon Jefferson, Bessie Smith, Jelly Roll Morton et al. helped make the blues part of American music.

2. LA is famous for smog, Watts, the Lakers and Dodgers, earthquakes, oranges, freeways, and the Calif. mystique.

3. On 5/18/81 Mt. St. Helens erupted with such force that it felled trees ten miles away.

4. After mother's death that Tues. in Aug., the family's dynamics changed considerably.

5. The Epilogue of H. Melville's *Moby Dick* opens with this quotation from Job: "And I only am escaped alone to tell thee."

6. The S. Korean city of Kwangchu boasts a pop. of over 700,000.

7. Rising near Cumberland, MD, the Potomac R. winds its way through the nation's capital before eventually emptying into Chespk. Bay.

8. After weeks and months of planning, yrs. of scientific progress, and centuries of dreaming, on July 20, '69, a member of the human species walked on the moon.

9. South of the U.S. and north of Guatemala, Mexico covers some 761,600 sq. mi. of land.

10. The New England area (Vermont, New Hampshire, etc.) still exports real maple syrup—the best thing that ever topped pancakes.

ASSIGNMENT 34B **WRITING NUMBERS**

Read the passage below for any errors in the presentation of numbers. Underline any errors you find, and make your corrections in the space above the line.

Readers have either loved Ernest Hemingway or hated him.[1] Either way, they have bought his books.[2] By October nineteen twenty-nine, his then new novel *A Farewell to Arms* had sold twenty-eight thousand copies in less than a month.[3] By November, it was number 1 on the best-seller list—its nearest competitor a book by a German titled *All Quiet on the Western Front.*[4] Since that time, Hemingway's books have continued to sell.[5] His name is still a household word.[6]

Ernest Miller Hemingway was born at 8 o'clock in the morning in his parents' house at four thirty-nine North Oak Park Avenue in the town of Oak Park, Illinois, a suburb of Chicago.[7] The date was July twenty-first, 1899.[8] Hemingway weighed in at 9 and a half pounds.[9] In the next 60 years, he would live enough and work enough to write a score of books, 4 or 5 of which will be read as long as people read English.[10] Curiously enough, one of the best of them, *The Garden of Eden,* was first published fully 25 years after his death.[11]

35

Using Italics

Italic type—type that slants like *this*—is used by word processing programs and by printers in a variety of conventional ways. If you write and print your work using computer equipment, chances are you can produce actual italics.

If you are handwriting or typing, you underline rather than italicize, and you should mentally translate every mention of italicizing to mean underlining, or vice versa.

Using Italics for Titles |35a|

Writers identify titles either through italics or through the use of quotation marks. In general, italics are reserved for the titles of whole works, whereas quotation marks identify titles of parts of larger works. Thus, in a manuscript, a book title is underlined, but a chapter title is placed in quotation marks. The title of a book of poems is underlined, whereas the title of a particular poem is placed in quotation marks. The name of a television series is underlined, while the name of a particular episode is identified by quotation marks. (For a review of the use of quotation marks, see Chapter 31.)

- Underline book, magazine, journal, pamphlet, and newspaper titles.

Note that sacred books (the Bible or the Koran, for example) are not underlined, nor are the divisions within them. In general, writers do not underline the titles of public documents such as the Constitution, the Camp David Accords, or the Magna Charta.

Books *Native Son, The Awakening, Ulysses*

Magazines, Journals, and Newspapers *Newsweek, Journal of the American Medical Association, North American Review,* the *American Scholar,* the *New York Times,* the *Chicago Sun-Times*

Note that *the* is not italicized or capitalized before the name of a magazine even if it is part of the official name. Similarly, the word *magazine* is not italicized or capitalized following the name. Only when the name of a city is part of the official name of a newspaper is the city name italicized (thus *New York Times,* New York *Daily News*).

- Underline the titles of plays, long poems, long musical works, choreographed works, paintings, and sculpture.

Plays *A Midsummer Night's Dream, Christmas at the Juniper Tavern*

Long Poems *Paradise Lost, Audubon: A Vision*

Long Musical Works *The Joshua Tree, The Wall, La Bohème, Messiah*
Note that classical works identified by form, number, and key are not italicized (for example, Sonata in F Minor).

Choreographed Works Martha Graham's *Frontier,* Agnes De Mille's *Rodeo*

Paintings *Starry Night, The Peaceable Kingdom*

Sculpture *David,* the *Pietà*

- Underline the titles of television series, other television programs, and radio programs.

Television Series and Programs *Mister Ed, Nightline*

Radio Programs *Morning Edition, A Prairie Home Companion*

Using Italics for Words, Letters, and Numbers Referred to as Such |35b|

Use italics whenever you want readers to see that you refer to a particular word, letter, or number not for its meaning but for itself.

How many *m*'s are there in *accommodate*?

In the inscriptions on some old buildings, the *u*'s look like *v*'s.

The binary system contains only *0*'s and *1*'s.

Also use italics to indicate a word you are about to discuss or define.

The word *prognosticate* has Latin origins.

Turn now to Assignment 35A at the end of this chapter for practice with italics.

Using Italics for Foreign Words and Phrases |35c|

Sometimes writers wish to use foreign words as part of English prose. Words or phrases like *Gesundheit* (German) and *gracias* (Spanish) are commonly understood by many English speakers and writers, even though these expressions are not part of English itself. When you do use words such as these, italicize them (except as noted in the discussion that concludes this section).

> Recently, *pro bono* work has been added to course requirements for law students studying at the University of Pennsylvania. [Pro bono *is a shortened version of* pro bono publico, *which means literally "for the public good." Thus,* pro bono *legal work is done without charge.*]

> In the Gorbachev era, the buzzword in Soviet-American relations is *glasnost.*

> That puppy has more energy and *joie de vivre* than it can handle.

However, notice this example: *The way the clerk treated me, I felt like a peon.* In this example, the word *peon* is not given special treatment. Some originally foreign words are now so commonly used that they do not need to be italicized simply because of that foreign origin. When in doubt about whether or not to italicize a particular word, consult a good dictionary.

EXERCISE 35.1 USING ITALICS FOR FOREIGN WORDS OR PHRASES

Choose and circle five of the words or phrases from the list below. On your own paper, use each in a sentence. If the word or phrase should be italicized as foreign, be sure it is underlined in your sentence. You may need to consult a good dictionary for this exercise.

habeas corpus	sans souci
idée fixe	ex post facto
a priori	bon mot
gemütlichkeit	glasnost
habitué	bona fide

Using Italics for Names of Vehicles |35d|

Italicize the specific names of ships, trains, aircraft, or spacecraft but not generic names like *cruiser, battleship, fighter plane,* or *subway.* The names of specific production models are capitalized as products, but not italicized. The initials *S.S.*, *U.S.S.*, *H.M.S.*, and so on are capitalized but not italicized. Do not italicize the word *the* before the name of a vehicle.

Ships   the *Golden Hinde*, the U.S.S. *Missouri*, the trawler *Alice III*

Trains   the *Golden Zephyr*, the *City of New Orleans*

Aircraft and Spacecraft   *Columbia*, *Echo I*, the *Graf Zeppelin*

Specific Production Models   Learjet, Volkswagen Rabbit

EXERCISE 35.2   ITALICIZING THE NAMES OF VEHICLES

Read the following sentences. Underline each name that should be italicized.

EXAMPLE

The battleship <u>Arizona</u> remains in Pearl Harbor as a memorial to those who died there on December 7, 1941.

1. The U.S.S. Constitution remains a living part of American history.

2. In 1937, the explosion of the Hindenburg effectively ended the use of airships for passenger service.

3. Small passenger planes, Cessnas cruise at about 175 mph.

4. Lindbergh's famous flight in the Spirit of St. Louis took him over thirty-three hours.

5. The first Mercury capsule, Freedom 7, carried astronaut Alan Shepard at speeds exceeding 5,000 miles per hour.

Using Italics for Special Emphasis |35e|

Especially in informal writing and in writing dialogue, the judicious and sparing use of italics can help readers actually hear the intonations of a person speaking. Note the differences in the following sentences:

The workers insisted they could not finish until at least Monday afternoon. [*no special emphasis*]

The *workers* insisted they could not finish until at least Monday afternoon. [*The workers insist one thing, but perhaps someone else is saying something else.*]

The workers insisted they could not finish until *at least* Monday afternoon. [*This version suggests that the job will take longer than the Monday afternoon deadline.*]

Here is another example; this time the emphasis is straightforward:

If we want to achieve our objectives, we *must* vote, and together we *will* win.

EXERCISE 35.3 USING ITALICS SPARINGLY FOR EMPHASIS

Briefly analyze the emphasis created by the use of italics in the following sentences. Use your own paper for this exercise.

EXAMPLE

> *I* heartily agree with you.
> *Analysis:* Italicizing *I* suggests that although the speaker agrees, someone else disagrees; italicizing *I* implies and highlights a contrast.

1. Will you ask the Johnsons to bring hamburgers *and* a potato salad?
2. When the scores were shown, it was clear that the judges could not find *anything* wrong with her diving performance.
3. With perseverance and care, we will *defeat* AIDS.

Write a sentence that contains one word italicized for emphasis, and explain what the emphasis is.

EXAMPLE

> The *evidence* seems to suggest that Arnold is the culprit here.
> *Analysis:* The sentence implies that something other than the evidence, perhaps Arnold's character, suggests he is not the culprit.

Now write the same sentence, but this time italicize a different word. Explain the new emphasis.

EXAMPLE

> The evidence *seems* to suggest that Arnold is the culprit here.
> *Analysis:* This version implies that the speaker does not believe the evidence; it is not what it seems.

ASSIGNMENT 35A USING ITALICS FOR TITLES AND FOR WORDS, LETTERS, OR NUMBERS REFERRED TO AS SUCH

Most (but not all) of the following sentences contain titles or other words that should be italicized. Underline these words. If the sentence is correct as written, simply go on to the next sentence.

EXAMPLES

As a result of his extensive travel covering events like the Olympics for television's Wide World of Sports, Jim McKay has seen the world.

The word separate is one that many people misspell.

1. TV Guide's cover story discussed some of the old westerns: Bonanza, Death Valley Days, The Lone Ranger, and others.
2. After the fire, we had to replace our copies of the concertos by Beethoven as well as those of the Messiah by Handel.
3. Arthur Miller's play Death of a Salesman opened in 1949; today it's a classic of the American theater.
4. When Kate Chopin wrote The Awakening, she couldn't have realized how many college students would respond to that book.
5. Native English speakers in French or German classes finally find out the difficulties nonnative speakers encounter here in the United States.
6. I'm reading Hugo's book Death and the Good Life for my English 205 class.
7. Boys' Life, Sports Illustrated, Better Homes and Gardens, the Saturday Evening Post, Redbook, and Life—all those magazines arrived in the mails when I was a kid, and I read them all.
8. Last year we saw one of the four original, handwritten, fifteenth-century copies of the Magna Charta on temporary display at the Huntington Library.
9. Overlooking the town, a large M is painted on the face of Mount Sentinel.
10. I decided to submit poems titled "Recognition" and "Tired" to Poetry magazine.
11. Due to its consistent popularity with concert goers, Beethoven's Symphony No. 5 frequently appears in the repertoires of major orchestras.
12. The Lawsons renewed their subscription to Smithsonian magazine.

36

Using Hyphens

Writers use hyphens to divide words at the end of a typed line, to form compound words (like *after-school* in the phrase *my after-school activities*), to write out fractions and two-digit numbers, and to prevent misreading. This chapter will discuss each of these uses.

Using Hyphens to Divide Words at the Ends of Lines |36a|

One of the very last things writers do is produce a final copy. Often this copy is typed; more and more frequently, it is printed via computer equipment. Most computer software will take care of the problem of end-of-line hyphenation by eliminating it either through justification or word wrap (moving the whole word to the next line). However, if you are typing, you may find that you do not have enough room to fit a word on a line. If you must break a word, use the following generally accepted writers' conventions:

1. Place the hyphen after the last letter on the line, not at the beginning of the next line.
2. Divide words only between syllables. If the word has only one syllable, either squeeze it onto the end of the line or shift it to the next. If you are not sure about the syllabic breaks for a particular word, check your dictionary.
3. Whenever possible, begin the part of the divided word on the new line with a consonant (*medi-tate* rather than *med-itate*).
4. Divide words that contain doubled consonants between the doubled letters (as in *sug-gest*) *unless* the doubled consonants are part of the root word (not *cal-ling* but *call-ing*) or make up a single syllable (not *signal-ed* but *sig-naled*).
5. Never divide the last word on a page. (Thus, you will never begin a new page with part of a word.)

6. Never leave a single letter at the end of a line or fewer than three letters at the beginning of a line.
7. Do not divide contractions, numerals, acronyms, or abbreviations.

UNACCEPTABLE

Though the eclipse was scheduled to begin at 9:-
38 A.M., a heavy cloud cover made observation impossible.

Ellen called to let you know that she would-
n't be able to meet with you until after 2 P.M.

After an exile that lasted several years, the AFL-
CIO allowed the Teamsters Union to rejoin.

8. Words that already contain hyphens should be divided only at a hyphen.

UNACCEPTABLE

The corporate plane seated twelve and was equipped with a jet-pro-
pelled engine.

ACCEPTABLE

The corporate plane seated twelve and was equipped with a jet-
propelled engine.

EXERCISE 36.1 USING HYPHENS TO DIVIDE WORDS AT THE ENDS OF LINES

Many of the following sentences employ unacceptable hyphenation. Read each sentence, and underline any improperly hyphenated word; make your correction in the space above the line. On the line below the sentence, explain briefly what is wrong with the use of the hyphen. If the sentence is acceptable as written, write *C* on the line. (Note: Treat proper nouns like all other nouns.)

EXAMPLE

                                    wouldn't
  Ellen called to let you know that she <u>would-</u>

  <u>n't</u> be able to meet with you until after 2 P.M.

  Contractions should not be hyphenated.

1. This afternoon, the four of us enjoyed a sunny October day at the coast.

2. If between now and the end of the month no precipitation falls, this will be the driest October since 1895.

---

3. While we have been enjoying this spate of unseasonable weather, other parts of the country have received snow.

---

4. Weather forecasters are predicting heavy rains and hur-
ricane-force winds for this afternoon.

---

5. The very first books, those printed during the fif-
teenth century, are known as *incunabula.*

---

6. Some fish possess modified muscle tissue that is capable of generating 450 to 600 volts of electricity.

---

7. The widely acclaimed actress Gertrude Lawrence had a career that spanned more than two decades.

---

8. In recent years, novelist Toni Morrison has solidly established herself as one of America's foremost writers.

---

9. The first set of ratings figures for the fall season shows NB-
C leading its two network rivals.

---

10. Baseball trivia buffs will recall the 1987 St. Louis vs. Minnesota World Series as the first in which the home team won every game.

Using Hyphens with Compound Words |36b|

> English is full of words (such as *backpack, underline,* and *payday*) that
> frequent usage has joined together to make single words. In other cases, such
> combination words are formed using hyphens, as in *simple-minded.* And
> sometimes, these combinations retain the normal space between words, as in

lame duck and *mountain range.* When it comes to specific compound words, you may simply have to consult a dictionary. If your compound word is a noun and your college dictionary does not list it, the compound word is probably two words and should be written as such. However, you may sometimes wish to construct and use compound words as modifiers; to do so correctly, see the discussion that follows.

Forming Compound Modifiers |36b1|

Suppose that you wish to describe a picture that you are sending to family or friends. You are in the picture, and the look on your face is not exactly cheerful. You might write, "Don't worry about that down-on-my-luck expression." You have strung four words together with hyphens. By so doing, you are telling your readers that these four words combine in one meaning. In theory, you could replace *down-on-my-luck* with a single adjective like *sour,* as in *Don't worry about that sour expression.*

Note that a series of compound modifiers sharing the same word (or words) can be shortened by using suspended hyphens:

> This summer, the eight-, nine-, and ten-year-old campers were placed in a single group.

- Hyphenate a compound adjective appearing before a noun; do not hyphenate such an adjective when it follows the noun.

In the example, *down-on-my-luck* (an adjective) precedes *expression* (a noun). The hyphens are appropriate in that example. However, if you rewrite the sentence so that the adjective follows the noun, hyphens are not used.

> That expression makes me look down on my luck—don't worry about it.

- Never use a hyphen to join an adverb ending in *ly* to another word.

> Her radically different approach produced excellent results.
>
> A crowd of morbidly curious onlookers gathered at the accident scene.

- Do not hyphenate a compound modifier if the first word is a comparative or a superlative, such as *more, better, best.*

> The second course provides more extensive coverage. [More extensive *should never be hyphenated.*]

Using Hyphens to Create Your Own Compounds for Special Effect l36b2l

When speaking or writing informally, we often create our own spur-of-the-moment compounds. While informal (and hence not always appropriate in formal writing situations), such compounds do add flair and can make for more interesting prose.

> We enjoyed another August-in-October day.

> After four hurry-up-and-wait hours in the airport, I was ready to fly anywhere.

Again, note that the hyphens connect words that form essentially a single adjective positioned in front of a noun. Sometimes the same words use hyphens when functioning as an adjective but use no hyphens when functioning as separate adjectives and nouns.

> The stained glass cast colorful shadows on the pews. [stained glass = *adjective + noun*]

> Stained-glass artistry made the church distinctive and inspiring. [stained-glass = *single adjective*]

> Officials estimate we need a month of rain to replenish the city's water supply. [water supply = *adjective + noun*]

> The plumber says our water-supply pipe has corroded and needs replacing. [water-supply = *single adjective*]

Turn now to Assignment 36A at the end of this chapter for practice with hyphens in compounds.

Using Hyphens with Fractions and Compound Numbers l36b3l

Writers conventionally use hyphens to spell out fractions. The fraction *3/4* would be spelled out as *three-fourths.* Here the hyphen acts (as it always does) to connect separate words in order to form one unit, one thing—in this case, one fractional number.

Compound numbers from *twenty-one* to *ninety-nine* are also written out using hyphens. Numbers higher than *ninety-nine* are not hyphenated, no matter how long they may be when written out, except for parts from *twenty-one* to *ninety-nine.* (Remember that numbers expressed in more than two words can also be written using numerals.) For example, to reproduce the number 300,354 in words, write *three hundred thousand two hundred fifty-four.* Note that the one hyphen occurs only with the part of the number between *twenty-one* and *ninety-nine.*

Using Hyphens with Prefixes and Suffixes |36c|

Over the years, many prefixes and suffixes have been so frequently attached to some words that now no hyphen is used to connect them. *Unusual, disinterested, predestined*—these are all examples of words containing prefixes and no hyphens.

However, several prefixes and suffixes do commonly take hyphens. Prefixes attached to numerals or to capitalized words always take hyphens, as in *pre-1914*, and *un-Christian*. When a prefix is attached to a compound word, use a hyphen, as in *pro-civil rights*. Other prefixes that commonly take hyphens include the following:

all- as in *all-inclusive*   *quarter-* as in *quarter-hour*
ex- as in *ex-softball player*   *quasi-* as in *quasi-complete*
half- as in *half-convinced*   *self-* as in *self-employed*
mid- as in *mid-afternoon*

Such suffixes include the following:

-elect as in *treasurer-elect*   *-odd* as in *forty-odd years old*

Unfortunately, there are several exceptions to this general guideline. *Midnight, halfback,* and *quarterfinalist* are exceptions; over time, the hyphen has been dropped from these words. The only way to be certain of such exceptions is to consult a dictionary.

Finally, some suffixes, such as *-like* and *-wise*, sometimes take hyphens and sometimes do not (for example), *warlike, giraffe-like*). Again, your surest bet is to check a good dictionary.

Turn now to Assignment 36B at the end of this chapter for practice in using hyphens when writing words and numbers.

Using Hyphens to Clarify Meaning

Suppose that you are reading this sentence:

Kevin sells men's clothing for Macy's, and Michael is a bus-
boy at the Ringside.

For at least a moment, the word *bus* appears to be part of that sentence; for just a moment, it sounds like Michael is a transportation vehicle. Although such hyphenation follows the guidelines presented earlier in this chapter, in this case it still leads to confusion. Whenever you hyphenate at the end of a line, make sure that you do not inadvertently send a confusing message. Here is another example:

When I get up late and have early morning appointments, I may carelessly skip breakfast.

In the two examples just given, end-of-line hyphens create momentary
confusion. However, sometimes hyphens are crucial to meaning. Consider
these sentences:

The couch needs to be recovered after the flood.

The couch needs to be re-covered after the flood.

The first sentence says that the couch is lost (perhaps washed away) and
needs to be found. The second sentence says that the couch's upholstery
needs repair. There are similarly significant differences between *procreation* and *pro-creation* and between *re-create* and *recreate*.

Hyphens are also commonly used to separate suffixes from their roots
whenever the combination would result in three identical consonants in a
row. Thus *skill + less = skill-less*.

When adding a prefix results in the repetition of a vowel (as in *anti-
imperialist*), a hyphen is often used. However, this practice is violated too
frequently to be considered a reliable guideline (consider *reenlist, cooper-
ate*, and the like); when in doubt, consult your dictionary.

Combinations of single letters and roots are nearly always hyphenated,
unless they form the names of musical notes. Here are some examples:
A-frame, I-beam, F sharp, B major.

Turn now to Assignment 36C at the end of this chapter for practice in
using hyphens correctly.

EXERCISE 36.2 USING HYPHENS TO CLARIFY MEANING

**Each of the questions below specifies a particular word. Use that word correctly in a
sentence. Consult your dictionary if necessary.**

EXAMPLE

pro-creation The pro-creation camp has definite opinions about how science ought to be
taught.

1. procreation
2. re-cover
3. recreation
4. re-creation
5. re-form
6. reform

ASSIGNMENT 36A USING HYPHENS WITH COMPOUND WORDS AND COMPOUND MODIFIERS

Many (but not all) of the sentences below use hyphens or compound words incorrectly. Read each sentence. If hyphens and compounds are used correctly, write _C_ on the lines provided. If the sentence needs revising, write your version on the lines.

EXAMPLES

Michael spent his afternoon entertaining the six-year-olds, seven-year-olds, and eight-year-olds.
Michael spent his afternoon entertaining the six-, seven-, and eight-year-olds. _____

Stained-glass artistry made the church distinctive and inspiring.
C _____

1. This is a brilliantly-argued position paper. _____

2. An Albany youngster was hospitalized yesterday after consuming a still to be determined quantity of mothballs. _____

3. Short-term forecasts indicate that we should plan for a rainstorm Wednesday.

_____

4. When you drop off your completed form, we will check to make sure that you have an up to date file. _____

5. Several drop offs of over sixty feet make the Eagle Creek Trail a potentially dangerous one. _____

_____

6. My grandparents left the mother-country in 1908. _____

7. Almost everything about U.S. elections is geared to the two party system.

_____

_____

8. Many argue that abortion is not just a two-sided or three-sided question.

_____

_____

9. After two days of pitching and yawing on a fishing boat, I feel weak-kneed,

windburned, and weather beaten. _____

_____

10. He decided his I don't care attitude was too easy; besides, it left him feeling

empty. _____

_____

ASSIGNMENT 36B USING HYPHENS WITH PREFIXES AND SUFFIXES AND WITH FRACTIONS AND COMPOUND NUMBERS

Each item below is either a number or a word with a prefix or a suffix. Construct sentences that use the specified words correctly. Consult your dictionary as needed.

EXAMPLE

thirty-six+odd
After thirty-six-odd years, she trusted her own judgment.

1. half+back _____

_____

2. self+control _____

_____

3. trans+continental _____

_____

4. quasi+professional _____

_____

5. machine+like _____

_____

6. mid+stream _____

_____

7. anti+freeze _____

_____

8. pre+adolescent _____

_____

9. post+Reagan _____

_____

10. un+important _____

_____

11. 2/3 (write using words) _____

_____

12. 405,222 (write using words) _____

_____

13. 4,000 (write using words) _____

_____

14. president+elect _____

_____

15. pre+high school _____

_____

Proofread the sentences that follow for confusing end-of-line hyphenation or other inaccurate hyphenation. Underline the errors you find, and correct each in the space above it. Consult a dictionary whenever necessary. If the sentence is acceptable as written, write *C* after it.

EXAMPLES

When I get up late and have early morning appointments, I may care-
carelessly

lessly skip breakfast.

I have never learned how to find B sharp.   *C*

1. Walking along the beach, we noticed that several homes were under-

cut by wave action.

2. We spent over a week in class discussing the various pro-

cedures relating to soil testing.

3. Several people have told me that the lead cabinet holds a radio-

active substance.

4. The lakefront was dotted with log cabins and A frames.

5. I was driving home in a soggy coat when I saw the most beautiful rain-

bow I've ever seen.

6. B flat and C-major are both musical notes.

7. With candy, cookies, cakes, nuts, and cider, our Halloween fes-

tivities were definitely high in calories.

PART

Doing Research and Using Sources

These questions are designed to help you, the student, decide what to study. Mark the following statements as either true or false.

1. A research paper is a long, argumentative paper that draws on a number of different sources. _____

2. A book that discusses and interprets another book in detail is a primary source. _____

3. The publisher and the date of publication of a work do not appear on its card catalogue entry. _____

4. Every book owned by a library will be listed under the following headings: the author's last name, the first significant word of the title, and at least one subject heading. _____

5. The original date of publication is not useful in evaluating a source. _____

6. A summary reproduces an author's meaning in different words and is approximately as long as the original; a paraphrase accurately records only the major points of the source and is significantly shorter. _____

7. Plagiarism is using the words or ideas of others without plainly acknowledging their origin. _____

8. Writing an explicit thesis statement is the final step in completing a research essay. _____

9. MLA style requires that writers set off quotations that run longer than four lines into block quotations, typing them as separate paragraphs that are indented ten spaces. _____

10. The introduction to a research paper ought to establish the specific topic and the range of discussion, as well as telling the reader what exactly the writer intends to accomplish. _____

Becoming a Researcher

Research is a part of everyday life, and most of us have conducted far more of it than we realize. If you have ever comparison shopped, even for small purchases such as toothpaste or school supplies, you have conducted research: you have investigated and compared the qualities (usefulness, price, cost effectiveness) of the products that were available and made a judgment as to which of them best suited your needs. By the same token, the rest of your life will probably present you with many situations in which you will need to research something, even if you never write another academic paper. If you ever have need of a doctor, you will probably investigate the credentials and practical advantages offered by several practitioners before deciding which to see. When you enter the job market, you may research different companies to which you are applying for jobs. Of course, research in daily life is apt to be less formal and involved than your college research will be. However, mastering the skills of academic research will make you that much more confident and capable when faced with these other research tasks.

Many college assignments require research. We will be focusing on one type of assignment, the research paper, because it involves all the phases of both the research process and the process of writing an essay based on research findings. But bear in mind as you study Chapters 37–41 that you can draw on many of the skills and techniques that they cover in completing other types of assignments as well.

The research paper most commonly is a long argumentative or interpretive essay that draws on primary and secondary source materials for support. When a teacher assigns a research paper, he or she has, broadly speaking, two major criteria for judging your work. First, have you learned enough through your research to become a credible expert on your subject?

Second, have you presented your findings in a clear, well-organized, and carefully reasoned essay? You have already practiced the writing skills you need for this project in the course of working through this book. This chapter, and the four following it, will give you some guidance in combining methods of research with your writing skills to produce a successful research paper.

The research process is rarely a straight line from ignorance to knowledge. Typically, researchers begin with an idea, a question, or a tentative hypothesis, and a plan for investigating it. After they begin their research, much of the information they uncover may alter their thinking on their topic and force them to modify their hypotheses and revise their plans. Like these researchers, you must be flexible. If you maintain an open mind, each new bit of information you find will deepen your understanding, producing new questions and provoking additional research.

EXERCISE 37.1   REVIEWING YOUR RESEARCH HISTORY

Think of one example of research that you have done. It could be anything from researching how to build something to preparing a term paper. Write a four- or five-paragraph essay describing the research that you did—how you conducted it, the information that you gathered, and how you used that information. End by describing what you learned through the experience, not only about your research subject but also about the research process—is there anything you might do differently next time, for instance?

Using Both Primary and Secondary Sources |37*a*|

Most research projects require both primary and secondary source materials. Primary sources are documents or things that you observe, study, or interpret yourself. These can include data from an experiment, surveys, or interviews you conduct; literary or historical documents (letters, diaries, maps, treaties) that you interpret for yourself; performances you attend; or objects, such as artworks, you examine yourself. On the other hand, secondary sources consist of the work of other people in your subject area: their laboratory or field work, or their analyses, critiques, studies, or interpretations of the primary sources you are considering.

A researcher examines and uses primary and secondary sources in different ways (these differences will be discussed in Chapter 39). Each research project you attempt will require a different amount of each type of source. Research papers in the physical sciences often require your own experimental results and observations (primary sources), as well as other scientists' findings and conclusions (secondary sources). A paper on a historical figure such as Rasputin or Charlemagne could, of necessity, rely entirely on secondary sources—there might be nothing in existence that qualifies as a primary source on such a topic. By the same token, if you are studying something quite new (the makeup of the rap music audience, for instance, or the reason for the popularity of a new board game), you might find that there is almost no secondary source material on your subject; it could well be that you are one of the first writers to address such a subject.

As you begin any research project, you should try to determine what primary and secondary sources are available to you and how much of each you should try to cover in your research. Bear in mind that when both are available to you, your readers will expect you to include both; if you do not, they will wonder if you have presented a complete account of your subject.

Understanding or Choosing a Research Topic |37b|

Analyzing an Assigned Topic |37b1|

As with any assignment, the first step in working on a research paper is making sure you know exactly what is expected of you. Section 2b of Chapter 2 presents many questions and some detailed discussion that should help in analyzing research paper assignments as well as other writing assignments. In research assignments, it is especially important to understand the practical requirements, such as the following:

- How long should the essay be?
- Are there specific requirements for the number or type of sources that must be used?
- What is the deadline for the final draft?
- Are there any related assignments, such as a working outline or preliminary bibliography, that must be turned in before the final draft is due?

The answers to these questions will help you predict the amount of work required of you. If you cannot answer these questions confidently, ask your instructor to clarify the assignment.

If your instructor assigns a specific topic for your paper, make certain you understand the meaning and implications of that topic. See Chapter 42 for guidelines in analyzing specific assignments in the disciplines (42a), and Section 2b for further discussion of understanding assignments.

Choosing Your Own Topic |37b2|

If you are allowed to choose your own topic for a research essay, your choice should be based not only on an awareness of the demands of the general assignment but also on some knowledge of the subject. Such knowledge often comes from the class itself, from class notes, in-class discussions, or assigned readings. If class time has been devoted to possible topic areas, begin your writing process by reviewing your notes, looking for any topic that has puzzled you or provoked your curiosity.

If little or no class time has been devoted to possible topics, ask yourself if you already possess enough knowledge to select a topic. Many writers will freewrite at this point, listing everything they know about a subject, and listing every possible source of information about it that they can remember.

If you know very little about a topic that intrigues you, you can obtain a general overview of a topic area from discussions with your instructor, other faculty members, or acquaintances who have some expertise in your subject. You can also consult less specialized sources. Textbooks (along with their "recommended reading" lists) and encyclopedias are especially useful at this stage. Moreover, popularized magazine and journal articles (most easily located through the *Readers' Guide to Periodical Literature*) and newspaper articles (located through the indexes to major newspapers such as the *New York Times*) can be helpful too.

EXERCISE 37.2 CHOOSING AND EXPLORING A RESEARCH TOPIC

Begin work on a research assignment by choosing a topic (unless your instructor prefers to assign one). Choose carefully; you will be working with this topic throughout the next five chapters of this book. On your own paper, answer the following questions.

1. What is your topic and why did you choose it? Freewrite for ten minutes about your topic, addressing such questions as what, where, and how you have learned about it.
2. What practical questions do you want to ask your instructor about your assignment?
3. How can you acquire an introduction to or a general understanding of your research topic? List one knowledgeable person with whom you could discuss your topic, as well as at least three textbooks or encyclopedias that could help you. Finally, use the *Readers' Guide* or the *New York Times Index* to locate at least one magazine or newspaper article on your subject. (Note: If these two reference guides do not list any articles related to your subject, try some of the many other periodical indexes mentioned in Chapter 38, or ask your librarian or instructor for help. Remember, however, that what you need right now is *general* information; try not to get sidetracked by source material covering very specific aspects of your topic.)

Narrowing and Focusing Your Topic |37c|

When you begin some preliminary reading in your general topic area, your immediate goal should be to find ways to limit your subject, focusing on one specific issue that can be discussed thoroughly in a relatively short essay (usually ten pages). For example, suppose you are intrigued by Henry VIII and his turbulent reign. After reading through your history textbooks and a couple of encyclopedia articles, you may decide that the interaction between his political and personal lives is particularly fascinating to you. Further, you have concluded that the event that most clearly illustrates this interaction is his marriage to Anne Boleyn. Your guiding research question could become: "Did Henry have Anne beheaded because of his belief that she had committed adultery, or was he motivated by political considerations?" After further reading, you would begin to form a tentative answer to that question, based on the evidence you uncovered. That answer would become your working hypothesis and eventually, after inevitable modifications, the thesis of your final paper.

A working hypothesis should meet the same standards that a working thesis must meet (see section 2f). It must be manageable, interesting, specific, and arguable. Sometimes the only way to find out whether your working hypothesis meets those criteria is to proceed with your research until you find something wrong with it. But if you can see a problem early on and can alter your hypothesis accordingly, you may save yourself a lot of time.

Another important factor in determining how you narrow and focus your general topic is the practical feasibility of your project. For example, your library might have very little information on one aspect of your subject but plenty on another, equally interesting aspect. Naturally, you would want to choose the more feasible aspect—the area in which you would have access to abundant source material.

Investigating What You Know about Your Topic |37d|

Your generalized research on your topic should have provided you with a certain amount of information on it. In addition, through that research and the process of narrowing and focusing your topic, you have probably developed a number of ideas, questions, insights, or hunches about this information or about the additional information you expect to uncover when you begin more specialized research. Take a few minutes to get this knowledge and all the ideas you have about it down on paper by using one of the basic prewriting techniques presented in Chapter 2: brainstorming, freewriting, and looping (see section 2e for instruction in these techniques).

These techniques will be most valuable if you try not to interrupt yourself or question whether a thought is worth writing down. If it crosses your mind, jot it down; ideas and musings that seem insignificant at first some-times lead to exploration and discoveries that are far more interesting than more obvious ideas. Remember, though, that this process should help you decide what you need to explore next. If, looking back over your ideas, you find that you do not know what the next step in your research should be, you may want to try a more focused prewriting activity: freewriting in fa-vor of your hypothesis, against it, or both. Doing this will take you through a verbal sketch of what your final paper might cover. It could also bring to your attention things your readers might find to criticize in your paper. This process should show you immediately any places where you need further background or expertise to back up your ideas.

EXERCISE 37.3 FOCUSING YOUR TOPIC AND FORMULATING A RESEARCH QUESTION

Assume that your assignment is to write a research paper of ten to fifteen pages, using both primary and secondary sources, due in one month. If you have completed Exercise 37.2, then you already have a research topic and a list of general sources on it. If you have not completed Exercise 37.2, choose a research area now, or ask your instructor to help you find one, and begin this exercise by locating the same general sources asked for in question 3 of Exercise 37.2. When you have your research topic and general sources, answer the following questions.

1. Do you think that you need to narrow or focus your topic? Explain why or why not.
2. Consult all the general sources you have located, and write a very brief summary (about one paragraph per source) of what you learn about your topic from each.
3. Review your summaries, and circle any points that you think will help you focus your topic or that apply to the focus you have already chosen. Based on this analysis of your general reading, what will your research question be?

EXERCISE 37.4 PLANNING FOR SPECIALIZED RESEARCH

Answer the following questions about your research question. (If you do not already have a research question, ask your instructor to help you.)

1. State your research question, and jot down important things that you know about it, as well as things you can think of that you *do not* know.
2. Think of a couple possible answers to your research question; even if they are unlikely or vague, these answers can help you decide what additional information you need for your paper.

3. Finally, identify two more sources that you think will provide additional information you need to answer your research question. Specify what you hope to learn from each source.

38

Conducting Research

Collecting Data in the Field |38*a*|

The first and most obvious way to begin research is with your own observations, perceptions, inferences, and judgment. For example, the core of any research paper in literature is your own analysis of a work. In other fields you can conduct your own experiment, construct and administer a survey, observe, or interview. For our purposes in this book, we will focus on observing and interviewing. Matters of experimentation—experimental design, survey design, and the like—are conveyed in detail in more specialized texts. If you elect to perform a formal experiment or survey in the natural or social sciences, you must satisfy the standards of that field. Seek out laboratory manuals and instructors in that discipline for assistance in fulfilling those standards.

Observing |38*a*1|

The kind of observation that is a primary research tool is considerably more formal and objective than what we do as part of our everyday lives. When researchers observe, they have a particular purpose in mind. They are seeking some specific information that they believe will help them answer a question or prove a point. To ensure that observation used for research provides exactly the information you are seeking—and that that information is sound and reliable—keep in mind the following general requirements as you are conducting it:

- Whatever you are observing should not be altered or affected in any way by the fact that you are observing it. For this reason, observers must often try to remain unobtrusive.

- The number of your observations should be large enough to be convincing; that is, you should conduct enough observations to provide a representative record of whatever you are observing.
- Your observational data should be systematized in some way. No observer can write down everything. Thus, it is important for you to know precisely what you are seeking and what you can safely ignore. You must also develop your own clear and consistent method for recording data.

EXERCISE 38.1 CONDUCTING OBSERVATION FOR RESEARCH

Begin this exercise by identifying a question you want to answer or a hypothesis you want to test (bear in mind that this exercise will be most useful to you if it relates to your research project, begun in Chapter 37). Next, determine what or whom you might observe in order to answer this question. For example, if you enjoy soap operas, can you figure out a way to observe and therefore determine which soap opera is most popular among your friends? Then, using your own paper, respond to the following questions.

1. What question will this observation help you answer? Why will this data be significant?

2. Exactly what will you be observing? What specific behavior? What kind of data will you be collecting? Will you be counting something? If so, what? Be as specific as you can.

Acting on your answers to questions 1 and 2, conduct your observation. Collect your data and, finally, answer these questions:

3. Did your observation proceed as you expected it to? If not, what happened differently?

4. Did this research answer the question you hoped it would? If not, or if it answered it only partially, what further questions should you now investigate in order to explore your subject?

Interviewing | 38a2 |

As a college student, you have a wealth of education and experience concentrated in a relatively small number of people—your school's faculty. Besides finding potential interviewees among the faculty, you can use your school's alumni directory, local newspaper features, a current *Who's Who* or another biographical guide, and, of course, the telephone directory to find experts to interview.

When you have identified an expert you would like to interview, the next step is simply to contact the person, either by telephone or by letter. You should take care to present your request professionally. Prior to the interview itself, try to discover as much information as possible about your interviewee. If you are well informed, your interviewee will be even more interested in talking with you and giving you time, and you will be better equipped to ask interesting and insightful questions.

When you prepare for an interview, the most important goal is this: know what kinds of information you need when you begin the interview. In practical terms, this means preparing questions in advance—actually writing them down. In the midst of an interesting discussion, it is easy to forget important questions. Let us look at an example of effective preparation. A business major who interviewed a small-business owner about the advantages and disadvantages of owning a business prepared the following questions:

- On the average, how many hours per week do you work?
- On the average, how many hours per week do you spend engaged in work-related activities?
- Has the workload been about what you expected it would be?

Note that these questions ask for short, generally factual answers. Usually, researchers will also ask focused but more open-ended questions:

- What has been most rewarding about being a small-business owner?
- What has been least rewarding?
- Knowing what you know now, would you do it again? Why or why not?
- What sort of person makes a successful small-business owner?

As an interviewer, you want to stay away from questions that seem vague or unfocused. Asking a small-business owner to "tell me about what you do" might make it seem that you have not given the interview much thought and are not taking it seriously.

EXERCISE 38.2 INTERVIEWING

Answer the following questions to help you prepare for and conduct an interview.

1. Identify three areas of knowledge (relating, if possible, to the research project you undertook in Chapter 37) that you would like to research. Then identify a potential interviewee for each area with whom you would likely be able to arrange an interview.

2. From the possibilities you have listed, select one person whom you will actually contact.

3. Contact the person and arrange an interview. Limit the time you request for the interview to thirty minutes, unless the person suggests a longer time. If the first person you try is unavailable, select another person familiar with that area of knowledge or one of the two remaining possibilities from question 1.

4. Draw up a list of questions that you will ask your interviewee.

5. Conduct the interview, and record answers by taking accurate notes or using a tape recorder if you have the person's permission to record. Write up a summary of what you learned from the interview.

6. Finally, write a critique of the interview process itself. Did it go smoothly? Did you get the information you needed? Did you do a good job as an interviewer? Is there anything that you would do differently next time?

Using Library Resources |38b|

When you need to consult published sources in your library, begin by thinking about what you want to accomplish. Try to answer these two questions:

- What question or questions do you want your library research to answer?
- What materials (such as books, periodicals, or newspapers) are likely to provide answers?

Above all, you do not want to go to the library and aimlessly browse through the card catalog or the library shelves themselves. Such unstructured library time almost always proves frustrating and unproductive.

Locating Research Information

The reference section of your library will provide you with three very helpful types of resources: the librarians themselves, specialized indexes and bibliographies, and the card catalog. It also may have a computerized catalog and specialized databases. If so, ask your librarian to assist you in using those particular systems. If you begin your library research by asking a librarian for help, make sure you have defined your research project as precisely as possible so as not to make unfair demands on his or her time.

Using Specialized Indexes and Bibliographies   In the previous chapter we mentioned some of the ways you can find general information on your research topic—textbooks, general encyclopedias, the *Readers' Guide to Periodical Literature*, and the *New York Times* or other newspaper indexes. These nonspecialized sources are very useful in the early stages of a project.

They help you narrow a topic and develop research questions. Thus, they provide an avenue toward more specialized research.

When you are ready to explore a more specific research question, you will find in the library reference section a number of specialized indexes and bibliographies that list articles and books that address your interests. If you wish to see the full range of what is available or to find an index for a specific subject, consult a guide to reference works such as the tenth edition of the *Guide to Reference Books*, edited by Eugene P. Sheehy, published in 1986. There are many other similar guides as well.

Some of the most commonly used indexes to periodical literature are the *Humanities Index*, the *Social Sciences Index*, the *Essay and General Literature Index, Historical Abstracts*, and the *General Science Index*. There are also several microfilm indexes to periodical literature: *Magazine Index, National Newspaper Index*, and *Business Index*, among others. For biographical questions, consult, among other references, the *Dictionary of American Biography*, the *Dictionary of National Biography*, and the many volumes of the *Who's Who* series. For facts on current events or statistics, consult almanacs and yearbooks such as *Facts on File*, the *Statistical Abstract of the United States*, and the *World Almanac and Book of Facts*. There are also many bibliographies that are published yearly, such as the *MLA International Bibliography of Books and Articles on the Modern Languages and Literature*, which lists publications on literature, linguistics, and folklore. One useful index for any field is the *Book Review Digest*, which contains excerpts from selected reviews of books; it will give you a clear idea of the critical reception of a book in any field.

The books just mentioned are only a handful of the many reference works that are available in most libraries. For any subject you can name, you will probably find a specialized dictionary, an encyclopedia, a bibliographical index, a yearbook, and perhaps a book of abstracts. Your reference librarian will know of all these resources, so be sure to ask if you cannot locate them on your own.

EXERCISE 38.3   USING SPECIALIZED INDEXES AND BIBLIOGRAPHIES

Locate two specialized indexes or bibliographies relevant to your own research topic, to a topic assigned to you by your instructor, or to a topic that you choose from the following list: organ transplants, acid rain, stress in the workplace, taxes, Shakespeare's *Othello*, the fate of the Spanish Armada, the life of John Lennon. Answer the following questions about each of the two reference works you locate.

1. What is the title of the bibliography or index?
2. How frequently is it published?

3. Where in the library is it found?

4. List three magazines or journals whose articles are cited in this index or bibliography.

5. Find three articles related to your research topic in the three magazines or journals you listed or in others. Record the information provided about each article, copying out the entries exactly as they appear.

6. Now write out all three entries in full, using complete words rather than the abbreviations used in the bibliography or index. Consult the front of the volume you are using for definitions of any abbreviations that you do not recognize.

Using the Card Catalog or Circulation Computer Indexes and bibliographies help researchers identify and locate useful articles in journals; the card catalog performs the same function for books. Whether you are using a computerized catalog or the actual cards themselves, the catalog provides you with an inventory of your library's holdings.

Each card lists the following basic publication information for a book:

- the full title
- the author and/or editor
- the publisher
- the place of publication
- the date of publication
- the library's call number for the book

Every book owned by your library will be listed under three alphabetized headings: (1) the author's last name, (2) the first significant word of the title, and (3) at least one subject heading (you can use a reference book called the *Library of Congress Subject Headings* to find out how librarians classify subjects).

Libraries follow either the Library of Congress system or the Dewey Decimal system for assigning call letters or numbers to books. These call letters or numbers reflect groupings by subject; thus, if you glance at nearby titles when retrieving a book from the shelf, you are likely to find other useful sources in your subject area.

If you do not have a particular author or title to search for in the catalog, you can check the subject cards for your particular area. There you may find specific bibliographies in your subject area. If there are too many cards listed under a subject for you to read through them efficiently (this is usually not the case, especially in smaller libraries), ask a librarian or an instructor for guidance in locating useful books more quickly. Also bear in mind that every useful source you find can lead you to other books or articles; always check the notes and bibliography in any good source you find.

ASSIGNMENT 38A LOCATING AND USING A NEWSPAPER SOURCE

Locate and read the front page of a newspaper published the day you were born. Then provide the following information about it.

1. Name of newspaper: _____

2. Place of publication: _____

3. How much did that issue of the paper cost? _____

4. Summarize two of the largest articles on the front page:

   A. _____

   _____

   _____

   _____

   _____

   B. _____

   _____

   _____

   _____

   _____

ASSIGNMENT 38B USING THE LIBRARY

Make a trip to your library in order to answer the following questions. Note: Answer question 7 first; if you need to consult with an instructor, you will want to do so before going to the library.

1. At what library are you completing this exercise?

_____

2. Does this library use the Dewey Decimal or Library of Congress system?

_____

3. What is this library's call number for *Native Son* by Richard Wright?

_____

4. Cite the publisher and publication date of *Native Son*. _____

_____

5. Where would you find this book in your library? What floor? What part of the

building? _____

_____

6. Does your library contain other books by Richard Wright? If so, note one of the

titles. _____

_____

7. Now locate a book that pertains directly to your ongoing research project. If you
have trouble finding a book, ask a professor to suggest a title. Give the title and the

professor's name. _____

_____

8. Check your library. Is that book part of the library's holdings? If it is, give its call
number, the name of the author, all publication information, and the total number of

pages. _____

_____

_____

9. Use that book's bibliography or notes to find one more article or book that looks

useful to you, and write the title here. _____

_____

39

Evaluating and Using Source Materials

When you have located some specialized sources you believe will be useful, your research will become both more interesting and more demanding. Once you begin reading, you will constantly be assessing each source for its usefulness and its quality. And just as important, you will need to record the information you gather accurately and efficiently. This chapter will offer you some guidelines for handling your source material effectively. As you work, the most important principle to remember is this: always read with your central research question or working hypothesis firmly in mind. This is your basis for both judging your sources and deciding what information you will record.

Choosing Sources |39a|

Assessing a Source's Usefulness |39a1, 39a2|

If you keep your research question clearly in mind, it should be fairly easy for you to avoid wasting time in reading source material that is only marginally relevant. There are a few key features in any book or article that you can examine quickly to give yourself a fairly clear sense of its usefulness.

> **Key Features for Assessing a Source's Usefulness**
>
> 1. Examine both the title and the subtitle carefully; the subtitle in particular should give you a sense of the range covered by a source.
> 2. Examine the table of contents, the index, the notes, and the bibliography; these will provide you with a cross section, so to speak, of the source's content.
> 3. Quickly read the abstract, the introduction (or preface or foreword), and the conclusion; these will give you a fairly clear idea of the author's point of view, his or her coverage plans, and the study's level of specialization.

4. Pay attention to the original date of publication; particularly in the social and physical sciences, information becomes dated quickly. However, do not judge the usefulness of any source simply by its age. The most authoritative source in a given field may well have been published many years ago; if that is the case, you will find that that source is still frequently cited in more recent studies.

Skimming and Evaluating a Source   l39a3l

If, on the basis of the criteria just listed, you decide that a book or article is likely to be useful, begin skimming the source quickly. Look at the first sentences of paragraphs as well as any subheadings. Examine any charts, tables, or graphs. Pause to read more slowly any sections that pertain directly to your research question. Ask yourself these two questions:

1. Does the author discuss the material I need?
2. Does the source include facts, examples, research data, or expert opinions that I can use as evidence?

By quickly working through a source in this manner, you should gain a fairly clear idea of the author's tone and perspective. A sense of these elements will help you judge the reliability of a source. In particular, examine the validity of an author's argument; analyze it in light of the material covered in Chapter 4. Further, ask yourself the following questions:

3. On what basis has the author adopted his or her particular point of view? Does the author seem to approach the subject with a preestablished attitude and then interpret evidence in light of that attitude? Or does he or she seem to examine the evidence fairly and neutrally and then draw reasonable inferences and conclusions from it?
4. In what ways do I share the author's interpretation of the evidence?
5. In what ways does my view differ from the author's?

EXERCISE 39.1   EVALUATING SOURCE MATERIALS

Using the list of key features in section 39a, locate a source that is likely to be relevant to your research question (or to another question you and your instructor have agreed upon). On a sheet of paper, write down the work's full title, the author's name, and the publication information. Then skim the source quickly and answer the five questions posed in the section above as fully as possible. Will you use this source in your essay? Why or why not?   _____

Reading Your Sources and Taking Notes   l39b, 39cl

Most researchers find note cards the most practical way to record information because they can be easily grouped and organized (see Chapter 40 for suggestions on using grouped note cards to help compose a working outline and a first draft).

Building a Working Bibliography |39b1|

For every source you find useful, you should begin by creating a bibliography card containing the following information:

- the author's full name
- the title of the work (if an article, the titles of both the article and the journal in which it appears)
- any edition or volume number and any series title
- the publisher and place of publication
- the publication date
- the call number (in case you need to retrieve the book)

It is a good idea to arrange this information in the documentation style your final bibliography will use (see Chapter 41). When the time comes for you to compose your final bibliography, you will simply need to arrange your cards in alphabetical order and begin typing.

Recording Information

You can record information from a source by using direct quotation, paraphrasing, or summarizing. **Direct quotation** is the slowest method of recording information, since you must be scrupulously careful to record the source's words exactly as they are written. You should signal any direct quotations you record by using quotation marks consistently; if you forget them, you may forget that you have quoted a source directly. (See Chapter 32 on using ellipsis points and brackets to signal the few changes it is permissible to make when quoting directly from a source.) Because recording quotations is slow and painstaking, try to record only those quotations you are fairly certain to use in your essay (see 40d). A **paraphrase** accurately and thoroughly reproduces the meaning and details of a passage in your own words; it is about the same length as a source passage. A **summary** also uses your own words instead of the author's, but it accurately records only the major points in a passage and is therefore significantly shorter than the source passage.

When you record information on note cards, be sure to record the exact page number(s) where it appears in the source. You should key every information card to the proper bibliography card by using the author's last name and, if necessary, a short version of the title. Try to limit what you record on a card to one idea; that will make grouping the cards easier.

Use note cards also to record your own thoughts, speculations, and reactions to sources, as well as your ideas on how you might use the sources in your essay. As we noted in Chapter 37, your ideas will inevitably change as you cover more and more material. Your central research question will become more precisely focused, and your answer to it—your working hypothesis—will become clearer. Sometimes a thought or point that is fairly complex and already in more or less complete sentences may occur to you. Do not make the mistake of ignoring such thoughts because you think that it is too early to begin writing. Some of our freshest, most interesting ideas come to us suddenly in this way, and unfortunately, we are apt to forget them just as suddenly. If you cannot fit the entire thought on a note card, use paper instead. But do be sure to write down these random insights. Keeping a record of your thought process will help you move more easily into writing your first draft.

EXERCISE 39.2 PREPARING BIBLIOGRAPHY AND NOTE CARDS

Photocopy an important one- to two-page passage from a source. Prepare a bibliography card for the source. Then prepare three information cards, one recording a direct quotation from the passage, one paraphrasing a paragraph from it, and one summarizing two other paragraphs from it.

Crediting Your Sources: Avoiding Plagiarism |39e|

Keeping track of your sources and using them accurately is one of your major responsibilities as a research writer. You must maintain careful distinctions between your words and ideas and those of someone else. Writers are guilty of plagiarism whenever they use the words or ideas of others as if they were their own. Even well-meaning authors have been known to plagiarize unintentionally. However, plagiarism, whether it results from deceit or simple carelessness, is both illegal and grossly unethical. Those who are guilty of it stand to lose much more than they might imagine. Once a reader detects plagiarism in your writing, you will lose your credibility as a researcher, and you may face severe penalties. Remember, too, that your college instructor is probably very familiar with the sources you are using; he or she is likely to recognize immediately when a source has been used without being properly credited.

Here are some guidelines to help you avoid charges of plagiarism:

- All direct (that is, word-for-word) quotations require quotation marks (unless set off as a block quotation, as discussed in Chapter 32) and a citation. (See Chapter 41 for instruction in citation styles.)
- All material that is new must be documented. For example, in mentioning the discovery of a new comet, you must credit the source in which its discovery is documented. Also, any material that is unique to one source—the judgments, opinions, or claims of a particular writer in your research area—must be documented, even if you present the material in your own words.

- All statistics, charts, tables, and graphs must be documented. Even if the graphic presentation is your own, you will still be using someone else's information.
- You do not need to document information that is general common knowledge or that is available in a great many sources, such as the fact that water freezes at 32 degrees Fahrenheit or that Mozart lived from 1756 until 1791.
- Anyone not already mentioned among your sources who provided useful insights and guidance or significant help in conducting your research should be credited. This includes instructors who have provided access to equipment, facilities, or rare sources or have offered particularly helpful insights into your material. It also includes anyone who helped you conduct fieldwork or experimentation, as well as anyone who helped you revise and edit. If these names cannot be logically and gracefully mentioned within the essay itself, create a separate page for them and label it "Acknowledgments." Be sure to specify how each person helped you with your work.
- When in doubt about whether or not to document particular information, ask your instructor. If your instructor is unavailable, go ahead and cite the source. It is better to include an unnecessary citation than to be guilty of plagiarism. Note: For the purposes of Exercise 39.3, and in general when you are taking notes, drafting, or revising, handle citations by providing, in parentheses, the author's last name, the title of the work (a short version if the title is cumbersome), and the exact pages on which the material you are using can be found. It is best to impose the correct citation style (see Chapter 41) at a late stage in editing, when you will be dealing with other details such as capitalization and punctuation.

EXERCISE 39.3 CITING QUOTATIONS

The following passage is from page 16 of Rachel Carson's book *The Sea around Us*. Read the passage and then follow the directions after it, using your own paper. [Note: If you have a research project in progress, you may select a passage from one of your sources and use that instead of the Rachel Carson excerpt.]

Nowhere in all the sea does life exist in such bewildering abundance as in the surface waters. From the deck of a vessel you may look down, hour after hour, on the shimmering disks of jellyfish, their gently pulsating bells dotting the surface as far as you can see. Or one day you may notice early in the morning that you are passing through a sea that has taken on a brick-red color from billions upon billions of microscopic creatures, each of which contains an orange pigment granule. At noon you are still moving through red seas, and when darkness falls the waters shine with an eerie glow from the phosphorescent fires of yet more billions and trillions of these same creatures.

And again you may glimpse not only the abundance but something of the fierce uncompromisingness of sea life when, as you look over the rail and down, down into water of a clear, deep green, suddenly there passes a silver shower of finger-long fishlets. The sun strikes a metallic gleam from their flanks as they streak by, diving deeper into the green depths with the desperate speed of the hunted. Perhaps you never see the hunters, but you sense their presence as you see the gulls hovering, with eager, mewing cries, waiting for the little fish to be driven to the surface.

1. Write a one- or two-sentence summary of the passage. Do not quote any of the passage directly. At the end of your summary, include a citation you have created based on the instructions preceding this exercise. If you are using an excerpt from one of your own sources, create an appropriate citation for that source.

2. Write a paraphrase of the passage—again, do not quote directly—and include the same citation.

3. Write a brief passage that does quote Carson (or the author of your source) and uses the citation.

40

Organizing, Drafting, and Revising a Research Essay

Organizing Research Information and Taking Inventory |40a, 40b|

As you research, you amass a wealth of information: note cards recording bibliographic information, material from primary and secondary sources, and your own thoughts. Your working hypothesis becomes clearer. And at some point in the research process (maybe at several points throughout), you will need to take inventory to review the information you have gathered and make decisions about how to organize it and about the direction your remaining research should take.

Some of the research projects you may be assigned as a college student will have standardized organizational requirements—a lab report is one example of such a project. With this sort of project, the process of organizing and assessing the information you have gathered is quite straightforward. But with many other projects you will need to create your own organizational strategies. The following paragraph describes three useful methods for taking inventory that may help you with this organizational process. You may also want to review the strategies discussed in sections 2h and 2i.

The methods for taking inventory vary, but three are particularly useful. The first is the process of **grouping note cards**. Combine cards that seem to go together. If a card contains some information that seems entirely unrelated to that on any other card, set it off by itself. Eventually, you will be able to see how your information clusters. When you have grouped your cards, reread them and begin constructing an informal outline of the major ideas uncovered during your research. **Outlining**, the second inventory-taking method, will force you to make connections or to realize that you cannot make such connections and therefore need to conduct further research. Finally, you could decide, after reading through your notes, to begin **freewriting**. Like outlining, freewriting at this point should reveal any major gaps in your research, and it could become the basis for your full rough draft.

EXERCISE 40.1 ASSESSING AND ORGANIZING A RESEARCH SUMMARY

Here is a summary of one student's research in response to this assignment: "Explore the role of athletics in college life, and determine what role athletics *should* have in an academic setting." On your own paper, use this summary to respond to the questions following it.

RESEARCH SUMMARY

Interview with gymnast:
   --athletic scholarship only way to stay in school
   --athletics provide their own out-of-class education
Information from Chronicle of Higher Education:
   --NCAA guidelines for student athletes
   --ongoing debate among educators: education vs. the entertainment
      business
   --abuses of sports programs by boosters
   --statistics on the number of student athletes
Interview with faculty senator:
   --athletics have no place; money unwisely spent
   --huge imbalance between faculty's salaries and coaches' salaries
   --some say sports are a metaphor for American culture--"hogwash"
Ideas from card catalog, library shelves:
   --two titles discussing the "sociology" of sports in American life
   --America as a nation of winners and losers; sports just a
      concentrated version of society
   --Sports metaphors (being a "team player," "the Saturday night
      quarterback," etc.) tend to trivialize other endeavors. Everything
      becomes sport.
What do my friends (other students) think?
   --football/basketball spectator sports as central to college life ("I
      can't imagine college without varsity sports.")
   --intramural sports as a useful outlet for stress ("When you're
      playing, you can forget about tests and grades for a little while.")

1. List at least three pieces of information from any of the sources listed in this summary that seem to go together. If you can see more than three that fit together, include this additional information as well.

2. What unites the information in your list for question 1? What is the common thread? Identify it in one sentence.

3. List at least three other pieces of information that seem to go together.

4. What unites the information in this second list?

5. Your two single-sentence answers to questions 2 and 4 identify two separate directions this research paper could take. If you were the researcher, which direction would you choose? Why?

EXERCISE 40.2 ORGANIZING, OUTLINING FROM, AND RECONSIDERING YOUR RESEARCH

The preceding section of Chapter 40 identifies grouping note cards and outlining as two ways for researchers to take inventory. Using your own cards and paper, group your research note cards and draw up an informal outline. You may also create an informal outline based on the research summary provided in Exercise 40.1. Then answer the following questions.

1. At this point in your research process, what is your working hypothesis?

2. Identify three major categories of information you have formed through grouping your note cards.

3. What is the relationship of each of these three categories to each other and to your working hypothesis? Your outline should reveal this.

4. Which one of these categories is most likely to become a central point in your final essay? What further research do you need to do in this area; that is, what additional information do you need?

Considering the Audience of Your Research Paper |40a1|

After you have filled in any research gaps and before you begin composing your first draft, you should consider the question of your audience. In the opening section of Chapter 37 we discussed an instructor's two major criteria for judging your essay, which are the standards *any* educated reader will bring to a consideration of your work. First, based on the extent and quality of your research, is your stance as an expert on a particular issue convincing? Remember that any research essay is, implicitly or explicitly, an argument. You have gathered a mass of information, and you want to convince your audience that your interpretation of that information is correct. (Review section 4d on the importance of a writer's image in developing a persuasive argument.) Second, does the quality of your writing—its clarity and coherence, the integration of source material with your own ideas, the use of an appropriately formal tone—reinforce your stance as a competent researcher?

One consideration regarding audience is unique to the research essay. Your research has uncovered several perspectives on your topic. As you draw conclusions based on the information you have uncovered and refine your working hypothesis, you will find yourself allied with some experts in your field and opposed to others' points of view. In fact, your instructor, too, may be an expert in this field with a particular point of view. All these authorities are part of your potential audience, just as you are part of theirs. You need to consider how valid your treatment of the subject will seem to them, particularly to those opposing your point of view. You must demonstrate in your essay that you understand the major points of view regarding your subject and have clear reasons, based on valid evidence, for opposing the views of some experts and supporting those of others.

EXERCISE 40.3 EXAMINING YOUR RESEARCH FROM YOUR AUDIENCE'S PERSPECTIVE

Answer the following questions on your own paper. (If you do not have a body of research to base your answers on, use the research summary provided in Exercise 40.1, supplementing it with additional research if necessary.)

1. Sketch very briefly the major positions/opinions/perspectives you have uncovered during the course of your research.
2. Identify or characterize as clearly as you can the group holding each of the major positions/opinions/perspectives you described in response to the first question.
3. By identifying these groups, you have analyzed your potential audience. With which group(s) do you ally yourself? Which do you oppose?
4. What evidence can you cite to demonstrate that you have valid reasons for holding a different point of view from that of the group(s) you oppose? Do you think you need to do further research to answer this question? What direction will your research take?

Developing an Explicit Thesis Statement |40a2|

After you have finished and organized your research and considered the question of audience, it is time to begin writing. Look over your grouped note cards and refine your informal outline so that it will give you sufficient guidance when you begin to write. (Review the discussion on organizational strategies in sections 2h and 2i.) Finally, before you begin the draft, compose an *explicit thesis statement* to focus your thoughts. Often, this statement is simply a more formal way of answering your central research question or restating the working hypothesis that has been guiding your research. It should take this form (for an example of a completed explicit thesis statement, see Assignment 40A):

> In this essay, I plan to _____
> (explain, argue, analyze, and so on) for an audience consisting of _____
> and will argue or demonstrate that _____
> because of (1) _____, (2) _____,
> and (3) _____.

The process of composing the explicit thesis statement, like so many other stages in writing a research essay, may expose holes in your knowledge or in your argument. It may lead you to realize that that argument is not solid or that you have not fully grasped certain areas that you plan to cover. In short, you may have to turn back to further research at this point. Just remember that addressing the problem now will save you more time than waiting until you have begun to draft.

Now turn to Assignment 40A at the end of the chapter for practice in composing and testing an explicit thesis statement. Also, for additional guidance in writing and testing a working thesis, see section 2f.

Drafting Your Research Essay |40c|

With many research projects, it is not very helpful to start a rough draft by trying to write your introduction. Let your explicit thesis statement serve as your introduction for the time being. Once the body of your essay is written, you will be better able to construct an appropriate introduction and conclusion. (Note: As with all writing, learning to draft a research essay really means finding out what works best for you. One writer may have trouble drafting an introduction before drafting the body of the paper; another may find that drafting an introduction helps him or her get started on the body. Only you can discover which approach suits you.) As you write the body of the essay, remember that you will be using the structures you have already studied for developing arguments and paragraphs; review the material in Chapters 4 and 5 when necessary.

Here are some general suggestions to keep in mind as you draft:

- Try to write at least two pages at a time.
- Do not become derailed by small questions. Almost inevitably, you will discover some gaps in your research as you write. Make a note of such gaps, and continue writing, unless a gap is so large that you must find the information before you can write further.
- When you do stop, make a note to yourself explaining how to pick up where you left off.

EXERCISE 40.4 DRAFTING YOUR RESEARCH PAPER

Begin to draft your research paper. Start with any portion that you feel ready to write. Write at least two pages. Then answer the following questions on your own paper. (Note: In order to complete this exercise, you will have to have completed all the research steps covered in previous exercises.)

1. What portion of the research paper did you start drafting? Did you begin with the introduction, some part of the body, or the conclusion?
2. Why did you start there?
3. Did you discover that you still have substantial research questions to answer? If so, what are they?
4. What will you do next? Will you do more research? If so, identify a likely source for the information you need. Will you continue drafting? If so, do you anticipate any problems with completing the draft? Explain.

Incorporating Source Materials into Your Draft |40d|

Even the most experienced research writers wrestle with the problem of incorporating sources into a rough draft. Material can be incorporated in the form of summarized or paraphrased material or in the form of a direct quotation (see Chapter 39). (Note: All sample parenthetical citations shown in this chapter follow Modern Language Association style; see Chapter 41 for other styles.) Most writers and readers agree that source material should not overpower one's own words. Allowing your essay to become a patchwork of quotations, paraphrases, and summaries loosely held together by your transitions will damage your stance as an expert.

Quotations can be particularly dangerous in this regard. You should use them only when they are strictly necessary or when you honestly believe you could not make the point your source has made in as effective a way. It would be silly, for instance, to use direct quotation in this way:

> Roper conjectures that Pocahontas may have been born "in 1595"
> (Pocahontas 297).

Clearly, there is nothing outstanding or memorable about the quoted phrase "in 1595." It is far better in a case like this to write a new sentence if yours is at all close to your source's wording or organization, and simply include the citation:

> Roper believes Pocahontas was born in 1595 (Pocahontas 297).

No book can tell you precisely when to quote material. However, the best methods of incorporating quotations into the body of your essay can be illustrated. (See also Chapter 31, which discusses quotation marks, and Chapter 32, which discusses brackets and ellipses.)

Using Direct Quotations A short quotation can often be built right into the structure of the sentence you are writing. You construct your sentence in such a way that the quotation carries out the sentence's grammatical sense. Try to present a short quotation in this way whenever you can; it helps your writing flow smoothly and lets your reader feel that you are in charge of your material.

EXAMPLE

An element of friction, resulting in a slight "edge" to the vocal tone, is inherent in and essential to a healthy singing process. This friction is directly caused by "the regular, rapid, and intermittent meeting of the vocal cords between tiny releases of air, which is propelled towards, through, and past the cords by muscular, diaphragmatic action upon the inflated lungs" (Bishop et al. 15).

When you want to call attention to the source of a quotation—when it is significant that a particular researcher or writer has said what you are about to quote—you may want to identify the person directly as you introduce the quotation. In addition, you may sometimes need to introduce a quotation by providing information about who or what your source is. When this is the case, it is often best to allow a short quotation to retain its original sentence structure within your prose. Do make certain, when using short quotations in this way, that the quotation consists of a complete grammatical sentence or sentences and that it fits logically into the surrounding sentences that you have written.

EXAMPLE

One of the most horrifying books in American literature is Tom Kromer's Waiting for Nothing. Published in 1935, the book draws heavily on the author's own experience as one of the homeless during the Depression. In the introduction, Kromer says, "I had no idea of getting Waiting for Nothing published, therefore, I wrote it just as I felt it, and used the language that stiffs use even when it wasn't always the nicest language in the world" (ii).

Long quotations, called **block quotations**, are set off as separate paragraphs and typed without quotation marks. Different documentation guidelines define block quotations differently. The Modern Language Association (MLA) calls for quotations that run longer than four lines to be set off as block quotations. The American Psychological Association (APA) defines a block quotation as any quotation that has more than 40 words. (See Chapter 41 for further discussion of the different styles of documentation.) Block quotations are indented ten spaces (MLA style) or five spaces (APA style) from the left margin. Since the indentation itself signals a quotation, no quotation marks are necessary. Use block quotations sparingly; they tend to break up the flow of your text. The following is an example of a block quotation that follows MLA style:

> Accompanying the text of Waiting for Nothing is a short autobiograph-
> ical statement by its author, Tom Kromer. He describes the life that
> formed the basis of his book:
>
>> I remained on the fritz for five months and came home. There was
>> no work at home. I bummed to California and then back again to
>> New York and Washington, D.C. I was sentenced to sixty days in
>> Occoquam Prison in Washington for sleeping in an empty building
>> during a storm. (ii)

Turn now to Assignment 40B at the end of the chapter for practice in using quotations in your writing.

EXERCISE 40.5 ANALYZING YOUR USE OF QUOTATIONS, PARAPHRASES, AND SUMMARIES

Assuming you have drafted the body of your research paper, review your draft, paying particular attention to how you have handled quotations, paraphrases, and summaries. Then, using your own paper, answer the following questions. Be specific.

1. What forms do the quotations take? Does the draft use mostly short quotations, quotations that are introduced by references to the source, or block quotations?
2. Do you think the draft quotes often enough? Does it quote too much? Can you cut any quotations without hurting the paper? If so, which ones? Should you add any quotations? If so, where?
3. Count the number of paraphrased and summarized passages from sources in the draft. Do you think there are too many or too few? If so, what should you cut or add?
4. Do you have the bibliographical information for each of the quotations, paraphrases, and summaries you use? If not, which ones do you need to obtain? Make a list.

Completing the Rough Draft: Introduction and Conclusion |40c1, 40c2|

Introduction The material for your introduction lies in your own experience early in your research process. If you can re-create your own initial feeling about your research question—your curiosity, surprise, or anger—you will hook your readers. Your introduction should also clearly set forth your topic and your point of view concerning that topic, and relate your plans for discussion. If you have already written the body of your draft, you know the writing that will follow the introduction. Most frequently, introductions to research papers follow a general-to-specific format (see section 5d).

Another way to look at introductions is to consider what questions they should answer for a reader. In general, introductions should (directly or indirectly) answer these questions, often in this order:

- On what topic does this writing focus?
- What is it about this topic that provokes discussion?
- What will be discussed? (What will not be discussed?)
- What kind of organization can readers expect?

Besides clearly establishing your thesis and the material you will be covering in the body of your essay, your introduction should serve to establish in your readers' minds your own credibility as a researcher and writer (refer to section 4d for more on establishing credibility). This means that you should demonstrate your overall understanding of your topic area and the completeness of your research. It is also important to establish a tone in your introduction that will make your audience feel ready and willing to continue reading. If you begin your essay with offensive language or statements that are unreasonable or carelessly worded, your readers will be inclined to distrust everything else that you say. If your thesis is novel or controversial, be especially careful to establish that you will be presenting detailed and convincing support for your thesis in your essay. (See Chapter 26 for a complete discussion of appropriate tone in college writing.)

If you have real difficulties writing an introduction, your research project may not yet be entirely focused. What specifically are you writing about? Return to your notes and draft, and take inventory again. You may need to do further research.

EXERCISE 40.6 DRAFTING AN INTRODUCTION

Assuming you have drafted the body of your research paper, now draft an introduction. In the left margin, label the major sections, using the questions in the preceding section. Then, referring to Chapter 5, identify the format of the paragraph(s) in your introduction.

Conclusion A conclusion should remind readers of what the writer has told them, give readers ideas about what they should think or do about the issue that has been discussed, and end the essay gracefully. Thus, a conclusion often begins with a summary or restatement of the essay's overall thesis. After working hard on the small points in the body of your paper, you may have trouble restating that overall thesis yourself. One useful strategy here is simply to reread your own writing. Read quickly, and focus on the overall structure of your ideas.

The conclusion also provides you with an opportunity to make a final point. This final point may be a call for agreement, or it may be a call for action; in either case it should arise naturally and directly from the body of your paper. A conclusion is not the place to introduce an entirely new subtopic.

EXERCISE 40.7 DRAFTING A CONCLUSION

You have already drafted the introduction and body of your essay. Now, using your own paper, draft a conclusion. Once you have a complete draft of the conclusion, note its major sections in the left margin.

Reviewing Your Draft |40e|

As you move from information gathering and drafting to revising (which may also include some additional research), you need to make a mental shift. From now on, you need to be both writer *and* reader. What writers try to do at this point is to imagine readers' responses. Better yet, many writers actually seek and use readers' comments. We will discuss two ways you and a reader can work together. Both ways assume you will have at least twenty minutes to devote to one draft; if you and your reader are going to respond to each other's drafts, plan on forty minutes.

Method 1 Begin by asking your respondent to read some parts of your draft aloud to you, particularly any sections you found especially difficult to write. Then ask your reader what he or she understands from that reading. Do not argue with your reader, and do not defend your draft. Your aim is to listen and understand how your writing comes across. Later you will decide which responses you will act on and which you will not.

Method 2 Draw up a list of specific questions you want a reader to address. Drawing up such a list serves two useful purposes. First, it forces you as a writer to determine what qualities you most want your paper to have, which provides you with criteria for revising. Second, it helps your reader focus on the issues that concern you most. Here is a list of generic questions. You could simply use this list, but it would be better for you to develop your own.

Introduction

1. What is the specific topic of this research paper?
2. What do you expect this paper to include in its discussion?
3. Does the introduction include material that tells readers what the writer plans to accomplish in the pages that follow?

Body

4. Is the transition from the introduction to the body smooth or rough?
5. Do the major sections or points in the paper raise questions that the paper does not answer?
6. Does the paper do a good job of relating the major sections or points to each other?

Conclusion

7. Does the conclusion clearly remind the reader of the overall thesis of the paper?

Overall Questions

8. What are the best parts of this draft as it is written?
9. What parts would you *particularly* advise this writer to work on before handing in the final product?

(For additional guidance in seeking and focusing reader response to a rough draft, see section 3c.)

EXERCISE 40.8 ASSESSING READER RESPONSE

Using your own paper, provide answers to the following questions.

1. Examine your completed draft, and then compose a list of at least six questions that you want a respondent to address while reading your paper.
2. Following the directions of your instructor, locate a respondent and use the questions you developed to focus the discussion of your draft. Ask further questions to make sure that you understand your reader's response.
3. Finally, act as a respondent for another research writer. Read carefully and critically, and be as articulate as you can in discussing what you do and do not understand.

Revising, Editing, and Proofreading Your Draft |40f|

Whatever your respondents have told you about your rough draft, you will certainly need to revise it, perhaps many times. Many accomplished writers will revise their work as often as ten or fifteen times; such devotion to the revision process may in fact be a major reason for their success as writers. In college writing you may not need to revise quite so repeatedly, but if you want your work to succeed, do plan to invest a good deal of time in revision.

Chapter 3 covers the revision and editing processes quite thoroughly. The strategies and guidelines it provides, along with ideas from readers, should tell you most of what you need to do in your first revisions. In addition, you may want to ask yourself the following questions before or as you revise:

- Have I presented a reasonable, balanced, and convincing argument in favor of my thesis?
- Have I made as much use of my sources as I might? Conversely, have I established that this draft represents an adequate amount of my own thinking on my subject, as opposed to simply presenting the thinking of others?
- Have I clearly expressed all the points that I need to make?
- Have I made the connections between all those points quite clear?

If you answer no to any of these questions, you should ask yourself what you need to add, delete, reorganize, or reword in order to correct the problem. At this stage of revision, try to concentrate strictly on the content of your essay. If you allow yourself to pay much attention to things like spelling, punctuation, and mechanics, you will lose your train of thought and it may be difficult to regain this focus. Also, do not be discouraged if you conclude during this early revision that you must conduct further research or that your draft is disorganized and must be heavily cut and rewritten. Such efforts may seem monumental, but they are terribly important. If you do not make them, the time you have invested so far will have been fruitless; if you *do* make them, the rewards will be considerable.

As you are revising your research paper, remember: revision is a circular process that you repeat several times until you are satisfied that you have done as much as you can. Keep looking critically at your draft, finding problems or areas for improvement and revising each one as you come to it. Do not try to rewrite every word of your draft from start to finish each time you revise—you will get very bored with your own writing if you do! Work on one section at a time, as the ideas for revision occur to you; then, when you have finished, you can go back and read the whole thing through.

Editing

In editing you address the specific details of writing style and mechanics. Nearly all of these details are covered elsewhere in this book. The following lists address them; you can use these lists to help you determine what you need to do in editing your draft. Also included are cross-references to the chapters in which each detail is covered, so that you can review the material if necessary. (See also Chapter 3 for more on the editing process itself.)

Paragraphing and Sentence Grammar

- Is each of your paragraphs logically complete and carefully organized? (Review Chapter 5.)
- Is each of your sentences grammatically complete? (Review Chapter 6.)
- Have you avoided common grammatical errors such as lack of pronoun-antecedent agreement, incorrect verb forms, fused sentences, shifts in verb tense or in tone, and misplaced or dangling modifiers? (Review Chapters 7–16.)

Style and Tone

- Is your writing interesting and enjoyable to read? Have you done your best to draw your reader into your material? If your answer to either question is no or only partially yes, move on to the following concerns.
- Have you used vivid, memorable language whenever possible? (Review Chapter 21.)
- Have you varied sentence structures and lengths so that your prose does not all sound the same? (Review Chapter 20.)
- Have you subordinated secondary ideas to primary ones so that readers will follow your organization? (Review Chapter 18.)
- Have you used parallel structures correctly? (Review Chapter 19.) Have you established and maintained appropriate diction and tone throughout your draft? (Review Chapters 25 and 26.)

Punctuation and Mechanics

- Finally, examine your draft for correct use of:

    - punctuation (Review Chapters 27–32.)
    - abbreviations and numbers (Review Chapter 34.)
    - italics or underscoring (Review Chapter 35.)
    - hyphenation (Review Chapter 36.)
    - documentation: citation style, bibliography or list of works cited (See Chapter 41.)

In research writing, the editing of punctuation and mechanics requires particular care. Make a point of double-checking all titles, authors' names, periodical names, publication information, and direct quotations to be sure that you have spelled, capitalized, and punctuated each exactly as it appears in the original source. The last thing you should do in editing is to read your entire final draft through slowly and carefully. It takes real patience to find all of your own mistakes, and by this point you may feel like tuning out your own words. If you feel you just cannot look at your work with a fresh eye, this may be a good time to ask a friend or classmate to help out. When this final read-through is done, you will be ready to begin typing, and it is best to begin that work feeling that everything in your draft can now stay exactly as it is.

Chapter 46 will give you instructions on typing and formatting your manuscript. You may want to check with your instructor to see if he or she has any special requirements regarding manuscript formats. Do try to begin this work at a time when you are well rested and alert; you will make fewer errors that way. Also, consider proofreading each paragraph that you type as you complete it. Any mistakes you have made can be corrected at that point without affecting other paragraphs or pages, and this will spare you a good deal of frustration. Note: If you are working on a word processor, you can be more flexible about finding and correcting errors—doing so rarely involves more than a few keystrokes. But you still need to edit and proofread carefully (see Chapter 45).

ASSIGNMENT 40A COMPOSING AN EXPLICIT THESIS STATEMENT

Working with the information you have gathered on your research topic or with another body of information provided by your instructor, complete the following explicit thesis statement by filling in the blanks.

EXAMPLE

In this essay, I plan to examine the theory that there was a conspiracy behind John F. Kennedy's assassination for an audience consisting of my instructor (as well as my classmates and, hypothetically, scholars of twentieth-century American history) and will argue that such a conspiracy must have existed because of (1) extensive, conclusive evidence provided by those who knew Lee Harvey Oswald, (2) analysis of the logistics of the shooting itself, and (3) evidence of a vendetta that developed against Kennedy following the Bay of Pigs incident.

In this essay, I plan to _____

_____

for an audience consisting of _____

_____

and will argue or demonstrate that _____

_____

because of (1) _____,

(2) _____, and

(3) _____ .

Answer the following questions about the sample thesis statement provided at the beginning of this assignment.

1. Is this thesis statement focused enough? Why or why not?

_____

_____

2. Are the three supporting points specified at the end of the thesis statement likely to provide adequate evidence in favor of the writer's argument? Why or why not?

_____

_____

_____

3. Can you imagine any points that might refute this writer's argument? If so, what are they, and how should the writer deal with them and still present a credible case for his or her thesis?

_____

_____

_____

Now answer the following questions about the thesis statement you yourself have written for this assignment.

4. Is your thesis statement focused enough? Why or why not? _____

_____

_____

5. Are your three supporting points likely to provide adequate evidence in favor of your argument? Why or why not?

_____

_____

_____

6. Are there points not mentioned in your thesis statement that might refute your argument? If so, what are they, and how do you plan to deal with them and still present a credible case in favor of your thesis?

_____

_____

_____

7. Has writing this thesis statement made you aware of any gaps in your research? If so, what are they, and how do you plan to fill them?

_____

_____

_____

_____

ASSIGNMENT 40B **USING QUOTATIONS IN YOUR WRITING**

Use either a passage you have found in one of your research sources or one found elsewhere to compose the following three types of quotations: (A) a short quotation that is run in with your own sentence structure; (B) a short quotation for which you provide explanation and introduction but which is not run in with your own sentence; and (C) a long, block quotation. Make sure that you use quotation marks correctly and that your block quotation uses correct margins. Indicate the author, title, and page number for each quotation either in your introduction to the quotation or in a citation following the quoted material. (For now, do not worry about citation style, which will be covered in the next chapter.)

EXAMPLES

A. "A sudden blow" is precisely what one feels on reading those words in Yeats's visionary rendition of Greek myth, "Leda and the Swan." (*Selected Poems* 114)

B. The biographer Phyllis Lee Levin feels that the conditions of Abigail Adams's upbringing may have helped shape her remarkable attitude toward education: "It was a challenging atmosphere, which seemed to inspire young Abigail with . . . a nervous need to acquire valuable knowledge before it eluded her reverent grasp" (*Abigail Adams* 3).

C. Among the most haunting of Shakespeare's songs is the one sung by Ariel in *The Tempest*. It begins

> Full fathom five thy father lies;
> > Of his bones are coral made;
> Those are pearls that were his eyes:
> > Nothing of him that doth fade
> But doth suffer a sea-change
> Into something rich and strange. (1. 2. 397–402)

A. _____

_____

B. _____

_____

_____

_____

C. _____

_____

_____

_____

_____

_____

41

Documenting Sources

The format you use for citing sources and constructing your bibliography depends largely on the discipline you are working in. To be safe, always ask your instructor which format you should use. This chapter will discuss several documentation formats and will present sample references for each. However, when you document your own research paper, you may need to consult the style manual appropriate to your field and chosen format for further information.

The four most commonly used documentation styles, and sources of further information on them, are listed below.

- The Modern Language Association (MLA) style, widely used in the humanities, uses parenthetical source references within the paper. These references lead readers to items listed at the end of the paper under *Works Cited*. (Consult *MLA Handbook for Writers of Research Papers*. 3rd ed. New York: Mod. Lang. Assoc., 1988.)
- The American Psychological Association (APA) style, used in the social sciences, also uses parenthetical source references within the paper. These references lead readers to full source information listed at the end of the paper under *References*. (Consult *Publication Manual of the American Psychological Association*. 3rd ed. Washington: Amer. Psych. Assoc., 1983.)
- The number style, used in the sciences, assigns a number to each source listed at the end of the paper under *Literature Cited*, then includes parenthetical references to the numbers only within the text. (Consult the *CBE Style Manual*. 5th ed. Bethesda: Council of Biology Editors, 1983; the *Handbook for Authors of Papers in American Chemical Society Publications*. Washington, D.C.: American Chemical Society, 1978; the *Style Manual for Guidance in Preparation of Papers*. 3rd ed. New York: American Institute of Physics, 1978; or ask your instructor to recommend a manual.)

- The note-and-bibliography (old MLA) style, used in the humanities, uses superscript numbers that refer readers to a list of notes at the end of the paper. These notes provide source information for each citation. In this documentation style, a separate *Bibliography*, following the *Notes*, lists all the author's sources alphabetically. (Consult the *MLA Handbook*, mentioned previously.)

Modern Language Association (MLA) Style |41a|

MLA Format for the List of Works Cited

To construct your list of works cited, alphabetize your sources by their authors' last names. When a work is unsigned, use the first word of its title, or the second if the title begins with *a, an,* or *the*. If the work is an interview, alphabetize it by the last name of the interviewee.

Begin typing the list on a new page, with the title *Works Cited*, centered, at the top. Do not underline or italicize this title or put it in quotation marks. Leave three blank lines below it before the first list entry.

Type the first line of each entry flush against the left margin. Indent each subsequent line within a single entry five spaces. Type each entry in three sections, each ending with a period: one giving author information, one giving title information, and one giving publication information. Many sources will require only these three sections. Some sources, however, will require that you include additional information, such as editors' and translators' names or original publication information if the edition you are using is a reprint (see Exercise 41.3 for examples of such variations). Consult the *MLA Handbook* for guidance in such cases.

A book with one author

```
Goedicke, Patricia.  The Wind of Our Going.  Port Townsend: Copper Canyon
      Press, 1985.
```

A book with two or three authors

```
Kennedy, X. J., and Dorothy M. Kennedy.  The Bedford Guide for College
      Writers. New York: St. Martin's, 1987.
```

Note that the first author's last name determines the alphabetic placement; the second author's name is typed first name first. Do not use the ampersand (&) as a substitute for *and*, even if the source itself does so. If you have a work by more than three authors, give only the first one listed, and follow it by the Latin abbreviation *et al.*, which means "and others": Britton, James, et al. *The Development of Writing Abilities*. London: Macmillan, 1975. Note that the title of the work is underlined or italicized.

A book edited by one individual

Kazin, Alfred, ed. The Open Form: Essays for Our Time. New York: Har-
court, 1961.

The abbreviation *ed.* identifies Kazin as this book's editor.

A book with an editor (or translator) and an author

Bush, Douglas, ed. Selected Poems and Letters. By John Keats. Riverside
Editions. New York: Houghton, 1959.

This entry indicates that the researcher has cited some portion of Bush's
editorial work (compare to the next example, which indicates that the researcher has *not* cited the editor's work). This book also happens to be part
of a series; the name of the series (Riverside Editions) appears after the title
and the editor's and author's names, and it is not underlined or italicized. If
you were using a translated work, the abbreviation *trans.* would appear
after the translator's name, in the same position as *ed.* in the preceding
entry.

A book with an author and an editor (or translator)

Keats, John. Selected Poems and Letters. Ed. Douglas Bush. Riverside
Editions. New York: Houghton, 1959.

This entry indicates the researcher cited Keats's work, not that of the
editor. If both the editor and the author are cited in the paper, both should
be listed in the *Works Cited*, which means including two entries.

A work in an anthology

Pound, Ezra. "The River-Merchant's Wife: A Letter." The Pocket Book of
Modern Verse. Rev. 3rd ed. Ed. Oscar Williams. New York: Simon and
Schuster, 1972. 251-252.

This format applies to any work in an anthology or reader, whether it is a
poem, story, essay, article, or anything else.

An article in a journal with continuous pagination

Isern, Thomas D. "An American Dream: The Family Farm in Kansas." The
Midwest Quarterly 26 (1985): 357-367.

Here the number 26 indicates the volume number; the year of publication
follows in parentheses, and a colon precedes the page numbers.

An article in a journal that pages issues separately

```
Jacobs, Naomi.  "Lies, Libels and the Truth of Fiction."  Missouri Review
     8.2 (1985): 164-178.
```

The number 8 refers to the volume, and the number 2 refers to the issue.

An article in a weekly or biweekly publication

```
Daugherty, Tracy.  "Low Rider."  New Yorker 23 Nov. 1987: 40-48.
```

Notice that the day, month, and year are specified.

Interviews

```
Vars, Mayor John.  Personal Interview.  9 Dec. 1987.
```

Here the researcher has personally interviewed Mayor John Vars.

EXERCISE 41.1 PREPARING A LIST OF WORKS CITED

Below you will find publication data for a variety of sources. Use this information to draw up a list of works cited.

1. Book title: *Naked Poetry*
   Editors: Stephen Berg and Robert Mesey
   Poem quoted: "A Day Begins"
   Poem's author: Denise Levertov
   Publisher: Bobbs-Merrill
   Date of publication: 1969
   Place of publication: Indianapolis, Indiana
   Poem found on page 140
2. Personal interview with Professor Heather Emberson on May 23, 1987
3. Story by Louise Erdrich
   Title: "The Plunge of the Brave"
   Published in the *New England Review and Breadloaf Quarterly* in the first issue of the seventh volume in the Autumn of 1984 (This journal pages issues separately.)
   Appeared on pages 120–136
4. Book title: *Tell Me a Riddle*
   Author: Tillie Olsen
   Date of publication: 1961
   Publisher: Dell Publishing Co., Inc.
   Place of publication: New York

MLA Format for Parenthetical Citations

MLA style features source citations enclosed in parentheses. The information you include in the parentheses varies. You need to include enough information in the parentheses so that your readers can locate the correct source in your list of works cited. Use Table 1 to determine what should be included in your parenthetical citation.

Suppose the following is a portion of your research paper:

> As Rachel Carson says in The Sea around Us, "Nowhere in all the sea does life exist in such bewildering abundance as in the surface waters."

This quotation is introduced by the author's name and the work's title. Assume this is the only work by Carson that you cite in your paper. Reading from the first line of Table 1, you can see that your parenthetical citation need only include a page number:

> ". . . the surface waters" (16).

Note that the parenthetical citation is placed *between* the closing quotation mark and the end punctuation. A parenthetical citation is always placed at a logical break in your sentence's syntax between the closing quotation mark and the next punctuation mark, whether it is a period, comma, semicolon, colon, or dash. The only exception to this rule is the citation for an indented display quotation, which, as you recall, does not

What information do you provide in introducing the material you are citing?		Is this the only source by the author(s) you are citing?		Your parenthetical citation should include:		
author's name	work's title	yes	no	author's name	work's title	page no.
X	X	X				X
X	X		X		X	X
		X		X		X
			X	X	X	X
X		X				X
X			X		X	X
	X	X		X		X
	X		X	X	X	X

Table 1 MLA Parenthetical Source Citations: What to Include

have quotation marks. In this case, the parenthetical citation follows the end punctuation of the quoted passage (see section 40d for an example).

Here is another variation:

```
As one author suggests, "Nowhere in all the sea does life exist in such
bewildering abundance as in the surface waters" (Carson, Sea 16).
```

This time, the introduction does not include the author's name or the work's title. Further, we are assuming that you are citing at least two works by Carson in your paper. Reading from the fourth line of Table 1, we can see that the citation should include the author's last name, a shortened version of the work's title, and the page number. (Make certain, by the way, that when you cite a work's title more than once, you always use the same shortened version—otherwise readers will believe you are referring them to other works.)

All MLA parenthetical references use the same general format. Here are the specifications for a few more complex references. For works by two or three authors, list all the authors' last names in the order in which they appear in the source. The word *and* precedes the last name listed:

```
"Vertical thin lines, for example, make a package appear taller, while
horizontal wide stripes cause it to appear shorter" (Pride and Ferrell
332).
```

For works by more than three authors, list only the name of the first author followed by *et al.*:

```
"The imagination of Romantic writers was, indeed, preoccupied with the
fact and idea of revolution" (Abrams et al. 5).
```

Sometimes you will want to quote something that another author has also quoted. In such cases, use *qtd. in* ("quoted in") to show where you found this material:

```
Charlotte Brontë apparently found Jane Austen's novels too tame for those
revolutionary times: "She ruffles her reader with nothing vehement . . ."
(qtd. in Abrams et al. 21).
```

For multiple-volume works, list the volume number first, followed by a colon and then the page number:

```
"Modernist writers prized experimentation, and gradually even sought to
blur the line between poetry and prose" (Foerster et al. 3: 150).
```

Note that when the author's name, the work's title, and the page number are all included in the text that introduces or identifies a quotation, no parenthetical citation is necessary.

American Psychological Association Style |41b|

APA *Format for References*

When following APA style, you must include all sources referred to by author or publication date in your list of references. (Your instructor may ask that you list all works you have consulted, rather than only those you have cited. If so, title your list *Bibliography*.) The list of references falls after the body of your essay, but before any appendixes you may be including. To alphabetize and type your list of references, follow the instructions for the MLA list of works cited, with the following exceptions:

- Title your list *References* rather than *Works Cited*.
- Allow only one blank line between the title and the first list entry.

Your entries should follow this format:

```
Last name of author, first name or initial and middle initials, if
    available. (Year of publication). Title. Publication Location:
    Publisher.
```

Note the following specific examples.

A book with one author

```
Coon, D. (1980). Introduction to psychology: Exploration and application.
    New York: West Publishing.
```

Note that book titles are underlined or italicized and that only the first word of the title and the first word of the subtitle are capitalized. Proper nouns, of course, are also capitalized.

A book with two or more authors

```
Newcombe, F., and Ratcliff, G. (1978). Defining females: The nature of
    women in society. New York: Wiley.
```

Note that names of publishers are shortened—here we have *Wiley* for *John Wiley and Sons*. However, names of university presses should be spelled out.

A book with an editor

```
Waggoner, H. H. (Ed.).  (1970).  Selected tales and sketches. New York:
    Holt.
```

An article in a journal with continuous pagination

```
Leder, G. C. (1984).  Sex differences in attributions of success and
    failure.  Psychological Reports, 54, 57-58.
```

Note that *both* the journal title and the volume number are underlined or italicized. Also note that neither underlining nor quotation marks are used with the article title, and that the first letter of all major words in the periodical title is capitalized.

An article in a magazine

```
Wallach, L. (1983, September).  Sex and the naked brain.  Science Digest,
    p. 87.
```

Note that the month of publication is included with the year. If the issue date included a specific day, it would also be included as follows: (1983, September 7). Note also that the page number follows the magazine title, and unlike the preceding example, includes an abbreviation—*p.* for a single page, *pp.* for more than one page.

EXERCISE 41.2 PREPARING A LIST OF REFERENCES

Preceding this exercise are several examples of APA format as it applies to specific kinds of reference entries. Locate three sources, each requiring a different sort of reference entry. Photocopy the title page (if your source is a book) or the first page (if your source is an article.) Also copy any other publication information you need from the source. Finally, using your own paper, draw up a three-entry list of references listing these three sources. Staple your photocopies to that list.

APA Format for Parenthetical Citations

As with the MLA style, source citations using the APA style must contain enough information to allow readers to locate the source in the list of references. Most of the time that means providing readers with the author's name and with the year of publication, either in the text or in a parenthetical citation. Note the following examples.

Both author and year included in text; no citation needed

```
George Steiner asserted in 1971 that music and mathematics hold special
status as amazing and uniquely human endeavors.
```

Citation with date only

Steiner (1971) asserts that music and mathematics are two particularly
amazing and uniquely human endeavors.

Citation with author and date

One critic and essayist identifies music and mathematics as sources of awe
(Steiner, 1971).

Citation with author, date, and page number

One critic and essayist argues that "music and mathematics are among the
preeminent wonders of the race" (Steiner, 1971, p. 50.)

Note that the APA style does allow for citations that include page references when specific passages are being cited and when direct quotations are
used.

The APA style has special provisions for sources with multiple authors
and for more than one source by the same author. If a work has two authors,
cite both by last name only, and link them with an ampersand: *(Ede &
Lunsford, 1987)*. If a work has more than two authors, cite every author (up
to five) in the first reference, and in subsequent references cite only the first
author together with *et al.* The first citation would look like this: (*Young,
Becker, & Pike, 1970*). Subsequent citations would look like this: (*Young et
al., 1970*). If your source has more than five authors, use only the name of the
first author followed by *et al.* for all citations.

Suppose an author has written two articles or books published in the
same year, and you wish to cite both. Identify the first source using a small *a*
following the date, and use a small *b* following the date of the second. Thus,
the first of two sources by Linda Flower would be cited as (*Flower, 1982a*),
while the second would be cited as (*Flower, 1982b*). If the same author has
written two of your sources but the publication dates are different, the
different dates will distinguish the two sources.

The APA style groups personal interviews, letters, memos, and the like
under the general category of personal communications. Anything in this
category is cited in the paper itself but does *not* appear on the *References*
page. A citation for a personal interview would look like this: (*T. Brussat,
personal communication, Dec. 10, 1987*).

Number Style |41c|

If your instructor requires that you document your paper following the
number style, be sure to get explicit guidelines from him or her, as this style
varies from discipline to discipline. In number-style documentation, citations are signaled by a number in parentheses, which corresponds to an

entry in the *Literature Cited* list at the end of the paper. The following are fictional samples of a number style citation and its corresponding Literature Cited entry.

Text reference

Studies have proven that the sun's ultra-violet (UV) rays contribute measurably to the risk of skin cancer (1).

Literature Cited *entry*

1. Livermore, T. Causes of Skin Cancer, Harbinger Press, Plainfield, 1982.

Note-and-Bibliography Style |41d|

Writers using the note-and-bibliography style signal a citation by typing a small number that is raised above the line of type, like this:[1]. Each citation has its own number, and each number corresponds to a footnote (listed at the bottom of the page) or an endnote (listed on a separate page at the end of the paper). A bibliography listing all works cited in alphabetical order follows both the paper and the endnotes. The format for this bibliography is the same as that for the MLA Works Cited list.

Note-and-Bibliography Format for Notes

Footnotes are typed four lines below the last line of text on a page. Individual notes are single-spaced, but an additional space should be allowed between notes. The first line of any note (foot- or end-) indents five spaces, and subsequent lines within the note are typed flush against the left margin. A note should contain the following information:

Books

- citation number
- author's name, first name first, followed by a comma
- title of book, underlined or italicized
- opening parenthesis, followed by place of publication, followed by a colon
- name of publisher, followed by a comma
- year of publication, followed by closing parenthesis
- page number(s)

Articles

- citation number
- author's name, first name first, followed by a comma
- title of article followed by a comma, and in quotation marks
- title of magazine, underlined or italicized
- volume and/or issue number (for articles from scholarly journals)
- date of publication, followed by colon (for journals, the year enclosed in parentheses)
- page number(s)

Once a source's full information has been presented in a note, subsequent references to it can be abbreviated. See the examples that follow.

Note citing a book

    ¹John Barron, <u>KGB Today: The Hidden Hand</u> (New York: Reader's Digest Press, 1983) 25.

Note citing an article

    ²Janice Flanagan, "Politicians Losing Heart," <u>Heartland Gazette</u> 13 July 1988: B27.

A subsequent reference to the same source

    ³Barron 98.

If another work by the same author is listed among your notes, include an abbreviated form of the title of the work you are citing for a second time, as in

    ³Barron, <u>KGB</u> 98.

Finally, if you will be citing a particular source many times, you may indicate this in your first note on it. Later citations can then be documented by providing page references in parentheses in the text; there is no need to include further notes. Here is an example:

    ¹Anthony Trollope, <u>The Prime Minister</u> (New York: Oxford UP, 1983) 245. All subsequent references to this work will appear in the text.

REVIEW EXERCISE 41.3 DOCUMENTING SOURCES

Photocopy three passages from your research essay or draft three brief passages in which you quote or otherwise draw on sources that require documentation. On a separate piece of paper, document all three, constructing an MLA-style citation and an APA-style citation for each one. Then construct bibliographical listings for all three passages in the two styles. See the following examples.

PASSAGE

    Einstein finds Constanze Weber to have been an undeserving, ill-chosen wife to Mozart. He describes her as "wholly uneducated" and as having had "no sense of the fitness of things."

MLA CITATION

One scholar finds Constanze Weber to have been an undeserving, ill-chosen wife to Mozart. He describes her as "wholly uneducated" and as having had "no sense of the fitness of things" (Einstein 70).

APA CITATION

One scholar finds Constanze Weber to have been an undeserving, ill-chosen wife to Mozart. He describes her as "wholly uneducated" and as having had "no sense of the fitness of things" (Einstein, 1945/1971, 70).

MLA BIBLIOGRAPHICAL LISTING

Einstein, Alfred. Mozart: His Character, His Work. Trans. Arthur Mendel and Nathan Broder. New York: Oxford UP, 1971.

APA BIBLIOGRAPHICAL LISTING

Einstein, A. (1971). Mozart: His Character, His Work (A. Mendel and N. Broder, Trans.). New York: Oxford University Press. (Original work published 1945)

Academic Writing

42

Writing in Different Disciplines

Every discipline uses its own vocabulary, its own writing conventions, and its own standards of proof. Whenever you enter a new discipline—whether history or experimental psychology or computer science—you will need to become familiar with its vocabulary and expectations as quickly as possible. This chapter will help you devise strategies for exploring new areas of knowledge.

Analyzing Academic Assignments and Expectations |42a|

When a college instructor presents you with an assignment, that instructor is also conveying a set of requirements—a set of expectations particular to that discipline and to that assignment. The following six questions should help you analyze any college writing task:

1. What does this assignment ask me to do—summarize? explain? argue? evaluate? interpret? illustrate? define? If it asks me to do more than one of these activities, does it specify an order in which they should be done?
2. Do I understand the vocabulary of the assignment? (For example, do I know what is meant by the term *case study*?)
3. What do I need to know or find out in order to complete this assignment? Will this assignment require that I reread or do research?
4. Does the assignment require, suggest, or exclude a particular organizational format? Is there a suggested length?
5. What tone is appropriate for this assignment? Should the writing be formal or informal?
6. Can I locate an example of this assignment? Will the instructor provide copies of superior papers?

EXERCISE 42.1 ANALYZING ASSIGNMENTS IN DIFFERENT DISCIPLINES

On a separate sheet of paper, copy down two writing assignments from two of your other courses—for example, psychology and biology, or art history and economics. Analyze each, answering in as much detail as possible the previous six questions for analyzing a college writing task. Then answer the following questions.

1. What common elements do these two assignments have?
2. What differences do they have?
3. How are their differences related to the fact that they are from two separate disciplines?

Understanding Disciplinary Vocabularies |42b|

Whenever you enter a class devoted to a new field of knowledge or read a textbook in a new field, you will encounter specialized terminology. How can you learn the meaning of these new terms efficiently? The following four strategies can help:

1. As you take notes from class discussions or lectures, write down and circle any terms that are unfamiliar. Look for these terms in your assigned reading for this class; they may be defined there.
2. Read with your notebook handy, and again note any unfamiliar terms. Write down the sentence, or at least the phrase, that provides a context for the word. After seeing a term two or three times, you should be able to write a tentative definition.
3. Ask your instructor or a librarian if this particular field has a specialized dictionary or handbook of terms. Perhaps one of your textbooks has a glossary. Use those resources to look up all the unfamiliar terms you have listed, even if you think you know their meanings.
4. Begin to use the new terms whenever you can, both in speech and in writing.

EXERCISE 42.2 MASTERING NEW TERMINOLOGY

On a separate sheet of paper, respond to the following instructions and questions.

1. Write down at least three new terms you have learned this semester in your courses, and provide a definition for each.
2. Explain how you learned the meanings of these terms.
3. Write down any new terms for which you have not yet learned the meanings. How will you find out what these terms mean?

4. Carry out the plan you have devised for learning the new terms that you listed in your answer to question 3. End this exercise by listing the new meanings you have found.

_____

Identifying a Discipline's Style |42c|

Along with learning the specialized terminology in a new field, you should become familiar with the writing style commonly used in that discipline. Your most immediate examples of writing in a discipline will most likely be your required texts. Textbooks are often written to help those new to a particular field. Your required reading for a particular course may also include original sources. For example, for an anthropology course you might read a work by Margaret Mead; for an economics course you might read a work by John Maynard Keynes. Such original sources should give you an idea of what written communication typically looks like in this new discipline. When you read original sources, you should pay particular attention to matters of style, content, and form. The best way to do this is to find a representative piece of writing in that field and to answer the following questions about it:

1. In general, how long are the sentences and paragraphs?
2. Are verbs generally active or passive—and why?
3. Does the writer use the first person (*I*) or prefer another term of self-reference, such as *one* or *the investigator*?
4. How would you describe the overall tone—formal? informal?
5. Does the writer include graphic aids, such as charts or diagrams?

Understanding the Use of Evidence in Different Disciplines |42d|

A writer in a particular discipline must be aware of the kinds of content (arguments and evidence) that readers in the discipline will find persuasive. Objective, quantifiable data is usually the best kind of evidence in the physical and social sciences; however, the same kind of data may be inappropriate—or even impossible to obtain—in a literary study, in which the writer's opinion is likely to be of the greatest importance. As you study a particular field, you will gradually become aware of its standards of proof. As you read your sources, ask yourself the following questions about the evidence they provide:

1. How are precedents and authority used in this discipline? What or who counts as an authority?
2. Is data obtained through fieldwork or formal experimentation important to writings in this discipline? If so, what are the specific standards such data must meet? How are such data presented in the writings?

3. How does this discipline use logical reasoning? How are definition, cause and effect, analogies, and examples used?
4. How are primary and secondary sources used in this discipline?

You may want to discuss these issues with your instructor in addition to analyzing them on your own.

Using Conventional Patterns and Formats |42e|

Once you have become familiar with the generally accepted writing style and the standards of proof in a new field, you need to consider the generally accepted ways of organizing and presenting information. The typical laboratory report in a discipline will generally follow a set format that will be presented to you in your laboratory manuals. A model case study appearing in a business text might be divided into a series of subheadings: *Introduction, Problem Analysis, Conclusions,* and *Recommendations*. A case study in sociology would follow its own typical organizational plan.

When you are required to follow a prescribed format, you should ask your instructor for models, or locate a model for yourself by looking at major scholarly journals in the field. When examining these models, ask yourself the following questions:

1. What types of essays are common in this field? What is the purpose of each type?
2. What does a reader expect to find in each type of essay?
3. How is each particular type of essay organized? What are the main parts of each type? Are these labeled with conventional headings?
4. How does each particular type of essay show connections between ideas? What points does the organization of each type emphasize?

EXERCISE 42.3 INVESTIGATING WRITING STYLE IN A NEW DISCIPLINE

Identify a discipline that is entirely new to you or one to which you have only recently been introduced. Perhaps one of your classes this term constitutes your introduction to that field. Using your own paper, provide the information asked for in the following instructions and questions. You will need to have access to one journal in the particular field you are discussing. You may also need to interview a professional in this field. Make your answers as detailed and specific as possible.

1. Name the field you are investigating.
2. Name a major journal read by professionals in that field.
3. What does this journal publish—articles, stories, reviews, experimental results, discussions of theory, personal essays? Describe the contents of a typical issue.

4. Look through the journal and identify one representative article. Give the article's title, author, and publication data.

5. Comment on the organization of this article. Has the writer used charts, graphs, or other illustrations? Has the writer used subheadings? So far as you can tell, has the writer invented this particular organization, or has he or she used a conventional format that you see repeated in similar articles? Explain your answers, referring to at least one other article in the journal you are using.

6. Photocopy the first page of the article, and refer to it as you respond to the following questions. Attach the copy to your answers.

> **a.** Does this writing depend heavily on vocabulary that is unfamiliar to you, or does it employ vocabulary that persons who are new to this field could understand? Quote a sentence to support your answer.
>
> **b.** Does the writing call attention to the writer, or does it have the opposite effect? Explain, and again quote a sentence to support your answer.
>
> **c.** Does this writing refer frequently to the writing of others? If it does, quote one such reference.

7. Think about yourself as a writer in this discipline. How would doing this kind of writing be different from the writing you have done in the past?

43

Writing Essay Examinations

An essay examination demands a deeper understanding of a subject than a true/false or multiple-choice test does. It also demands that writers manage their test-taking time wisely. This chapter will help you to meet both of these requirements.

Preparing for Essay Examinations |43a|

With the first lecture you listen to, the first discussion you participate in, the first reading you do in textbooks, you are generally preparing for a later examination. Taking careful notes to highlight important concepts and pertinent details is one of the most reliable ways to prepare yourself for a later test. If your own note-taking habits are intuitive and nonsystematic, you may need to adopt a more disciplined approach.

Consider, for instance, recording notes and phrases on one page in your notebook and your questions and comments on these notes and phrases on the facing page. (Or divide a single page down the middle and arrange your notes on the right-hand side and your comments and questions on the left, following the instructions given in Exercise 43.1.) The key here is to force yourself, if necessary, to add those questions and comments. This approach will lead you to examine and reflect upon what you are recording, rather than simply copying it down mindlessly. Practiced consistently, inquiring note taking also yields another benefit: your subject becomes more interesting because you become more involved in it.

As you become more involved in and knowledgeable about your subject, try anticipating the questions you might be asked about it on your examination. Which points have been emphasized in your lectures? Which points are complex—perhaps so complex that there was not time to cover them completely during class itself? Once you have formulated possible questions, you will naturally begin considering how you would answer them. Actually writing out answers will help you understand your material even more clearly. If you time yourself as you write out practice answers, you will have the added benefit of seeing how long it takes you to consider, organize, and write your answers.

EXERCISE 43.1 PREPARING FOR AN ESSAY EXAMINATION

For this exercise, divide a sheet of your own paper vertically down the center. Then follow these instructions.

1. Take your own notes from one of your classes and copy them onto the left-hand side. In the right-hand column, add as many comments and questions as you can formulate (try to come up with at least four).
2. Based on these comments, write down three possible examination questions on another sheet of paper.
3. Now write out an answer to the second of your three possible questions. Allow yourself only twenty minutes.
4. How much did you write in twenty minutes? Did you finish the answer? Were you able to include details? Discuss how the time limit affected your writing.

Analyzing Essay Examination Questions |43b|

During an essay examination itself, the first thing you do is quite obvious: you read the directions and the questions. Knowing the kinds of questions that often appear on examinations should give you more time to call to mind and organize your content.

Most essay examination questions are composed of two kinds of terms: strategy terms and content terms. The strategy terms are often imperative verbs such as *analyze, contrast, define, discuss, argue,* and *describe.* Each of these terms defines both a pattern of thinking and a pattern of organization. When you realize this, you can outline an answer quickly. The content words give you your topic. Paying close attention to content words helps ensure that you will answer the question as it has been asked.

Consider this example:

strategy term	content terms
Discuss	affirmative action as it affects you and society.

What content does this question specify as the focus for your answer? If you look closely, you will see it defines two content areas: *affirmative action as it affects you* and *affirmative action as it affects society*. Thus two related questions have been posed in one sentence. Readers who do not analyze this question carefully might answer only the first half.

In addition, many essay questions are made up of several questions following one number. For example, a professor might easily combine these two questions:

> Define capital punishment as applied and administered in the state of Utah. Is the Utah law just?

Notice that the second question does not contain a strategy term, even though one is implied. In such cases, you must decide what the question seeks. In this example, the question seems most likely to call for an evaluation.

EXERCISE 43.2 ANALYZING ESSAY EXAMINATION QUESTIONS

Using your own paper, write a brief description of what you believe each of the following strategy terms asks you to do; then discuss how you would organize an essay in response to that term.

    1. Analyze   **4.** Discuss
    2. Contrast   **5.** Argue
    3. Define   **6.** Describe

For each of the following sample essay questions, identify the strategy term(s) and explain each. Then identify the content term(s).

7. Explain the major events of Huck's education in *Huckleberry Finn*.
8. Define the word *Zen* as you now understand it based on your readings.
9. Analyze Lincoln's Gettysburg Address; explain what has made this speech so enduring.
10. Evaluate the Monroe Doctrine in light of current events in Central and Latin America. Is the Monroe Doctrine applicable today?
11. Compare post–World War I Germany with post–World War II Germany.

Thinking Through Your Answer, Sketching Its Organization, and Beginning to Write | 43c, 43d |

When you write an essay exam, how you use your time becomes almost as important as how much you know about your subject. For example, if the test contains two questions and each is worth 50 percent of your grade, you must be careful not to devote all your time to just one of them. Always begin by looking over the entire test and calculating how much time you should spend on each part of it.

When you have planned how to divide your time, begin by answering the question that seems easiest. (Answering one question successfully will give you energy and confidence for the rest.) Evaluate the question in terms of what it specifically asks you to do, and begin to sketch the answer in outline form. This outline should be quite informal: simply position major points at the left and explanations beneath each point. The essay itself then becomes a matter of following the outline, using sentences and paragraphs to make yourself understood as clearly and completely as time allows.

EXERCISE 43.3 A PRACTICE ESSAY EXAMINATION

Assume that you must respond to the following sample question in an essay examination. Use your own paper to answer the questions after the sample question.

Compare the process of writing an essay examination as presented in this chapter with the process you have used for essay questions in the past. Discuss the differences and similarities.

1. Analyze the question by following these two steps:

    a) Identify the strategy terms and indicate what they ask you to do.
    b) Identify the content terms.

2. Sketch an outline based on your analysis.
3. Now write your answer. Work quickly, note how long you take, and do not revise.
4. Based on your answers to questions 1–3, describe your overall performance in answering the sample question. Use the following questions as guidelines in preparing your description.

    a) What part of the process worked particularly well for you? Why?
    b) What do you still need to practice? Do you need to work more quickly, or more slowly?

Revising and Editing Your Answer |43e|

Essay examinations rarely provide time for wholesale revision. This fact makes your outline even more important than it might have appeared at first. Though large-scale revision is usually not possible in a timed examination, smaller scale rewording and correcting are certainly possible. You should try to save some time for such rewording and correcting.

The first step in revision is rereading your answer. In most cases, we think more quickly than we write. This disparity often results in words being omitted or whole sentences being left out. As you reread, keep the following questions for revision in mind:

- Has my answer been worded so that it clearly responds to the question?
- Are all the major points of my outline included in my answer?
- Are the transitions from point to point clear and logical?
- Are the major points developed with sufficient clarity and detail?
- Have any sentences or words been left out?
- Has punctuation been used correctly?
- Is my handwriting legible?

Under tight constraints, you will probably be able to reread and revise only once, so that means keeping all of these questions in mind as you read.

EXERCISE 43.4 REREADING AND CORRECTING YOUR ANSWER

Using the draft you wrote for Exercise 43.3, respond to the following instructions and questions on your own paper.

1. Reread and correct your draft, keeping the preceding questions for revision in mind. Do not recopy the draft; simply make your corrections on the original. Check the clock before you begin, and write down your starting time; also note the time when you finish.

2. List the four most important changes you had to make.

3. How long did it take you to make these changes?

4. When reading over and revising your answers in an essay examination in the future, what will you particularly need to watch for?

EXERCISE 43.5 TIMED SAMPLE ESSAY EXAMINATION

PART ONE

You have forty-five minutes to respond to the following question, using your own paper. Time yourself, and do not exceed the limit.

Discuss the writing process you believe will be most useful to you when you are required to write essay examinations. Detail this process step by step.

PART TWO

1. Evaluate your performance in completing Part One. What worked well for you and what did not?

2. Given all you know about yourself as a writer and all you know about essay examinations, what two pieces of advice do you have for yourself when it comes to completing essay examinations? Be specific.

PART

Writing for Nonacademic Audiences

Writing for Business

Preparing Business Communications: Style and Format |44a|

Business writing differs considerably from academic writing, particularly in the question of audience. Consider the general standards of most college instructors as they read essays. Most teachers value the careful presentation of background information, which leads to the focus of an essay—a thesis, which is then illustrated or proved by means of ample detail. The pace of an academic essay is thoughtful, certainly not hurried.

Business writers have little patience with writing based on the academic model. For business readers, time is literally money. They read in order to act. They read only as much as they need. They prefer reading summaries to reading long discussions; they would rather read recommendations first, not the lengthy analysis that leads to them. These are the main features of much business writing:

- It is written for a particular (often small) audience.
- It is written to be used by that audience in practical ways.
- It is structured carefully and presented with the use of subheadings, lists, illustrations, or graphs so that it can be read and understood quickly.
- It places great emphasis on formal correctness, which involves both using the proper conventional form for a given situation and using correct grammar, punctuation, and spelling.

The classic business memo epitomizes these features of business writing. It has a set form that is easy to skim quickly. It opens with a line identifying the writer, then one identifying the audience, and finally one indicating the subject or point of the memo. There usually follows a paragraph offering additional information needed by the audience to understand the significance of the communication. The memo is a model of brevity. Any errors in form or language are glaring in this type of communication.

Business Writing Style

Like any other specialized field of activity, business does possess its share of specific terms. Using specialized terminology is both common and necessary if it makes your content accurate and is familiar to your readers. That does not mean that business writing should sound pretentious or evasive. Here are six guidelines for clear business writing.

1. Anticipate your readers' need for detail and explanation, and tailor your content accordingly. If you are not sure what your readers need, ask.
2. In memos longer than a page, make your organization clear by using subheadings to identify blocks of content. That way, a reader can skim your headings and see the overall picture. Subheadings also make it easier for readers to locate specific details.
3. Keep sentences and paragraphs relatively short, so that your readers can work quickly through the text.
4. Though keeping sentences relatively short, try to vary sentence length and structure.
5. Use simple and specific wording rather than complex, vague, abstract phrasing. Is not *overspending* the same thing as *utilization in excess of available budgetary resources*, for example?
6. Use active verbs wherever possible. The active voice often results in more concise prose.

EXERCISE 44.1 REVISING TO CREATE APPROPRIATE BUSINESS PROSE

Each of the following sentences is wordy and unnecessarily convoluted. Using your own paper, translate the sentences into clearer business prose.

1. A marketing approach specifically designed to reach particular market segments ought to be implemented at the earliest point in time following the achievement of financial backing and the decision by management to commence production.

2. Currently it is estimated by the manager of the quality assurance group that the level of nondesirable outcomes resulting from stress conditions will be kept at an acceptable minimum level assuming the adoption of numerous nonmajor alterations in current design specification.

3. We regret to inform you that we are forced by rapidly escalating operational expenditures to seek from you an increased infusion of capital into the company in exchange for an unchanged, identical level of service.

4. The unexpected onset of illness in several personnel together with the arrival of unseasonably difficult and unexpected meteorological conditions has resulted in the loss of several working days.

Writing Business Letters

Courtesy and the efficient presentation of information are the most crucial elements of any business correspondence. To be sure that you have achieved these elements, check the following in your business letters.

Recipient's Name, Job Title, Company, and Address It is essential that you spell and punctuate all of these items correctly. Double check each by phoning the company, or consulting a business directory at the library. Remember, too, that men should be addressed as *Mr.* and women as *Ms.*, unless you know for a fact that a given woman prefers *Miss* or *Mrs.* It is also acceptable to use a person's full name only, without *Mr.* or *Ms.*, in an address.

The Tone of Your Prose Your business writing should be formal but simple, respectful but not apologetic (unless you truly owe your recipient an apology for a specific reason).

The Content of Your Letter Be sure you have stated all that your recipient needs to know (this may be quite different from all that you would like to tell him or her), but have not included anything unnecessary or extraneous. Remember to state who you are, where you can be contacted, why you are writing, and what you are asking of your recipient. Also remember to thank him or her for any time or effort reading and responding to your letter may involve.

Your Complimentary Close Choose simple, standard closing sentiments—such as *Sincerely yours*, and *Very truly yours*,—rather than long and elaborate ones. Signing off in innovative and clever ways will not generally impress your readers.

Business Letter Formats

Successful business writers know that business readers expect certain kinds of formats for written communication. Several letter formats are in current use. This chapter will discuss three: the traditional indented format, the modified block format, and the full block format.

The Traditional Indented Format This letter format (shown in Figure 3) features paragraphs that are indented five spaces, and double spacing between paragraphs. The writer's address and the date are positioned at the top of the page, aligned at the center. The writer's signature block is also aligned at the center of the page, at the bottom of the letter. At least one or as many as four line spaces should separate the date line from the line on which you type the recipient's name. One line space should separate the last paragraph from the line on which you type your complimentary close; three line spaces separate the complimentary close from the line on which you type your name (your signature then goes in that three-line space).

```
                                    Writer's Street Address
                                    Writer's City, State  Zip Code
                                    Date


   Recipient's Name, Title
   Recipient's Organization
   Organization Street Address
   Organization City, State  Zip Code

   Dear Name of Recipient:

       First sentence of the first paragraph of the body goes here, indented
   five spaces. Paragraph continues X X X X X X X X X X X X X X X X X X X X
   X X X X X X X X X X X X X X X X X X X X X X X X X X X X X X X X X X X X X
   X X X X X X X X X X X X X X X X X X X X X X X X X X X X X X X X X X X X X
   X X X X X X X X X X X X X X X X X X X X ...

       Second paragraph X X X X X X X X X X X X X X X X X X X X X X X X X X X
   X X X X X X X X X X X X X  X X X X X X X X X X X X X X X X X X X X X X X X
   X X X X X X ...

       Third paragraph X X X X X X X X X X X X X X X X X X X X X X X X X X X X
   X X X X X X X X X X X X X X X X X X X X X X X X X X X X X X X X X X X X X X
   X X X X X ...

                                    Yours sincerely,


                                    (Writer's signature here)


                                    Writer's name typed
                                    Writer's title (optional)
                                    Writer's phone number (optional)

   ABC:xyz: (initials of writer; initials of secretary or typist)
   Enc: names of documents enclosed (optional)
   cc: names of other individuals who will receive copies of this letter (used
       only if you are sending copies)
```

Figure 3   The Traditional Indented Format

The Modified Block Format The modified block format is perhaps the most frequently used in business correspondence. It is prepared exactly as the traditional indented format is, except that it eliminates paragraph indentations. The first line of each new paragraph is aligned with the left-hand margin of the letter.

The Full Block Format The full block format uses no indentations at all; it arranges everything—the writer's name and address, the date, the writer's signature, and the first lines of each new paragraph—along the left-hand margin of the letter. (Figure 5 on page 528 shows a letter that was typed using the full block format.)

The Envelope Use a standard-size white envelope, 4 by 9½ inches (a number 10 business envelope). Type the return address in the upper left-hand corner (single-spaced): your name on line one; your street address on line two; and your city, state abbreviation, and zip code on line three. Leave about eight line spaces below the return address. Then, just to the left of the center of the envelope, type the following (single-spaced): recipient's name on line one; recipient's job title on line two; the name of the recipient's organization on line three; street address on line four; and the city, state abbreviation, and zip code on the last line. Arrange all lines on the envelope in block format—that is, using no indentations.

EXERCISE 44.2 FOLLOWING BUSINESS LETTER TYPING FORMATS

Write a letter to a fictional company or institution requesting information on its products or operations (you may wish to say that you are researching organizations of that type or business procedures or something similar). Be specific about what you are requesting, and include all the information your letter's recipient will need to answer your questions. Using one of the three formats for typing business letters, type your letter on white 8½-by-11-inch paper. Invent whatever address information you need, and type an envelope for your letter as well. Proofread carefully, and make sure that both your letter and your envelope look professional.

Writing Complaint Letters |44c|

Perhaps the hardest task in writing an effective complaint letter is shelving your anger. Antagonizing the recipient, however, is not in your best interest. Instead of giving free reign to your venom, state your claim clearly and firmly, in a tone that does not sound angry. Be sure to include all pertinent identifying information about the problem, followed by the supporting facts of your claim, and a statement relaying what action you would like taken to remedy the situation. Conclude by stating your confidence in the reader's ability and willingness to comply with your request. Remember that most businesses want their customers to be happy. (For an exercise in writing complaint letters, see Exercise 26.1.)

Writing Job Applications |44e|

Before you begin any of the writing that is involved in applying for a job, you should do quite a bit of thinking, even if you believe that you know exactly what you want to say to prospective employers. Thinking things through will help you to clarify your own goals and intentions. Begin by asking yourself the following questions and exploring your answers to them by brainstorming or freewriting:

- What am I interested in? What subjects do I most enjoy in school? What sorts of jobs sound appealing and exciting to me?
- What am I good at? (The answer to this question may differ considerably from your answer to the first question!) What subjects or tasks have I been successful at? What general sorts of responsibility do I gravitate toward—managing people? scheduling? selling things? analyzing situations or tasks? detail work? training or instructing people? meeting people and putting them at ease? Do I draw, write, speak other languages, solve problems effectively? What sorts of jobs are there in which my abilities would be valued?
- Do I prefer making my own decisions and following my own ideas, or would I rather someone else had that responsibility?
- What is most important to me in the quality of my life: a certain level of income? security and stability? regular change and new challenges? the feeling of being important and respected? Think, also, about questions like these: Do I want to travel or not? Where do I prefer to live? Do I mind being asked regularly to move?

Careful, thoughtful answers to these questions should help you formulate a picture of the job and living situation that you are looking for. Once you have that picture relatively clearly in mind, you can tailor your résumé and your letters of application to communicate what your real goals, strengths, and values are. Consideration of these factors is more important than simply landing any job you can. If you end up in a job that does not suit your own needs and interests, you will be a dissatisfied employee, and that is not what either you or your potential employer really wants.

One last important point: the job that best suits your interests and values may not be within your reach as an entry-level applicant. If you do not have the experience or skills required for your ideal job, you should begin by looking for a position that will help you gain that experience or those skills.

Career Objectives

One of your goals at this stage should be to formulate a fairly explicit career objective. For some people this is not difficult; for others it is just not possible. Many of us truly do not know what kind of job we would most like to have. In such a case your career objective could be quite basic: *to obtain an entry-level position in the film industry*, or even simply *to obtain an entry-level position*. If the only thing you care about is living in Houston, your career objective may be just that: to obtain an entry-level position in Houston. Whatever your objective turns out to be, it is wise to decide upon it while you are planning your résumé, because much of what you include and what you stress in a résumé should be determined by what you are looking for.

If you cannot formulate any career objective this soon, do not worry. Just keep coming back to it as you gather information for your résumé and begin to think about its organization. And remember that the purpose of your career objective is not to impress anyone with your ambitions but to help you to focus and streamline your job search.

Compiling Résumé Information

One of the best ways to begin work on a résumé is to take a personal inventory. This inventory should particularize many of the personal traits, interests, and skills that you have already identified in yourself. It may even lead you to refine your assessment of those traits and to alter, expand, or focus your career objective. You may discover, for example, that you had forgotten about something in your background that makes you uniquely qualified for a certain type of job. The information you set down on your inventory, meanwhile, should form the rough notes for the first draft of your résumé. The following are guidelines for taking a personal inventory.

Personal Inventory List

1. *Education:* List here all the schools you have attended since high school (unless you went to a specialized high school at which you received significant instruction in your chosen job field). If you attended schools as part of military training or some other specific training program or workshop, include those as well. List the dates you attended all these institutions, your major areas of study, and any degrees or certifications that you received. Also list any honors or academic awards you received, your overall grade point average (G.P.A.), your G.P.A. for upper division (junior and senior) courses, and your G.P.A. for courses in your major area of study only.

2. *Work Experience:* List every job you have had since high school (if you are a recent high school graduate, list those you had during high school). List everything, including any part-time, temporary, or volunteer positions. For each job, try to answer these questions:

   - What did you do regularly?
   - What did you do only sometimes?
   - Did you ever train anyone, either formally or informally?
   - Did you receive a raise?
   - Were you promoted?

- Who was your immediate supervisor? Would this person recommend you?
- Did you handle money?
- Did you use machinery or computers of any sort? If so, what kinds?
- What did you learn from this job?

3. *Personal Interests, Activities, Skills, and Awards:* Think of other things you know how to do, even if you have not been paid to do them. Do you have any hobbies? One way to identify such areas of interest is to ask this question: *What could I teach someone?*

Note that obtaining references or recommendations from people who know you is an essential step in preparing a résumé. You should begin work on this step well in advance, to allow these people time to think about what they would like to say on your behalf. And think carefully about whom you ask for recommendations: it is best to ask only people who really know you as a worker or a student and who you know have approved of your work. Be sure to acknowledge that these people will be doing you a real service if they agree to write letters of recommendation for you; remember to thank them.

EXERCISE 44.3 CREATING YOUR PERSONAL INVENTORY

On your own paper, answer the questions in the preceding *Personal Inventory List*. Do not censor yourself; if it occurs to you that some bit of information might be useful, include it. If possible, return to this exercise several times over the course of a week; you will probably remember more as the week progresses. Keep in mind that some of the questions may not apply to you; simply answer those that do.

Writing the Résumé

Organizing Once you have a clear sense of all the material that could appear on your résumé, you must decide what you should actually use and how it should be organized. The more specific you can be about your career objective, the more finely tuned your résumé can be. If, for example, you are interested in a job involving only one specific kind of electronics, write your résumé to stress your expertise in that area, perhaps omitting experience you have in other, unrelated disciplines. On the other hand, if you are willing to consider a variety of jobs, you might want to include a variety of details about your background and interests, stressing your general talents, interests, and skills.

Whether you decide on a specific or a general résumé, you can present your background either chronologically (beginning with your most recent jobs and studies and ending with the ones you completed longest ago) or functionally (beginning with the material most likely to interest or impress prospective employers and ending with material that is less certain to be of interest or that might interest only a few of your prospective employers).

Writing Once you have decided what to include and how to organize it, you will begin the actual writing of your résumé. It is standard in résumé writing to use short, telegraphic statements (often phrases and clauses) rather than full, detailed sentences. This style saves your readers time, which they will generally appreciate. However, remember that rules of grammar and clear communication apply even when you are not writing complete sentences; be careful to maintain parallel structures, to check agreement between subjects and verbs and between pronouns and their antecedents, to place modifiers correctly, and to establish clear pronoun references, among other things. If your résumé does not follow conventions in these areas, your prospective employers will find it carelessly prepared and may suspect that you will be a careless employee. Plan to draft and revise your résumé as carefully and as exhaustively as you would any other demanding writing assignment; this is, after all, one of the most important writing assignments you will tackle.

Appearance Clearly, the content of your résumé and the way in which you word or present that content are terribly important. But the appearance of your résumé is also quite important. In fact, a careless typing job, the wrong color of paper, or any of a number of other seemingly superficial concerns can all but ruin the positive impact the content of your résumé might otherwise have made. So take extra care in arranging, typing, printing, duplicating, and mailing your résumé. In general, choose plain white paper for most applications; and unless you are applying for a job in graphic arts or some related field, stay away from fancy typefaces—they will not enhance your résumé's effectiveness. Above all, proofread your résumé very carefully, and check any copies of it that you send out to make sure they are clean, readable, and free of errors.

Figure 4 is a résumé for an imaginary college student. She is majoring in business with an emphasis on accounting. She wants to work for an accounting firm after graduation. Her résumé is designed to highlight her accounting experience and expertise. A discussion of the sections included in most résumés, and of how Elizabeth has handled these sections, follows.

CAREER OBJECTIVE

Ms. Porter has omitted this section, as many people do. Generally, include a line stating your career objective at the beginning of your résumé only if you feel it is important that anyone interviewing you know what your specific aspirations are.

EDUCATION

Ms. Porter has decided that her educational credentials are her most important asset; they appear first. For most college graduates looking for

```
                    Elizabeth Jane Porter
                    Street Address
                    City, State  Zip Code
                    Phone Number


EDUCATION
B.A., Business (Accounting Concentration), University of Someplace, June
      1989
Upper Division G.P.A.  3.58
Course work in accounting, marketing, and international business
Also attended Local Community College, 1986-87


ACCOUNTING AND BUSINESS EXPERIENCE
Internship, Top Ten Accounting Firm, City, State.  Discussion of major ac-
tivities observed and performed during this internship.  More details of
this experience.  Supervisor will provide a recommendation (consider men-
tioning that supervisor by name here).  Dates of internship.

Office Receptionist, Dr.  D.  Dentist, City, State.  Discussion of major du-
ties, particularly including anything having to do with billing or with the
handling of money.  Summers, 1987, 1988.

Salesperson, Major Department Store.  Met public, answered questions, oper-
ated NCR register.  Responsible for tallying daily receipts.  December holi-
day work, 1988.


OTHER EXPERIENCE
Coach, City Recreational League, 4th-grade team.  Full responsibility for
practices, scheduling, reporting of scores, dealing with players and with
parents.

Fast Food Sales, Local Hamburger Store.  Promoted from counter sales to su-
pervisory position.  Worked closely with assistant manager.  Summers 1985,
1986.

PERSONAL DATA
Born August 1, 1966.  Graduated from Home Town High, 1984.  Willing to relo-
cate.


REFERENCES: Available on request from the University of Someplace Placement
Center, address of placement center, phone number of placement center.
```

Figure 4   A Sample Résumé

career positions, educational credentials are crucial. Ms. Porter has also listed a G.P.A. figured on upper division courses only. That G.P.A. is probably higher than her overall average. There is nothing deceptive in doing this, as long as you identify the figure for what it is—something other than a cumulative G.P.A. Ms. Porter has mentioned attending a community college but has chosen not to stress this fact. The courses she took there probably had nothing to do with accounting.

EXPERIENCE

Ms. Porter has labeled her next category *Accounting and Business Experience*. Under this category we find two listings, one for an internship position and one for an office receptionist position. Since these are the first and therefore the most important entries relating to noneducation credentials, Ms. Porter has detailed her duties carefully. Details count. Without such details, employers will not know what duties and responsibilities were assumed by the applicant.

The internship was actually part of Ms. Porter's educational experience; she received course credit for her work. But placing it under *Accounting and Business Experience* allows her to stress the importance of the on-the-job learning she did there. The résumé asserts that the internship was as valuable as a salaried job. It also allows her to construct a category that contains the word *accounting*. An employer scanning category titles would probably read material under a category identified specifically in this way. The same material under a category labeled simply *Experience* might not be noticed.

Two jobs are listed under *Other Experience*. The label here indicates these jobs are less important than the preceding ones. The coaching experience was a volunteer one, though that fact is not mentioned and need not be. The duties are mentioned because they show an ability to work with people and assume responsibility. The fast food sales position receives the least attention, reflecting Ms. Porter's decision to downplay that experience and highlight other things.

PERSONAL DATA

Ms. Porter's *Personal Data* section is short, and she could have chosen to omit it altogether. Federal law prohibits job discrimination on the basis of sex, religion, race, age, or national origin, and it is not necessary to provide such information in a résumé.

REFERENCES

Finally, Ms. Porter's résumé indicates that her recommendations can be obtained through her college placement center. Making these documents available through a third party is a good idea because it makes them easy to obtain; an employer can obtain several through one telephone call.

Ms. Porter has not mentioned any outside interests or skills on her résumé. Some people do include a section titled *Interests*, where they list such things as performing arts background, foreign language skills, and hobbies. It is best to limit such a section to two lines or less, but it is rarely a mistake to include it, if only to give people a fuller idea of what sort of person you are.

EXERCISE 44.4 WRITING A RÉSUMÉ

Based on the material you generated for Exercise 44.3, and your analysis of the sample résumé in Figure 4, write a résumé to fit your own needs and aspirations. Type or print your résumé on high-quality white bond paper.

Writing an Application Letter

Once you have done all the work involved in assembling a résumé, writing a letter of application to accompany it is not very difficult. Think of an application letter as your opportunity to present one page (no more) of information that an employer must see. Some readers will not read your résumé unless the content of your letter convinces them to do so. You can almost construct a formula for a successful application letter:

- The opening consists of a sentence or two indicating which job you seek and how you found out about it.
- The body is made up of two or three paragraphs indicating your particular qualifications for the job. What have you done successfully? How do these experiences combine to make you uniquely qualified? (This will repeat information in your résumé.)
- The closing consists of a sentence or two indicating what the next step in your application process will be. If you say you will call the employer by a certain date, be sure to do so.

An application letter designed to accompany Elizabeth Porter's résumé is shown in Figure 5.

EXERCISE 44.5 WRITING AN APPLICATION LETTER

Locate a job opening in which you are now interested or one that would interest you at graduation. Use the résumé you drafted in Exercise 44.4, and write an application letter expressing your interest in the position. Type or print your letter on high-quality white bond paper. Be scrupulous in checking for errors.

```
123 Street Name
Town, State  Zip Code
Date


Recipient's Name, Title
Recipient's Company
123 Street Name
Town, State  Zip Code

Dear Ms./Mr. Name:

The current issue of the San Francisco Chronicle lists your advertisement
for an entry level accounting position--one for which I feel particularly
qualified.  In addition to my Bachelor of Arts in Business from the Univer-
sity of Someplace, I have worked in a variety of business settings, each of
which has given me valuable experience.

During my internship with Big Ten Accounting Firm, I worked closely with
personnel in both the corporate and personal accounting divisions.  I gained
valuable experience in computer data analysis, cost accounting, and inven-
tory valuation. During this time I was also interested to see how my courses
in tax law applied in actual work situations.  I particularly enjoyed work-
ing closely with Mr. John Accountant, my intern supervisor.  His recommenda-
tion is a part of my dossier available through the University of Someplace
Placement Center.

In addition to my internship experience, I have acted as office receptionist
for Dr. D. Dentist for two straight summers.  In this capacity I have had
full responsibility for scheduling, routine billing, and the ordering of a
wide variety of dental and office supplies.  As receptionist, I have also
gained valuable experience dealing with many kinds of people.

My education and my work experience combine to give me both theoretical and
practical knowledge I will be able to use as I work with you and continue to
learn.  I look forward to hearing from you.

Sincerely yours,

Elizabeth Jane Porter

Elizabeth Jane Porter

Enc.: Resume
```

Figure 5 A Sample Application Letter (Full Block Format)

Working with Your Text

45

Using Computers in Writing

During the last ten years, the personal computer has become an increasingly common tool for writers. This chapter will briefly discuss the ways you can use computers during all the stages of the writing process.

Using the Computer for Planning and Invention |45a|

A relatively small number of invention or planning programs have been designed to help writers by asking them questions. As discussed in Chapter 2, invention or planning questions can often prove useful as writers begin the writing process.

Obviously, a computer-generated list of questions frees you from having to generate such questions yourself. However, you need no special invention program to discover the joys of freewriting or invisible writing on the computer. Doing freewriting at the computer keyboard carries one significant advantage. Word-processing programs allow for the easy correction of errors. Knowing how easy it is to correct errors often makes composing at the keyboard even freer than it might otherwise be. In addition to freewriting, you might try invisible writing. Turn the brightness control down on your monitor so that what you type is not visible, and begin composing. Once you have exhausted your train of thought, turn up the brightness and read what you have written.

EXERCISE 45.1 PLANNING, INVENTING, AND FREEWRITING ON A COMPUTER

Respond to either A or B.

A. If you have an invention program available to you, use it to help you identify what your precomputer planning habits have been. What writing activities have you used to help you get started? Will you be able to transfer these activities to the computer? Can you see any advantages or disadvantages to switching to computer use? Once you have used your invention program to address these questions, use your word-processing program to respond to this question: Did using the invention program help you generate information you would not otherwise have obtained? Explain.

B. If you have no invention program available, use your word-processing program to try either freewriting or invisible writing. Respond to this question: In the past, what have you typically done to begin the writing process? Then use the program to evaluate your freewriting or invisible writing. What differences do you see between computer freewriting and your normal writing habits? Would you consider this first attempt at computer freewriting successful? Why or why not? Once you have answered these questions, print out your answers.

Using the Computer for Organizing and Outlining |45b|

Chapters 2 and 3 discuss outlining as both an invention and a revision strategy. Outlining is easy to do on the computer. In fact, there are outlining programs that make it easy for you to construct or modify an outline.

Whether you use an outlining program or your word-processing program, writing an outline on your computer gives you considerable flexibility. Computers make it quite easy for writers to change the order in which material appears; if one section of your outline seems out of place, you can simply move it by using a few commands.

This flexibility makes outlining particularly useful as you draft and revise and draft some more. Suppose you have printed out a hard copy of a draft, and you want to check its organization. You can outline each page. With that outline in front of you, you should be able to see whether or not your material has been organized logically.

EXERCISE 45.2 ORGANIZING AND OUTLINING ON A COMPUTER

This exercise involves using the computer to get started on an essay. Though you are not asked to complete the essay, this exercise should give you a fairly complete idea of how that essay would look.

1. Consider this question: What are the qualities of a truly fine college teacher? Freewrite on this topic at the keyboard for at least ten minutes. Print this material out, saving the hard copy. (If you are progressing through this entire chapter, make a backup copy on your disk, and save it for the first part of Exercise 45.4.)

2. Use the computer to construct an outline of your freewrite. Some material will not seem to fit, and other parts may seem out of order. Do not let that worry you; simply outline the material as it appears in your freewrite. Then print it out.

3. Retaining a backup copy in its original form, revise your outline. Add or cut anything necessary; reorder the points so that they follow a more logical sequence. Then print it out. Turn in all three printouts.

Using the Computer for Drafting, Revising, and Editing |45c|

Besides making it easier for you to correct errors during proofreading, the computer allows you to add or cut material without resorting to any kind of cumbersome cut-and-paste process. If you leave out a word, the word-processing program will allow you to add it and will adjust the rest of your text accordingly. The same holds true for changes of an entire paragraph or several pages.

Still, there are several things that you should be careful to incorporate into your working process and train of thought as you draft, revise, or edit on a computer:

1. Working with a word-processing program will only allow you increased flexibility to the extent that you familiarize yourself with how your particular program works. Mastering the ins and outs of a word-processing program takes some time and practice; if you invest that time and practice early—before you are actually trying to produce a document—you will have done yourself a great favor.

2. A word-processing program allows you to create and change a draft in a number of ways, but until you use the *save* command, it will not actually store any of what you have done. Practically every writer using a word-processing program has had the harrowing experience of inputting or editing several paragraphs or pages, thinking a good deal of work was done, leaving the computer for a time, and then coming back to find that all that work was lost because the writer had forgotten to save it. Write yourself a note and tape it to your keyboard if necessary, but remember to use the save command after every few paragraphs or so.

3. It is also important to make backup copies of any document files you are working on. If you make significant changes in a document and then wonder whether an earlier passage was better, or if you mistakenly delete a section of your document, you will be very grateful to have a backup copy of your previous version. By the same token, each time you have completed a draft or a revision, it is a good idea to print out a copy of it. Doing so will protect you against such mishaps as the data loss caused by a bad sector developing in your disk.

4. It is especially important that you do not allow the neatness and legibility of all word-processed documents to fool you into thinking that your writing is finished and complete before it really is. A document that is flawless in appearance can be riddled with misspellings, grammatical errors, poor punctuation, and so on. Be sure to proofread and edit your word-processed document at least as closely and carefully as you would any other.

5. With all the advantages word processing offers, it is still wise to work on printed copies of your writing from time to time in your revising and editing process. At the very least, working with a printed copy will give you an idea whether your draft needs further formatting before you print a final copy.

Using The St. Martin's Hotline

As a student using this book, you have available to you a unique software package called *The St. Martin's Hotline.* This program is compatible with most word-processing programs, and it provides you with an on-line, abbreviated version of *The St. Martin's Handbook,* sections of which will "pop up" upon command as reference aids while you are actually working on a document. Thus if you are revising a sentence and are not sure whether you need to include a comma, you can call up a concise version of the *Handbook*'s rules on comma usage to find out. This program should be especially helpful during revision, editing, and proofreading.

EXERCISE 45.3   REVISING ON A COMPUTER

Take one recently written paragraph with which you are dissatisfied, and, using your word-processing program, enter it as a new file exactly as it was written, errors and all. Revise it, correcting all mechanical errors, adding material that now seems necessary, deleting material that now seems unnecessary or unrelated, and generally improving the paragraph's style and tone. Then print out the revised paragraph.

Using the Computer to Proofread

Chapter 3 discusses the use of an editing checklist as one way you can help yourself identify and eliminate errors. Working from your checklist, you can use your word-processing program to help you identify possible errors. Many programs possess commands that let you search for a particular word, phrase, or punctuation mark. Suppose, for example, that you know that when you draft, you do not pay close attention to comma usage, particularly before the word *and.* Using the *search* capability of your program, you could ask the computer to read through your draft and stop at each comma. You can then make a correction if necessary and continue.

Many writers also use the *search-and-replace* command, especially for words that are consistently misspelled. You can have the computer locate each instance of the error and replace it with the correct spelling. You can also use the search-and-replace command to speed up your drafting. For example, if you are writing a report analyzing several word-processing programs, you will probably need to use the phrase *word processing* several times. Instead of typing it out in full each time, you could type only *wp.* Then, when you have finished drafting, you could replace each instance of the abbreviation with the full phrase.

EXERCISE 45.4 EDITING ON A COMPUTER

Exercise 45.2 asked you to freewrite on the topic of what qualities a truly fine college teacher possesses. Use that freewrite to follow these directions.

1. Use your computer's search command to check for accurate comma usage. Correct any errors you find.

2. Use your computer's search-and-replace command to locate every use of the word *teacher* and replace it with the word *instructor*.

3. Think about errors in grammar, spelling, and punctuation you commonly make. List four of those common errors, and add this list below the freewriting you worked on in questions 1 and 2.

4. Now print out the freewriting version you generated in question 2 above, together with the list from question 3, and save this data on your disk. You will need it for Exercise 45.5.

Using Spelling Checkers and Text-Analysis Programs

Some word-processing programs include **spelling checkers**. All spelling checkers work by examining each word of a document and comparing it to a dictionary that is part of the program. Spelling checkers have two important drawbacks:

1. A spelling checker will not be able to tell the difference between words that are often confused, such as *accept* and *except* and *principle* and *principal,* since all are standard words correctly spelled. It cannot check for usage. In addition, a spelling checker will often miss typing errors that result in perfectly correct English words, such as *on* for *in.*

2. Because spelling checkers take up an enormous amount of a computer's memory, their dictionaries are relatively small. They will identify any word not in their dictionary as incorrectly spelled. If your vocabulary is specialized, a spelling checker could label a number of correctly spelled words as incorrect.

You can still make good use of spelling checkers while realizing their limitations. Their only danger is that they may lull you into believing that all your proofreading has been done for you.

Text-analysis programs look for and identify various kinds of patterns in sentences. Some count words and identify lengthy sentences; some identify use of the passive voice; others identify phrasing as either formal or colloquial. However, text-analysis programs cannot determine the appropriate tone or sentence length in your writing situation; they cannot grasp a writer's intentions.

EXERCISE 45.5 PROOFREADING ON A COMPUTER

If you completed Exercise 44.4, you should have saved the answer to question 4. Return to that answer now. If you have not completed Exercise 44.4, freewrite for ten minutes on this topic: What one class that you have taken has left the most lasting and positive impression on you and why? Then use your own paper to answer the following questions.

1. Use your spelling checker to analyze and identify spelling errors in your freewrite. Correct each error.

2. Now print out a copy of your freewrite and proofread it. Has the spelling checker missed any errors? Make a note of these.

3. How effective do you think your spelling checker will be for you?

4. If a text-analysis program is available to you, use it to analyze your freewrite. What does the program tell you about your draft?

5. Do you agree or disagree with the conclusions of your text-analysis program? How useful will this program be for you?

46

Preparing Your Manuscript

Even before they begin to read, your readers will judge your finished manuscript on its physical appearance and readability. This chapter presents guidelines to help you make a good first impression. But the most important general rule is this: follow the manuscript guidelines established by your instructor.

- Submit typed or printer-produced papers whenever possible.

If you are using a printer, a letter-quality or near-letter-quality font is best. Remember that many readers strongly object to reading draft-mode print from a dot-matrix printer. Always consult your audience before submitting any work printed in draft mode.

- Consult a manuscript style sheet.

Anyone writing for publication must submit manuscripts that follow particular stipulations for margins, spacing, and the like. The various academic disciplines also follow their own sets of such rules, and these rules are published by the major professional organization for a particular discipline. The guidelines of the Modern Language Association are published in *The MLA Handbook,* and those of the American Psychological Association are published in its style manual.

The following manuscript style sheet will be appropriate for many college essays and long papers. But again, always follow your instructor's guidelines, even if they are different from those in this style sheet.

Manuscript Style Sheet

Typed or printed papers:	*Handwritten papers:*

PAPER

Use 8½-by-11-inch white, heavyweight bond paper. Type on one side only.

Use 8½-by-11-inch loose-leaf ruled paper. Write on one side only.

INK

Use a fresh ribbon for dark, clear impressions.

Write in pen (never pencil) and use black or blue ink.

TYPEFACE

Use pica or elite typefaces, nothing fancy.

Be legible. If necessary, print.

MARGINS

Use 1- to 1½-inch margins at top, bottom, and on both sides.

SPACING

Double-space between lines. Skip two spaces after end punctuation. Leave one space after colons, commas, and semicolons. Leave no space before or after a dash or an apostrophe, unless the apostrophe ends the word. Brackets and apostrophes are "invisible"—they do not change the normal spacing of the text. Ellipsis marks are three periods, each separated by a single space. Do not surround a slash with space unless it divides two lines of poetry.

PARAGRAPH INDENTATIONS

Five spaces from left margin.

About three-fourths of an inch from the left margin.

LONG (BLOCK) QUOTATIONS

Triple-space between the main text and the quoted material. Double-space the quoted material itself. Do not use quotation marks to enclose block quotations.

BINDING

Instructors frequently prefer that you use only paper clips to keep the pages of your paper together. Avoid stapling and plastic folders.

PAGINATION

Number each page after the first one. Place the number in the upper right corner, and print or type your name after it.

TITLE PAGE

Most college essays do not require a separate title page. If your instructor has made no mention of one, you can probably assume it is not required. If it is not required, include your name, course and number, course instructor, and the date in the upper left corner of the first page of your paper; type these items double-spaced and on separate lines. Then center your title four lines down. Finally, begin your essay four lines down from the title. If your instructor does require a separate title page, follow these specifications: Your title should be centered and positioned three inches down from the top of the page; if your title is lengthy, use two double-spaced lines. Your name should appear two inches down from the title, centered. Finally, centered and two inches down from your name, type or write the course name and number, the name of your instructor, and the date on separate, double-spaced lines.

EXERCISE 46.1 CREATING A MANUSCRIPT STYLE CHECKLIST

Generate your own checklist for evaluating a manuscript, based on the guidelines presented in the preceding style sheet. Then, using essays you have written for this or another class, exchange essays with a fellow student. Evaluate one another's manuscripts using your checklists.

■ Follow a standard proofreading procedure for every paper.

Whether or not you proofread as you type, it is essential that you do a final proofreading after you have finished typing. Proofread the final paragraph, the next-to-final paragraph, and so on, until you get to the first paragraph. Reading in this way should help you focus on checking for correctness rather than on the content of your paper. In addition, read slowly. Look at each word and each punctuation mark. Whenever you have found a mistake or are not sure if something is correct, circle the word or mark it in pencil. If you have only one or two such circles on a page, you may be able to correct by hand, through careful erasure. Never make corrections below the line or in the margins. If you must insert a word, position the word above the line, and use a caret (∧) to indicate the insertion. If you have more than two errors on a page, it is best to retype the page.

EXERCISE 46.2 PROOFREADING A SAMPLE MANUSCRIPT

Proofread and correct the following passages from student papers.

1.   While Donne places most of his innovative efforts into the creation of

imagery, Herbert placed most of his into the creation of the poem's form.

We find this difference illustrated in the two poems the poets

respectively have written dealing with the death and resurrection of

Christ. Donne's 'Good Friday, 1613, Riding Westward' is in a very straight

forward, ordinary form: rhymed couplets throughout. But his imagery

and language are unusual and interesting:

> O think me worth Thine anger: punish me;
> Burn off my rusts and my deformity;
> Restore Thine image so much, by Thy grace,
> That Thou mayst know me, and I"ll turn my face. (pp. 1205-6)

What is most striking about 'Good Friday' is the different

perspective Donne gives us in the Easter story: his reaction is to

turn away from seeing it, to be humbled by it, rather than to find in

it a source of exhiliaration, as most people do. This latter

feeling, the ususal, expected one is expressed by Herbert in his

'Easter Wings'

> With thee
> O let me rise
> As larks, harmoiously
> And sing this day thy victories:
> Then shall the fall further the flight in me. (p. 1258)

The sentiment is one of sympathetic spiritual rebirth at the

witnessing of Christ's resurrection and ascension into Heaven.

Herbert makes the whole thing new not in his imagery - that of larks and flying - which is again an expected image in this subject, but in the from he puts it all into. There are two stanzas, each beginning with a long line and working through shorter and shorter lines and then back to a long line again, with apause in the middle between the two shortest lines. This form is symbolic of the death and resurrection. In each stanza the first half describe's man's decay, downfall, or something of the nature. The second half beins in goth cases with the words "With thee". And in the company of God both the poem and the man it describes are resurrected.

2.   At the end of A Separate Reality, Castaneda still has "...an overwhelming urge to ask for explanations." (Reality 262) Don Juan says, "There's nothing to undertsand. Understaading is only a very small affair, so very small." (260) And a new feeling comes to Carlos: "For the first time in my life I felt the encumbering weight of my reason." (162) It is this reason, with it's insatiable appetite for explnations, that is the most important threat to Carlos' progress toward knowledge. He must budge it. It is because he has not done so that don Juan's las words in this second book tell him that although he has worked hard and developped the"'...need to live like a warrior...Nothing has really changed in you.'" (p.263)

Answers to Preview Questions

Compare your answers to Part Preview Questions with those provided here. If you were unable to answer a question, or if your answer conflicts, find the first bracketed chapter reference following the answer given below. That chapter will be one that you should study closely.

PART 1 1) F 2) F [Chapter 1] 3) T 4) F 5) F [Chapter 2] 6) T 7) T 8) F 9) T [Chapter 3] 10) T 11) T 12) F 13) T 14) F [Chapter 4] 15) T 16) T [Chapter 5]

PART 2 1) Meryl, car, supermarket 2) Washingtons, pet, doctor 3) will get, finishes 4) might speak, going 5) Anybody, those who, his 6) Which, you 7) Until, under, up [Chapter 6] 8) I 9) whom 10) Whom 11) he, she 12) me [Chapter 7] 13) am 14) doesn't 15) gave 16) lay 17) would 18) wants [Chapter 8] 19) its 20) a 21) travels 22) have 23) is [Chapter 9] 24) well 25) most 26) really 27) nicer, nicest [Chapter 10]

PART 3 1a) no 1b) no 1c) no 1d) yes [Chapter 11] 2a) yes 2b) no 2c) yes 2d) yes [Chapter 12] 3a) yes 3b) no 3c) no 3d) yes [Chapter 13] 4a) no 4b) yes [Chapter 14] 5a) no 5b) no 5c) no [Chapter 15] 6a) no 6b) yes 6c) yes 6d) yes [Chapter 16]

PART 4 1a) yes 1b) no [Chapter 17] 2a) so 2b) but 3) no 4a) When the rain started 4b) who gave me this watch 4c) even though she left an hour early [Chapter 18] 5a) no 5b) yes 5c) no [Chapter 19] 6a) wordiness 6b) C 6c) passive verbs, wordiness 6d) weak verb 6e) passive verb [Chapters 20 and 21]

PART 5 1) Their (They're) 2) definately (definitely), desert (dessert) 3) herd (heard), developped (developed) 4) rein (reign), righters (writers), dyed (died) 5) nucular (nuclear), treatey (treaty) [Chapter 22] 6) Latin, *adjudicatus*, past part. of *adjudicare*, to judge 7) premature dementia, schizophrenia 8) trend, drift, current, inclination, tenor 9) six–ten [Chapter 23] 10a) *for instance*: biology, biography 10b) *for instance*: juror, jurisdiction, jurisprudence, justice, justify 11) -ly 12) -ive, -ic, -able, -ful, -ish [Chapter 24] 13) eludes (alludes) 14) stink (*fragrance, aroma*, or *scent* would be better) 15) continuously (continually), continual (continuous) 16) C [Chapter 25] 17) X ("tons" is informal language) 18) (sentence acceptable) 19) X ("he's just wrong" is too extreme; readers who disagree may feel offended) [Chapter 26]

PART 6 1) . . . shared much, they . . . 2) . . . cousin, lives . . . 3) . . . china was totally . . . [Chapter 27] 4) . . . at first; however . . . 5) . . . positions: short-order . . . 6) . . . a "bookhouse," I . . . [Chapter 28]   7) . . . Marisa asked.   8) T. S. Eliot . . . J. Alfred . . .   9) . . . one's writing?" they . . .   10) . . . shouted "Stop!"   [Chapter 29]   11) . . . judges' . . . defense's . . . 12) . . . just doesn't want . . .   13) . . . eight o'clock . . .   14) C   15) . . . was theirs. [Chapter 30] 16) "I did not know . . . evening," Peter said.   17) . . . was 'very taxing,' " Vincent . . .   18) . . . windy," the . . .   19) . . . robbers "are now in custody."   20) . . . novel *Robinson Crusoe*. [Chapter 31]   21) . . . literature: good . . .   22) C [Chapter 32]

PART 7   1) capitalize *We*; do not capitalize *northwestern*   2) do not capitalize *they*   3) C   4) C 5) capitalize *Renaissance* and *Middle Ages*   [Chapter 33]   6) "a doctor" and "an M.D." say the same thing; use one or the other when referring to a single person or group   7) C   8) AD (A.D.)   9) # (number)   10) Cal., Ariz. (California, Arizona)   11) 6 (Six)   12) 10,000 (ten thousand) [Chapter 34]   13) *Hebrew Bible, Gospels, Koran* (none of these should be italicized)   14) "King Lear," "Shakespearean Negotiations" (italicize; do not use quotation marks)   15) C   16) C 17) "in medias res" (italicize; do not use quotation marks)   18) C   19) "Annie Hall" (italicize; do not use quotation marks) [Chapter 35]   20) best-known (do not hyphenate)   21) C   22) cloud-less (do not hyphenate), rain- ed (do not divide)   23) C   24) better-coverage (do not hyphenate) 25) C   26) man- uscripts (do not begin a new line with a vowel) [Chapter 36]

PART 8   1) T   2) F [Chapter 37]   3) F   4) T [Chapter 38]   5) F   6) F   7) T [Chapter 39]   8) F 9) T   10) T [Chapter 40]

Index

Note: Boldface numbers refer to definitions in the text. Page numbers preceded by *E* denote pages on which Exercises or end-of-chapter Assignments appear.